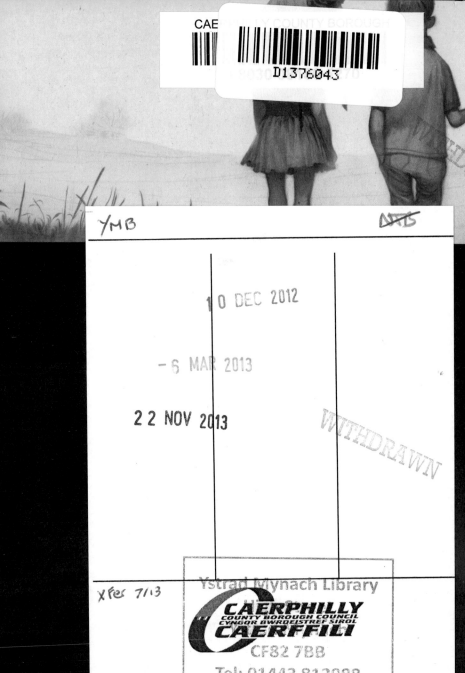

FABLES: SUPER TEAM

FABLES CREATED BY BILL WILLINGHAM

Bill Willingham
Writer

Mark Buckingham
Steve Leialoha
Eric Shanower
Terry Moore
Andrew Pepoy
Richard Friend
Artists

Lee Loughridge
Colorist

Todd Klein
Letterer

Joao Ruas
Cover Art and Original Series Covers

SHELLY BOND
Editor – Original Series

GREGORY LOCKARD
Associate Editor – Original Series

IAN SATTLER
Director – Editorial, Special Projects and
Archival Editions

SCOTT NYBAKKEN
Editor

ROBBIN BROSTERMAN
Design Director – Books

KAREN BERGER
Senior VP – Executive Editor, Vertigo

BOB HARRAS
VP – Editor-in-Chief

DIANE NELSON
President

DAN DIDIO and **JIM LEE**
Co-Publishers

GEOFF JOHNS
Chief Creative Officer

JOHN ROOD
Executive VP – Sales, Marketing and Business
Development

AMY GENKINS
Senior VP – Business and Legal Affairs

NAIRI GARDINER
Senior VP – Finance

JEFF BOISON
VP – Publishing Operations

MARK CHIARELLO
VP – Art Direction and Design

JOHN CUNNINGHAM
VP – Marketing

TERRI CUNNINGHAM
VP – Talent Relations and Services

ALISON GILL
Senior VP – Manufacturing and Operations

DAVID HYDE
VP – Publicity

HANK KANALZ
Senior VP – Digital

JAY KOGAN
VP – Business and Legal Affairs, Publishing

JACK MAHAN
VP – Business Affairs, Talent

NICK NAPOLITANO
VP – Manufacturing Administration

SUE POHJA
VP – Book Sales

COURTNEY SIMMONS
Senior VP – Publicity

BOB WAYNE
Senior VP – Sales

*This one is dedicated to my favorites of
the super men: Kirby, Ditko, Romita,
Kane, Kubert, Cardy, Aparo, Buscema,
Steranko, Adams and Byrne.*
— Bill Willingham

*For my very own super team of Bill, Steve,
Todd, Lee, Joao, Andrew, Greg, Shelly and
all our wonderful guest creators who
make this book a joy to work on every
month. This volume is also dedicated to
all the super hero books that inspired me
from a very early age, especially
the works of Jack Kirby.*
— Mark Buckingham

Logo design by Brainchild Studios/NYC

FABLES: SUPER TEAM

Published by DC Comics. Cover and compilation
Copyright © 2011 Bill Willingham and DC Comics.
All Rights Reserved.

Originally published in single magazine form
as FABLES 101-107. Copyright © 2011
Bill Willingham and DC Comics.
All Rights Reserved. All characters, their
distinctive likenesses and related elements
featured in this publication are trademarks of
Bill Willingham. VERTIGO is a trademark of
DC Comics. The stories, characters and incidents
featured in this publication are entirely fictional.
DC Comics does not read or accept unsolicited
submissions of ideas, stories or artwork.

DC Comics, 1700 Broadway, New York, NY 10019
A Warner Bros. Entertainment Company.
Printed in the USA. First Printing.
ISBN: 978-1-4012-3306-8

SUSTAINABLE
FORESTRY
INITIATIVE

Certified Fiber Sourcing

www.sfiprogram.org
Fiber used in this product line meets the
sourcing requirements of the SFI program.
www.sfiprogram.org SGS-SFI/COC-US10/81072

Table of Contents

WHO'S WHO IN FABLETOWN

BUFKIN

The reluctant but resourceful defender of Fabletown's lost business office.

FRANKIE

The remains of a certain doctor's most infamous experiment.

FLYCATCHER

The former Frog Prince and janitor, now the ruler of the Kingdom of Haven in the liberated Homelands.

BIGBY

The celebrated Big Bad Wolf and former sheriff of Fabletown.

THE NORTH WIND

Bigby's father, one of the four Great Winds.

MISTRAL

A servant of the North Wind

STINKY

Now renamed Brock Blueheart in honor of the fallen Boy Blue, in whose imminent return from the dead Brock has unshakable faith.

CLARA

A cunningly disguised dragon.

KING COLE

The once and future mayor of Fabletown.

BELLFLOWER

Once known as Frau Totenkinder, she led Fabletown's witches throug their greatest trials, includi an epic confrontation with Mister Dark.

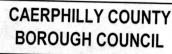

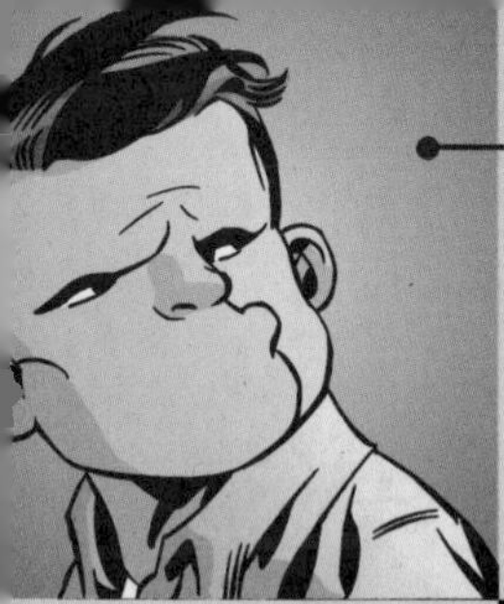

PINOCCHIO

Geppetto's first-carved son, transformed somewhat capriciously into an unaging boy.

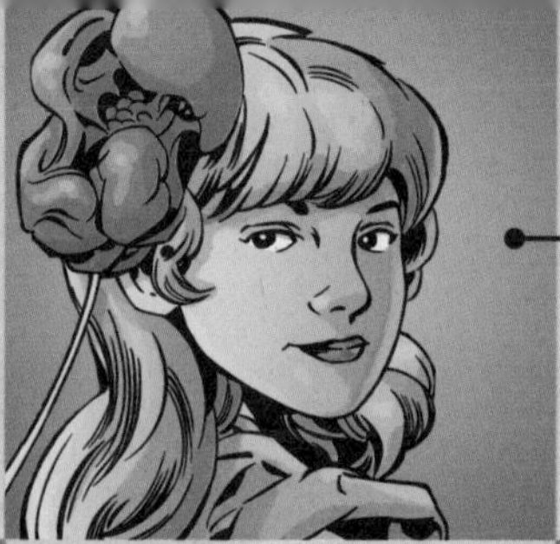

OZMA

The misleadingly youthful-looking leader of Fabletown's wizards and witches.

SNOW WHITE

Fabletown's former deputy mayor, wife of Bigby, and mother to their seven cubs.

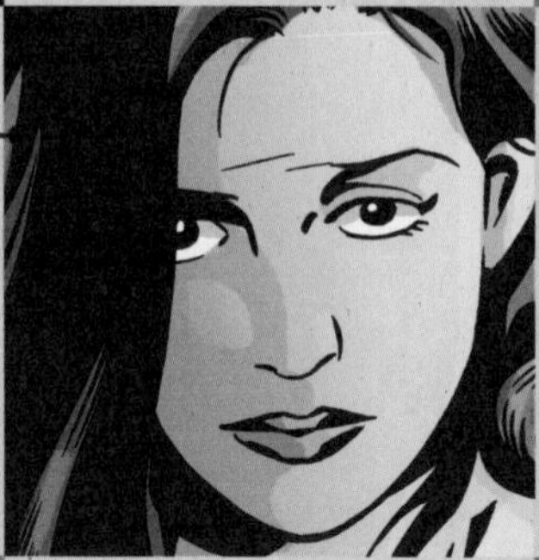

THE CUBS

Bigby and Snow's children; six are visible, one is hidden.

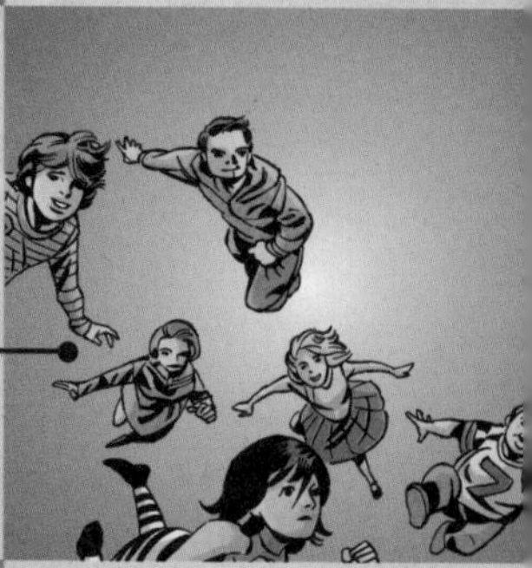

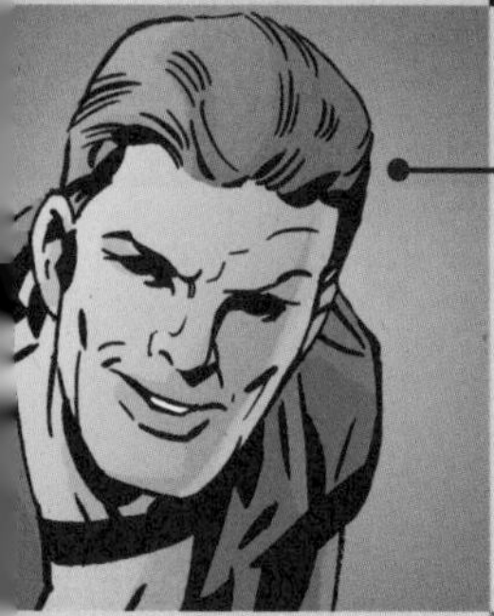

BEAST

Beauty's husband and the sheriff of Fabletown.

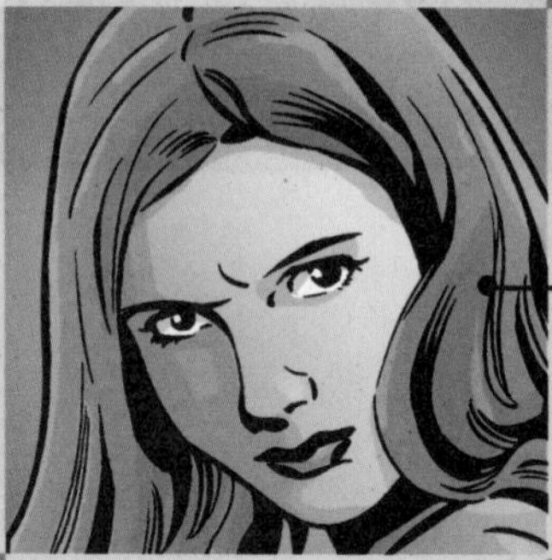

BEAUTY

The current deputy mayor, wife of Beast, and mother to their newborn.

GEPPETTO

Fabletown's former adversary, now a much-reviled fellow citizen.

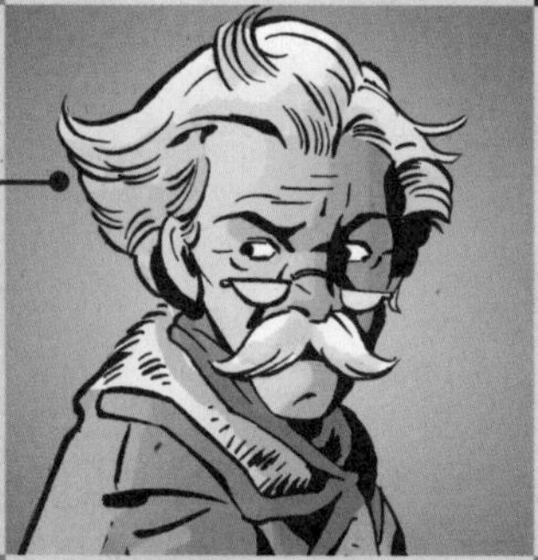

ROSE RED

Snow White's sister and the leader of the non-human Fable community known as the Farm.

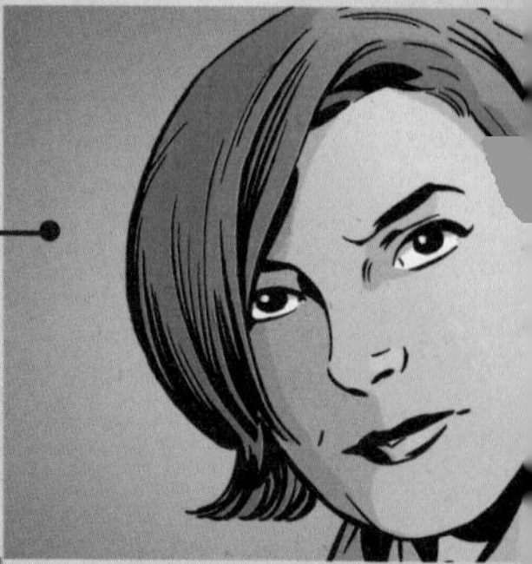

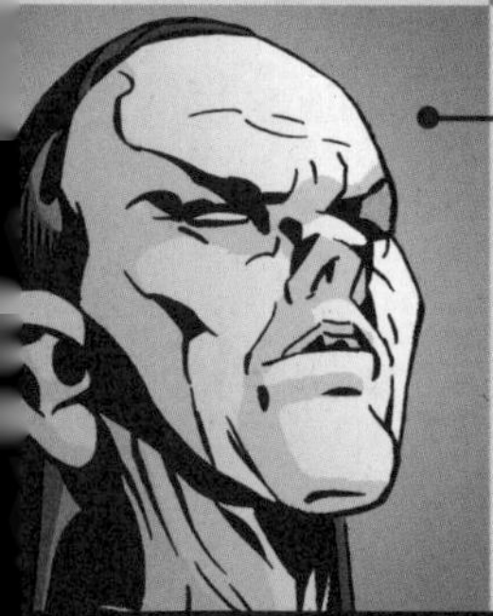

MISTER DARK

A Great Power imprisoned for centuries by the Adversary, he is the embodiment of all that is malign and corrupt in existence.

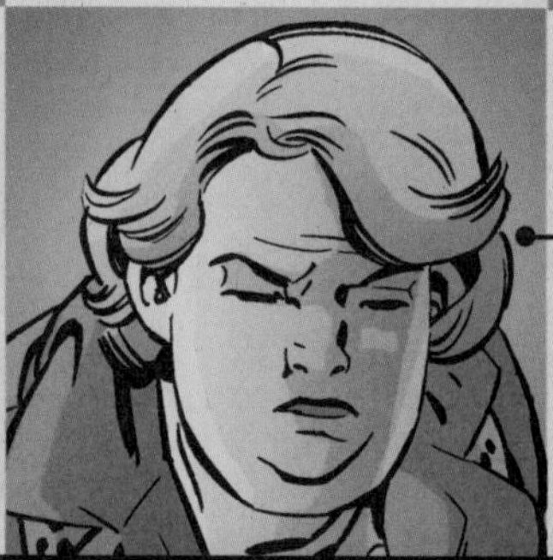

NURSE SPRATT

Jack Spratt's widow and an enthusiastic collaborator with Mister Dark.

THE STORY SO FAR

After seeing their beloved Fabletown laid waste and their hoarded treasures and defenses scattered, the Free Fables of the Mundane World rallied around their most powerful magical champion and mounted what they hoped would be a final assault on the elemental scourge of Mister Dark. For a brief moment it seemed that victory was theirs, but this latest adversary proved too powerful to be held for long. Soon Fabletown's survivors were obliged to retreat again — and with nowhere left to fall back to, the next stand they make against this enemy will be their last

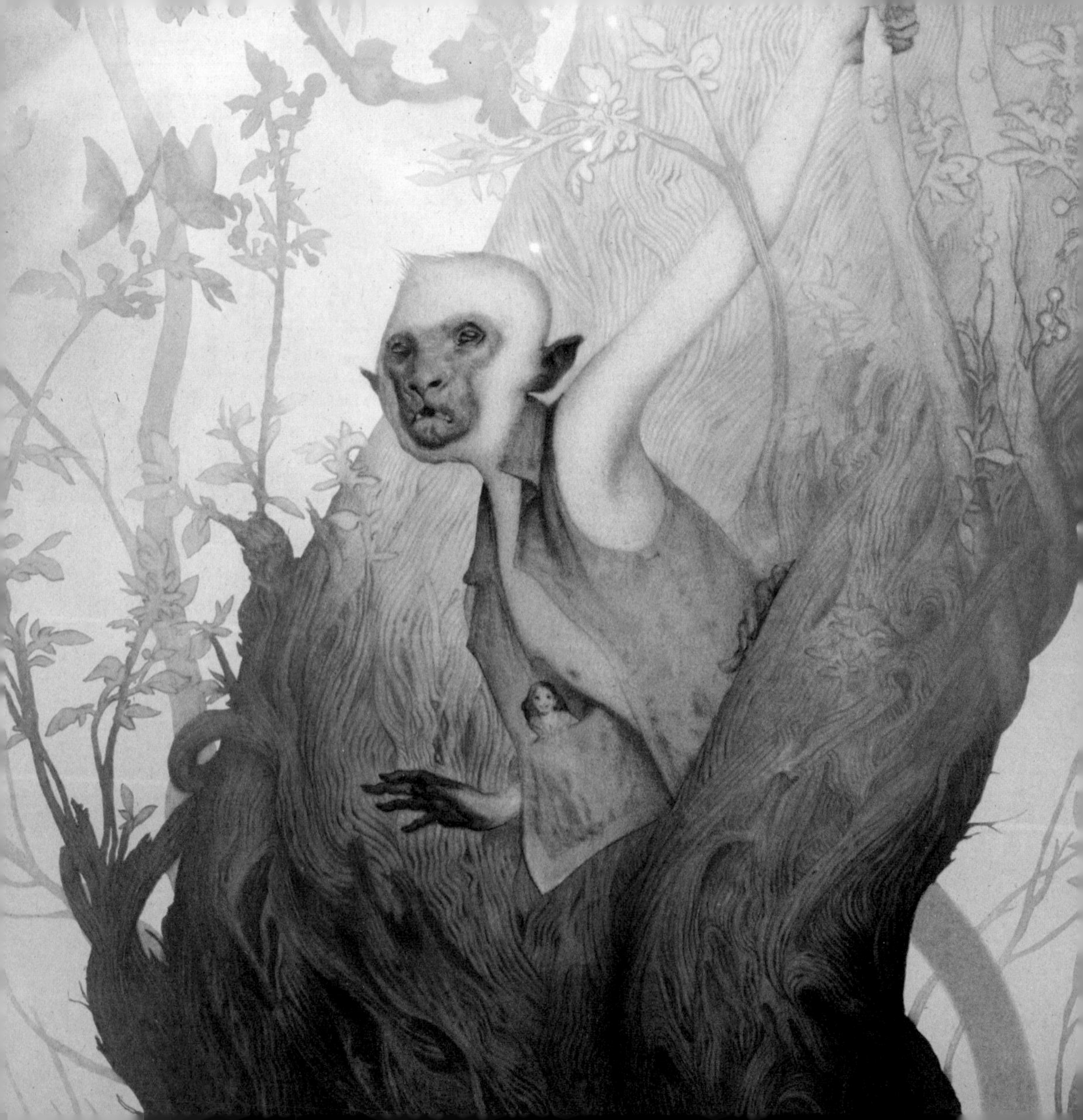

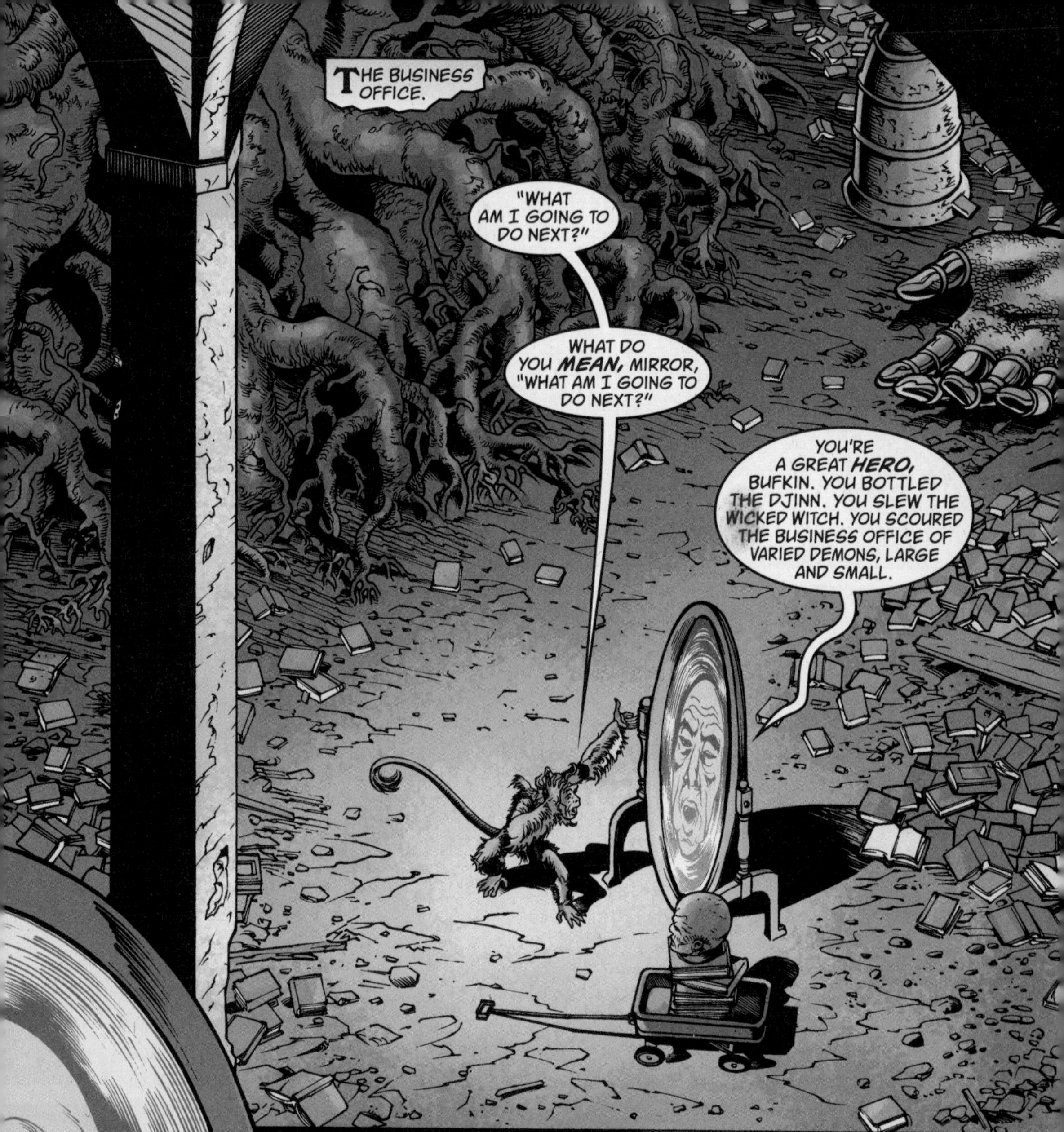
THE BUSINESS OFFICE.
"WHAT AM I GOING TO DO NEXT?"
WHAT DO YOU MEAN, MIRROR, "WHAT AM I GOING TO DO NEXT?"
YOU'RE A GREAT HERO, BUFKIN. YOU BOTTLED THE DJINN. YOU SLEW THE WICKED WITCH. YOU SCOURED THE BUSINESS OFFICE OF VARIED DEMONS, LARGE AND SMALL.

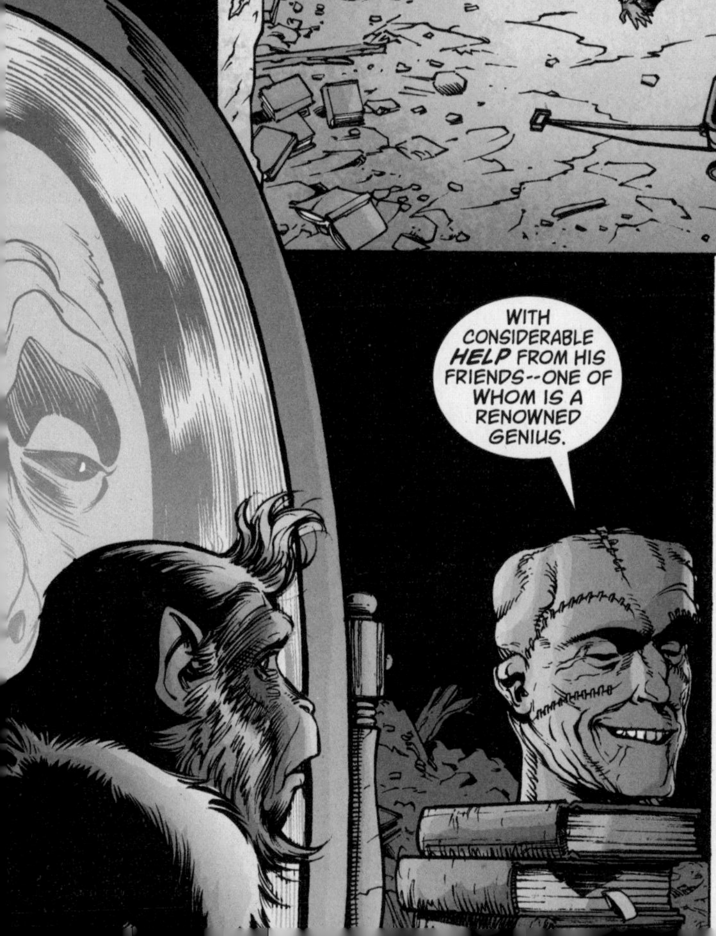
WITH CONSIDERABLE HELP FROM HIS FRIENDS--ONE OF WHOM IS A RENOWNED GENIUS.

The Ascent

In which we take a moment to see what's been happening in the Business Office lately.

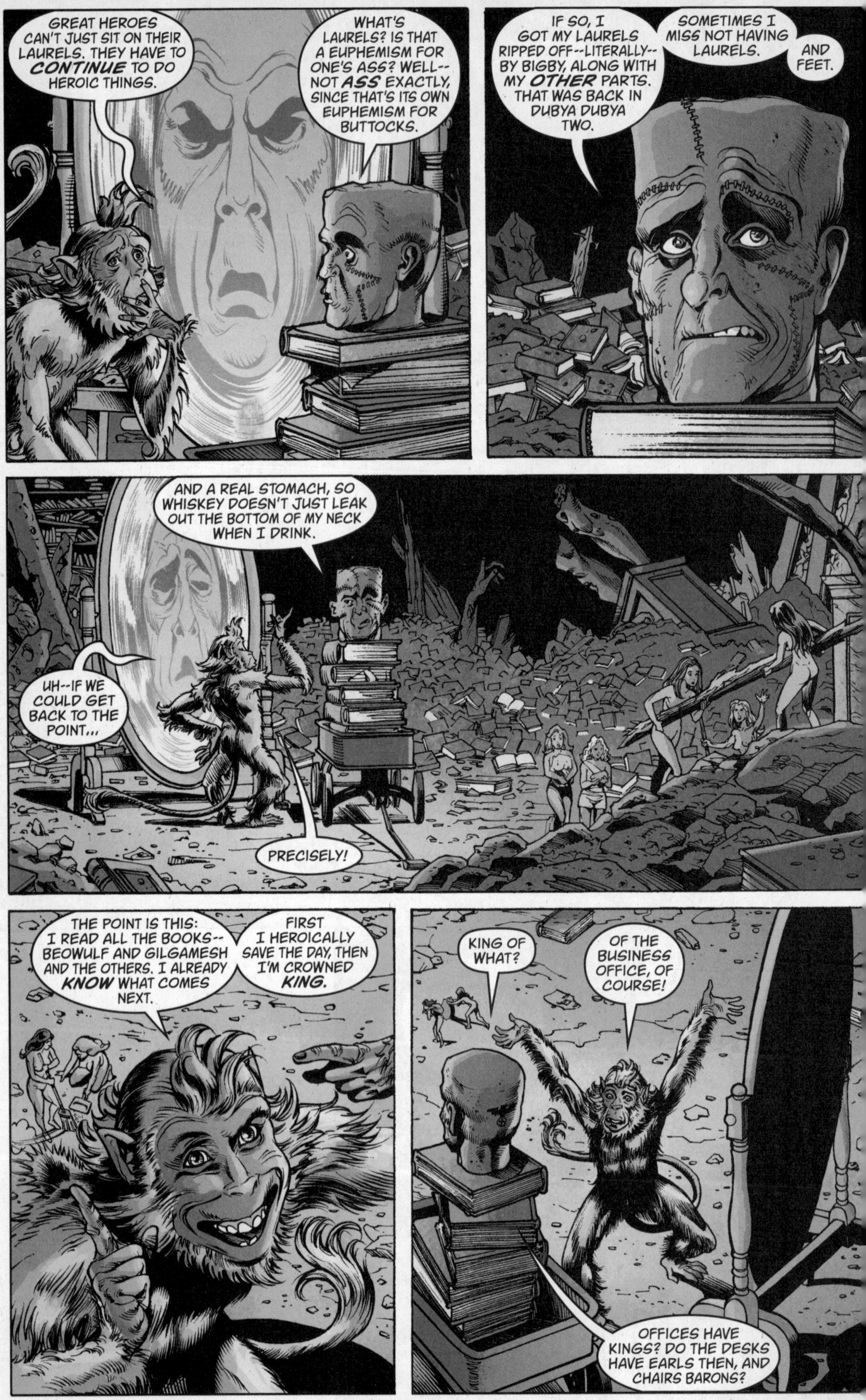
GREAT HEROES CAN'T JUST SIT ON THEIR LAURELS. THEY HAVE TO *CONTINUE* TO DO HEROIC THINGS.
WHAT'S LAURELS? IS THAT A EUPHEMISM FOR ONE'S ASS? WELL-- NOT *ASS* EXACTLY, SINCE THAT'S ITS OWN EUPHEMISM FOR BUTTOCKS.
IF SO, I GOT MY LAURELS RIPPED OFF--LITERALLY-- BY BIGBY, ALONG WITH MY *OTHER* PARTS. THAT WAS BACK IN DUBYA DUBYA TWO.
SOMETIMES I MISS NOT HAVING LAURELS.
AND FEET.
AND A REAL STOMACH, SO WHISKEY DOESN'T JUST LEAK OUT THE BOTTOM OF MY NECK WHEN I DRINK.
UH--IF WE COULD GET BACK TO THE POINT...
PRECISELY!
THE POINT IS THIS: I READ ALL THE BOOKS-- BEOWULF AND GILGAMESH AND THE OTHERS. I ALREADY *KNOW* WHAT COMES NEXT.
FIRST I HEROICALLY SAVE THE DAY, THEN I'M CROWNED *KING.*
KING OF WHAT?
OF THE BUSINESS OFFICE, OF COURSE!
OFFICES HAVE KINGS? DO THE DESKS HAVE EARLS THEN, AND CHAIRS BARONS?

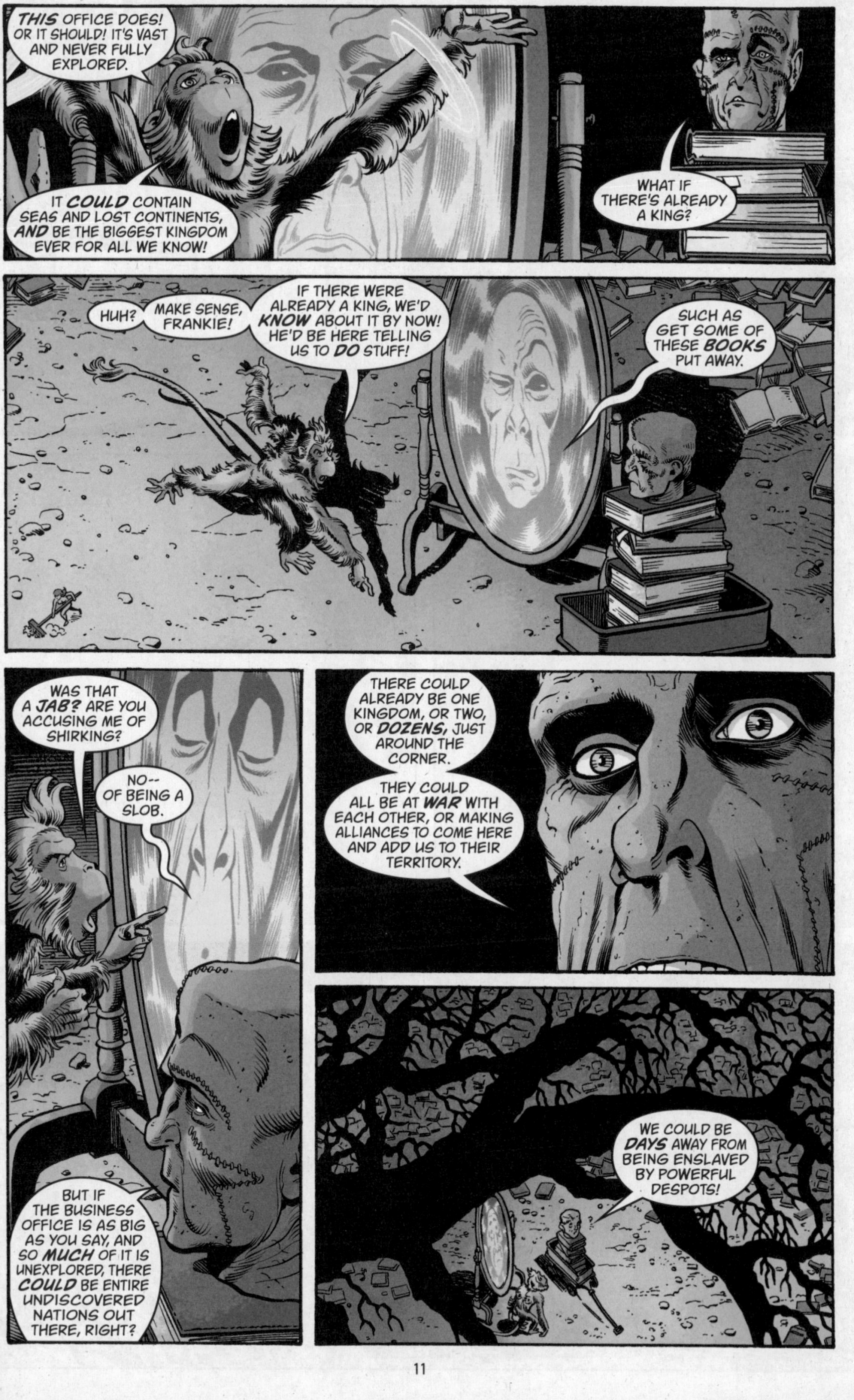
THIS OFFICE DOES! OR IT SHOULD! IT'S VAST AND NEVER FULLY EXPLORED.
IT COULD CONTAIN SEAS AND LOST CONTINENTS, AND BE THE BIGGEST KINGDOM EVER FOR ALL WE KNOW!
WHAT IF THERE'S ALREADY A KING?
HUH?
MAKE SENSE, FRANKIE!
IF THERE WERE ALREADY A KING, WE'D KNOW ABOUT IT BY NOW! HE'D BE HERE TELLING US TO DO STUFF!
SUCH AS GET SOME OF THESE BOOKS PUT AWAY.
WAS THAT A JAB? ARE YOU ACCUSING ME OF SHIRKING?
NO-- OF BEING A SLOB.
BUT IF THE BUSINESS OFFICE IS AS BIG AS YOU SAY, AND SO MUCH OF IT IS UNEXPLORED, THERE COULD BE ENTIRE UNDISCOVERED NATIONS OUT THERE, RIGHT?
THERE COULD ALREADY BE ONE KINGDOM, OR TWO, OR DOZENS, JUST AROUND THE CORNER.
THEY COULD ALL BE AT WAR WITH EACH OTHER, OR MAKING ALLIANCES TO COME HERE AND ADD US TO THEIR TERRITORY.
WE COULD BE DAYS AWAY FROM BEING ENSLAVED BY POWERFUL DESPOTS!

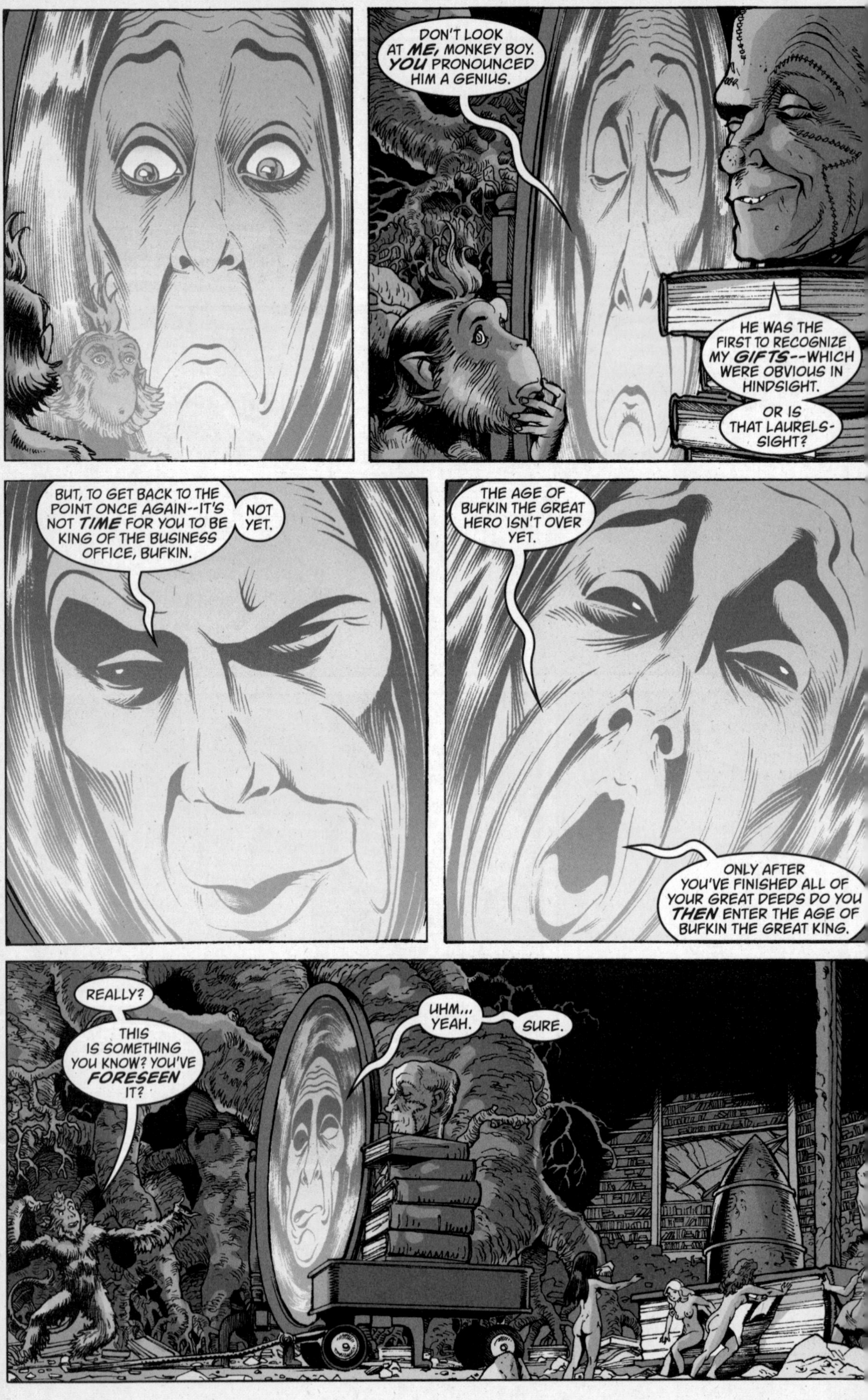
DON'T LOOK AT ME, MONKEY BOY. YOU PRONOUNCED HIM A GENIUS.
HE WAS THE FIRST TO RECOGNIZE MY GIFTS--WHICH WERE OBVIOUS IN HINDSIGHT.
OR IS THAT LAURELS-SIGHT?
BUT, TO GET BACK TO THE POINT ONCE AGAIN--IT'S NOT TIME FOR YOU TO BE KING OF THE BUSINESS OFFICE, BUFKIN.
NOT YET.
THE AGE OF BUFKIN THE GREAT HERO ISN'T OVER YET.
ONLY AFTER YOU'VE FINISHED ALL OF YOUR GREAT DEEDS DO YOU THEN ENTER THE AGE OF BUFKIN THE GREAT KING.
REALLY?
THIS IS SOMETHING YOU KNOW? YOU'VE FORESEEN IT?
UHM... YEAH.
SURE.

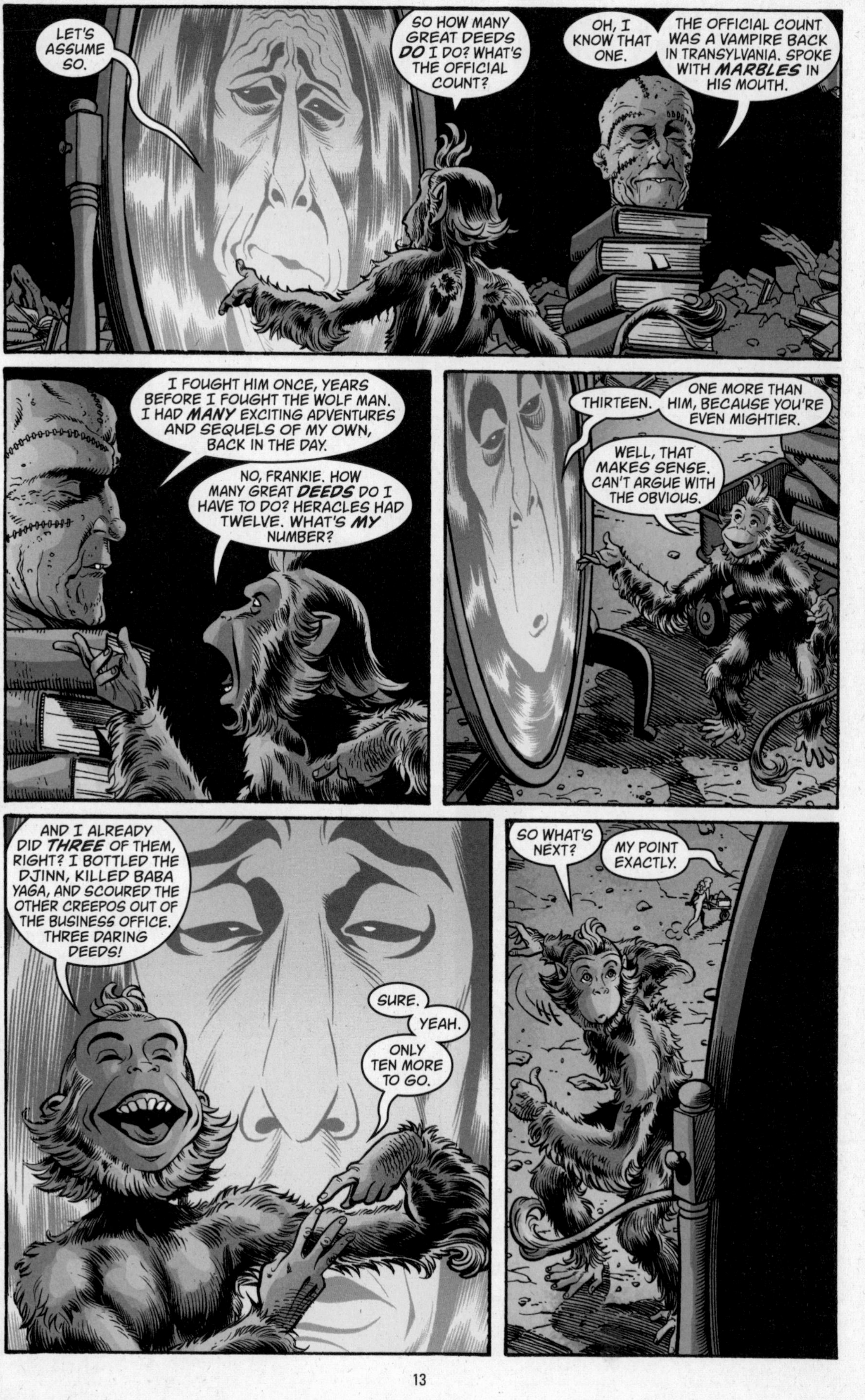
LET'S ASSUME SO.
SO HOW MANY GREAT DEEDS DO I DO? WHAT'S THE OFFICIAL COUNT?
OH, I KNOW THAT ONE.
THE OFFICIAL COUNT WAS A VAMPIRE BACK IN TRANSYLVANIA. SPOKE WITH MARBLES IN HIS MOUTH.
I FOUGHT HIM ONCE, YEARS BEFORE I FOUGHT THE WOLF MAN. I HAD MANY EXCITING ADVENTURES AND SEQUELS OF MY OWN, BACK IN THE DAY.
NO, FRANKIE. HOW MANY GREAT DEEDS DO I HAVE TO DO? HERACLES HAD TWELVE. WHAT'S MY NUMBER?
THIRTEEN.
ONE MORE THAN HIM, BECAUSE YOU'RE EVEN MIGHTIER.
WELL, THAT MAKES SENSE. CAN'T ARGUE WITH THE OBVIOUS.
AND I ALREADY DID THREE OF THEM, RIGHT? I BOTTLED THE DJINN, KILLED BABA YAGA, AND SCOURED THE OTHER CREEPOS OUT OF THE BUSINESS OFFICE. THREE DARING DEEDS!
SURE.
YEAH.
ONLY TEN MORE TO GO.
SO WHAT'S NEXT?
MY POINT EXACTLY.

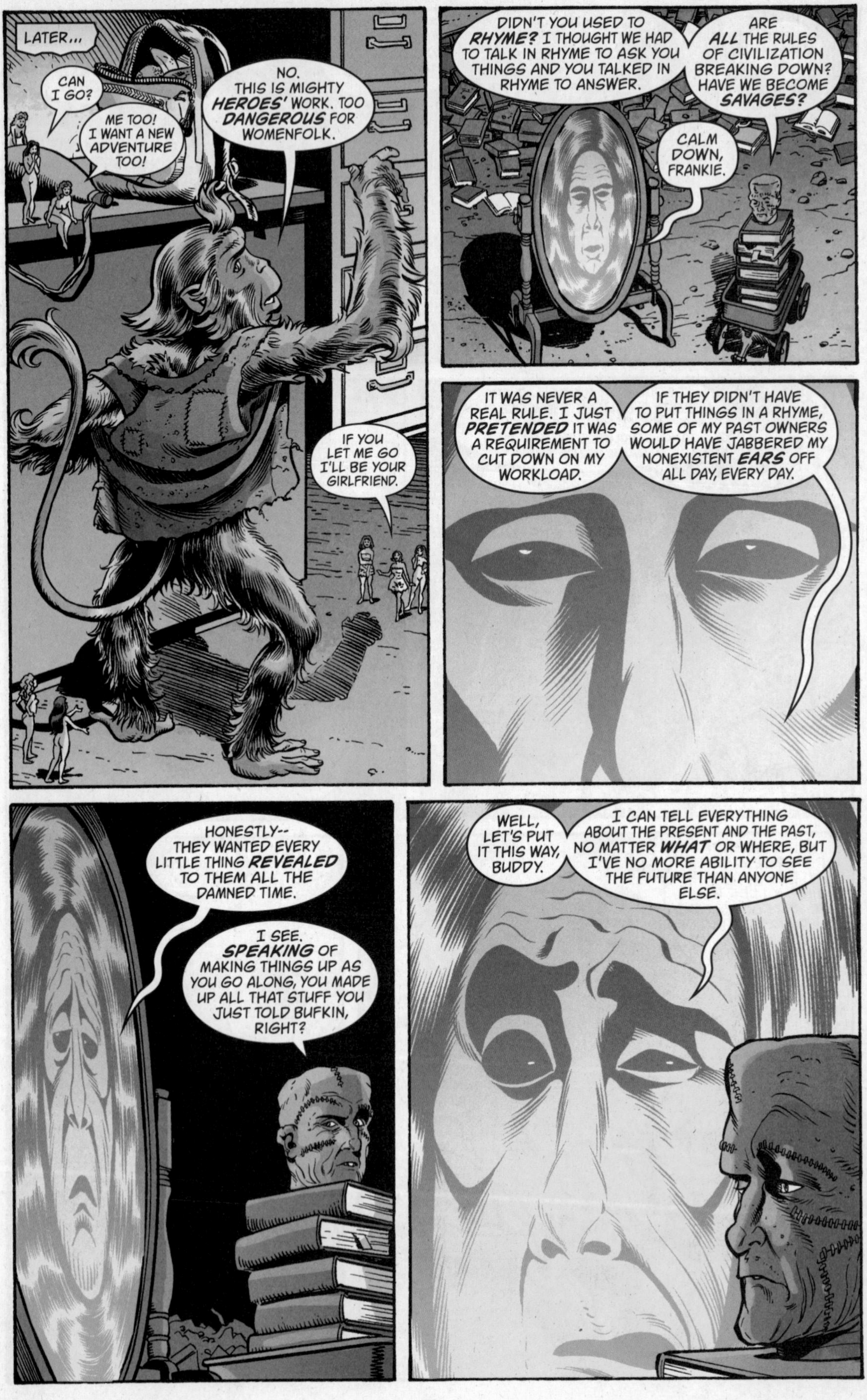
LATER...
CAN I GO?
ME TOO! I WANT A NEW ADVENTURE TOO!
NO. THIS IS MIGHTY HEROES' WORK. TOO DANGEROUS FOR WOMENFOLK.
IF YOU LET ME GO I'LL BE YOUR GIRLFRIEND.
DIDN'T YOU USED TO RHYME? I THOUGHT WE HAD TO TALK IN RHYME TO ASK YOU THINGS AND YOU TALKED IN RHYME TO ANSWER.
ARE ALL THE RULES OF CIVILIZATION BREAKING DOWN? HAVE WE BECOME SAVAGES?
CALM DOWN, FRANKIE.
IT WAS NEVER A REAL RULE. I JUST PRETENDED IT WAS A REQUIREMENT TO CUT DOWN ON MY WORKLOAD.
IF THEY DIDN'T HAVE TO PUT THINGS IN A RHYME, SOME OF MY PAST OWNERS WOULD HAVE JABBERED MY NONEXISTENT EARS OFF ALL DAY, EVERY DAY.
HONESTLY-- THEY WANTED EVERY LITTLE THING REVEALED TO THEM ALL THE DAMNED TIME.
I SEE. SPEAKING OF MAKING THINGS UP AS YOU GO ALONG, YOU MADE UP ALL THAT STUFF YOU JUST TOLD BUFKIN, RIGHT?
WELL, LET'S PUT IT THIS WAY, BUDDY.
I CAN TELL EVERYTHING ABOUT THE PRESENT AND THE PAST, NO MATTER WHAT OR WHERE, BUT I'VE NO MORE ABILITY TO SEE THE FUTURE THAN ANYONE ELSE.

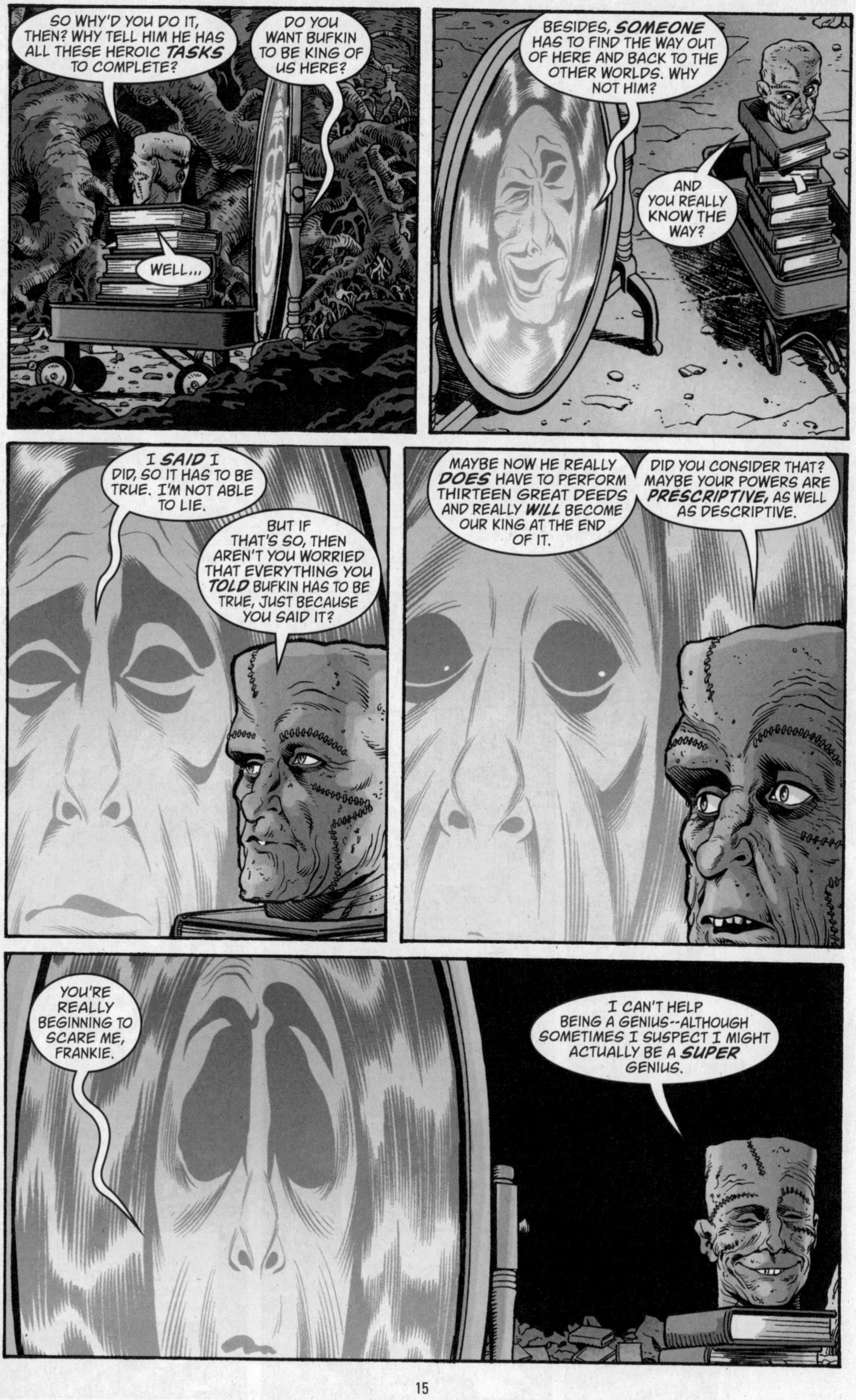
SO WHY'D YOU DO IT, THEN? WHY TELL HIM HE HAS ALL THESE HEROIC TASKS TO COMPLETE?
DO YOU WANT BUFKIN TO BE KING OF US HERE?
WELL...
BESIDES, SOMEONE HAS TO FIND THE WAY OUT OF HERE AND BACK TO THE OTHER WORLDS. WHY NOT HIM?
AND YOU REALLY KNOW THE WAY?
I SAID I DID, SO IT HAS TO BE TRUE. I'M NOT ABLE TO LIE.
BUT IF THAT'S SO, THEN AREN'T YOU WORRIED THAT EVERYTHING YOU TOLD BUFKIN HAS TO BE TRUE, JUST BECAUSE YOU SAID IT?
MAYBE NOW HE REALLY DOES HAVE TO PERFORM THIRTEEN GREAT DEEDS AND REALLY WILL BECOME OUR KING AT THE END OF IT.
DID YOU CONSIDER THAT? MAYBE YOUR POWERS ARE PRESCRIPTIVE, AS WELL AS DESCRIPTIVE.
YOU'RE REALLY BEGINNING TO SCARE ME, FRANKIE.
I CAN'T HELP BEING A GENIUS--ALTHOUGH SOMETIMES I SUSPECT I MIGHT ACTUALLY BE A SUPER GENIUS.

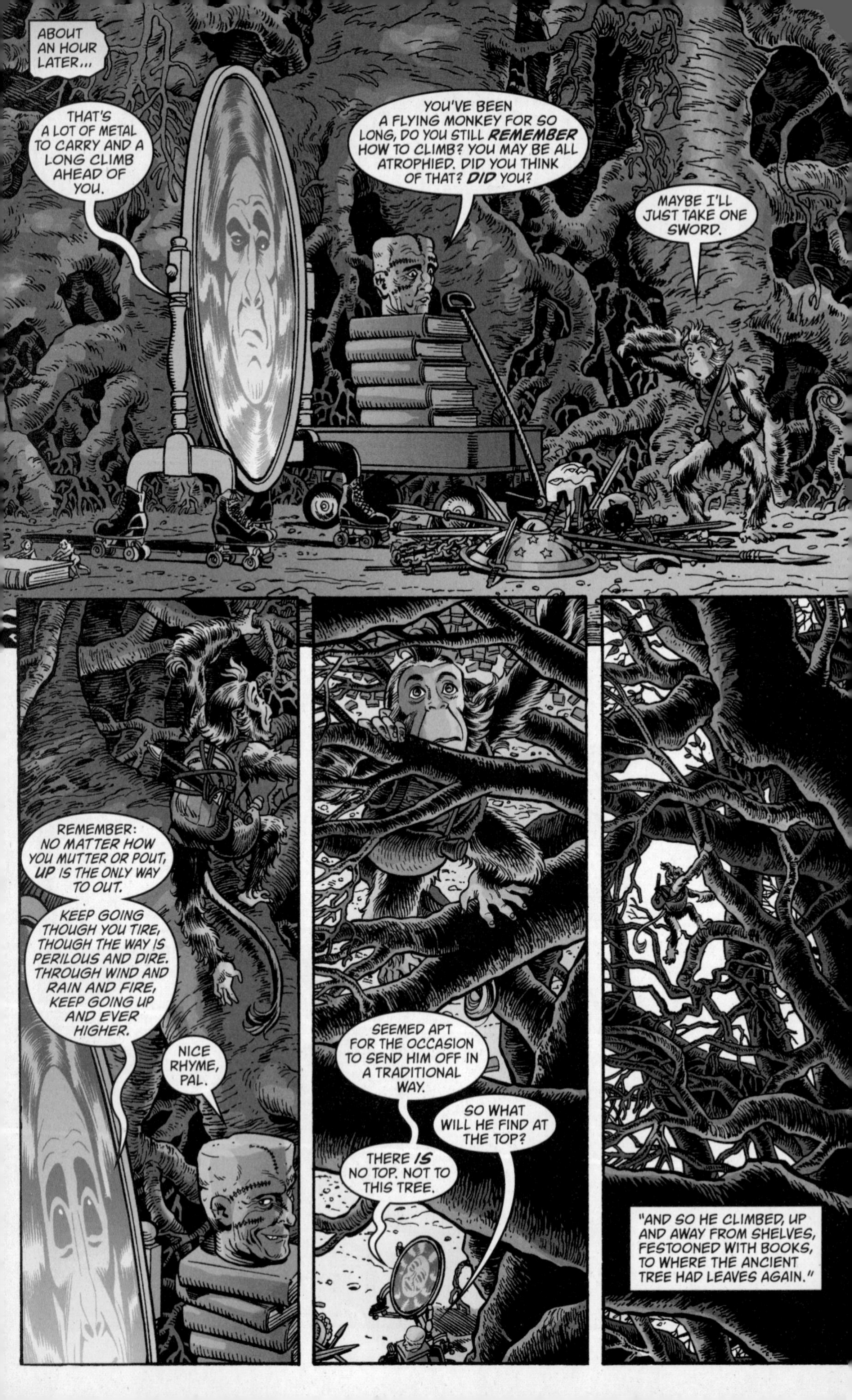
ABOUT AN HOUR LATER...
THAT'S A LOT OF METAL TO CARRY AND A LONG CLIMB AHEAD OF YOU.
YOU'VE BEEN A FLYING MONKEY FOR SO LONG, DO YOU STILL REMEMBER HOW TO CLIMB? YOU MAY BE ALL ATROPHIED. DID YOU THINK OF THAT? DID YOU?
MAYBE I'LL JUST TAKE ONE SWORD.
REMEMBER: NO MATTER HOW YOU MUTTER OR POUT, UP IS THE ONLY WAY TO OUT.
KEEP GOING THOUGH YOU TIRE, THOUGH THE WAY IS PERILOUS AND DIRE. THROUGH WIND AND RAIN AND FIRE, KEEP GOING UP AND EVER HIGHER.
NICE RHYME, PAL.
SEEMED APT FOR THE OCCASION TO SEND HIM OFF IN A TRADITIONAL WAY.
SO WHAT WILL HE FIND AT THE TOP?
THERE IS NO TOP. NOT TO THIS TREE.
"AND SO HE CLIMBED, UP AND AWAY FROM SHELVES, FESTOONED WITH BOOKS, TO WHERE THE ANCIENT TREE HAD LEAVES AGAIN."

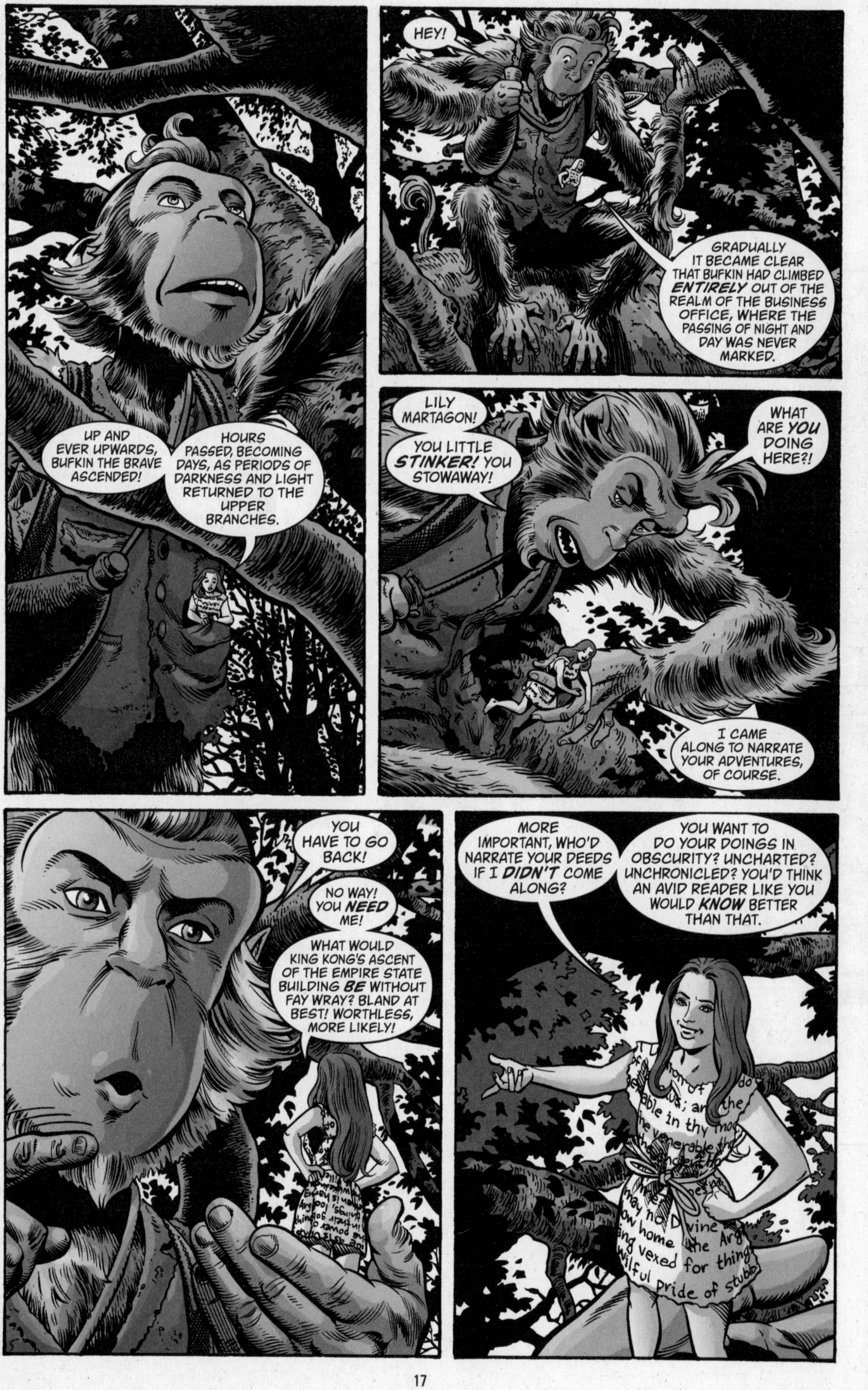

UP AND EVER UPWARDS, BUFKIN THE BRAVE ASCENDED!
HOURS PASSED, BECOMING DAYS, AS PERIODS OF DARKNESS AND LIGHT RETURNED TO THE UPPER BRANCHES.
HEY!
GRADUALLY IT BECAME CLEAR THAT BUFKIN HAD CLIMBED ENTIRELY OUT OF THE REALM OF THE BUSINESS OFFICE, WHERE THE PASSING OF NIGHT AND DAY WAS NEVER MARKED.
LILY MARTAGON!
YOU LITTLE STINKER! YOU STOWAWAY!
WHAT ARE YOU DOING HERE?!
I CAME ALONG TO NARRATE YOUR ADVENTURES, OF COURSE.
YOU HAVE TO GO BACK!
NO WAY! YOU NEED ME!
WHAT WOULD KING KONG'S ASCENT OF THE EMPIRE STATE BUILDING BE WITHOUT FAY WRAY? BLAND AT BEST! WORTHLESS, MORE LIKELY!
MORE IMPORTANT, WHO'D NARRATE YOUR DEEDS IF I DIDN'T COME ALONG?
YOU WANT TO DO YOUR DOINGS IN OBSCURITY? UNCHARTED? UNCHRONICLED? YOU'D THINK AN AVID READER LIKE YOU WOULD KNOW BETTER THAN THAT.

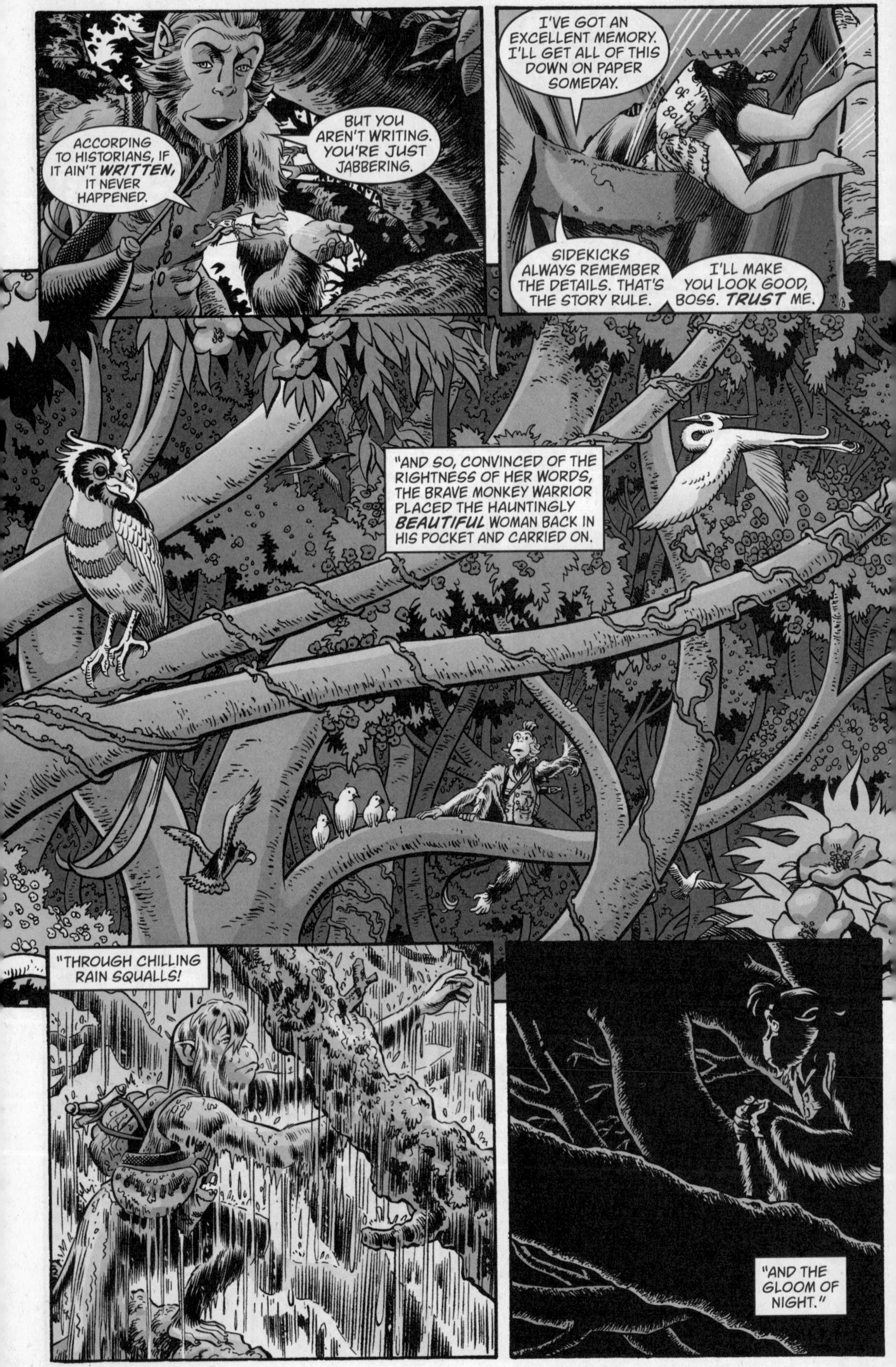

ACCORDING TO HISTORIANS, IF IT AIN'T WRITTEN, IT NEVER HAPPENED.
BUT YOU AREN'T WRITING. YOU'RE JUST JABBERING.
I'VE GOT AN EXCELLENT MEMORY. I'LL GET ALL OF THIS DOWN ON PAPER SOMEDAY.
SIDEKICKS ALWAYS REMEMBER THE DETAILS. THAT'S THE STORY RULE.
I'LL MAKE YOU LOOK GOOD, BOSS. TRUST ME.
"AND SO, CONVINCED OF THE RIGHTNESS OF HER WORDS, THE BRAVE MONKEY WARRIOR PLACED THE HAUNTINGLY BEAUTIFUL WOMAN BACK IN HIS POCKET AND CARRIED ON.
"THROUGH CHILLING RAIN SQUALLS!
"AND THE GLOOM OF NIGHT."

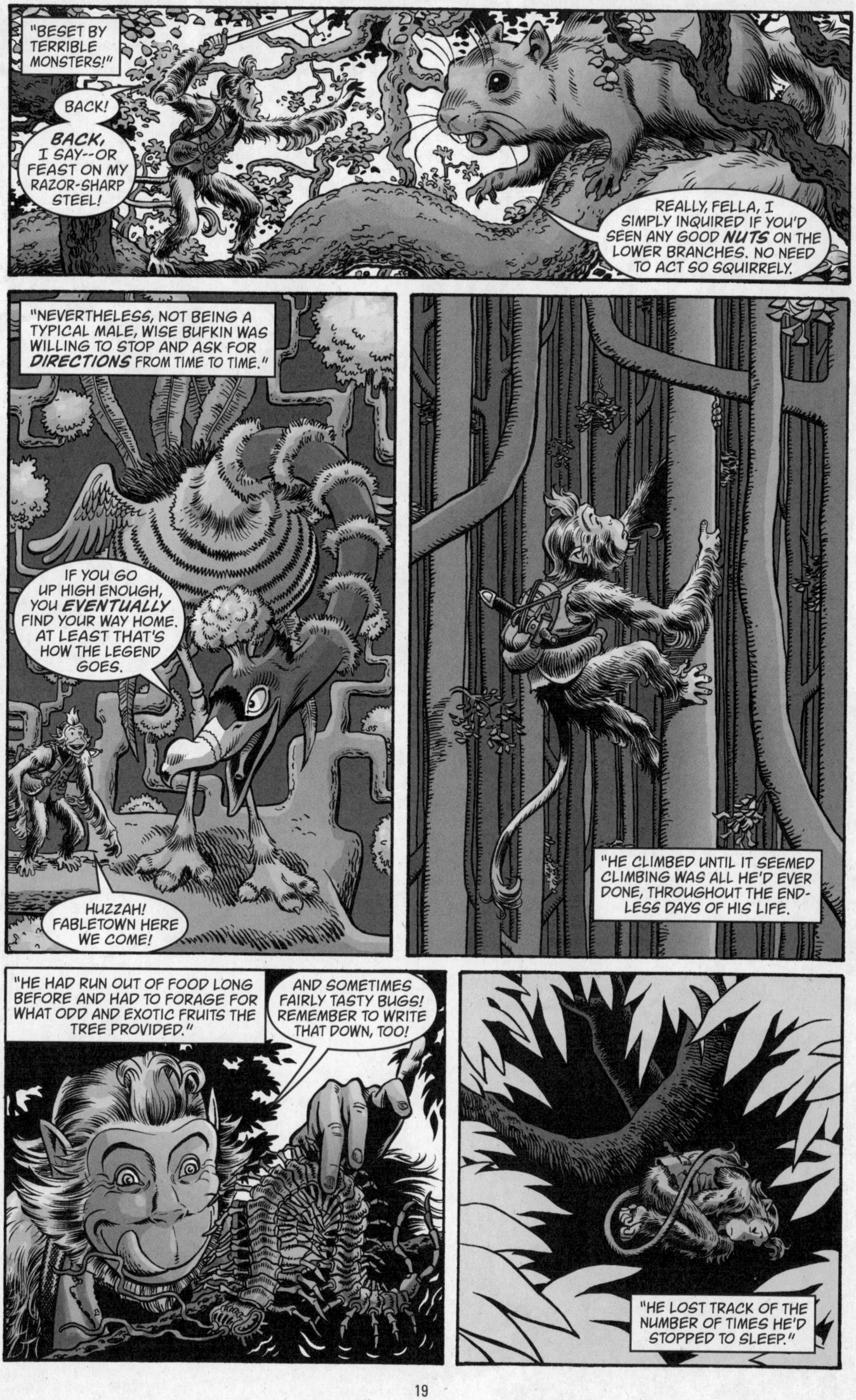
"BESET BY TERRIBLE MONSTERS!"
BACK!
BACK, I SAY--OR FEAST ON MY RAZOR-SHARP STEEL!
REALLY, FELLA, I SIMPLY INQUIRED IF YOU'D SEEN ANY GOOD NUTS ON THE LOWER BRANCHES. NO NEED TO ACT SO SQUIRRELY.
"NEVERTHELESS, NOT BEING A TYPICAL MALE, WISE BUFKIN WAS WILLING TO STOP AND ASK FOR DIRECTIONS FROM TIME TO TIME."
IF YOU GO UP HIGH ENOUGH, YOU EVENTUALLY FIND YOUR WAY HOME. AT LEAST THAT'S HOW THE LEGEND GOES.
HUZZAH! FABLETOWN HERE WE COME!
"HE CLIMBED UNTIL IT SEEMED CLIMBING WAS ALL HE'D EVER DONE, THROUGHOUT THE END-LESS DAYS OF HIS LIFE.
"HE HAD RUN OUT OF FOOD LONG BEFORE AND HAD TO FORAGE FOR WHAT ODD AND EXOTIC FRUITS THE TREE PROVIDED."
AND SOMETIMES FAIRLY TASTY BUGS! REMEMBER TO WRITE THAT DOWN, TOO!
"HE LOST TRACK OF THE NUMBER OF TIMES HE'D STOPPED TO SLEEP."

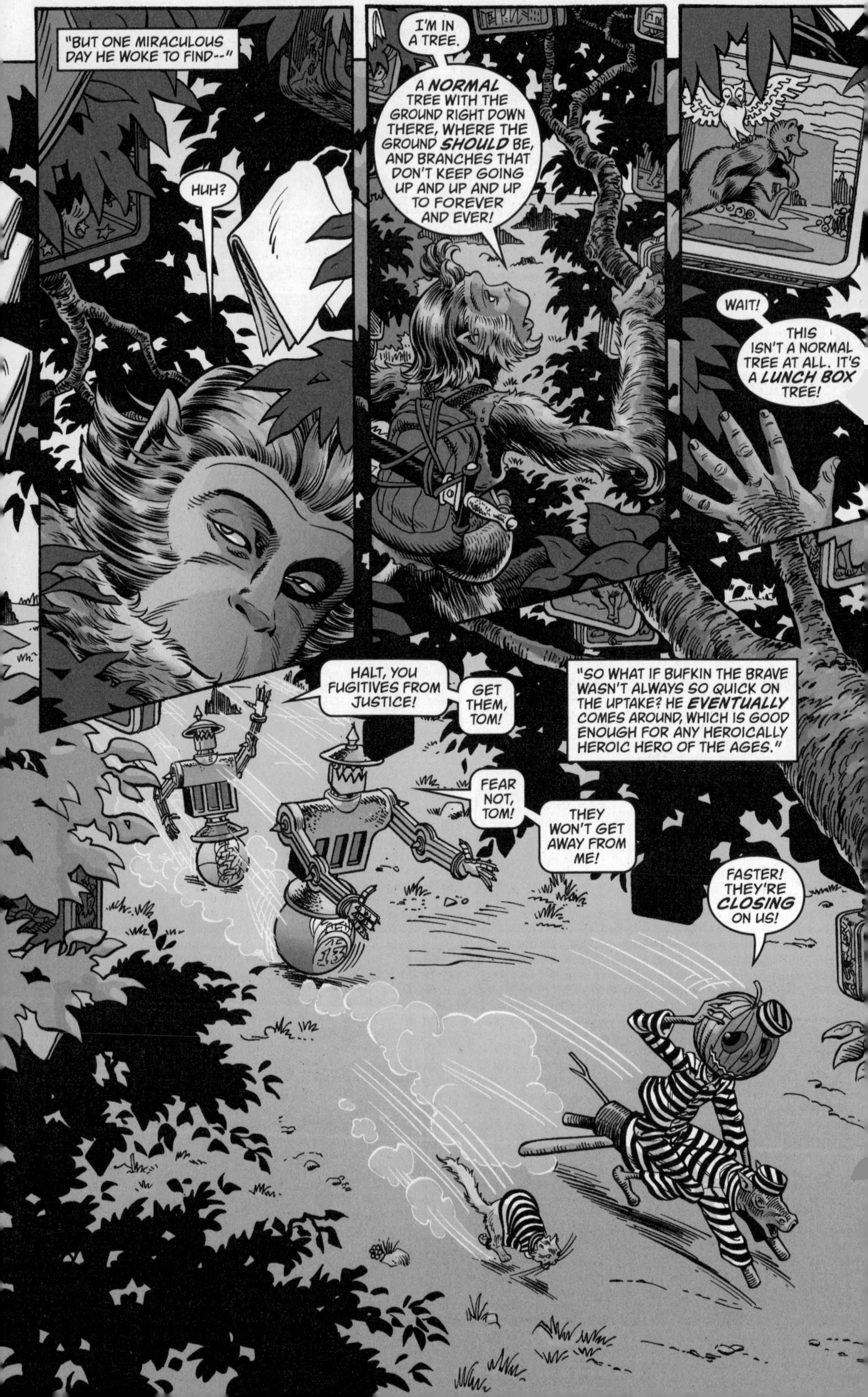
"BUT ONE MIRACULOUS DAY HE WOKE TO FIND--"
HUH?
I'M IN A TREE.
A NORMAL TREE WITH THE GROUND RIGHT DOWN THERE, WHERE THE GROUND SHOULD BE, AND BRANCHES THAT DON'T KEEP GOING UP AND UP AND UP TO FOREVER AND EVER!
WAIT!
THIS ISN'T A NORMAL TREE AT ALL. IT'S A LUNCH BOX TREE!
HALT, YOU FUGITIVES FROM JUSTICE!
GET THEM, TOM!
"SO WHAT IF BUFKIN THE BRAVE WASN'T ALWAYS SO QUICK ON THE UPTAKE? HE EVENTUALLY COMES AROUND, WHICH IS GOOD ENOUGH FOR ANY HEROICALLY HEROIC HERO OF THE AGES."
FEAR NOT, TOM!
THEY WON'T GET AWAY FROM ME!
FASTER! THEY'RE CLOSING ON US!

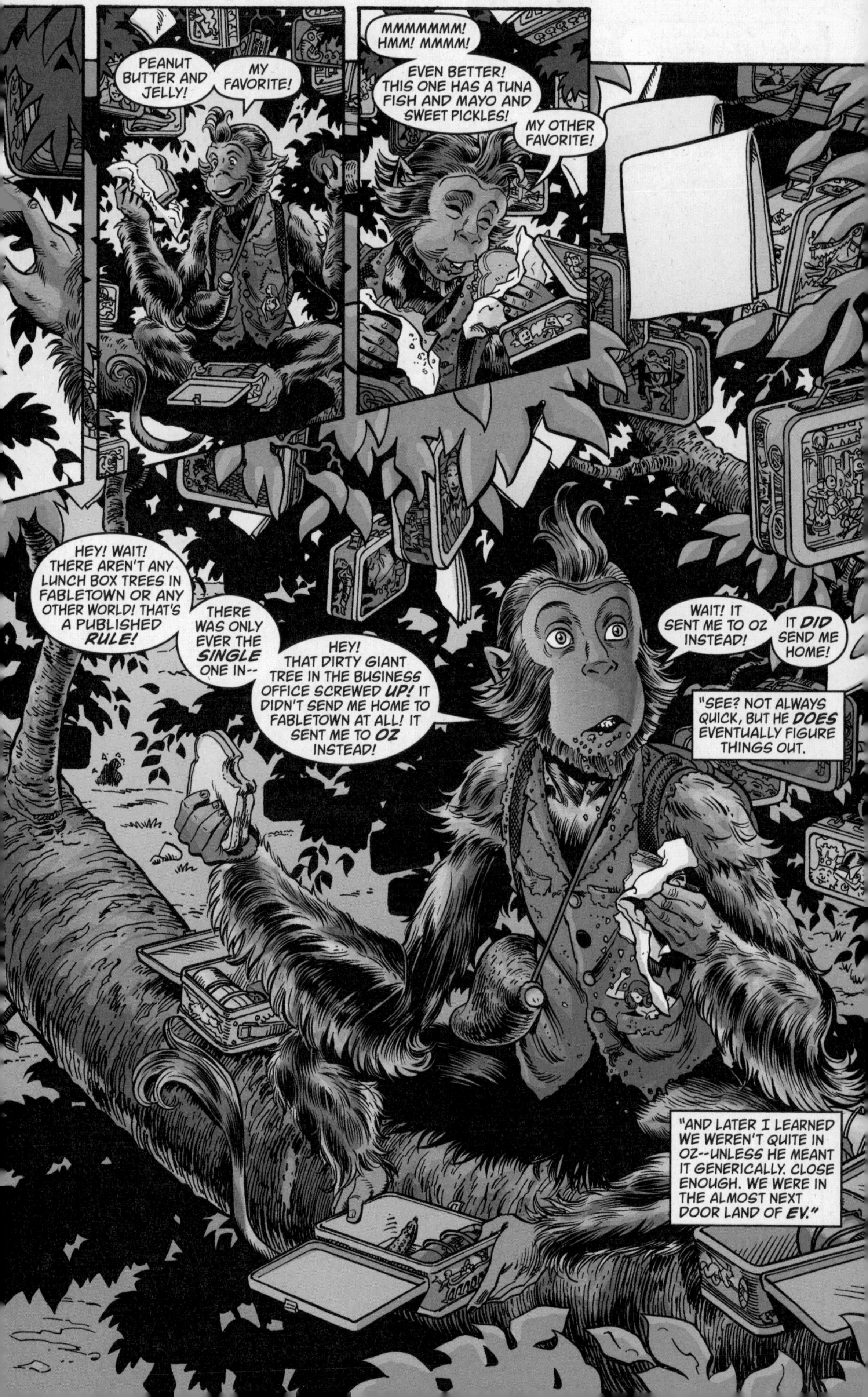
PEANUT BUTTER AND JELLY!
MY FAVORITE!
MMMMMMM! HMM! MMMM!
EVEN BETTER! THIS ONE HAS A TUNA FISH AND MAYO AND SWEET PICKLES!
MY OTHER FAVORITE!
HEY! WAIT! THERE AREN'T ANY LUNCH BOX TREES IN FABLETOWN OR ANY OTHER WORLD! THAT'S A PUBLISHED RULE!
THERE WAS ONLY EVER THE SINGLE ONE IN--
HEY! THAT DIRTY GIANT TREE IN THE BUSINESS OFFICE SCREWED UP! IT DIDN'T SEND ME HOME TO FABLETOWN AT ALL! IT SENT ME TO OZ INSTEAD!
WAIT! IT SENT ME TO OZ INSTEAD!
IT DID SEND ME HOME!
"SEE? NOT ALWAYS QUICK, BUT HE DOES EVENTUALLY FIGURE THINGS OUT.
"AND LATER I LEARNED WE WEREN'T QUITE IN OZ--UNLESS HE MEANT IT GENERICALLY. CLOSE ENOUGH. WE WERE IN THE ALMOST NEXT DOOR LAND OF EV."

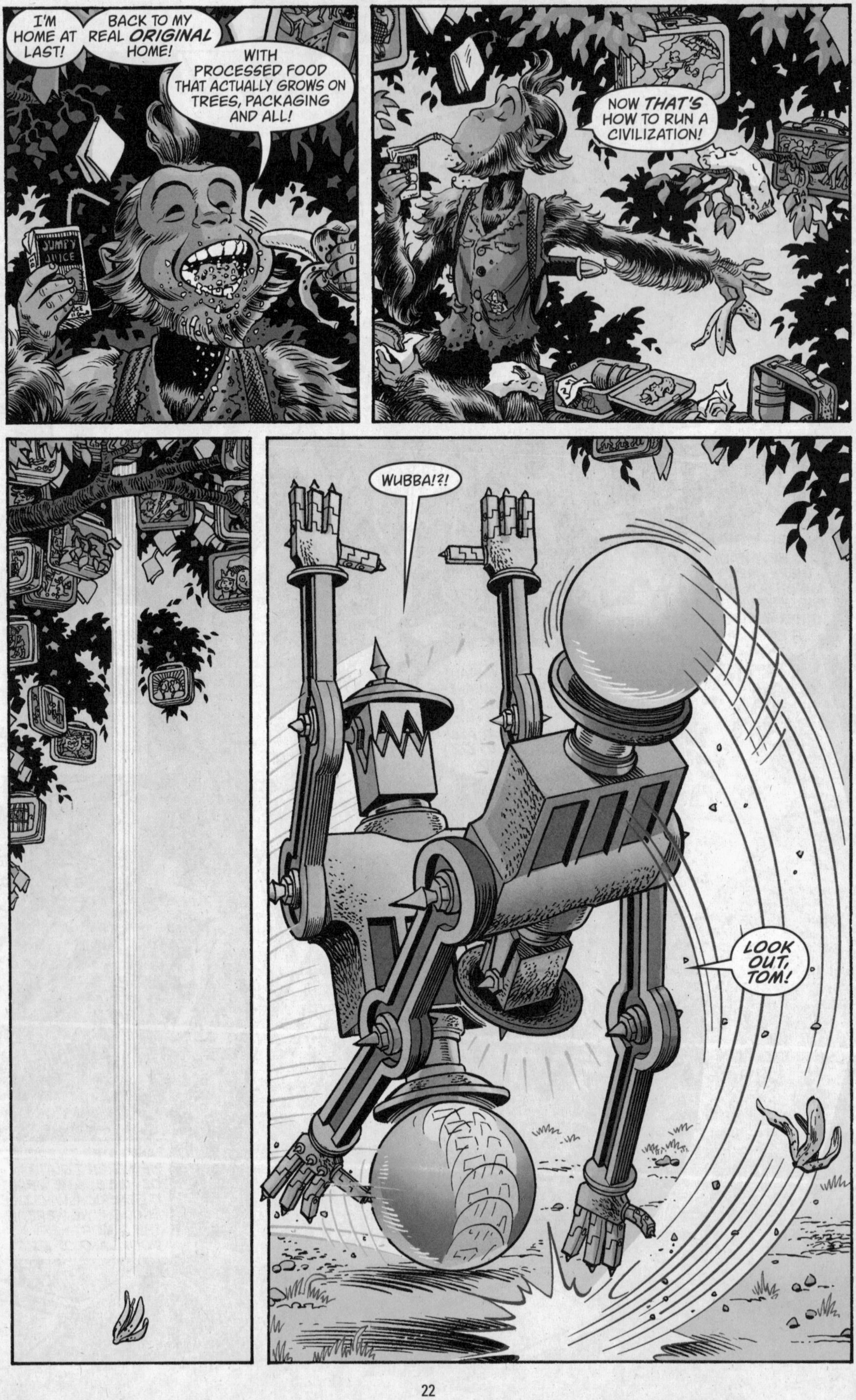
I'M HOME AT LAST!
BACK TO MY REAL ORIGINAL HOME!
WITH PROCESSED FOOD THAT ACTUALLY GROWS ON TREES, PACKAGING AND ALL!
JUMPY JUICE
NOW THAT'S HOW TO RUN A CIVILIZATION!
WUBBA!?!
LOOK OUT, TOM!

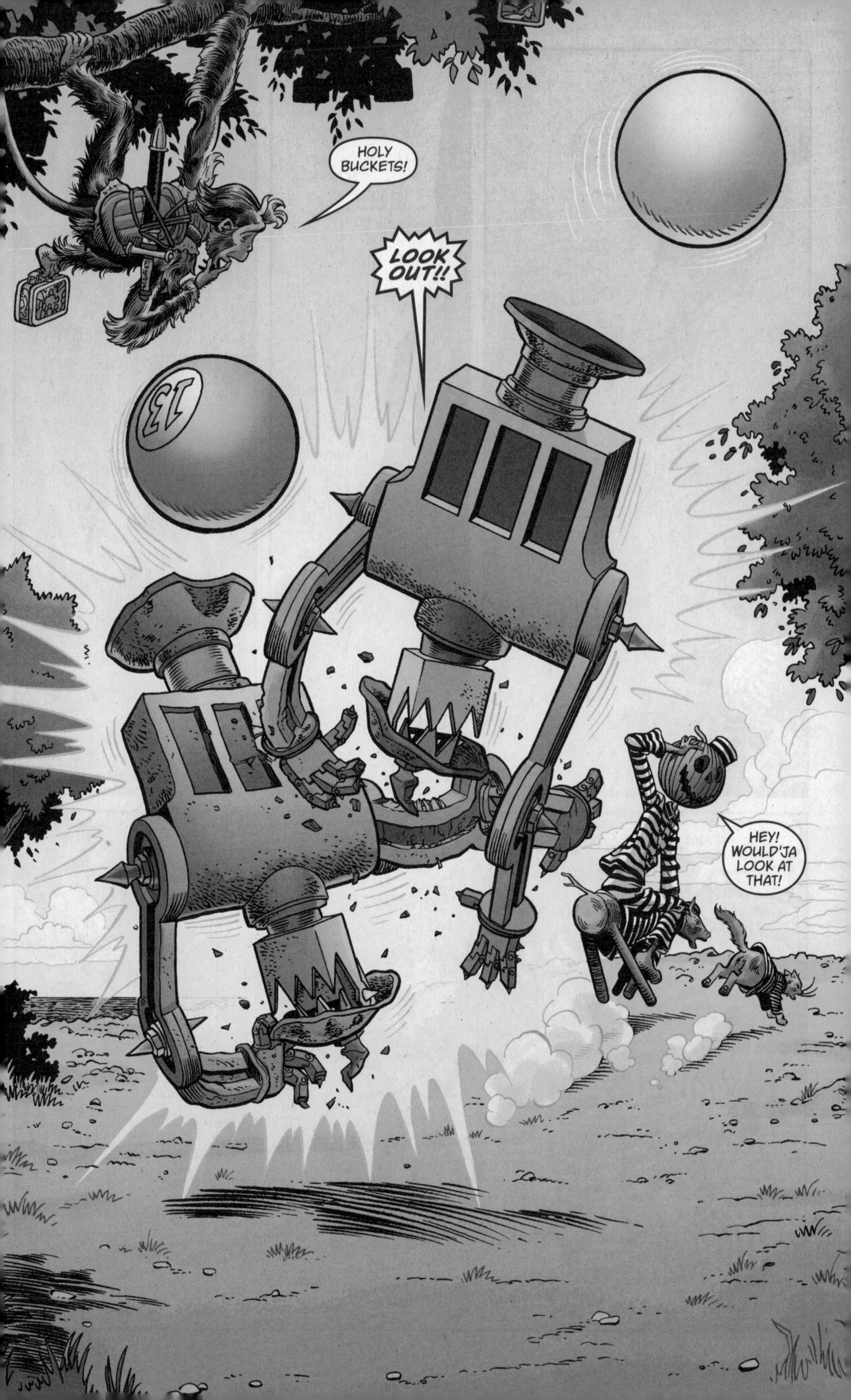
HOLY BUCKETS!
LOOK OUT!!
13
HEY! WOULD'JA LOOK AT THAT!

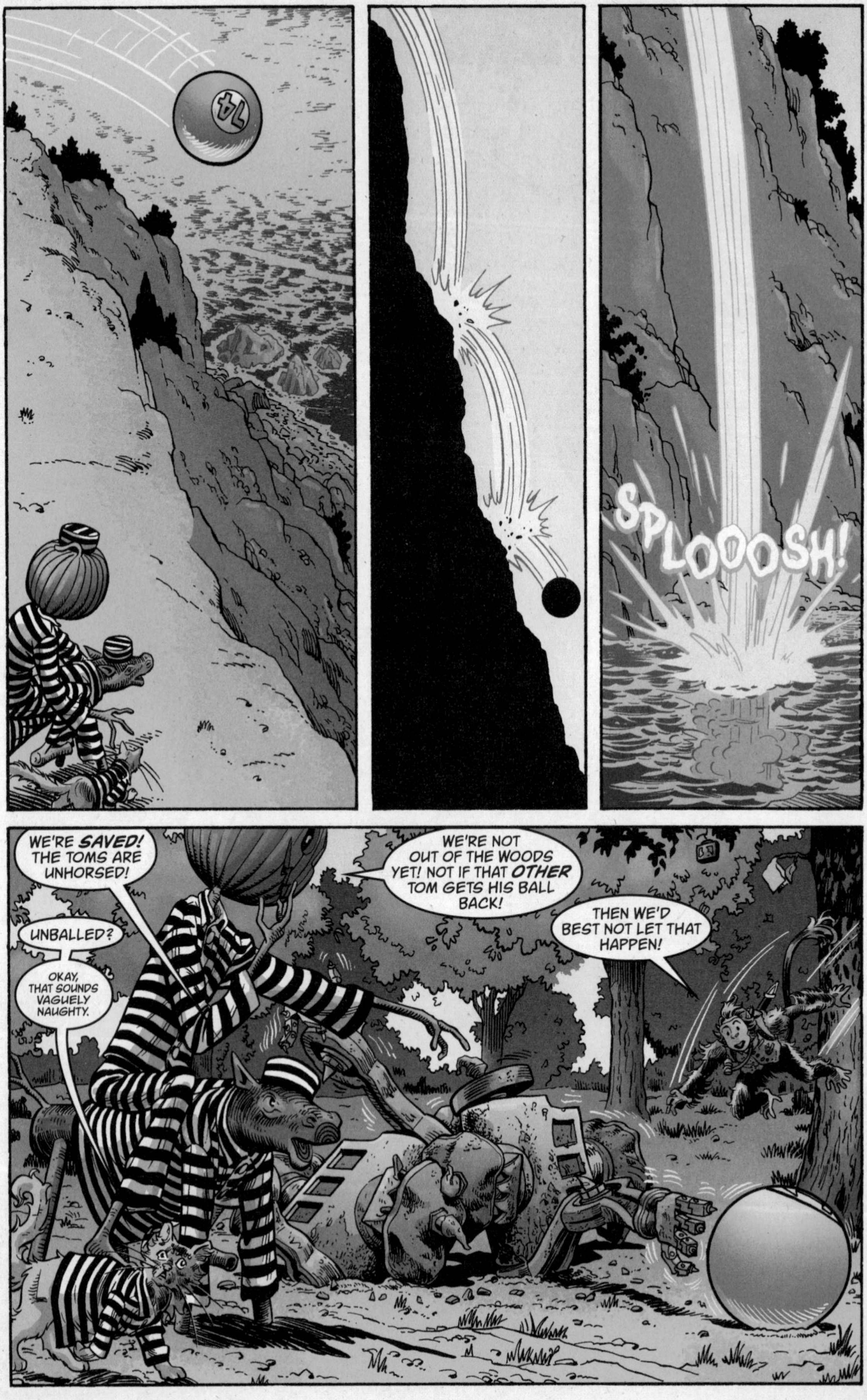

74
SPLOOOSH!
WE'RE SAVED! THE TOMS ARE UNHORSED!
UNBALLED?
OKAY, THAT SOUNDS VAGUELY NAUGHTY.
WE'RE NOT OUT OF THE WOODS YET! NOT IF THAT OTHER TOM GETS HIS BALL BACK!
THEN WE'D BEST NOT LET THAT HAPPEN!

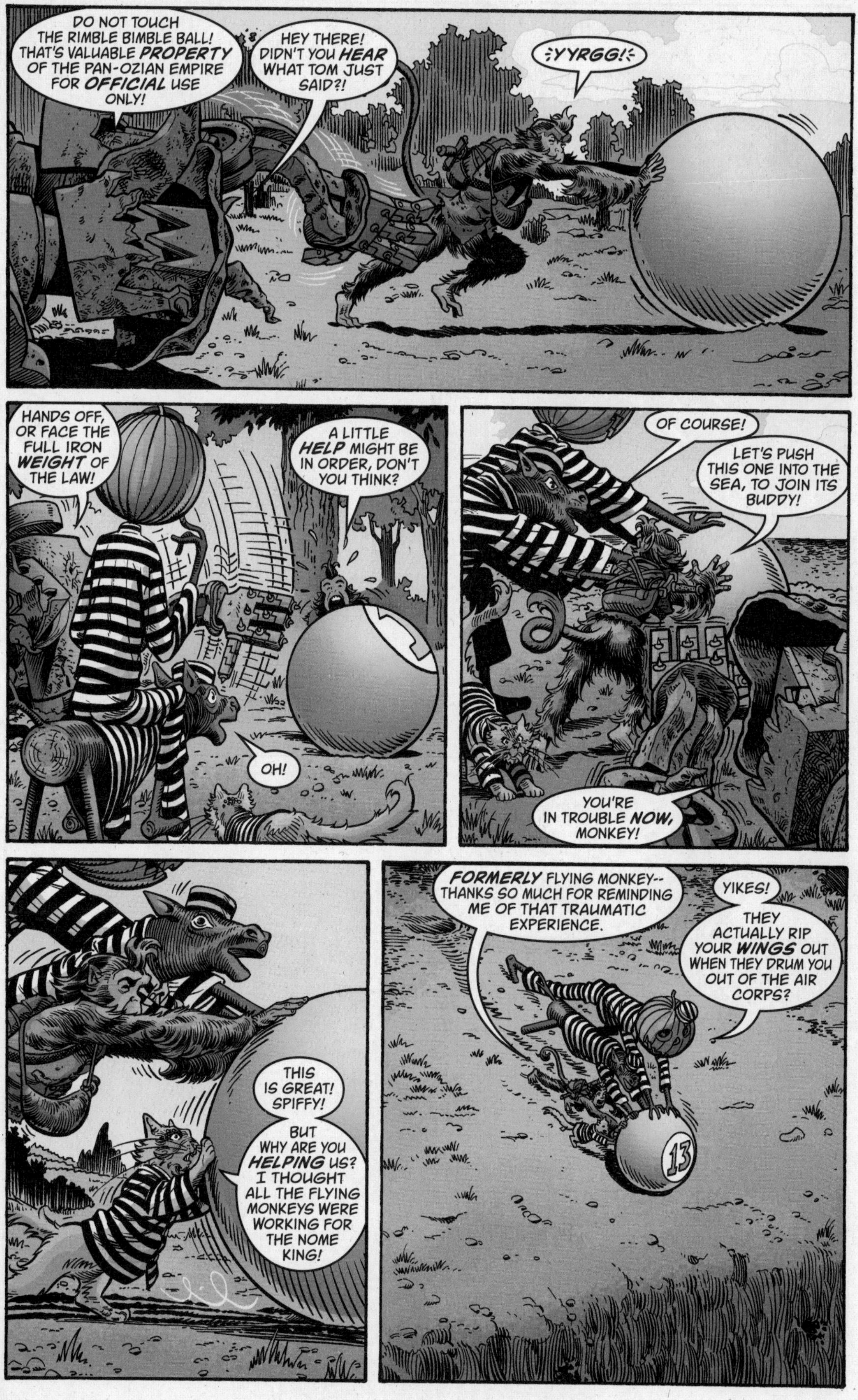
DO NOT TOUCH THE RIMBLE BIMBLE BALL! THAT'S VALUABLE PROPERTY OF THE PAN-OZIAN EMPIRE FOR OFFICIAL USE ONLY!
HEY THERE! DIDN'T YOU HEAR WHAT TOM JUST SAID?!
YYRGG!
HANDS OFF, OR FACE THE FULL IRON WEIGHT OF THE LAW!
A LITTLE HELP MIGHT BE IN ORDER, DON'T YOU THINK?
OH!
OF COURSE!
LET'S PUSH THIS ONE INTO THE SEA, TO JOIN ITS BUDDY!
YOU'RE IN TROUBLE NOW, MONKEY!
THIS IS GREAT! SPIFFY!
BUT WHY ARE YOU HELPING US? I THOUGHT ALL THE FLYING MONKEYS WERE WORKING FOR THE NOME KING!
FORMERLY FLYING MONKEY-- THANKS SO MUCH FOR REMINDING ME OF THAT TRAUMATIC EXPERIENCE.
YIKES!
THEY ACTUALLY RIP YOUR WINGS OUT WHEN THEY DRUM YOU OUT OF THE AIR CORPS?
13

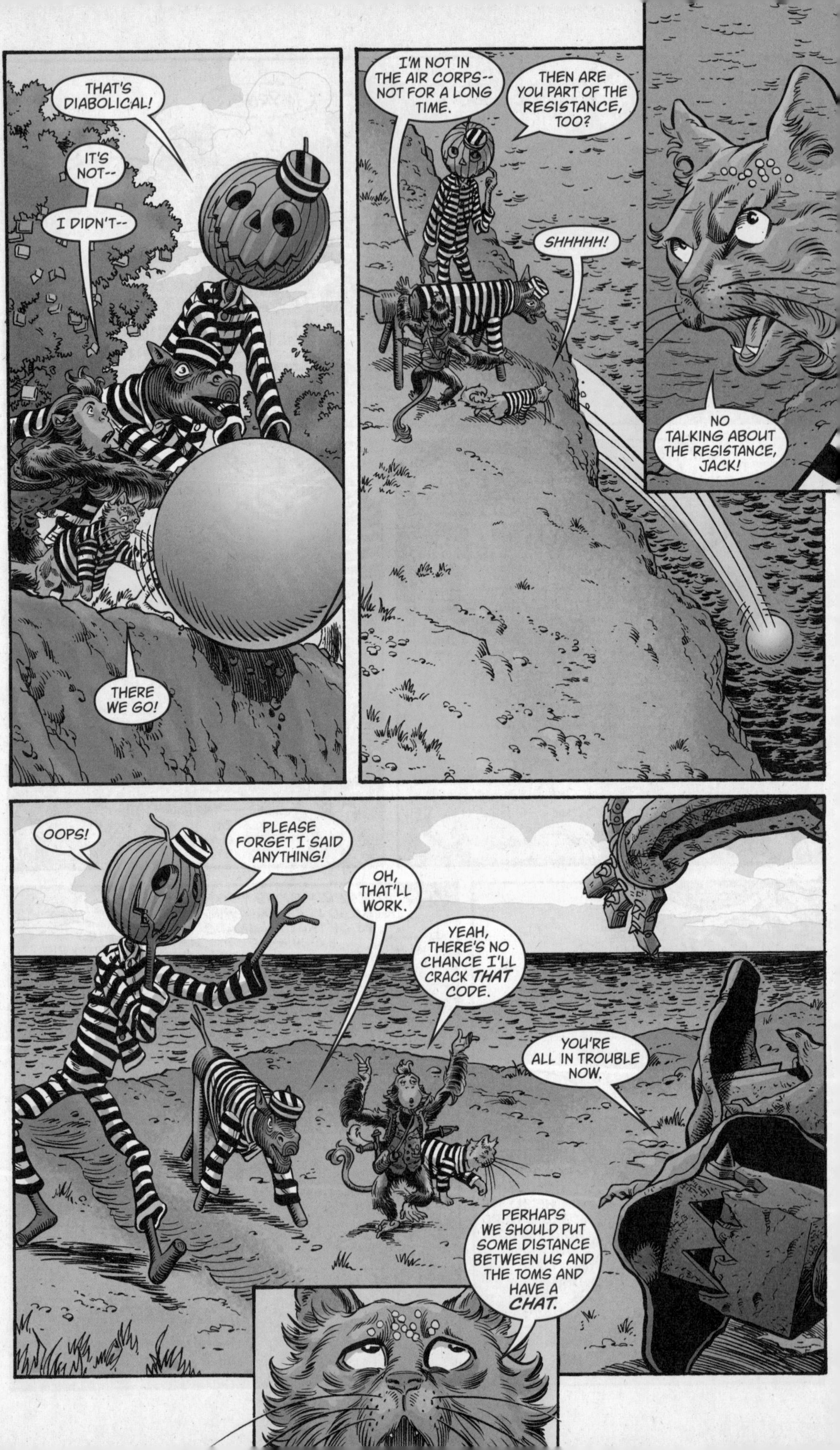
THAT'S DIABOLICAL!
IT'S NOT--
I DIDN'T--
THERE WE GO!
I'M NOT IN THE AIR CORPS-- NOT FOR A LONG TIME.
THEN ARE YOU PART OF THE RESISTANCE, TOO?
SHHHHH!
NO TALKING ABOUT THE RESISTANCE, JACK!
OOPS!
PLEASE FORGET I SAID ANYTHING!
OH, THAT'LL WORK.
YEAH, THERE'S NO CHANCE I'LL CRACK THAT CODE.
YOU'RE ALL IN TROUBLE NOW.
PERHAPS WE SHOULD PUT SOME DISTANCE BETWEEN US AND THE TOMS AND HAVE A CHAT.

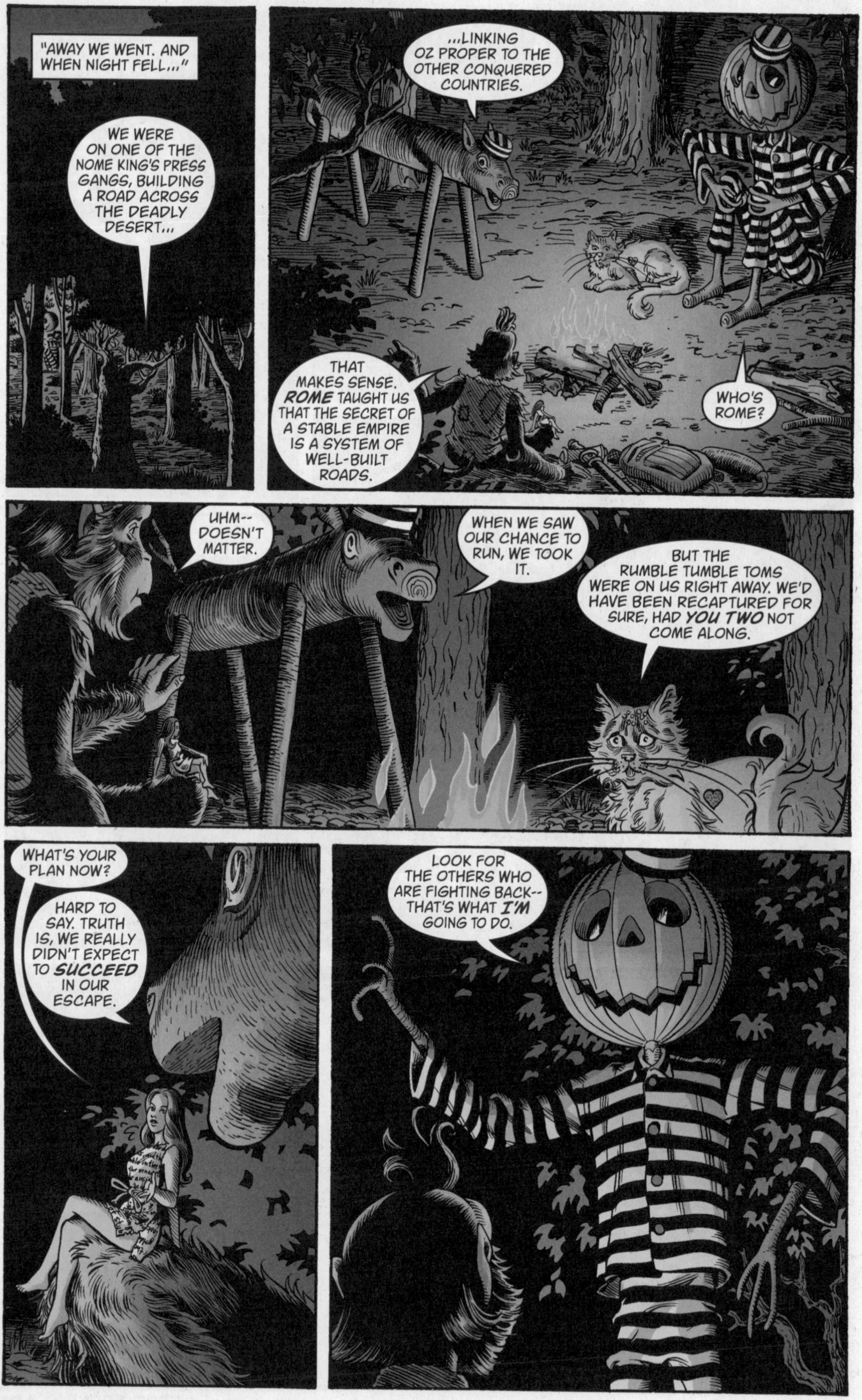
"AWAY WE WENT. AND WHEN NIGHT FELL..."
WE WERE ON ONE OF THE NOME KING'S PRESS GANGS, BUILDING A ROAD ACROSS THE DEADLY DESERT...
...LINKING OZ PROPER TO THE OTHER CONQUERED COUNTRIES.
THAT MAKES SENSE. ROME TAUGHT US THAT THE SECRET OF A STABLE EMPIRE IS A SYSTEM OF WELL-BUILT ROADS.
WHO'S ROME?
UHM-- DOESN'T MATTER.
WHEN WE SAW OUR CHANCE TO RUN, WE TOOK IT.
BUT THE RUMBLE TUMBLE TOMS WERE ON US RIGHT AWAY. WE'D HAVE BEEN RECAPTURED FOR SURE, HAD YOU TWO NOT COME ALONG.
WHAT'S YOUR PLAN NOW?
HARD TO SAY. TRUTH IS, WE REALLY DIDN'T EXPECT TO SUCCEED IN OUR ESCAPE.
LOOK FOR THE OTHERS WHO ARE FIGHTING BACK-- THAT'S WHAT I'M GOING TO DO.

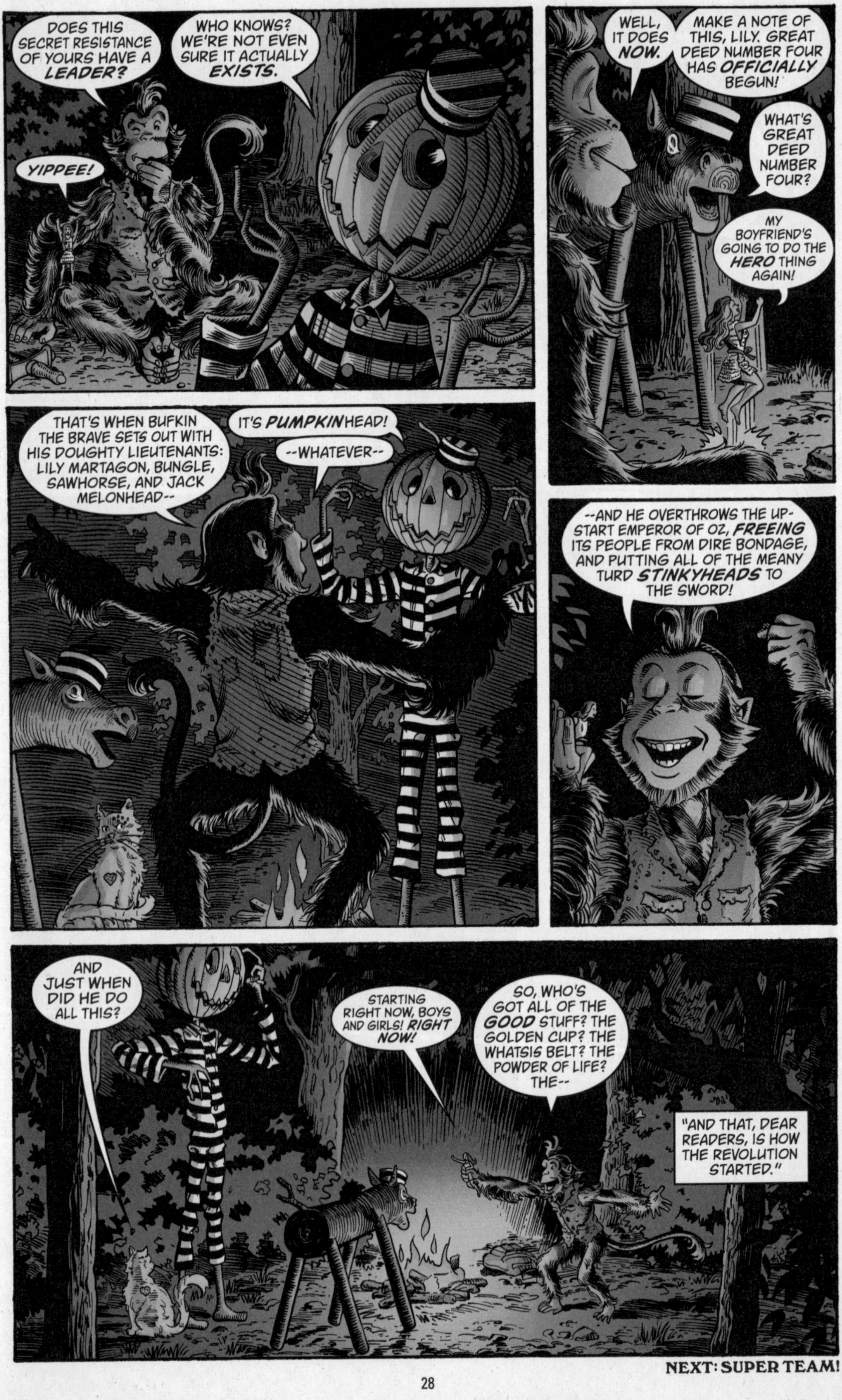
DOES THIS SECRET RESISTANCE OF YOURS HAVE A LEADER?
WHO KNOWS? WE'RE NOT EVEN SURE IT ACTUALLY EXISTS.
YIPPEE!
WELL, IT DOES NOW.
MAKE A NOTE OF THIS, LILY. GREAT DEED NUMBER FOUR HAS OFFICIALLY BEGUN!
WHAT'S GREAT DEED NUMBER FOUR?
MY BOYFRIEND'S GOING TO DO THE HERO THING AGAIN!
THAT'S WHEN BUFKIN THE BRAVE SETS OUT WITH HIS DOUGHTY LIEUTENANTS: LILY MARTAGON, BUNGLE, SAWHORSE, AND JACK MELONHEAD--
IT'S PUMPKINHEAD!
--WHATEVER--
--AND HE OVERTHROWS THE UP-START EMPEROR OF OZ, FREEING ITS PEOPLE FROM DIRE BONDAGE, AND PUTTING ALL OF THE MEANY TURD STINKYHEADS TO THE SWORD!
AND JUST WHEN DID HE DO ALL THIS?
STARTING RIGHT NOW, BOYS AND GIRLS! RIGHT NOW!
SO, WHO'S GOT ALL OF THE GOOD STUFF? THE GOLDEN CUP? THE WHATSIS BELT? THE POWDER OF LIFE? THE--
"AND THAT, DEAR READERS, IS HOW THE REVOLUTION STARTED."

NEXT: SUPER TEAM!

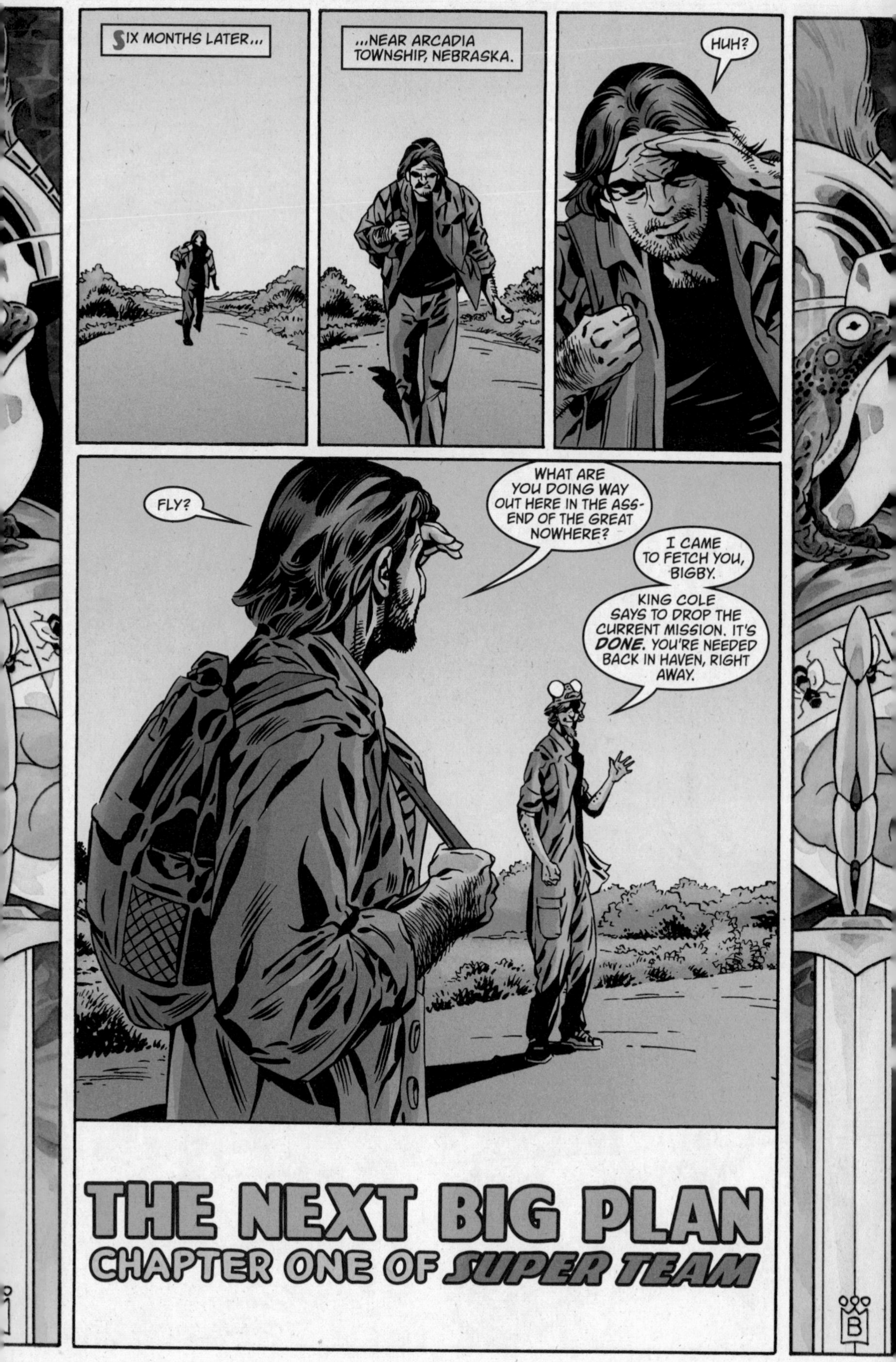
SIX MONTHS LATER...
...NEAR ARCADIA TOWNSHIP, NEBRASKA.
HUH?
FLY?
WHAT ARE YOU DOING WAY OUT HERE IN THE ASS-END OF THE GREAT NOWHERE?
I CAME TO FETCH YOU, BIGBY.
KING COLE SAYS TO DROP THE CURRENT MISSION. IT'S DONE. YOU'RE NEEDED BACK IN HAVEN, RIGHT AWAY.
THE NEXT BIG PLAN
CHAPTER ONE OF SUPER TEAM

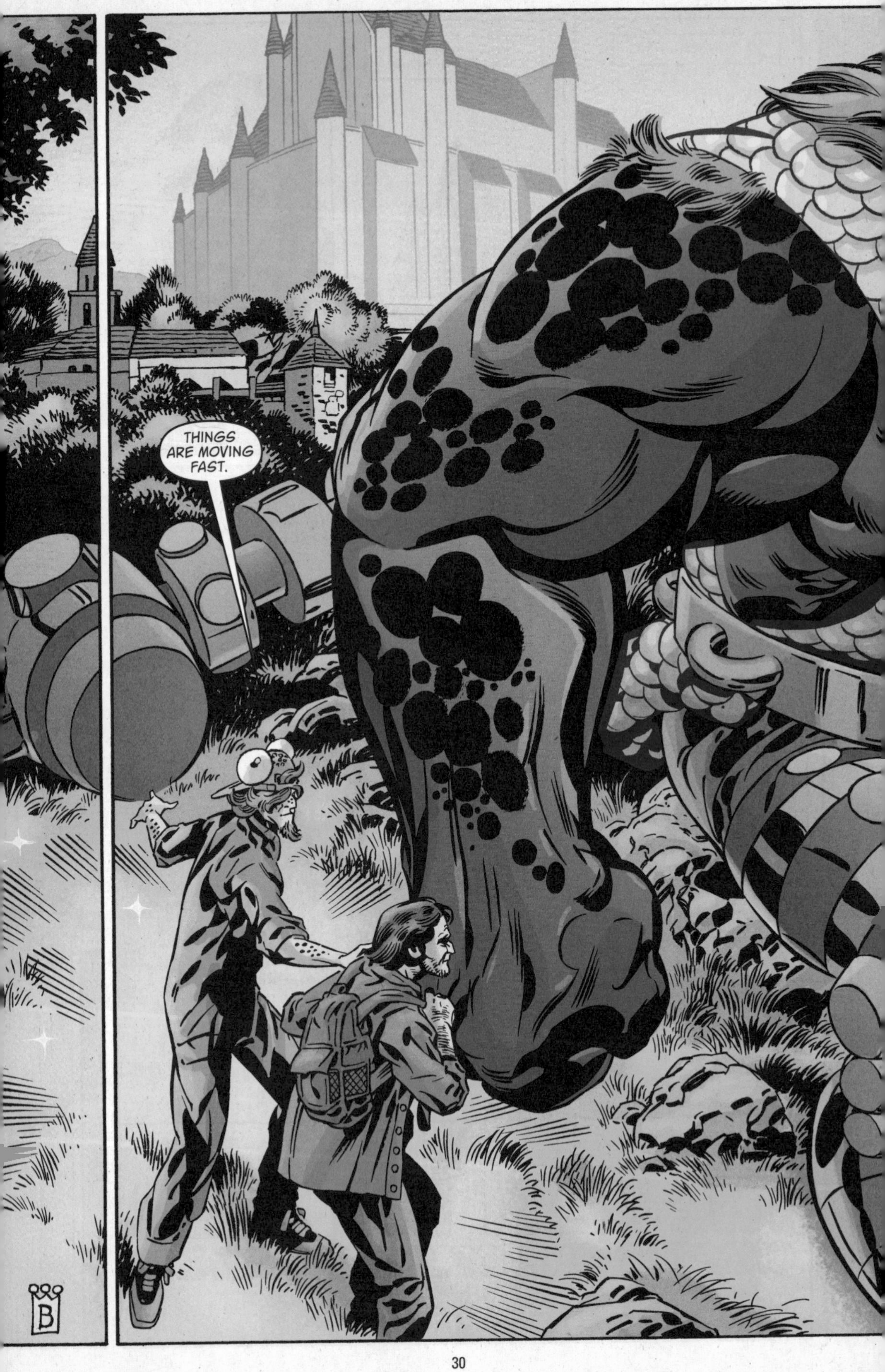
THINGS ARE MOVING FAST.

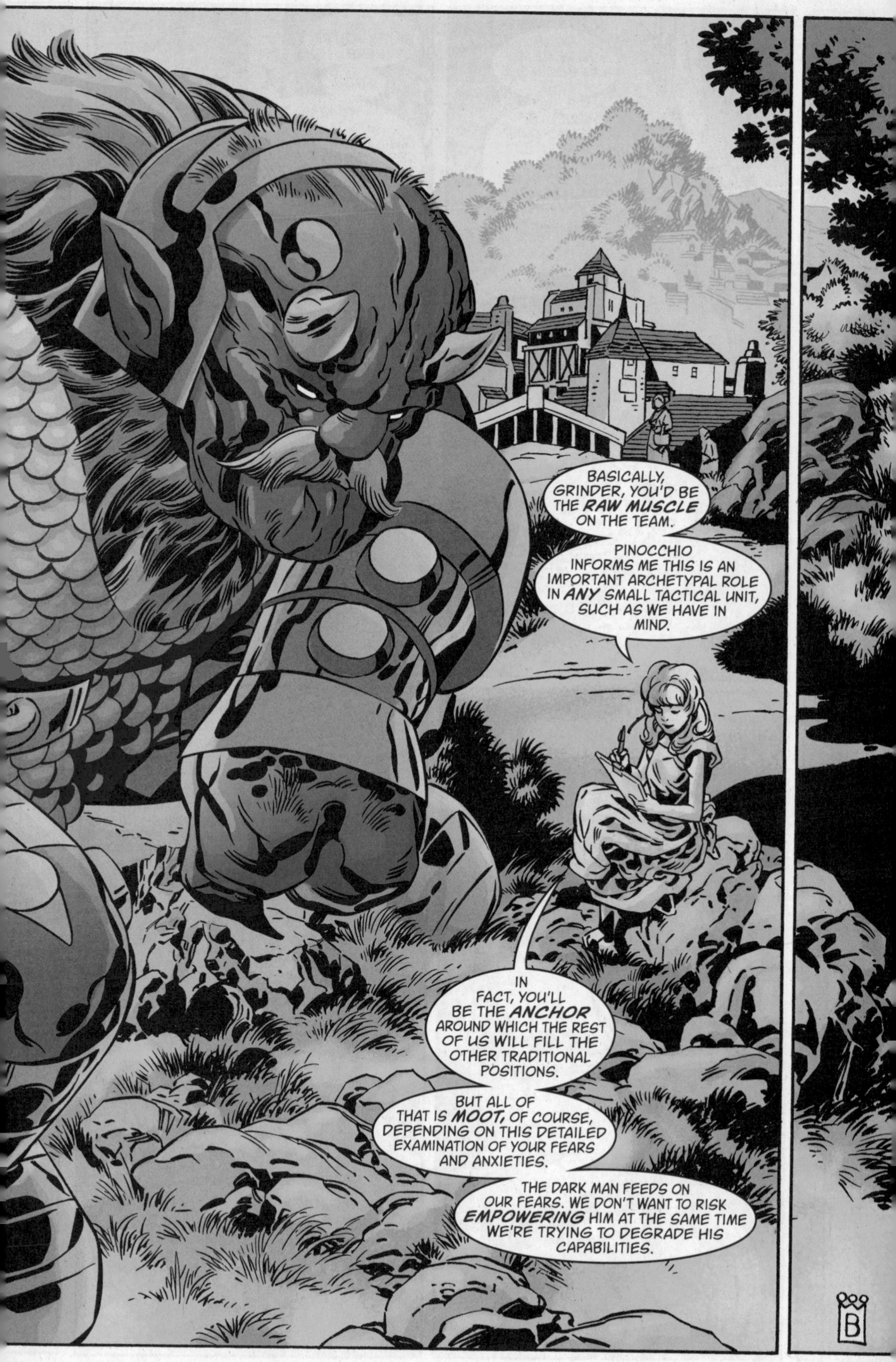
BASICALLY, GRINDER, YOU'D BE THE RAW MUSCLE ON THE TEAM.
PINOCCHIO INFORMS ME THIS IS AN IMPORTANT ARCHETYPAL ROLE IN ANY SMALL TACTICAL UNIT, SUCH AS WE HAVE IN MIND.
IN FACT, YOU'LL BE THE ANCHOR AROUND WHICH THE REST OF US WILL FILL THE OTHER TRADITIONAL POSITIONS.
BUT ALL OF THAT IS MOOT, OF COURSE, DEPENDING ON THIS DETAILED EXAMINATION OF YOUR FEARS AND ANXIETIES.
THE DARK MAN FEEDS ON OUR FEARS. WE DON'T WANT TO RISK EMPOWERING HIM AT THE SAME TIME WE'RE TRYING TO DEGRADE HIS CAPABILITIES.

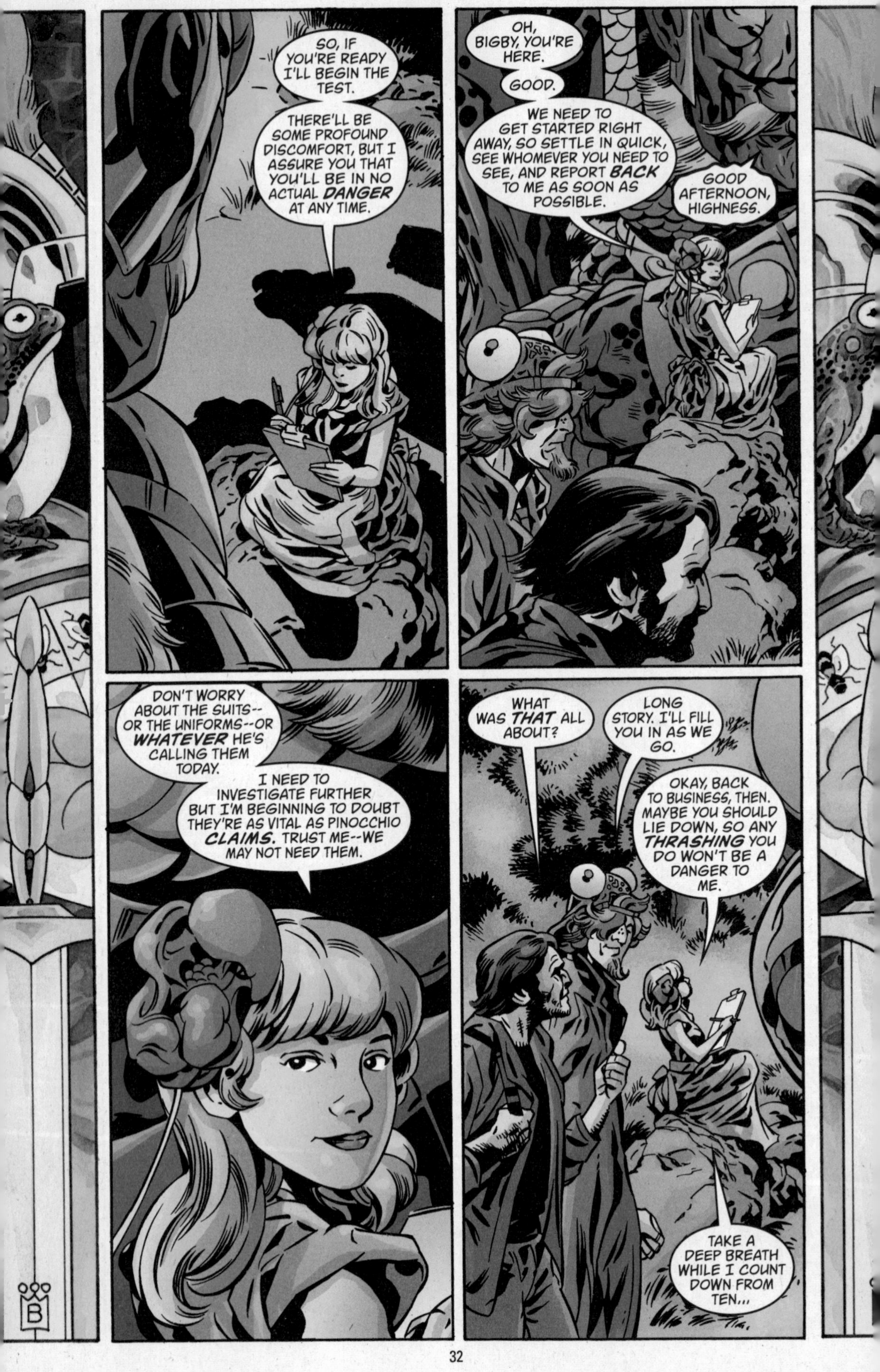

SO, IF YOU'RE READY I'LL BEGIN THE TEST.
THERE'LL BE SOME PROFOUND DISCOMFORT, BUT I ASSURE YOU THAT YOU'LL BE IN NO ACTUAL DANGER AT ANY TIME.
OH, BIGBY, YOU'RE HERE.
GOOD.
WE NEED TO GET STARTED RIGHT AWAY, SO SETTLE IN QUICK, SEE WHOMEVER YOU NEED TO SEE, AND REPORT BACK TO ME AS SOON AS POSSIBLE.
GOOD AFTERNOON, HIGHNESS.
DON'T WORRY ABOUT THE SUITS--OR THE UNIFORMS--OR WHATEVER HE'S CALLING THEM TODAY.
I NEED TO INVESTIGATE FURTHER BUT I'M BEGINNING TO DOUBT THEY'RE AS VITAL AS PINOCCHIO CLAIMS. TRUST ME--WE MAY NOT NEED THEM.
WHAT WAS THAT ALL ABOUT?
LONG STORY. I'LL FILL YOU IN AS WE GO.
OKAY, BACK TO BUSINESS, THEN. MAYBE YOU SHOULD LIE DOWN, SO ANY THRASHING YOU DO WON'T BE A DANGER TO ME.
TAKE A DEEP BREATH WHILE I COUNT DOWN FROM TEN...

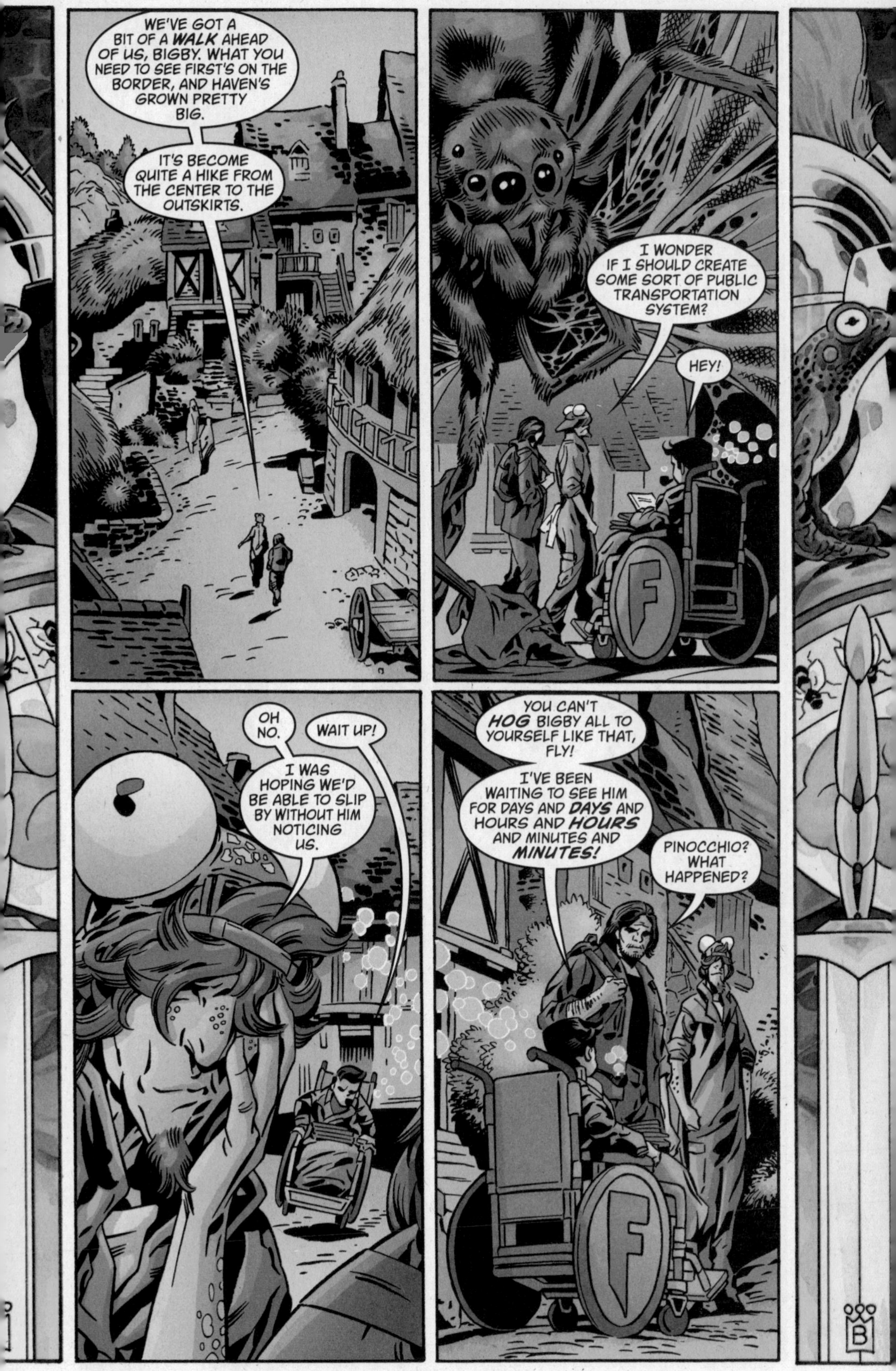
WE'VE GOT A BIT OF A WALK AHEAD OF US, BIGBY. WHAT YOU NEED TO SEE FIRST'S ON THE BORDER, AND HAVEN'S GROWN PRETTY BIG.
IT'S BECOME QUITE A HIKE FROM THE CENTER TO THE OUTSKIRTS.
I WONDER IF I SHOULD CREATE SOME SORT OF PUBLIC TRANSPORTATION SYSTEM?
HEY!
OH NO.
WAIT UP!
I WAS HOPING WE'D BE ABLE TO SLIP BY WITHOUT HIM NOTICING US.
YOU CAN'T HOG BIGBY ALL TO YOURSELF LIKE THAT, FLY!
I'VE BEEN WAITING TO SEE HIM FOR DAYS AND DAYS AND HOURS AND HOURS AND MINUTES AND MINUTES!
PINOCCHIO? WHAT HAPPENED?

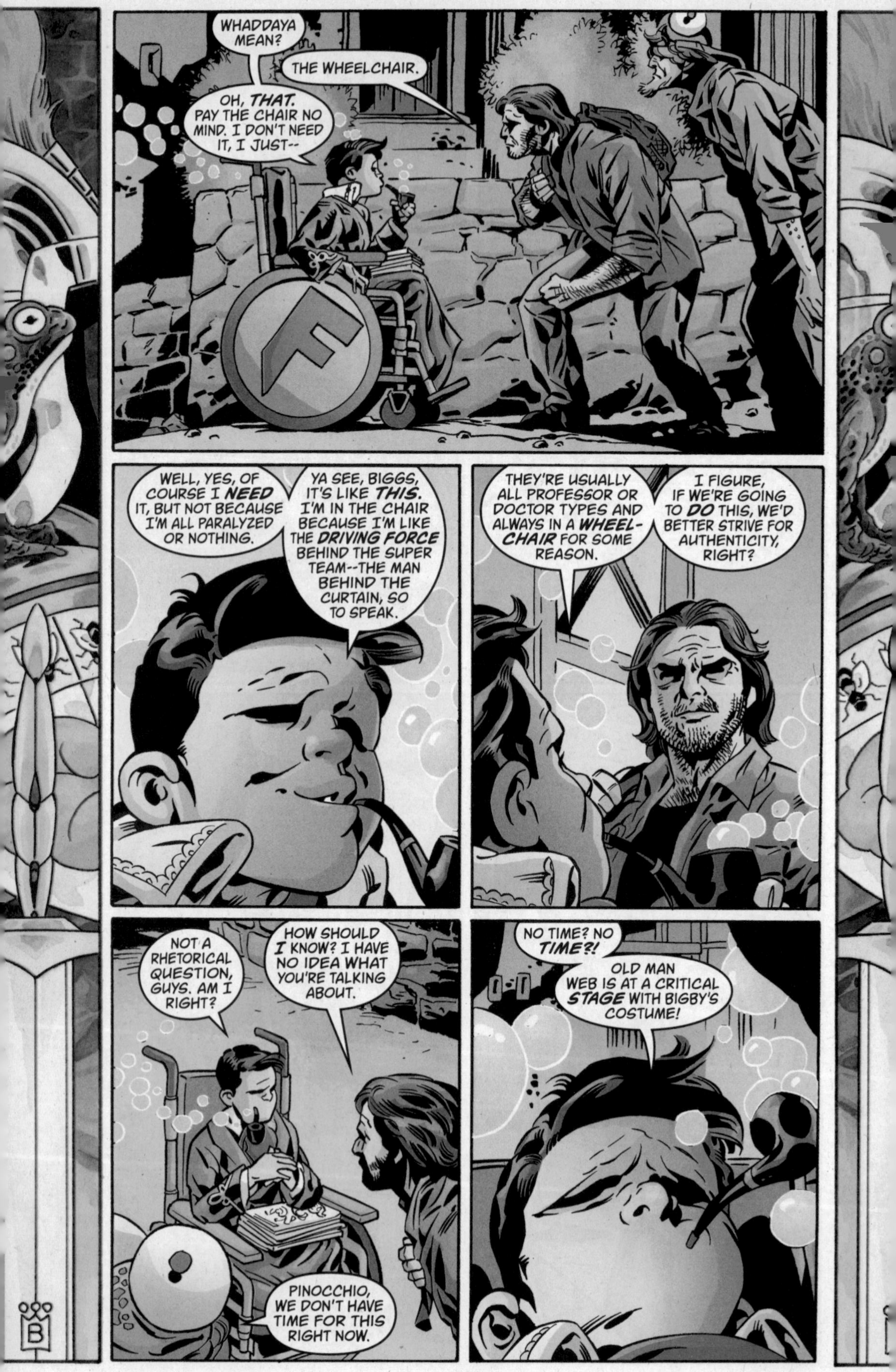
WHADDAYA MEAN?
THE WHEELCHAIR.
OH, THAT. PAY THE CHAIR NO MIND. I DON'T NEED IT, I JUST--
WELL, YES, OF COURSE I NEED IT, BUT NOT BECAUSE I'M ALL PARALYZED OR NOTHING.
YA SEE, BIGGS, IT'S LIKE THIS. I'M IN THE CHAIR BECAUSE I'M LIKE THE DRIVING FORCE BEHIND THE SUPER TEAM--THE MAN BEHIND THE CURTAIN, SO TO SPEAK.
THEY'RE USUALLY ALL PROFESSOR OR DOCTOR TYPES AND ALWAYS IN A WHEEL-CHAIR FOR SOME REASON.
I FIGURE, IF WE'RE GOING TO DO THIS, WE'D BETTER STRIVE FOR AUTHENTICITY, RIGHT?
NOT A RHETORICAL QUESTION, GUYS. AM I RIGHT?
HOW SHOULD I KNOW? I HAVE NO IDEA WHAT YOU'RE TALKING ABOUT.
PINOCCHIO, WE DON'T HAVE TIME FOR THIS RIGHT NOW.
NO TIME? NO TIME?!
OLD MAN WEB IS AT A CRITICAL STAGE WITH BIGBY'S COSTUME!

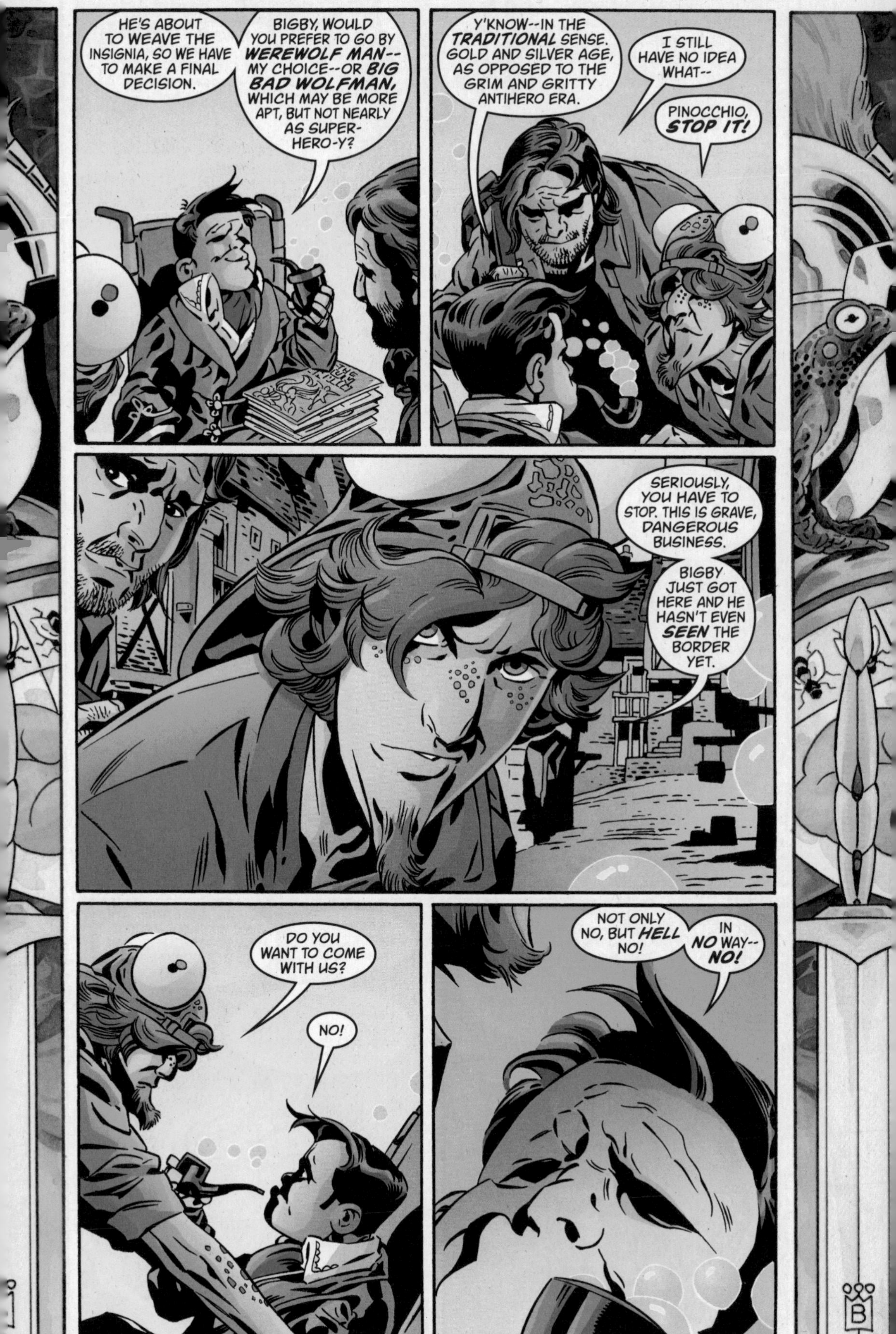
HE'S ABOUT TO WEAVE THE INSIGNIA, SO WE HAVE TO MAKE A FINAL DECISION.
BIGBY, WOULD YOU PREFER TO GO BY **WEREWOLF MAN**--MY CHOICE--OR **BIG BAD WOLFMAN**, WHICH MAY BE MORE APT, BUT NOT NEARLY AS SUPER-HERO-Y?
Y'KNOW--IN THE **TRADITIONAL** SENSE. GOLD AND SILVER AGE, AS OPPOSED TO THE GRIM AND GRITTY ANTIHERO ERA.
I STILL HAVE NO IDEA WHAT--
PINOCCHIO, **STOP IT!**
SERIOUSLY, YOU HAVE TO STOP. THIS IS GRAVE, DANGEROUS BUSINESS.
BIGBY JUST GOT HERE AND HE HASN'T EVEN **SEEN** THE BORDER YET.
DO YOU WANT TO COME WITH US?
NO!
NOT ONLY NO, BUT **HELL** NO!
IN **NO** WAY--**NO!**

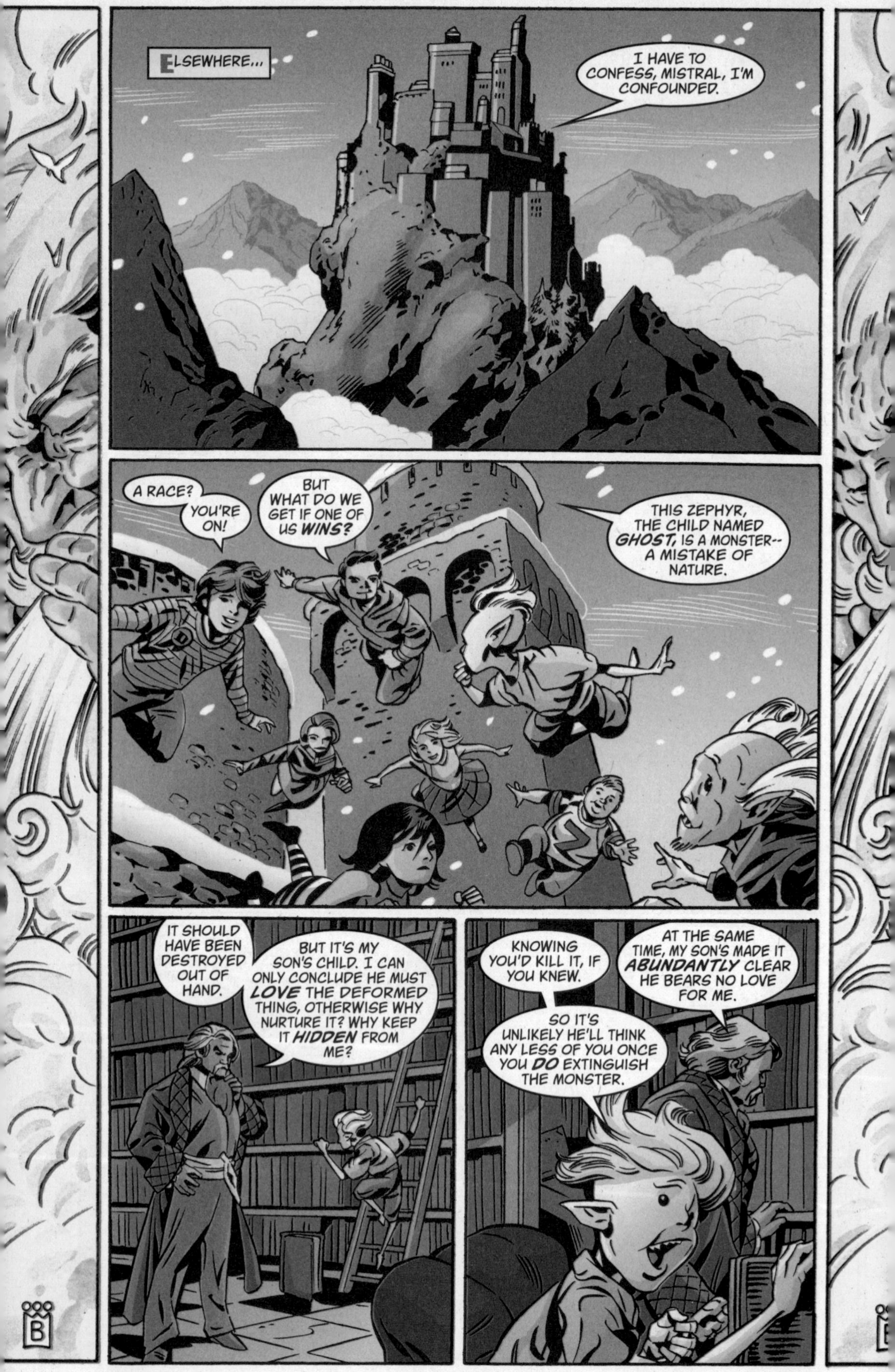
ELSEWHERE...
I HAVE TO CONFESS, MISTRAL, I'M CONFOUNDED.
A RACE?
YOU'RE ON!
BUT WHAT DO WE GET IF ONE OF US WINS?
THIS ZEPHYR, THE CHILD NAMED GHOST, IS A MONSTER-- A MISTAKE OF NATURE.
IT SHOULD HAVE BEEN DESTROYED OUT OF HAND.
BUT IT'S MY SON'S CHILD. I CAN ONLY CONCLUDE HE MUST LOVE THE DEFORMED THING, OTHERWISE WHY NURTURE IT? WHY KEEP IT HIDDEN FROM ME?
KNOWING YOU'D KILL IT, IF YOU KNEW.
AT THE SAME TIME, MY SON'S MADE IT ABUNDANTLY CLEAR HE BEARS NO LOVE FOR ME.
SO IT'S UNLIKELY HE'LL THINK ANY LESS OF YOU ONCE YOU DO EXTINGUISH THE MONSTER.

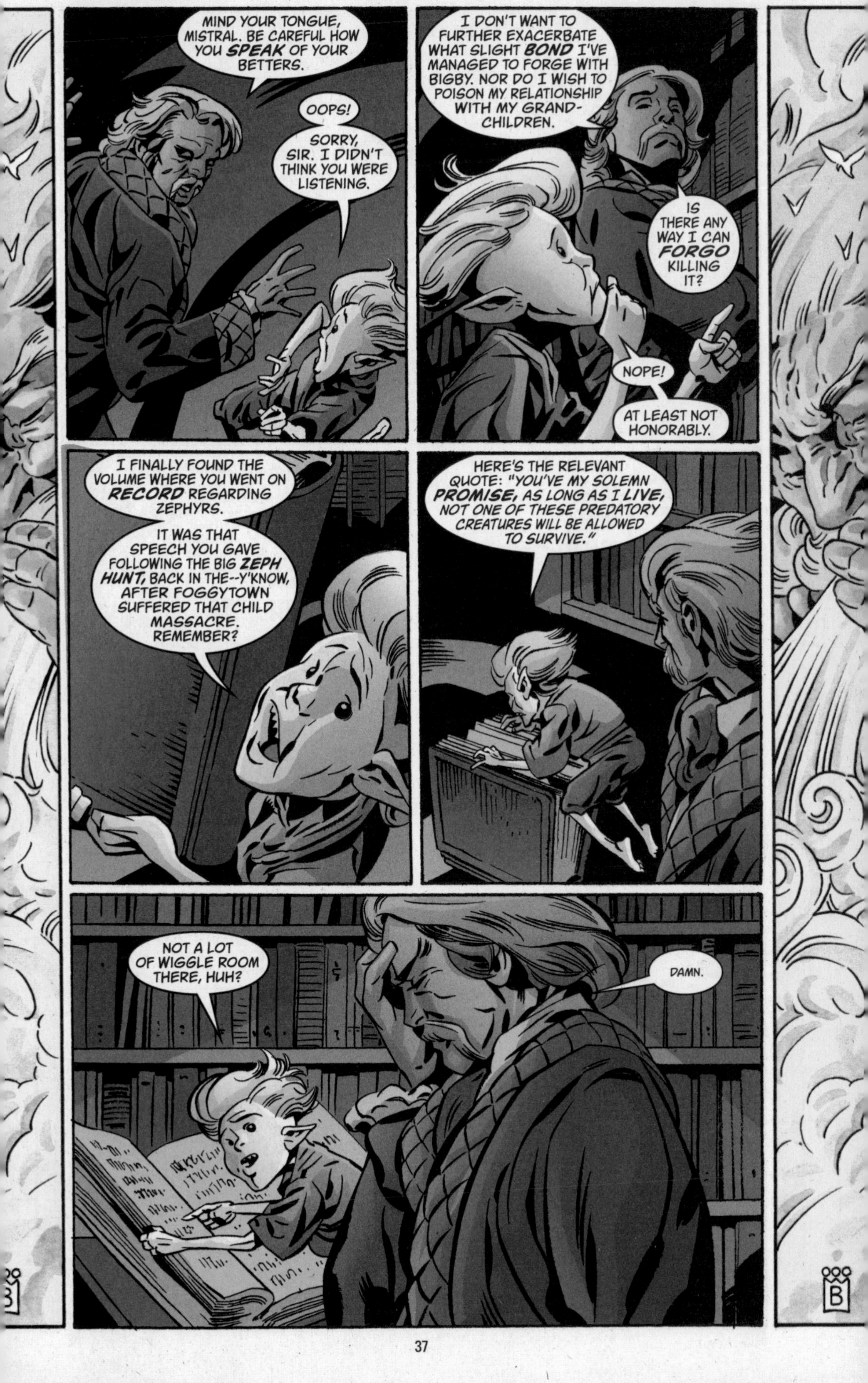
MIND YOUR TONGUE, MISTRAL. BE CAREFUL HOW YOU SPEAK OF YOUR BETTERS.
OOPS!
SORRY, SIR. I DIDN'T THINK YOU WERE LISTENING.
I DON'T WANT TO FURTHER EXACERBATE WHAT SLIGHT BOND I'VE MANAGED TO FORGE WITH BIGBY. NOR DO I WISH TO POISON MY RELATIONSHIP WITH MY GRAND-CHILDREN.
IS THERE ANY WAY I CAN FORGO KILLING IT?
NOPE!
AT LEAST NOT HONORABLY.
I FINALLY FOUND THE VOLUME WHERE YOU WENT ON RECORD REGARDING ZEPHYRS.
IT WAS THAT SPEECH YOU GAVE FOLLOWING THE BIG ZEPH HUNT, BACK IN THE--Y'KNOW, AFTER FOGGYTOWN SUFFERED THAT CHILD MASSACRE. REMEMBER?
HERE'S THE RELEVANT QUOTE: "YOU'VE MY SOLEMN PROMISE, AS LONG AS I LIVE, NOT ONE OF THESE PREDATORY CREATURES WILL BE ALLOWED TO SURVIVE."
NOT A LOT OF WIGGLE ROOM THERE, HUH?
DAMN.

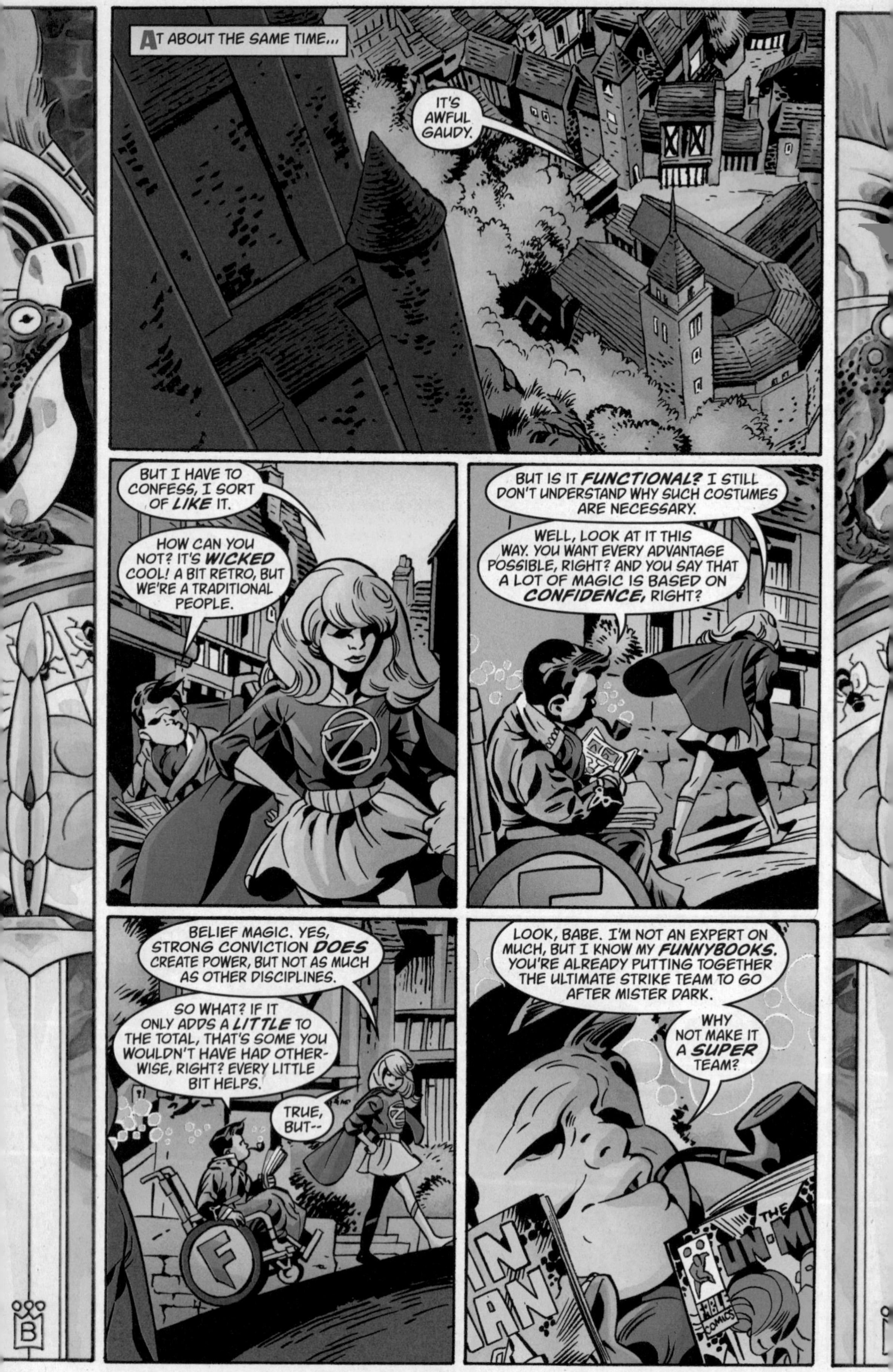
AT ABOUT THE SAME TIME...
IT'S AWFUL GAUDY.
BUT I HAVE TO CONFESS, I SORT OF LIKE IT.
HOW CAN YOU NOT? IT'S WICKED COOL! A BIT RETRO, BUT WE'RE A TRADITIONAL PEOPLE.
BUT IS IT FUNCTIONAL? I STILL DON'T UNDERSTAND WHY SUCH COSTUMES ARE NECESSARY.
WELL, LOOK AT IT THIS WAY. YOU WANT EVERY ADVANTAGE POSSIBLE, RIGHT? AND YOU SAY THAT A LOT OF MAGIC IS BASED ON CONFIDENCE, RIGHT?
BELIEF MAGIC. YES, STRONG CONVICTION DOES CREATE POWER, BUT NOT AS MUCH AS OTHER DISCIPLINES.
SO WHAT? IF IT ONLY ADDS A LITTLE TO THE TOTAL, THAT'S SOME YOU WOULDN'T HAVE HAD OTHER-WISE, RIGHT? EVERY LITTLE BIT HELPS.
TRUE, BUT--
LOOK, BABE. I'M NOT AN EXPERT ON MUCH, BUT I KNOW MY FUNNYBOOKS. YOU'RE ALREADY PUTTING TOGETHER THE ULTIMATE STRIKE TEAM TO GO AFTER MISTER DARK.
WHY NOT MAKE IT A SUPER TEAM?

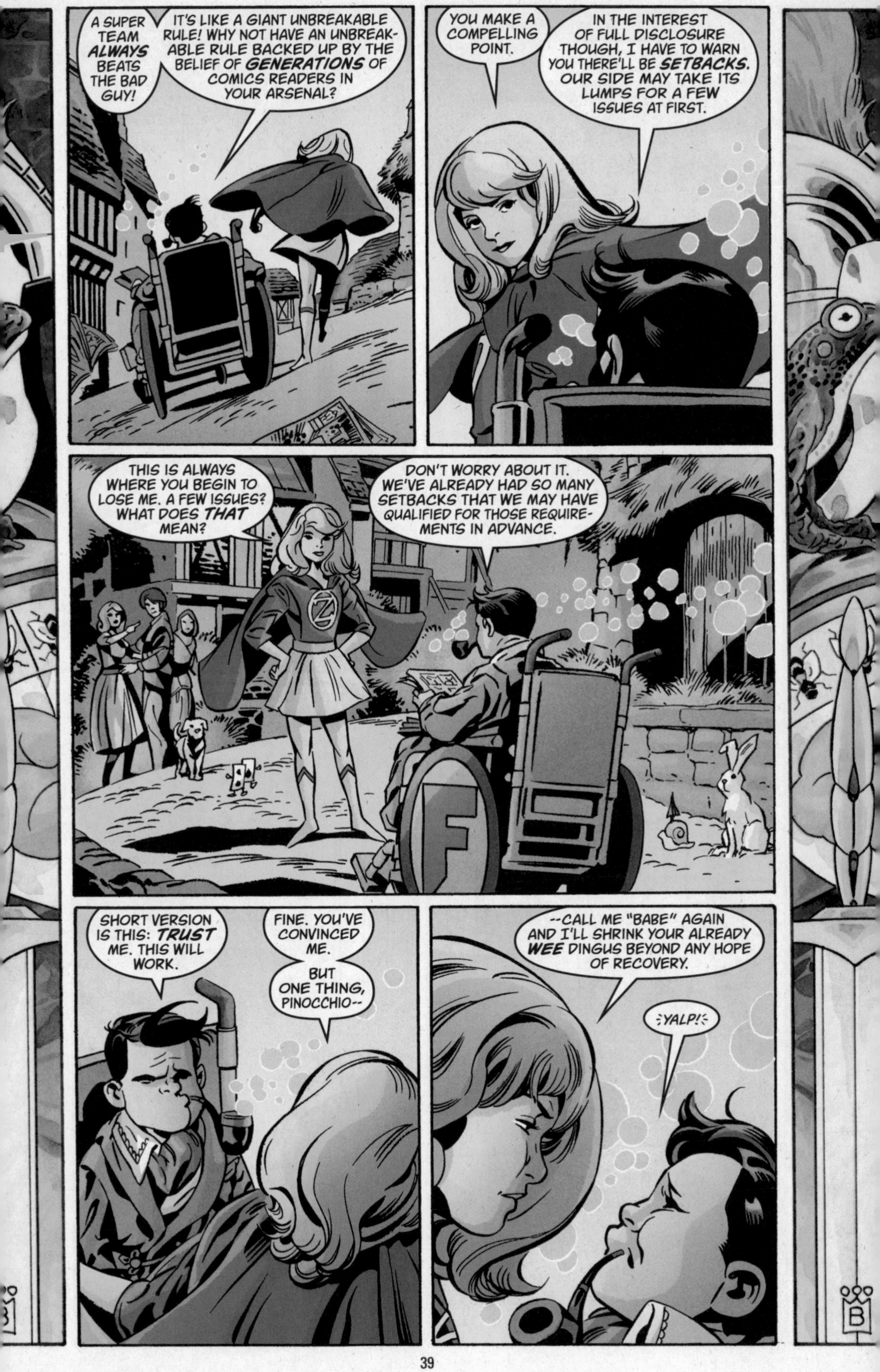
A SUPER TEAM ALWAYS BEATS THE BAD GUY!
IT'S LIKE A GIANT UNBREAKABLE RULE! WHY NOT HAVE AN UNBREAKABLE RULE BACKED UP BY THE BELIEF OF GENERATIONS OF COMICS READERS IN YOUR ARSENAL?
YOU MAKE A COMPELLING POINT.
IN THE INTEREST OF FULL DISCLOSURE THOUGH, I HAVE TO WARN YOU THERE'LL BE SETBACKS. OUR SIDE MAY TAKE ITS LUMPS FOR A FEW ISSUES AT FIRST.
THIS IS ALWAYS WHERE YOU BEGIN TO LOSE ME. A FEW ISSUES? WHAT DOES THAT MEAN?
DON'T WORRY ABOUT IT. WE'VE ALREADY HAD SO MANY SETBACKS THAT WE MAY HAVE QUALIFIED FOR THOSE REQUIREMENTS IN ADVANCE.
SHORT VERSION IS THIS: TRUST ME. THIS WILL WORK.
FINE. YOU'VE CONVINCED ME.
BUT ONE THING, PINOCCHIO--
--CALL ME "BABE" AGAIN AND I'LL SHRINK YOUR ALREADY WEE DINGUS BEYOND ANY HOPE OF RECOVERY.
YALP!

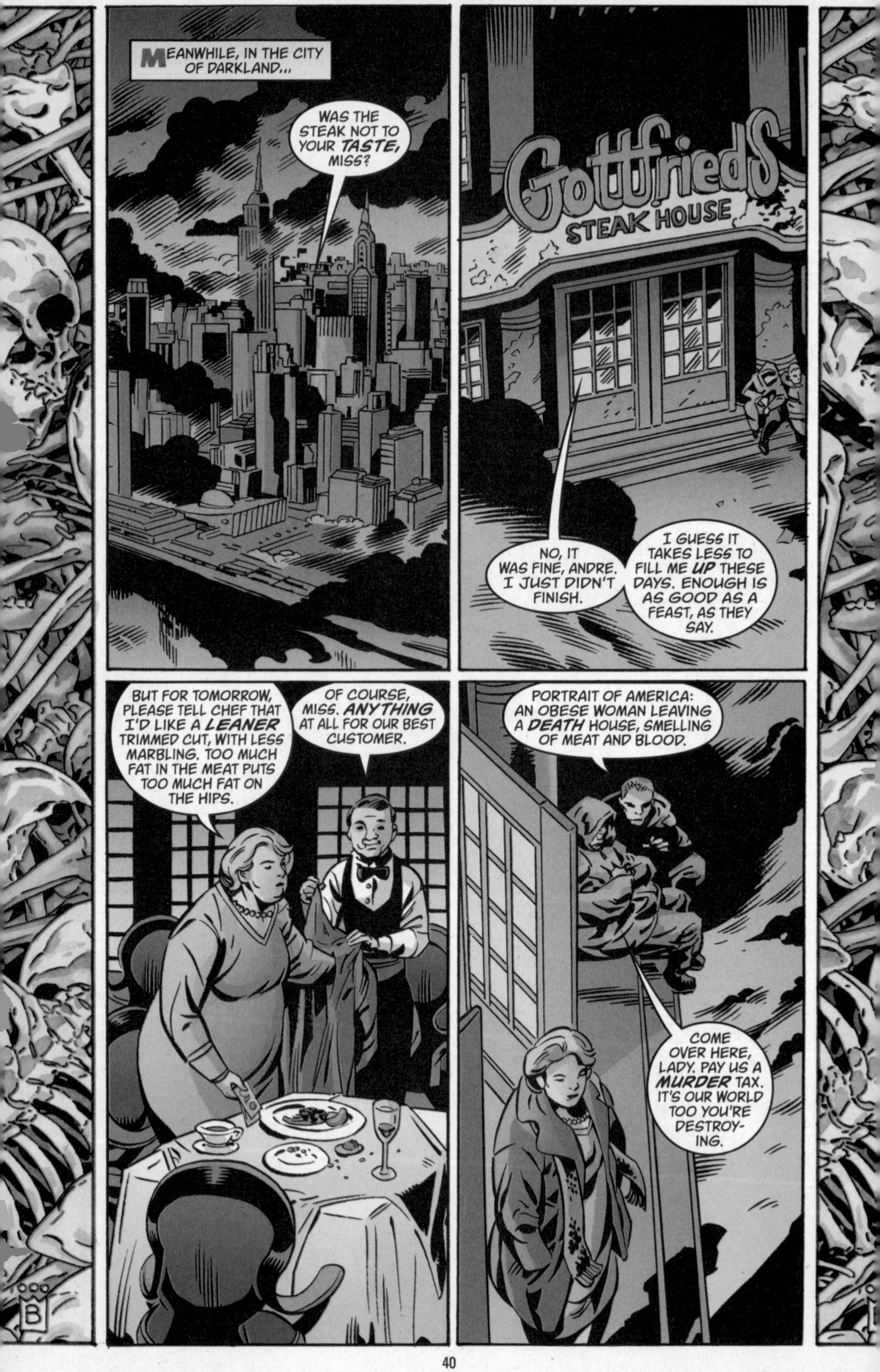
MEANWHILE, IN THE CITY OF DARKLAND...
WAS THE STEAK NOT TO YOUR TASTE, MISS?
Gottfrieds STEAK HOUSE
NO, IT WAS FINE, ANDRE. I JUST DIDN'T FINISH.
I GUESS IT TAKES LESS TO FILL ME UP THESE DAYS. ENOUGH IS AS GOOD AS A FEAST, AS THEY SAY.
BUT FOR TOMORROW, PLEASE TELL CHEF THAT I'D LIKE A LEANER TRIMMED CUT, WITH LESS MARBLING. TOO MUCH FAT IN THE MEAT PUTS TOO MUCH FAT ON THE HIPS.
OF COURSE, MISS. ANYTHING AT ALL FOR OUR BEST CUSTOMER.
PORTRAIT OF AMERICA: AN OBESE WOMAN LEAVING A DEATH HOUSE, SMELLING OF MEAT AND BLOOD.
COME OVER HERE, LADY. PAY US A MURDER TAX. IT'S OUR WORLD TOO YOU'RE DESTROY-ING.

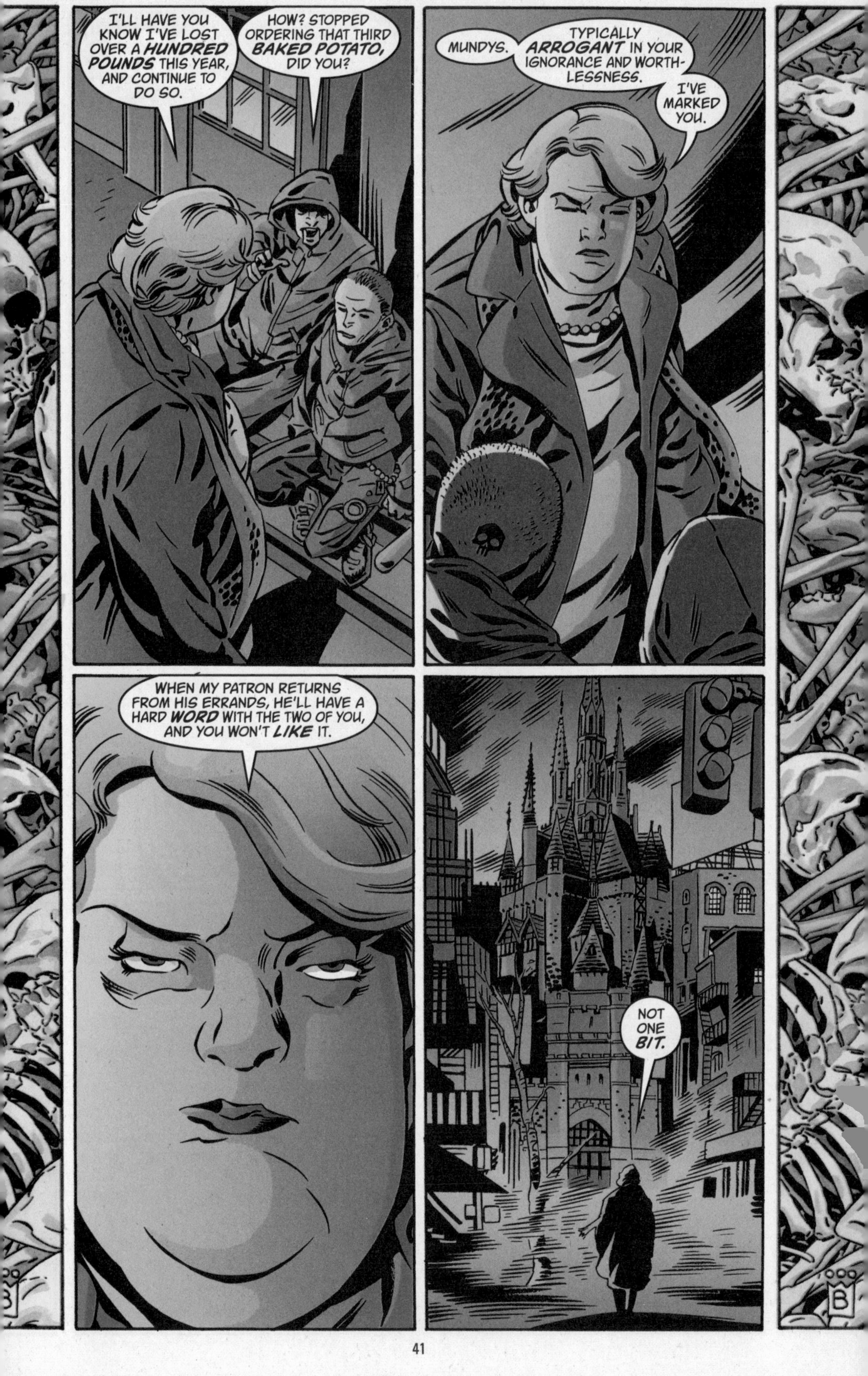
I'LL HAVE YOU KNOW I'VE LOST OVER A HUNDRED POUNDS THIS YEAR, AND CONTINUE TO DO SO.
HOW? STOPPED ORDERING THAT THIRD BAKED POTATO, DID YOU?
MUNDYS.
TYPICALLY ARROGANT IN YOUR IGNORANCE AND WORTH-LESSNESS.
I'VE MARKED YOU.
WHEN MY PATRON RETURNS FROM HIS ERRANDS, HE'LL HAVE A HARD WORD WITH THE TWO OF YOU, AND YOU WON'T LIKE IT.
NOT ONE BIT.

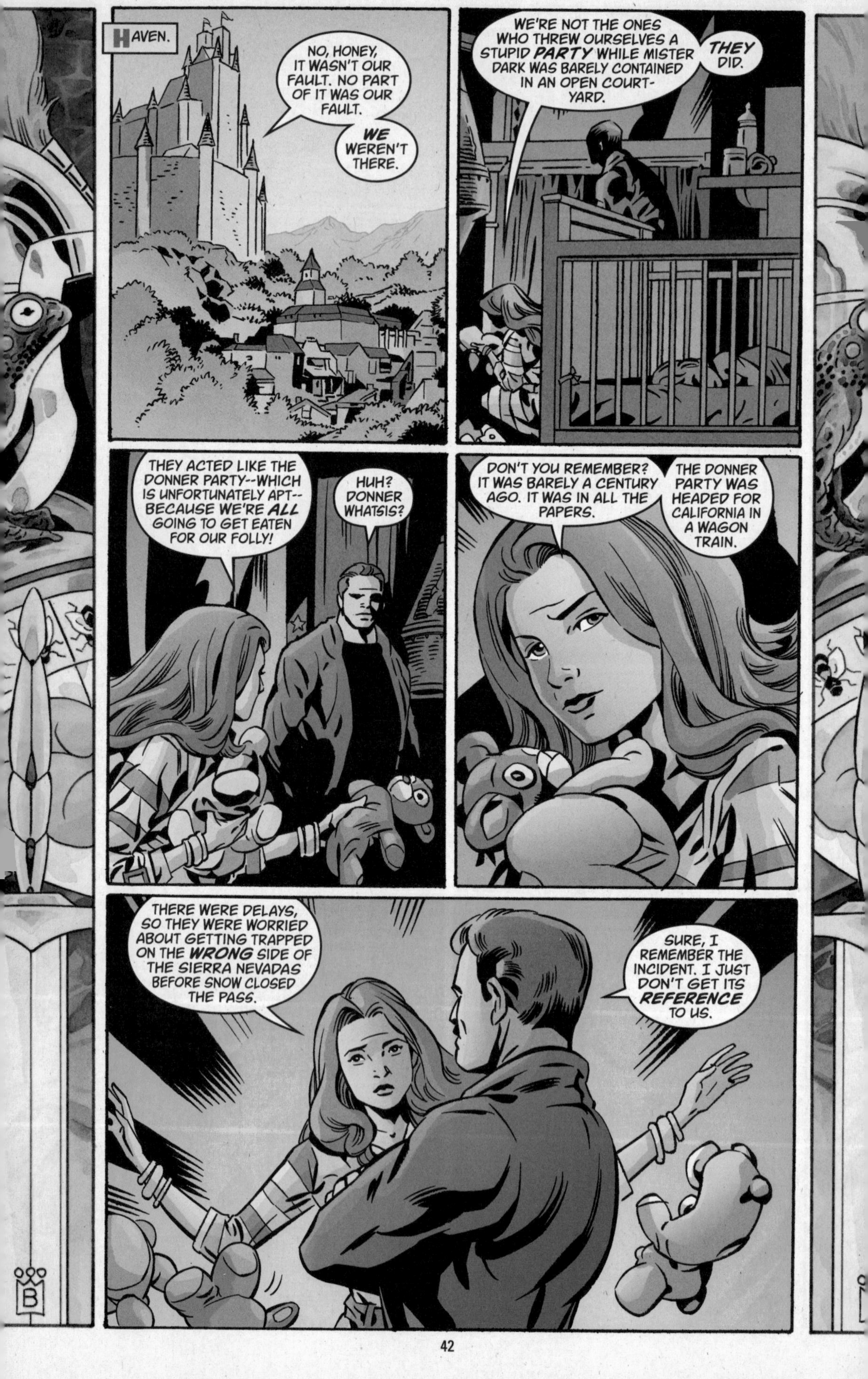
HAVEN.
NO, HONEY, IT WASN'T OUR FAULT. NO PART OF IT WAS OUR FAULT.
WE WEREN'T THERE.
WE'RE NOT THE ONES WHO THREW OURSELVES A STUPID PARTY WHILE MISTER DARK WAS BARELY CONTAINED IN AN OPEN COURT-YARD.
THEY DID.
THEY ACTED LIKE THE DONNER PARTY--WHICH IS UNFORTUNATELY APT--BECAUSE WE'RE ALL GOING TO GET EATEN FOR OUR FOLLY!
HUH? DONNER WHATSIS?
DON'T YOU REMEMBER? IT WAS BARELY A CENTURY AGO. IT WAS IN ALL THE PAPERS.
THE DONNER PARTY WAS HEADED FOR CALIFORNIA IN A WAGON TRAIN.
THERE WERE DELAYS, SO THEY WERE WORRIED ABOUT GETTING TRAPPED ON THE WRONG SIDE OF THE SIERRA NEVADAS BEFORE SNOW CLOSED THE PASS.
SURE, I REMEMBER THE INCIDENT. I JUST DON'T GET ITS REFERENCE TO US.

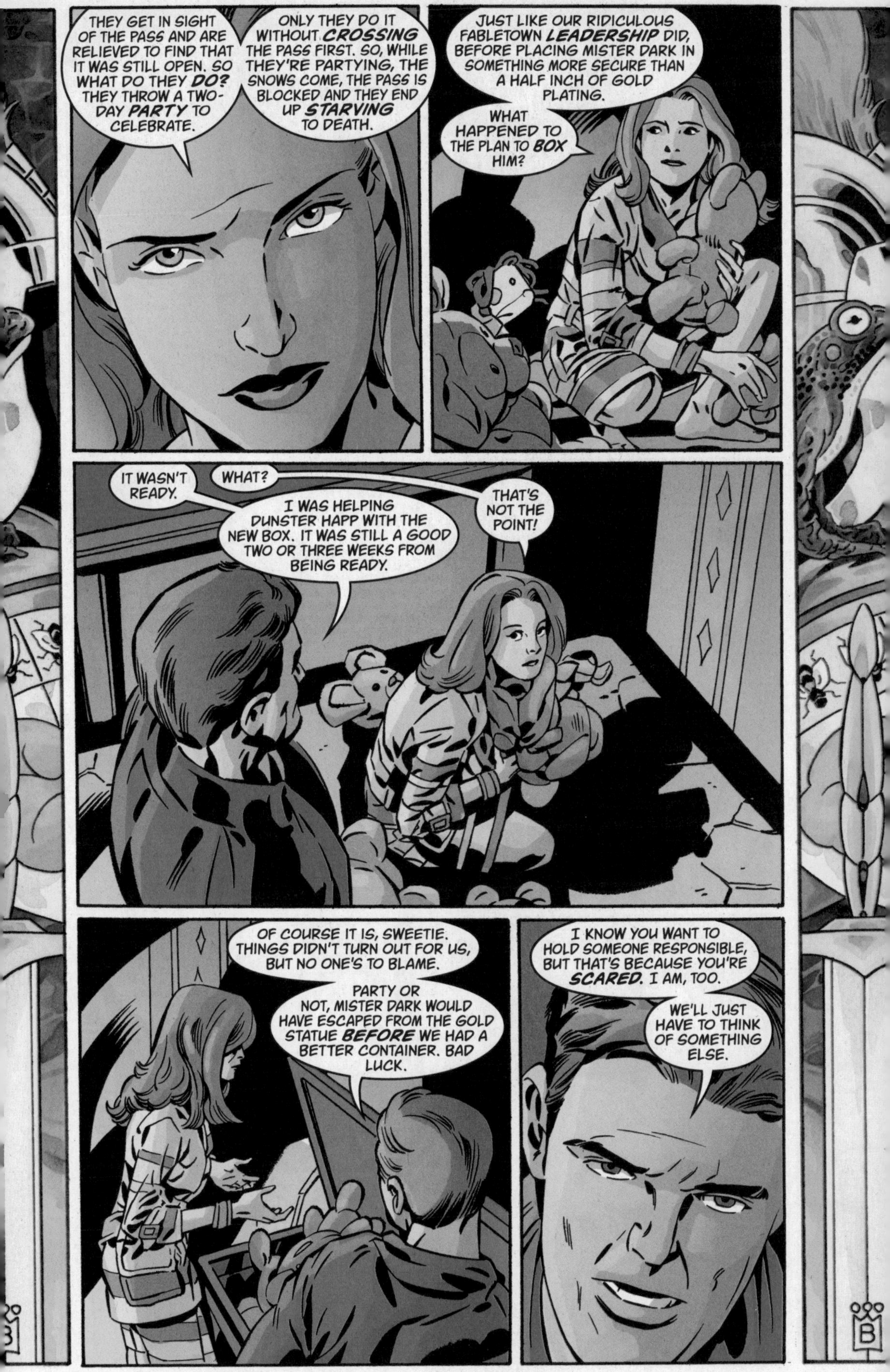

THEY GET IN SIGHT OF THE PASS AND ARE RELIEVED TO FIND THAT IT WAS STILL OPEN. SO WHAT DO THEY DO? THEY THROW A TWO-DAY PARTY TO CELEBRATE.
ONLY THEY DO IT WITHOUT CROSSING THE PASS FIRST. SO, WHILE THEY'RE PARTYING, THE SNOWS COME, THE PASS IS BLOCKED AND THEY END UP STARVING TO DEATH.
JUST LIKE OUR RIDICULOUS FABLETOWN LEADERSHIP DID, BEFORE PLACING MISTER DARK IN SOMETHING MORE SECURE THAN A HALF INCH OF GOLD PLATING.
WHAT HAPPENED TO THE PLAN TO BOX HIM?
IT WASN'T READY.
WHAT?
I WAS HELPING DUNSTER HAPP WITH THE NEW BOX. IT WAS STILL A GOOD TWO OR THREE WEEKS FROM BEING READY.
THAT'S NOT THE POINT!
OF COURSE IT IS, SWEETIE. THINGS DIDN'T TURN OUT FOR US, BUT NO ONE'S TO BLAME.
PARTY OR NOT, MISTER DARK WOULD HAVE ESCAPED FROM THE GOLD STATUE BEFORE WE HAD A BETTER CONTAINER. BAD LUCK.
I KNOW YOU WANT TO HOLD SOMEONE RESPONSIBLE, BUT THAT'S BECAUSE YOU'RE SCARED. I AM, TOO.
WE'LL JUST HAVE TO THINK OF SOMETHING ELSE.

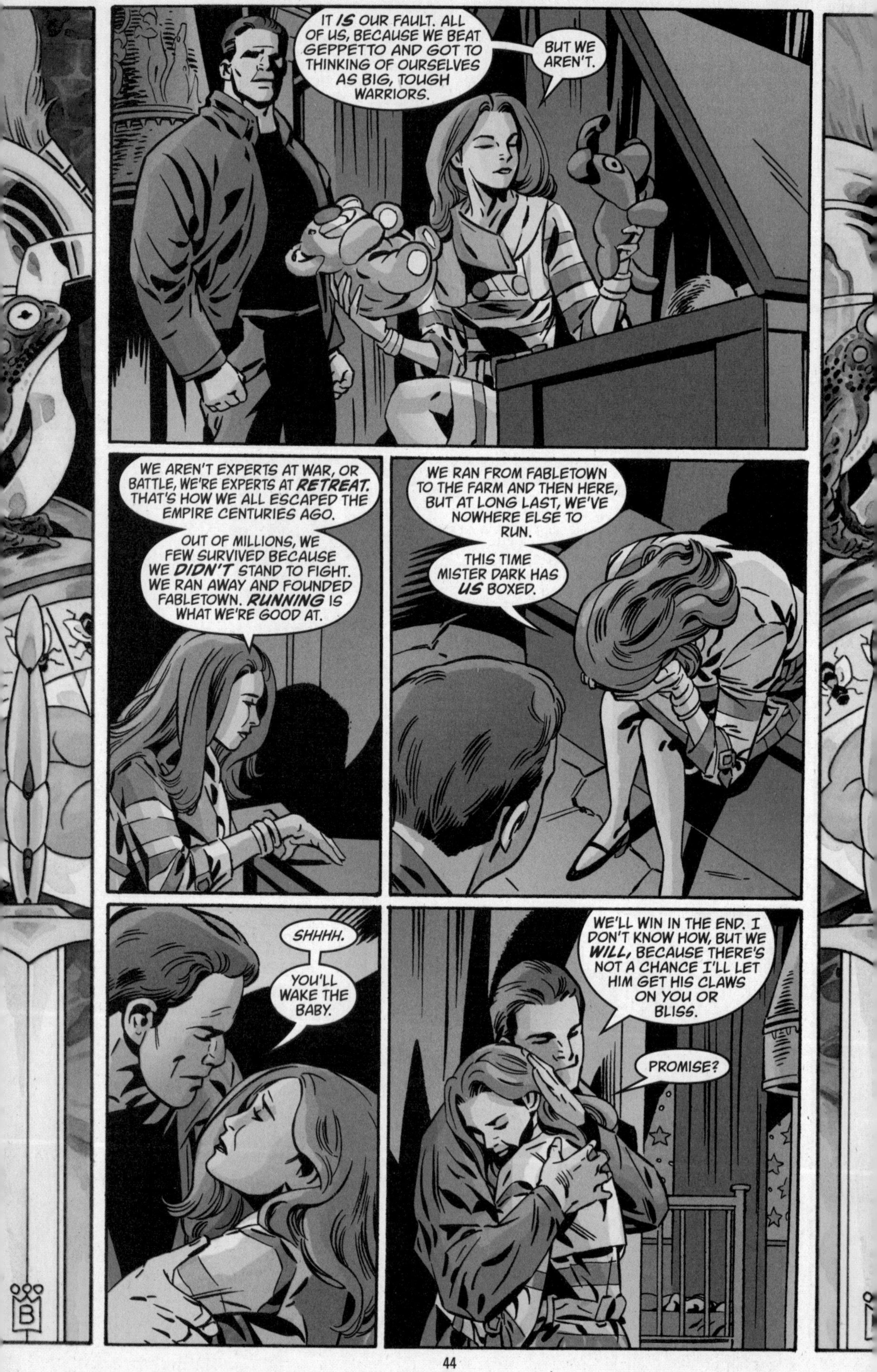
IT *IS* OUR FAULT. ALL OF US, BECAUSE WE BEAT GEPPETTO AND GOT TO THINKING OF OURSELVES AS BIG, TOUGH WARRIORS.
BUT WE AREN'T.
WE AREN'T EXPERTS AT WAR, OR BATTLE, WE'RE EXPERTS AT ***RETREAT.*** THAT'S HOW WE ALL ESCAPED THE EMPIRE CENTURIES AGO.
OUT OF MILLIONS, WE FEW SURVIVED BECAUSE WE ***DIDN'T*** STAND TO FIGHT. WE RAN AWAY AND FOUNDED FABLETOWN. ***RUNNING*** IS WHAT WE'RE GOOD AT.
WE RAN FROM FABLETOWN TO THE FARM AND THEN HERE, BUT AT LONG LAST, WE'VE NOWHERE ELSE TO RUN.
THIS TIME MISTER DARK HAS ***US*** BOXED.
SHHHH.
YOU'LL WAKE THE BABY.
WE'LL WIN IN THE END. I DON'T KNOW HOW, BUT WE ***WILL,*** BECAUSE THERE'S NOT A CHANCE I'LL LET HIM GET HIS CLAWS ON YOU OR BLISS.
PROMISE?

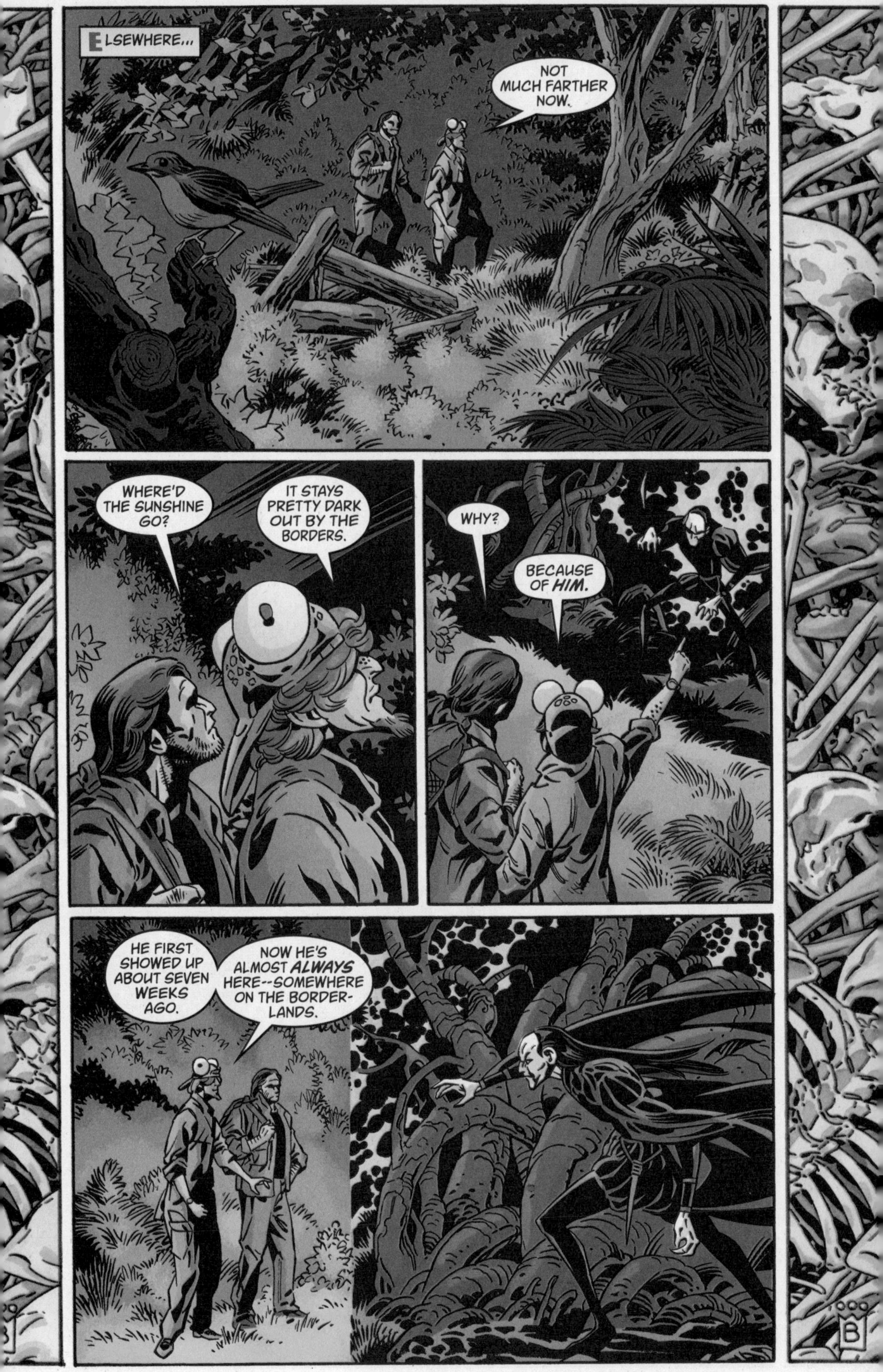
ELSEWHERE...
NOT MUCH FARTHER NOW.
WHERE'D THE SUNSHINE GO?
IT STAYS PRETTY DARK OUT BY THE BORDERS.
WHY?
BECAUSE OF *HIM.*
HE FIRST SHOWED UP ABOUT SEVEN WEEKS AGO.
NOW HE'S ALMOST *ALWAYS* HERE--SOMEWHERE ON THE BORDER-LANDS.

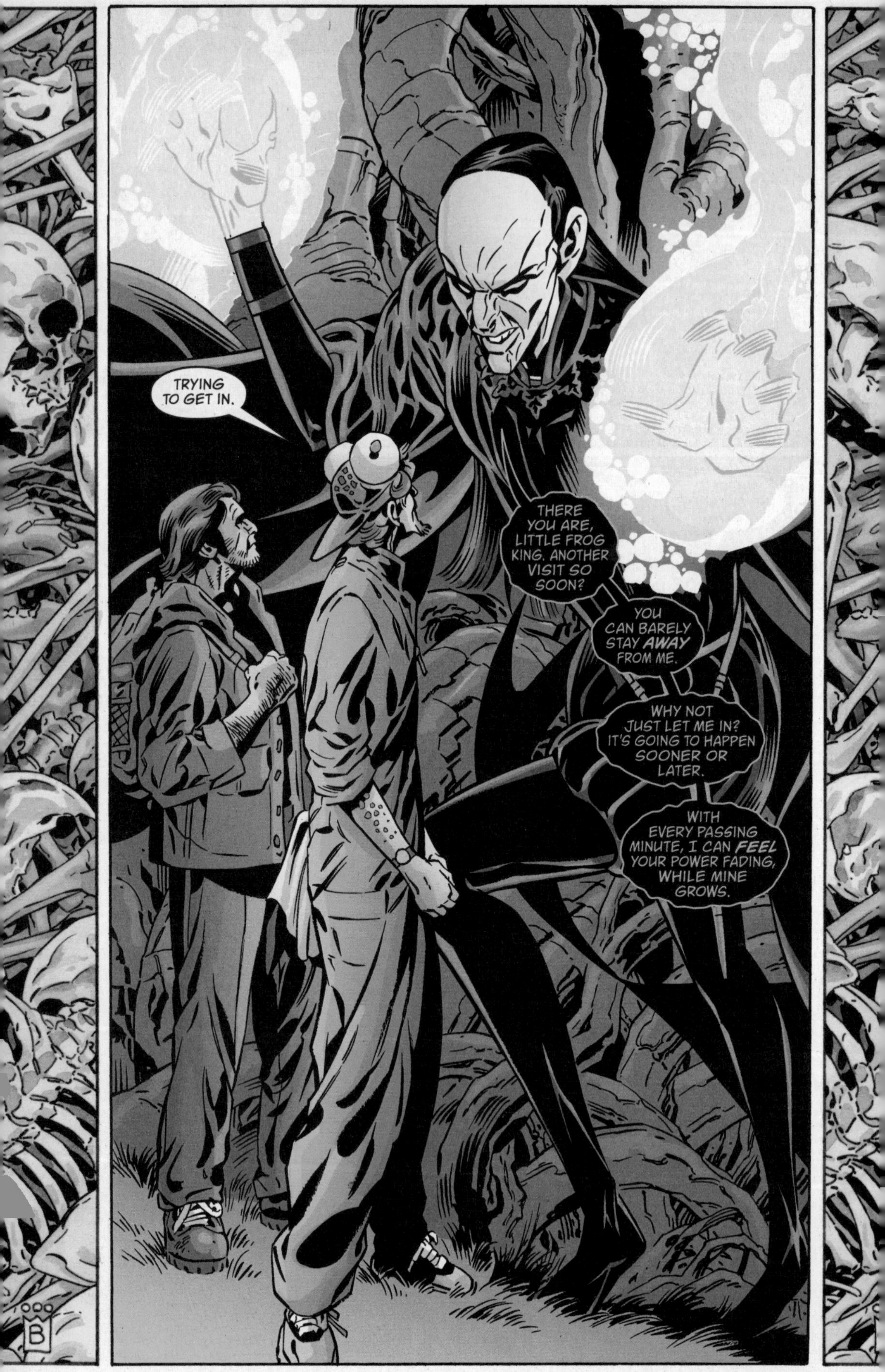

TRYING TO GET IN.
THERE YOU ARE, LITTLE FROG KING. ANOTHER VISIT SO SOON?
YOU CAN BARELY STAY AWAY FROM ME.
WHY NOT JUST LET ME IN? IT'S GOING TO HAPPEN SOONER OR LATER.
WITH EVERY PASSING MINUTE, I CAN FEEL YOUR POWER FADING, WHILE MINE GROWS.

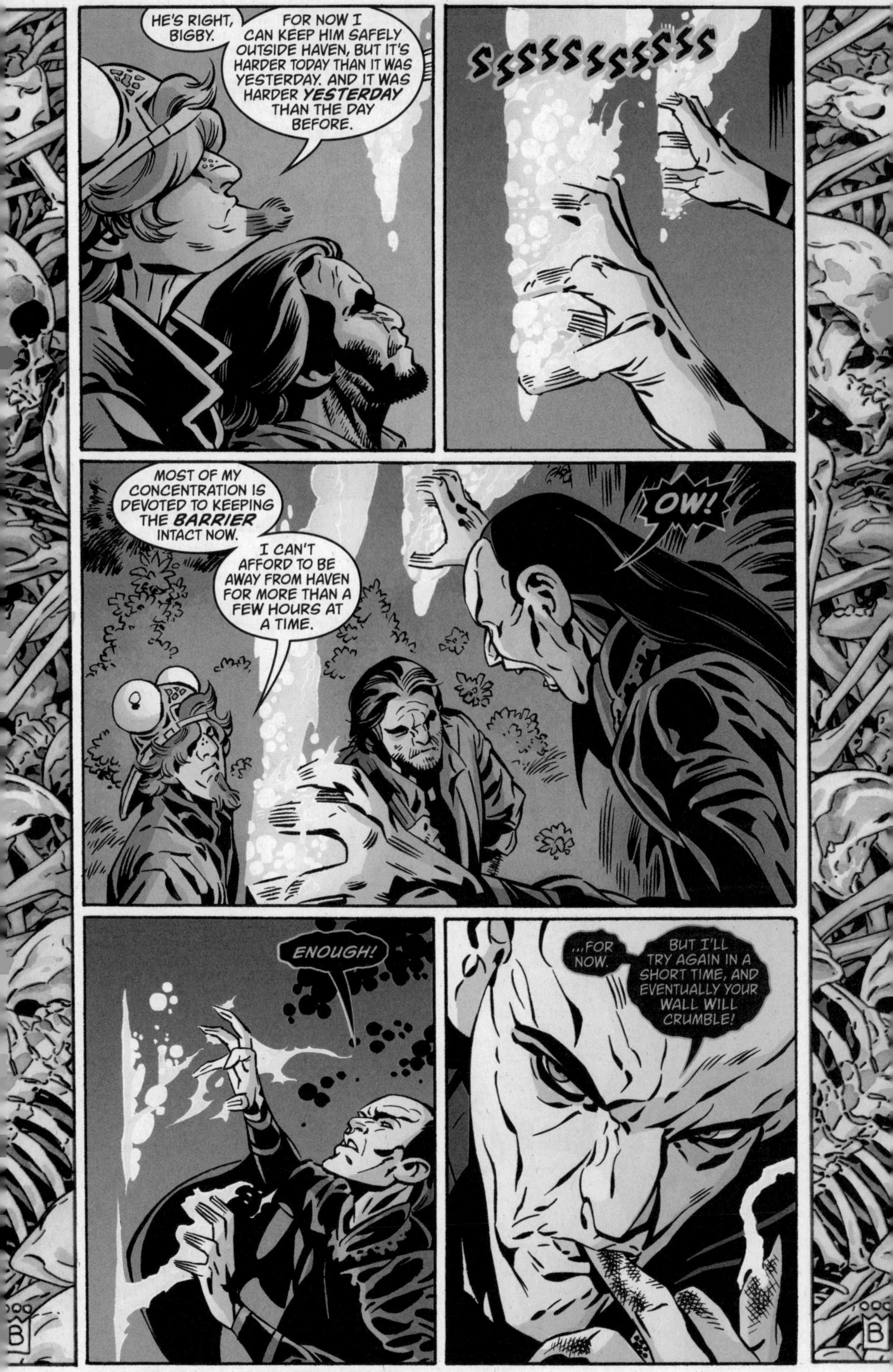
HE'S RIGHT, BIGBY.
FOR NOW I CAN KEEP HIM SAFELY OUTSIDE HAVEN, BUT IT'S HARDER TODAY THAN IT WAS YESTERDAY. AND IT WAS HARDER YESTERDAY THAN THE DAY BEFORE.
SSSSSSSSSSSS
MOST OF MY CONCENTRATION IS DEVOTED TO KEEPING THE BARRIER INTACT NOW.
I CAN'T AFFORD TO BE AWAY FROM HAVEN FOR MORE THAN A FEW HOURS AT A TIME.
OW!
ENOUGH!
...FOR NOW.
BUT I'LL TRY AGAIN IN A SHORT TIME, AND EVENTUALLY YOUR WALL WILL CRUMBLE!

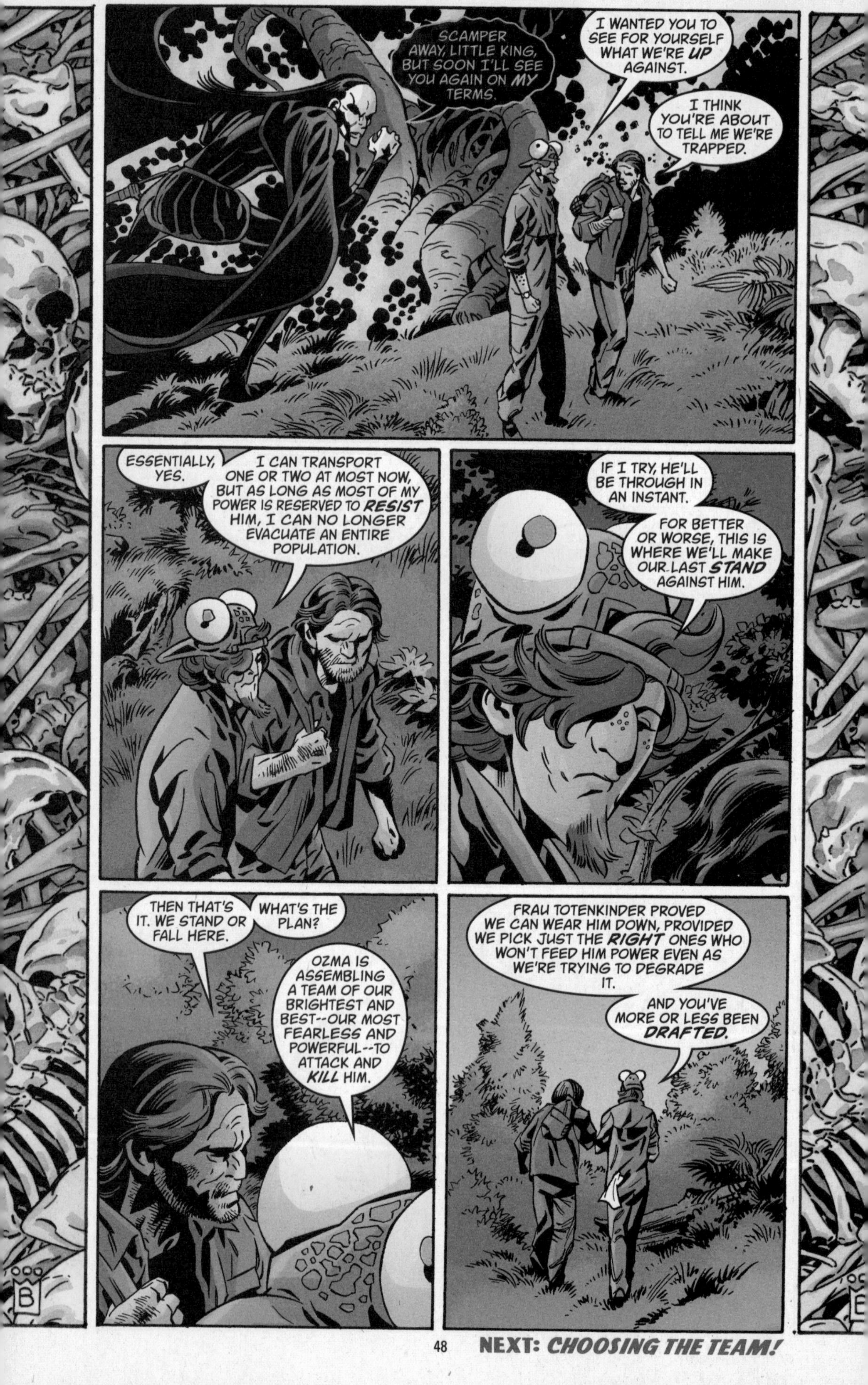
SCAMPER AWAY, LITTLE KING, BUT SOON I'LL SEE YOU AGAIN ON MY TERMS.
I WANTED YOU TO SEE FOR YOURSELF WHAT WE'RE UP AGAINST.
I THINK YOU'RE ABOUT TO TELL ME WE'RE TRAPPED.
ESSENTIALLY, YES.
I CAN TRANSPORT ONE OR TWO AT MOST NOW, BUT AS LONG AS MOST OF MY POWER IS RESERVED TO RESIST HIM, I CAN NO LONGER EVACUATE AN ENTIRE POPULATION.
IF I TRY, HE'LL BE THROUGH IN AN INSTANT.
FOR BETTER OR WORSE, THIS IS WHERE WE'LL MAKE OUR LAST STAND AGAINST HIM.
THEN THAT'S IT. WE STAND OR FALL HERE.
WHAT'S THE PLAN?
OZMA IS ASSEMBLING A TEAM OF OUR BRIGHTEST AND BEST--OUR MOST FEARLESS AND POWERFUL--TO ATTACK AND KILL HIM.
FRAU TOTENKINDER PROVED WE CAN WEAR HIM DOWN, PROVIDED WE PICK JUST THE RIGHT ONES WHO WON'T FEED HIM POWER EVEN AS WE'RE TRYING TO DEGRADE IT.
AND YOU'VE MORE OR LESS BEEN DRAFTED.

NEXT: *CHOOSING THE TEAM!*

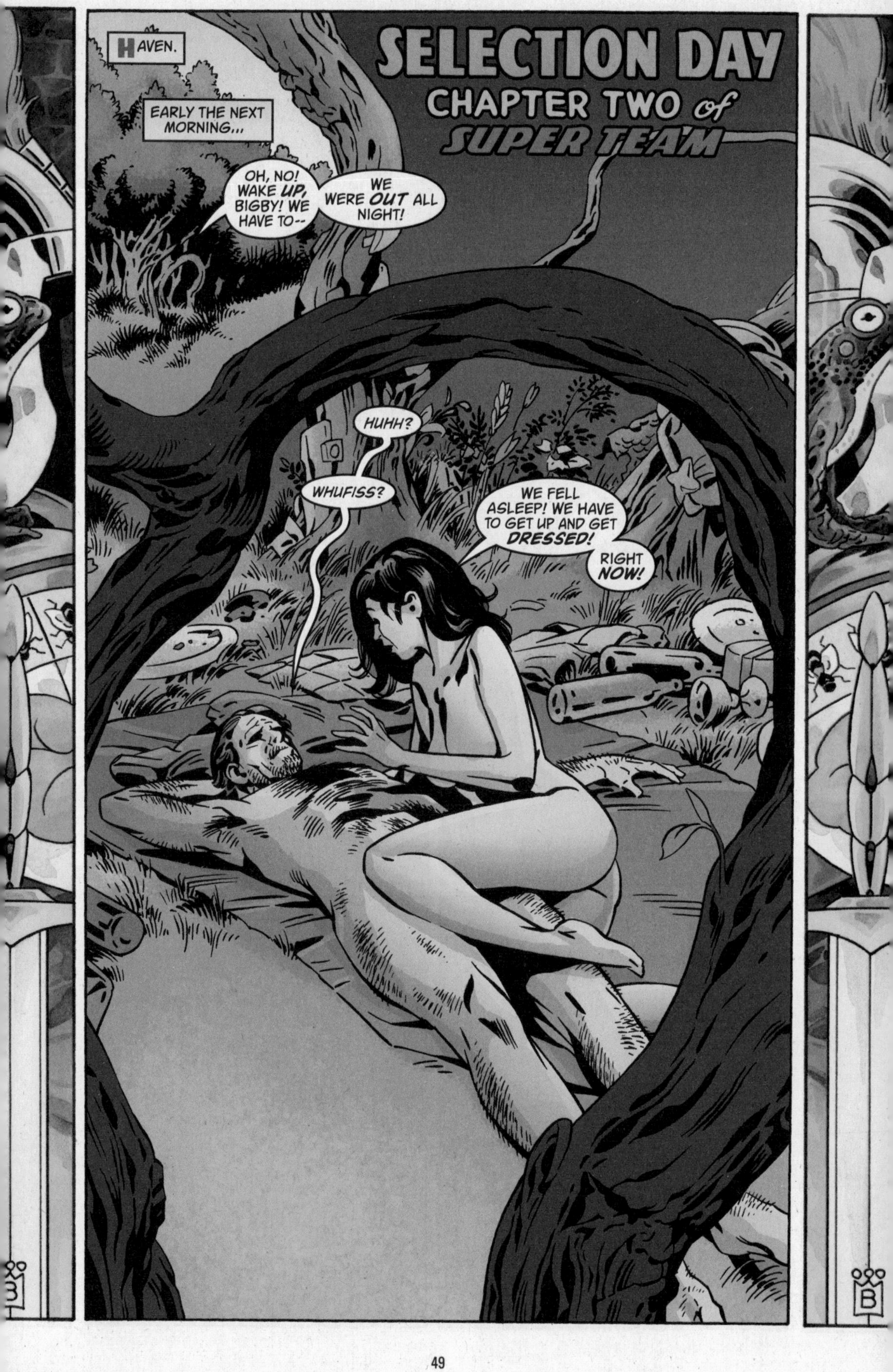
HAVEN.
EARLY THE NEXT MORNING...
SELECTION DAY
CHAPTER TWO of SUPER TEAM
OH, NO! WAKE UP, BIGBY! WE HAVE TO--
WE WERE OUT ALL NIGHT!
HUHH?
WHUFISS?
WE FELL ASLEEP! WE HAVE TO GET UP AND GET DRESSED!
RIGHT NOW!

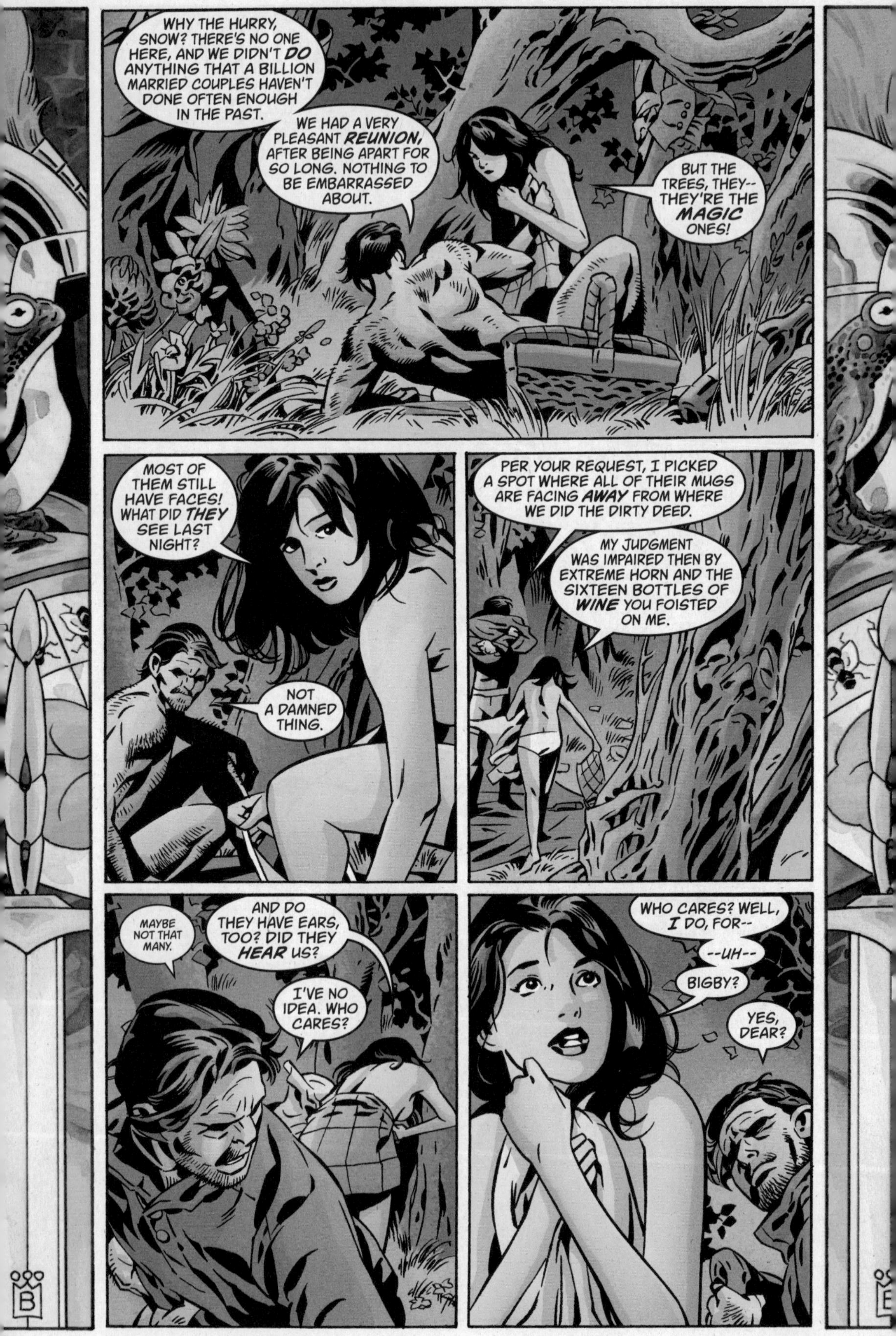

WHY THE HURRY, SNOW? THERE'S NO ONE HERE, AND WE DIDN'T DO ANYTHING THAT A BILLION MARRIED COUPLES HAVEN'T DONE OFTEN ENOUGH IN THE PAST.
WE HAD A VERY PLEASANT REUNION, AFTER BEING APART FOR SO LONG. NOTHING TO BE EMBARRASSED ABOUT.
BUT THE TREES, THEY-- THEY'RE THE MAGIC ONES!
MOST OF THEM STILL HAVE FACES! WHAT DID THEY SEE LAST NIGHT?
NOT A DAMNED THING.
PER YOUR REQUEST, I PICKED A SPOT WHERE ALL OF THEIR MUGS ARE FACING AWAY FROM WHERE WE DID THE DIRTY DEED.
MY JUDGMENT WAS IMPAIRED THEN BY EXTREME HORN AND THE SIXTEEN BOTTLES OF WINE YOU FOISTED ON ME.
AND DO THEY HAVE EARS, TOO? DID THEY HEAR US?
MAYBE NOT THAT MANY.
I'VE NO IDEA. WHO CARES?
WHO CARES? WELL, I DO, FOR--
--UH--
BIGBY?
YES, DEAR?

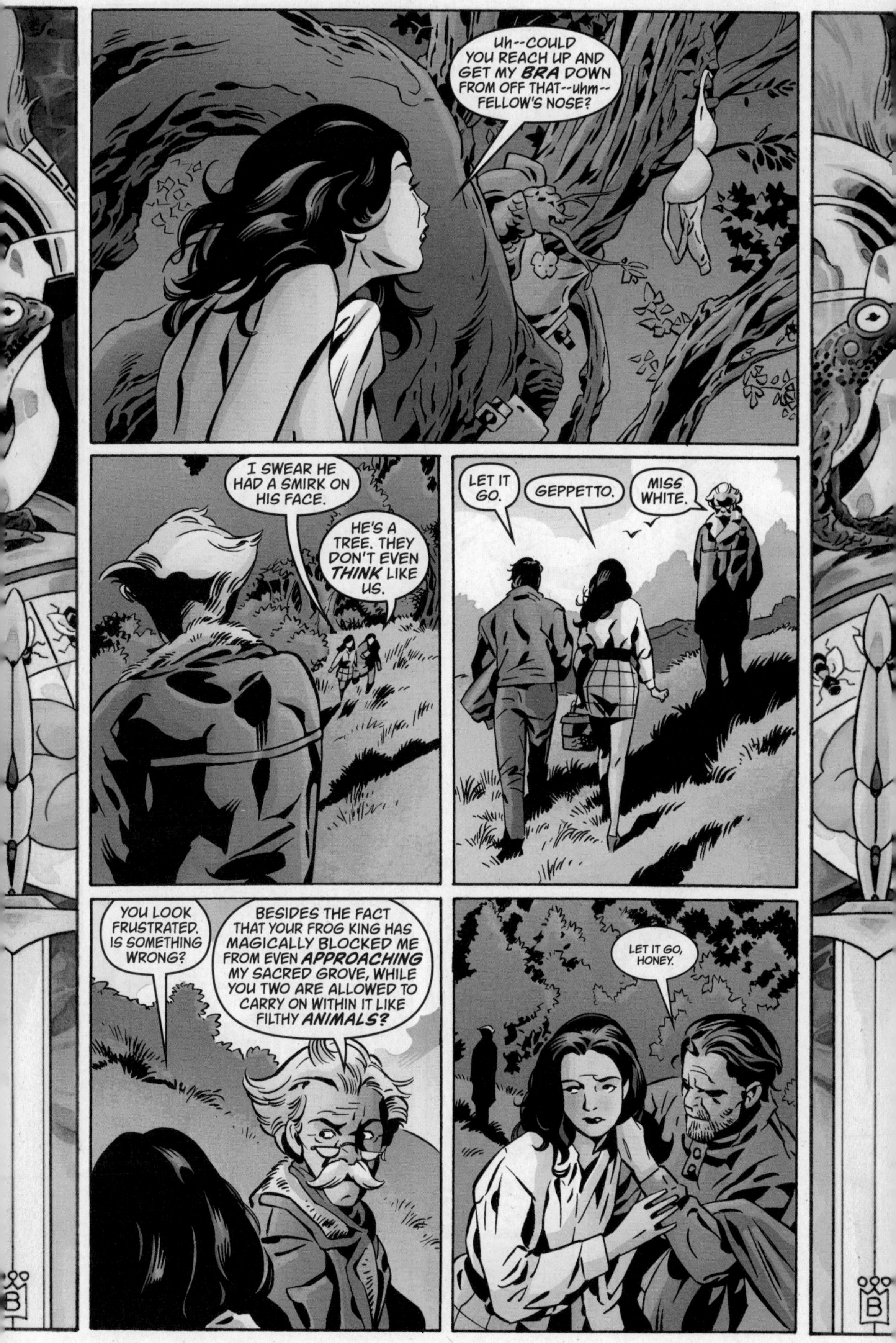
UH--COULD YOU REACH UP AND GET MY *BRA* DOWN FROM OFF THAT--*UHM*--FELLOW'S NOSE?
I SWEAR HE HAD A SMIRK ON HIS FACE.
HE'S A TREE. THEY DON'T EVEN *THINK* LIKE US.
LET IT GO.
GEPPETTO.
MISS WHITE.
YOU LOOK FRUSTRATED. IS SOMETHING WRONG?
BESIDES THE FACT THAT YOUR FROG KING HAS MAGICALLY BLOCKED ME FROM EVEN *APPROACHING* MY SACRED GROVE, WHILE YOU TWO ARE ALLOWED TO CARRY ON WITHIN IT LIKE FILTHY *ANIMALS?*
LET IT GO, HONEY.

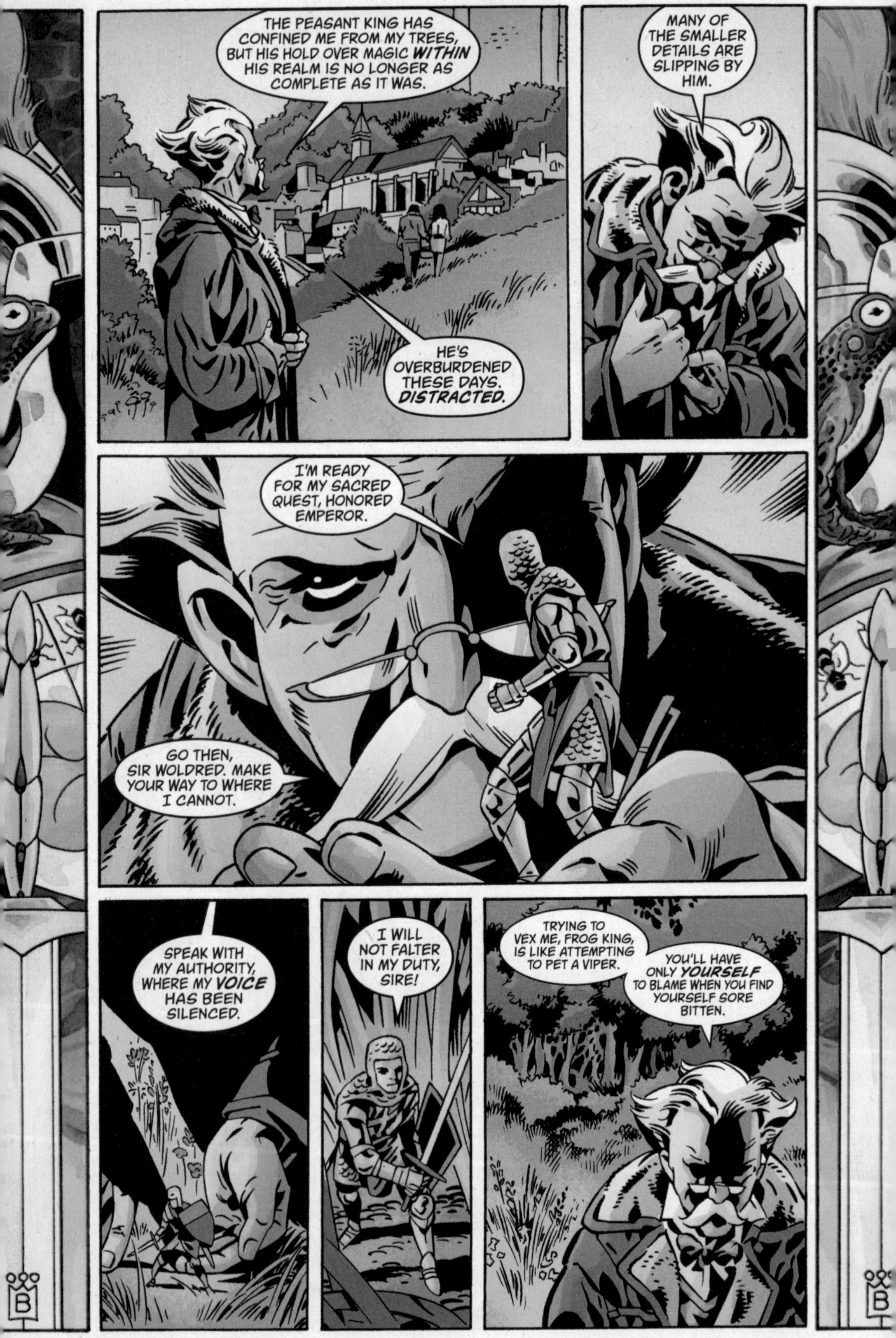
THE PEASANT KING HAS CONFINED ME FROM MY TREES, BUT HIS HOLD OVER MAGIC WITHIN HIS REALM IS NO LONGER AS COMPLETE AS IT WAS.
HE'S OVERBURDENED THESE DAYS. DISTRACTED.
MANY OF THE SMALLER DETAILS ARE SLIPPING BY HIM.
I'M READY FOR MY SACRED QUEST, HONORED EMPEROR.
GO THEN, SIR WOLDRED. MAKE YOUR WAY TO WHERE I CANNOT.
SPEAK WITH MY AUTHORITY, WHERE MY VOICE HAS BEEN SILENCED.
I WILL NOT FALTER IN MY DUTY, SIRE!
TRYING TO VEX ME, FROG KING, IS LIKE ATTEMPTING TO PET A VIPER.
YOU'LL HAVE ONLY YOURSELF TO BLAME WHEN YOU FIND YOURSELF SORE BITTEN.

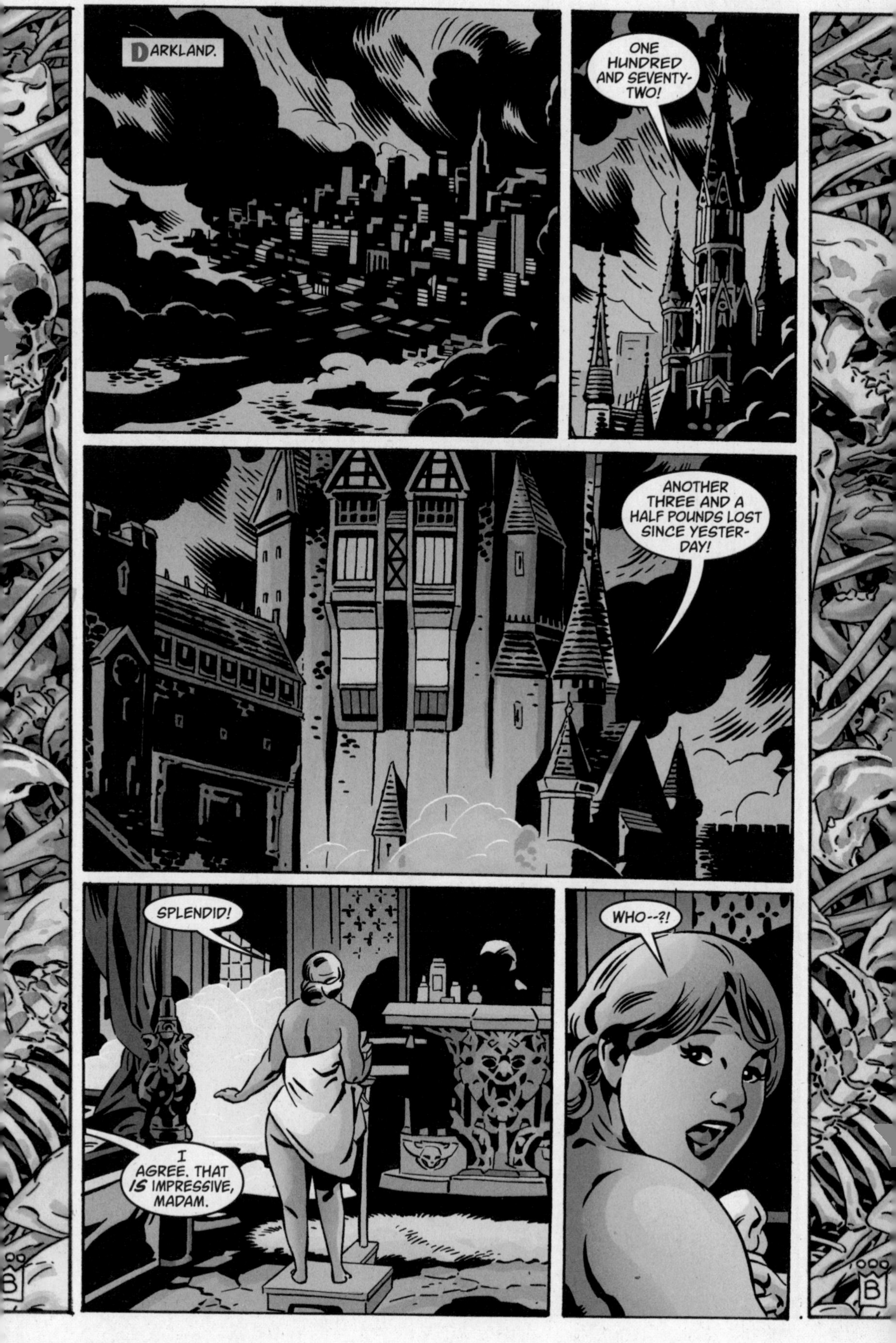
DARKLAND.
ONE HUNDRED AND SEVENTY-TWO!
ANOTHER THREE AND A HALF POUNDS LOST SINCE YESTER-DAY!
SPLENDID!
I AGREE. THAT IS IMPRESSIVE, MADAM.
WHO--?!

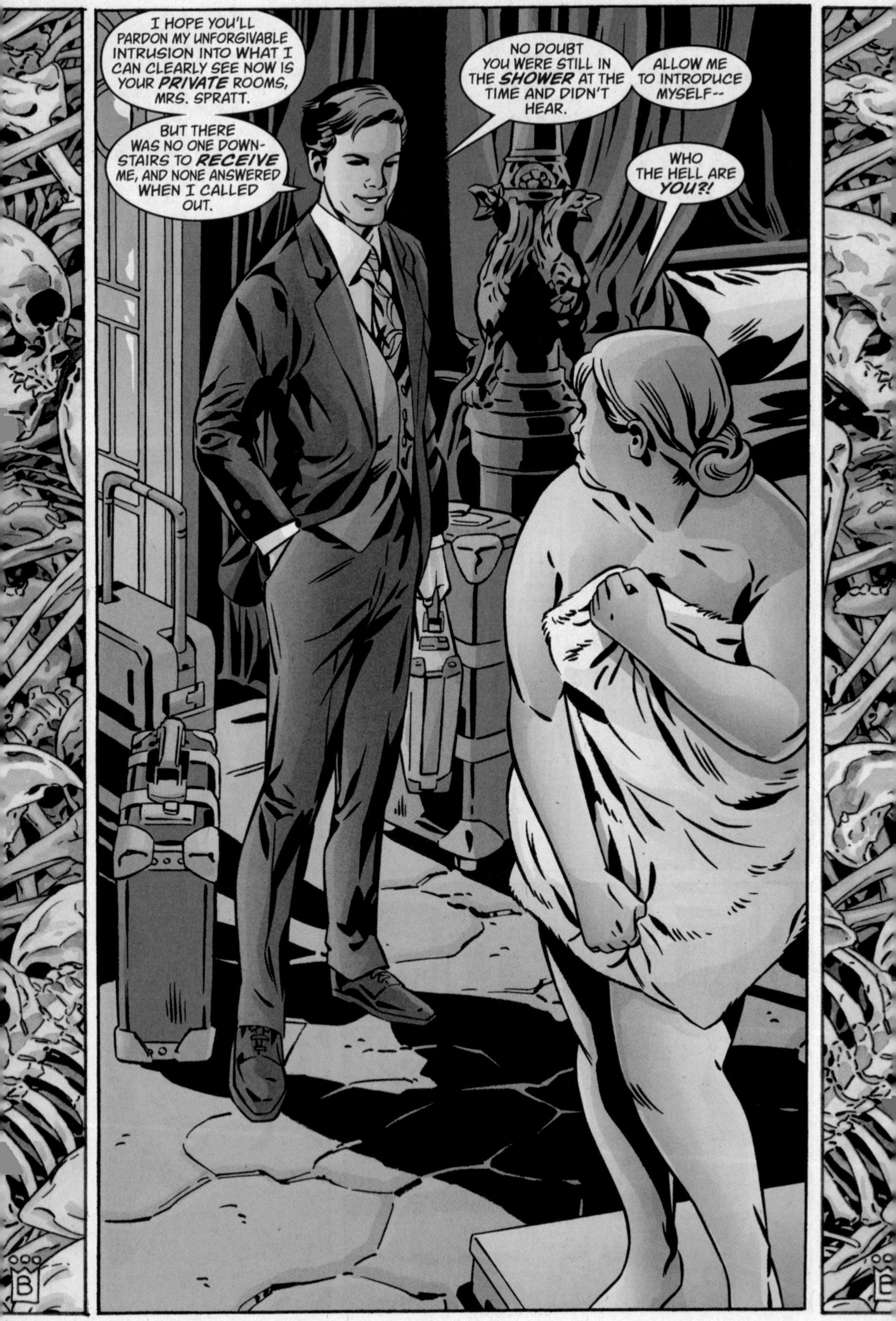
I HOPE YOU'LL PARDON MY UNFORGIVABLE INTRUSION INTO WHAT I CAN CLEARLY SEE NOW IS YOUR PRIVATE ROOMS, MRS. SPRATT.
BUT THERE WAS NO ONE DOWN-STAIRS TO RECEIVE ME, AND NONE ANSWERED WHEN I CALLED OUT.
NO DOUBT YOU WERE STILL IN THE SHOWER AT THE TIME AND DIDN'T HEAR.
ALLOW ME TO INTRODUCE MYSELF--
WHO THE HELL ARE YOU?!

YES, EXACTLY.

AS I WAS SAYING, I'M WERIAN HOLT, ESQUIRE. AS OUR MUTUAL *BENEFACTOR* PROMISED--

YOU'RE MY HANDSOME PRINCE?

AH--WELL, THANK YOU, MADAM. THAT'S *QUITE* FLATTERING.

BUT WHAT I MEANT TO SAY IS I'VE BEEN *ENGAGED*, BY MISTER DARK, TO HELP YOU ALONG ON HIS VOW TO TURN YOU INTO THE "FAIREST IN ALL THE LAND."

AS REMARKABLE AS YOUR WEIGHT LOSS HAS BEEN, AND *CONTINUES* TO BE, IT ISN'T BY ITSELF ENOUGH TO COMPLETE THE TRANSFOR-MATION.

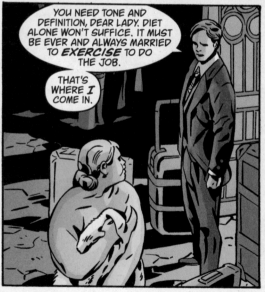

YOU NEED TONE AND DEFINITION, DEAR LADY. DIET ALONE WON'T SUFFICE. IT MUST BE EVER AND ALWAYS MARRIED TO *EXERCISE* TO DO THE JOB.

THAT'S WHERE *I* COME IN.

SO--?

I'M YOUR FENCING INSTRUCTOR.

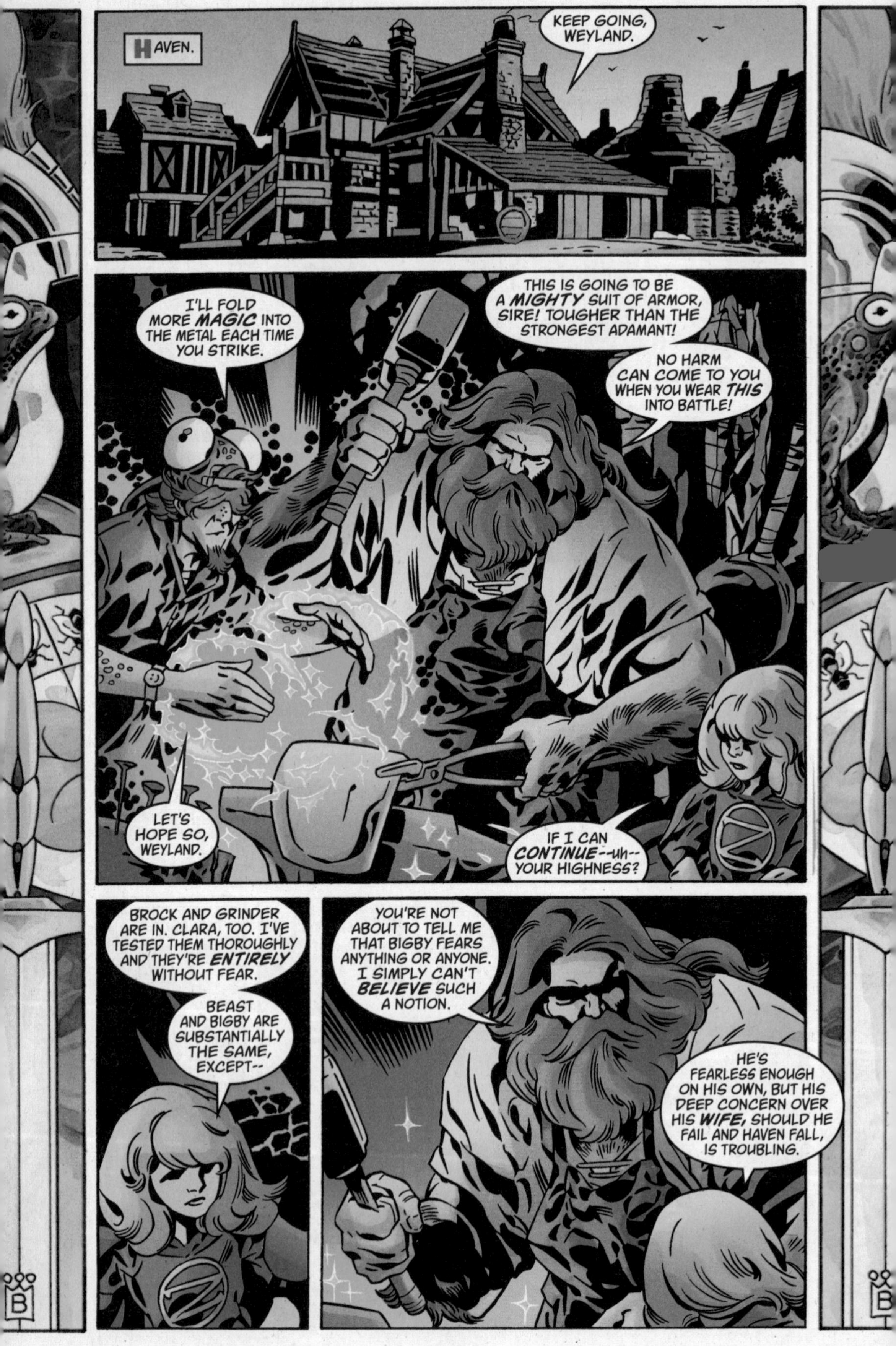
HAVEN.
KEEP GOING, WEYLAND.
I'LL FOLD MORE MAGIC INTO THE METAL EACH TIME YOU STRIKE.
THIS IS GOING TO BE A MIGHTY SUIT OF ARMOR, SIRE! TOUGHER THAN THE STRONGEST ADAMANT!
NO HARM CAN COME TO YOU WHEN YOU WEAR THIS INTO BATTLE!
LET'S HOPE SO, WEYLAND.
IF I CAN CONTINUE--uh--YOUR HIGHNESS?
BROCK AND GRINDER ARE IN. CLARA, TOO. I'VE TESTED THEM THOROUGHLY AND THEY'RE ENTIRELY WITHOUT FEAR.
BEAST AND BIGBY ARE SUBSTANTIALLY THE SAME, EXCEPT--
YOU'RE NOT ABOUT TO TELL ME THAT BIGBY FEARS ANYTHING OR ANYONE. I SIMPLY CAN'T BELIEVE SUCH A NOTION.
HE'S FEARLESS ENOUGH ON HIS OWN, BUT HIS DEEP CONCERN OVER HIS WIFE, SHOULD HE FAIL AND HAVEN FALL, IS TROUBLING.

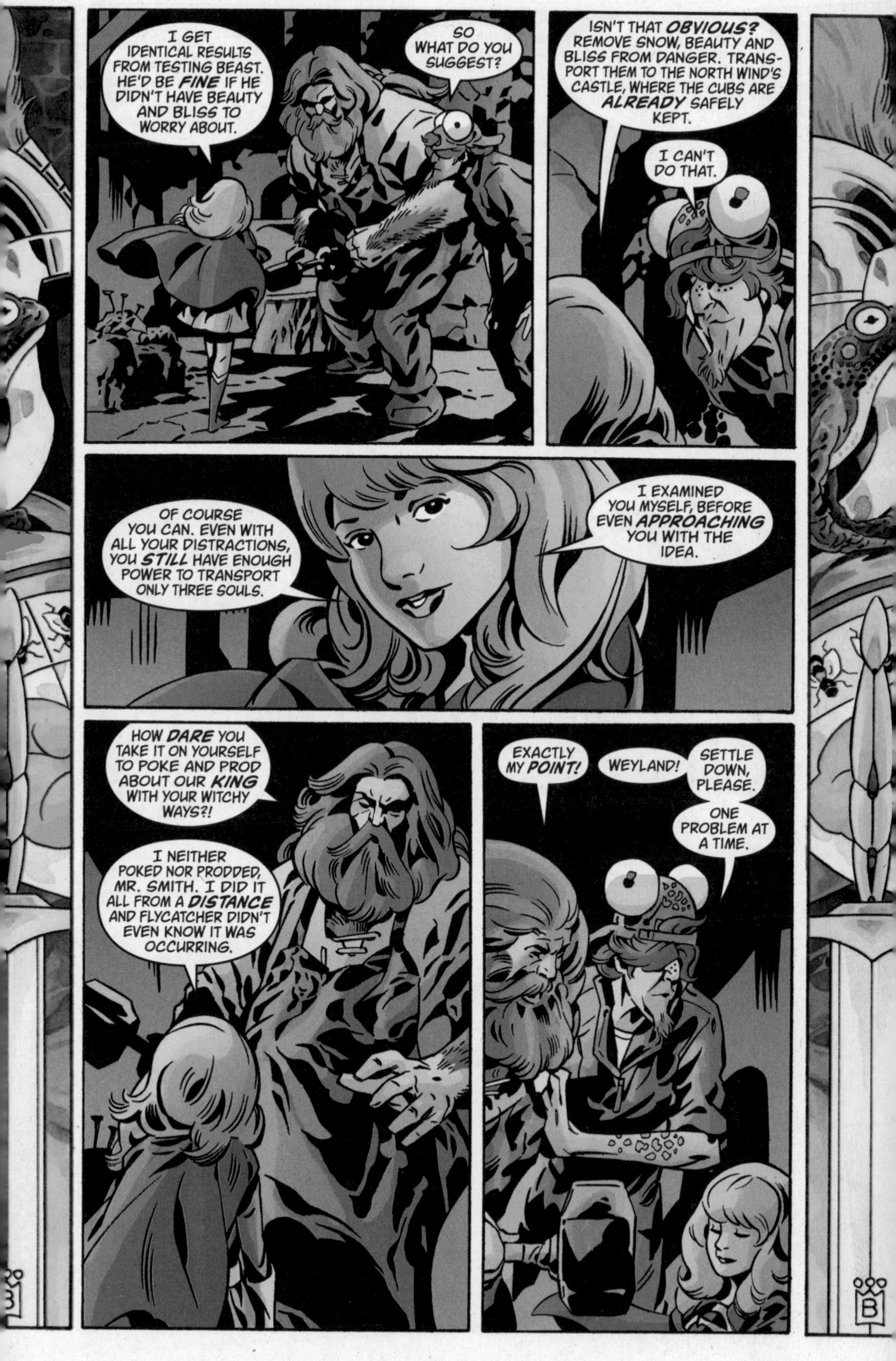
I GET IDENTICAL RESULTS FROM TESTING BEAST. HE'D BE FINE IF HE DIDN'T HAVE BEAUTY AND BLISS TO WORRY ABOUT.
SO WHAT DO YOU SUGGEST?
ISN'T THAT OBVIOUS? REMOVE SNOW, BEAUTY AND BLISS FROM DANGER. TRANSPORT THEM TO THE NORTH WIND'S CASTLE, WHERE THE CUBS ARE ALREADY SAFELY KEPT.
I CAN'T DO THAT.
OF COURSE YOU CAN. EVEN WITH ALL YOUR DISTRACTIONS, YOU STILL HAVE ENOUGH POWER TO TRANSPORT ONLY THREE SOULS.
I EXAMINED YOU MYSELF, BEFORE EVEN APPROACHING YOU WITH THE IDEA.
HOW DARE YOU TAKE IT ON YOURSELF TO POKE AND PROD ABOUT OUR KING WITH YOUR WITCHY WAYS?!
I NEITHER POKED NOR PRODDED, MR. SMITH. I DID IT ALL FROM A DISTANCE AND FLYCATCHER DIDN'T EVEN KNOW IT WAS OCCURRING.
EXACTLY MY POINT!
WEYLAND!
SETTLE DOWN, PLEASE.
ONE PROBLEM AT A TIME.

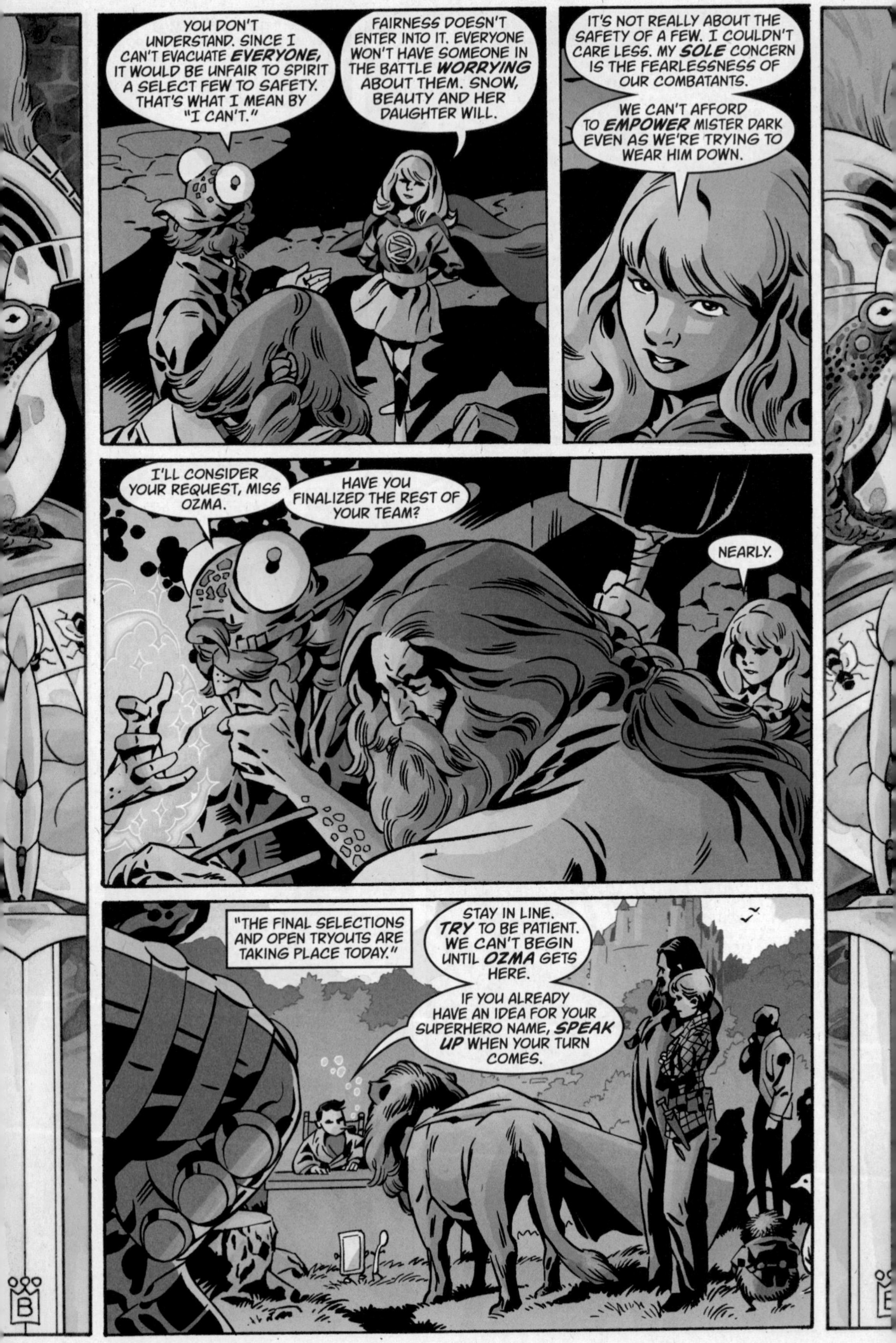

YOU DON'T UNDERSTAND. SINCE I CAN'T EVACUATE EVERYONE, IT WOULD BE UNFAIR TO SPIRIT A SELECT FEW TO SAFETY. THAT'S WHAT I MEAN BY "I CAN'T."
FAIRNESS DOESN'T ENTER INTO IT. EVERYONE WON'T HAVE SOMEONE IN THE BATTLE WORRYING ABOUT THEM. SNOW, BEAUTY AND HER DAUGHTER WILL.
IT'S NOT REALLY ABOUT THE SAFETY OF A FEW. I COULDN'T CARE LESS. MY SOLE CONCERN IS THE FEARLESSNESS OF OUR COMBATANTS.
WE CAN'T AFFORD TO EMPOWER MISTER DARK EVEN AS WE'RE TRYING TO WEAR HIM DOWN.
I'LL CONSIDER YOUR REQUEST, MISS OZMA.
HAVE YOU FINALIZED THE REST OF YOUR TEAM?
NEARLY.
"THE FINAL SELECTIONS AND OPEN TRYOUTS ARE TAKING PLACE TODAY."
STAY IN LINE. TRY TO BE PATIENT. WE CAN'T BEGIN UNTIL OZMA GETS HERE.
IF YOU ALREADY HAVE AN IDEA FOR YOUR SUPERHERO NAME, SPEAK UP WHEN YOUR TURN COMES.

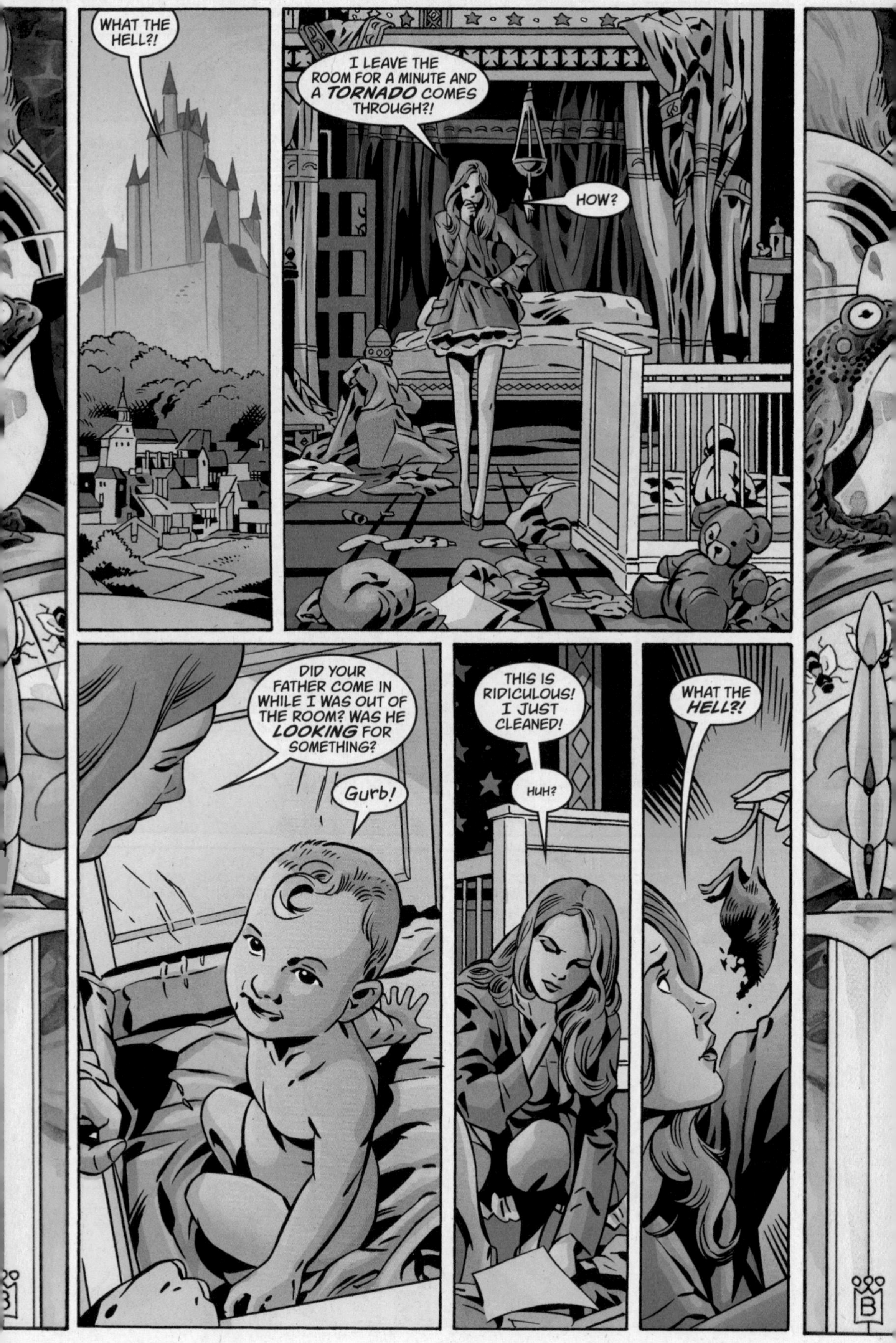
WHAT THE HELL?!
I LEAVE THE ROOM FOR A MINUTE AND A TORNADO COMES THROUGH?!
HOW?
DID YOUR FATHER COME IN WHILE I WAS OUT OF THE ROOM? WAS HE LOOKING FOR SOMETHING?
Gurb!
THIS IS RIDICULOUS! I JUST CLEANED!
HUH?
WHAT THE HELL?!

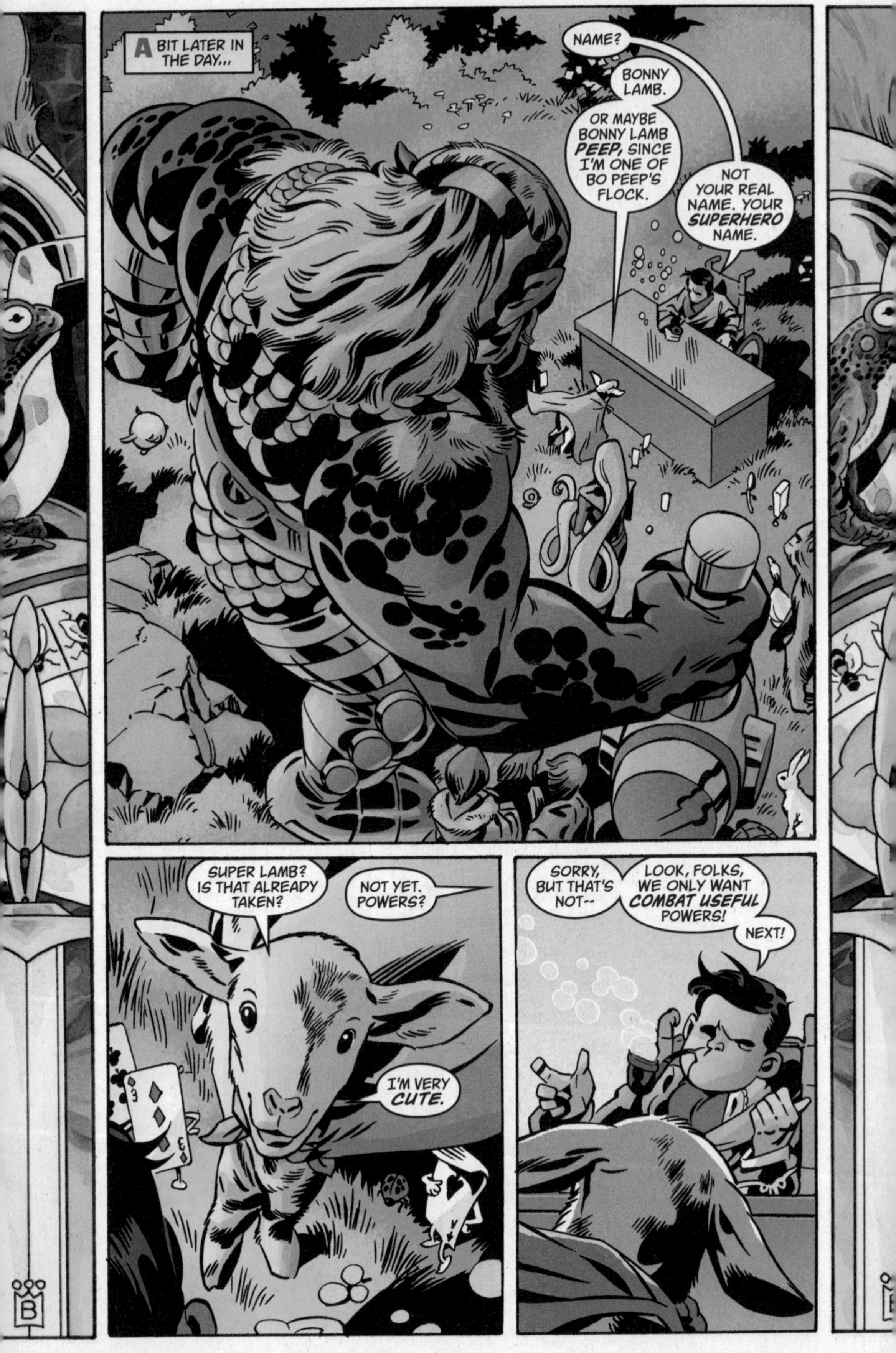
A BIT LATER IN THE DAY...
NAME?
BONNY LAMB.
OR MAYBE BONNY LAMB PEEP, SINCE I'M ONE OF BO PEEP'S FLOCK.
NOT YOUR REAL NAME. YOUR SUPERHERO NAME.
SUPER LAMB? IS THAT ALREADY TAKEN?
NOT YET. POWERS?
I'M VERY CUTE.
SORRY, BUT THAT'S NOT--
LOOK, FOLKS, WE ONLY WANT COMBAT USEFUL POWERS!
NEXT!

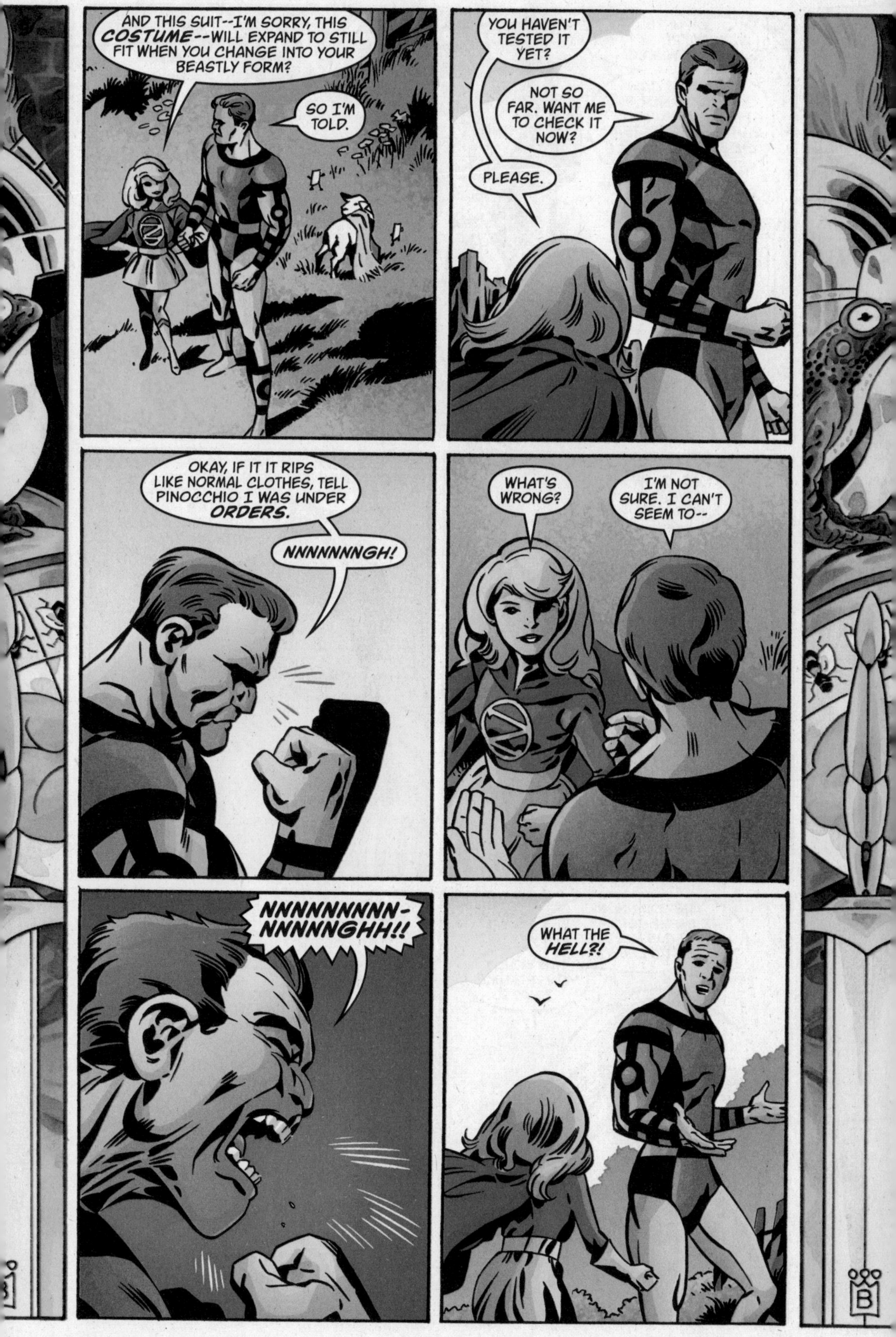
AND THIS SUIT--I'M SORRY, THIS COSTUME--WILL EXPAND TO STILL FIT WHEN YOU CHANGE INTO YOUR BEASTLY FORM?
SO I'M TOLD.
YOU HAVEN'T TESTED IT YET?
NOT SO FAR. WANT ME TO CHECK IT NOW?
PLEASE.
OKAY, IF IT IT RIPS LIKE NORMAL CLOTHES, TELL PINOCCHIO I WAS UNDER ORDERS.
NNNNNNNGH!
WHAT'S WRONG?
I'M NOT SURE. I CAN'T SEEM TO--
NNNNNNNNN-NNNNNGHH!!
WHAT THE HELL?!

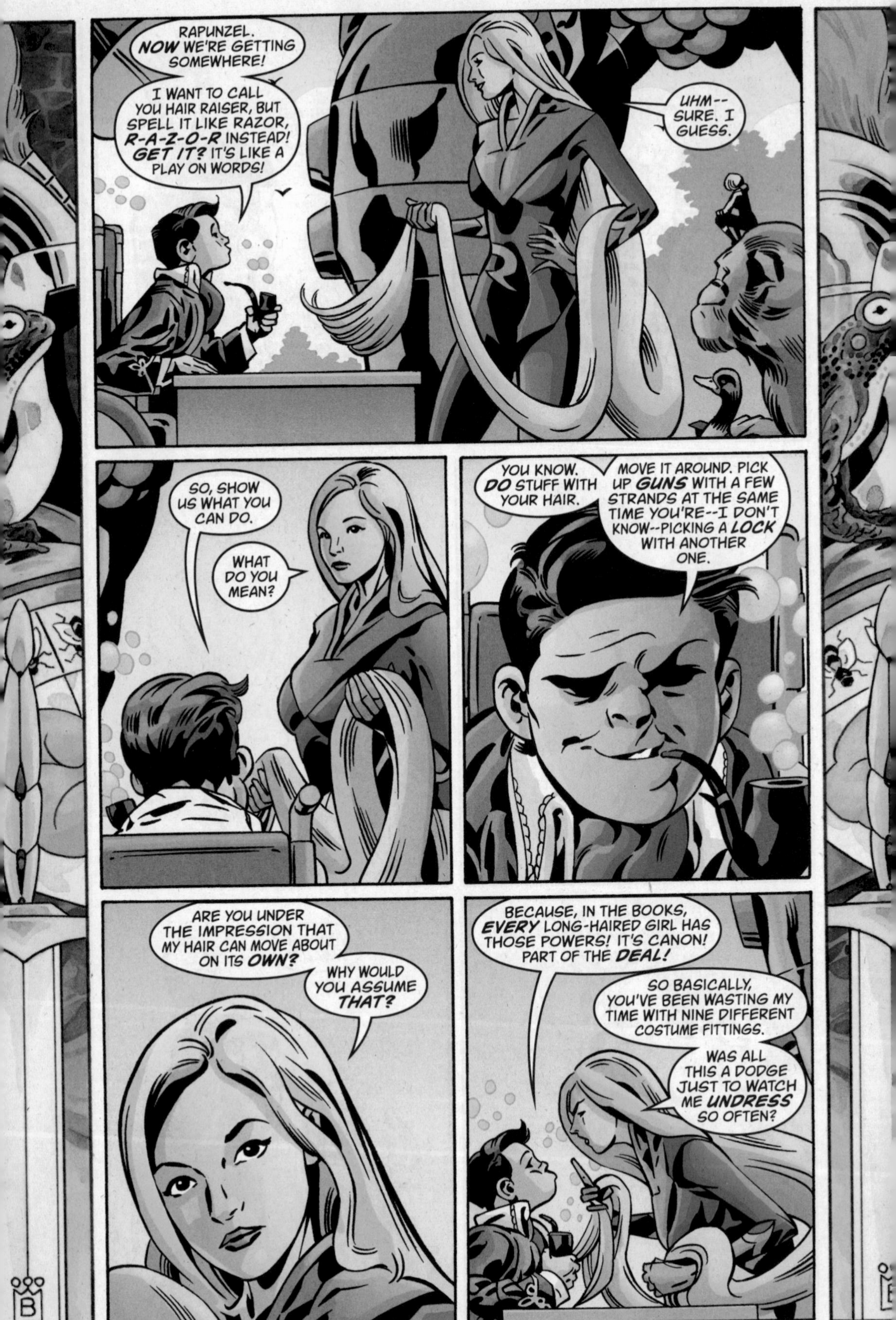
RAPUNZEL. NOW WE'RE GETTING SOMEWHERE!
I WANT TO CALL YOU HAIR RAISER, BUT SPELL IT LIKE RAZOR, R-A-Z-O-R INSTEAD! GET IT? IT'S LIKE A PLAY ON WORDS!
UHM-- SURE. I GUESS.
SO, SHOW US WHAT YOU CAN DO.
WHAT DO YOU MEAN?
YOU KNOW. DO STUFF WITH YOUR HAIR.
MOVE IT AROUND. PICK UP GUNS WITH A FEW STRANDS AT THE SAME TIME YOU'RE--I DON'T KNOW--PICKING A LOCK WITH ANOTHER ONE.
ARE YOU UNDER THE IMPRESSION THAT MY HAIR CAN MOVE ABOUT ON ITS OWN?
WHY WOULD YOU ASSUME THAT?
BECAUSE, IN THE BOOKS, EVERY LONG-HAIRED GIRL HAS THOSE POWERS! IT'S CANON! PART OF THE DEAL!
SO BASICALLY, YOU'VE BEEN WASTING MY TIME WITH NINE DIFFERENT COSTUME FITTINGS.
WAS ALL THIS A DODGE JUST TO WATCH ME UNDRESS SO OFTEN?

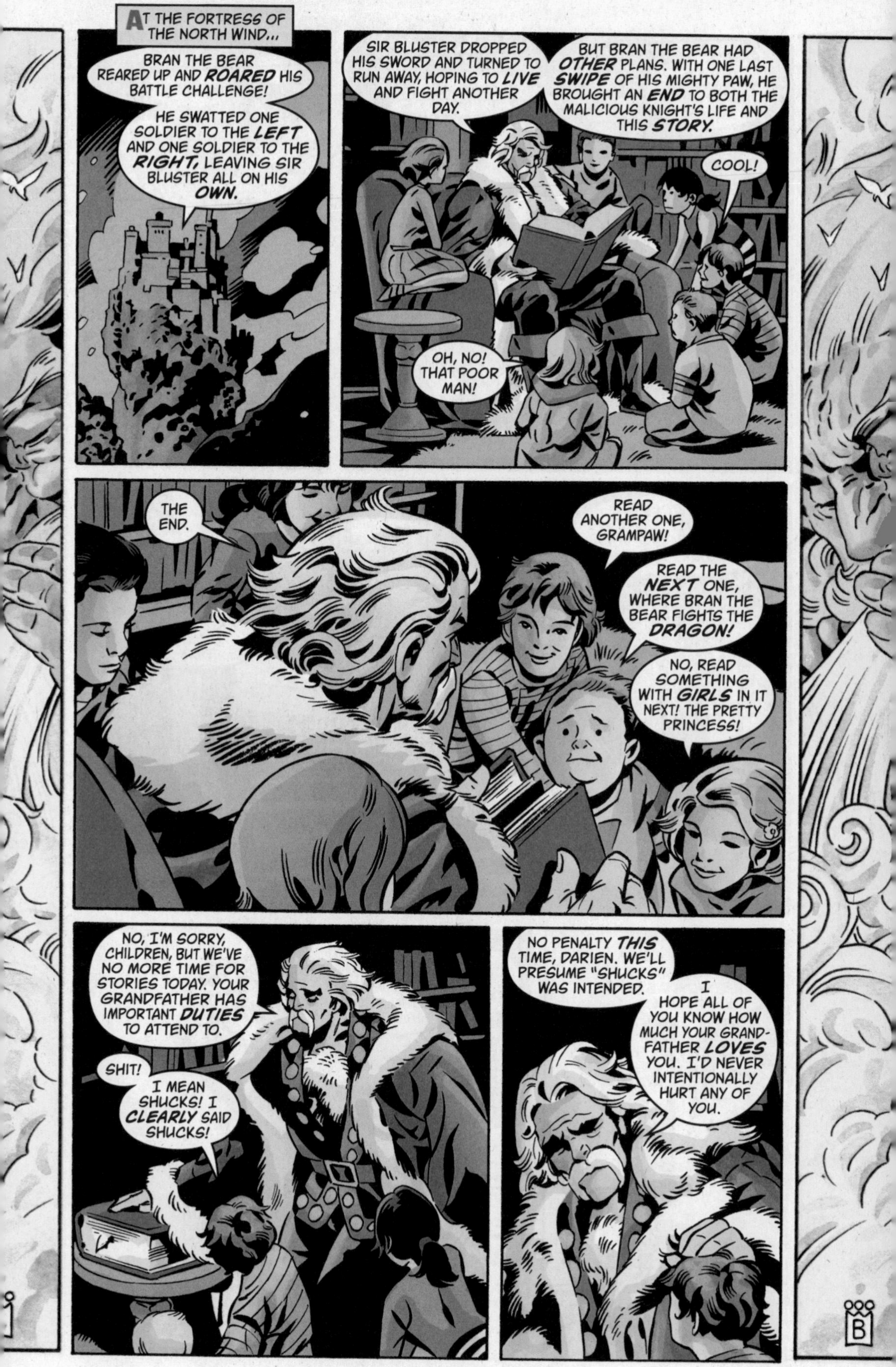

AT THE FORTRESS OF THE NORTH WIND...
BRAN THE BEAR REARED UP AND ROARED HIS BATTLE CHALLENGE!
HE SWATTED ONE SOLDIER TO THE LEFT AND ONE SOLDIER TO THE RIGHT, LEAVING SIR BLUSTER ALL ON HIS OWN.
SIR BLUSTER DROPPED HIS SWORD AND TURNED TO RUN AWAY, HOPING TO LIVE AND FIGHT ANOTHER DAY.
BUT BRAN THE BEAR HAD OTHER PLANS. WITH ONE LAST SWIPE OF HIS MIGHTY PAW, HE BROUGHT AN END TO BOTH THE MALICIOUS KNIGHT'S LIFE AND THIS STORY.
COOL!
OH, NO! THAT POOR MAN!
THE END.
READ ANOTHER ONE, GRAMPAW!
READ THE NEXT ONE, WHERE BRAN THE BEAR FIGHTS THE DRAGON!
NO, READ SOMETHING WITH GIRLS IN IT NEXT! THE PRETTY PRINCESS!
NO, I'M SORRY, CHILDREN, BUT WE'VE NO MORE TIME FOR STORIES TODAY. YOUR GRANDFATHER HAS IMPORTANT DUTIES TO ATTEND TO.
SHIT!
I MEAN SHUCKS! I CLEARLY SAID SHUCKS!
NO PENALTY THIS TIME, DARIEN. WE'LL PRESUME "SHUCKS" WAS INTENDED.
I HOPE ALL OF YOU KNOW HOW MUCH YOUR GRANDFATHER LOVES YOU. I'D NEVER INTENTIONALLY HURT ANY OF YOU.

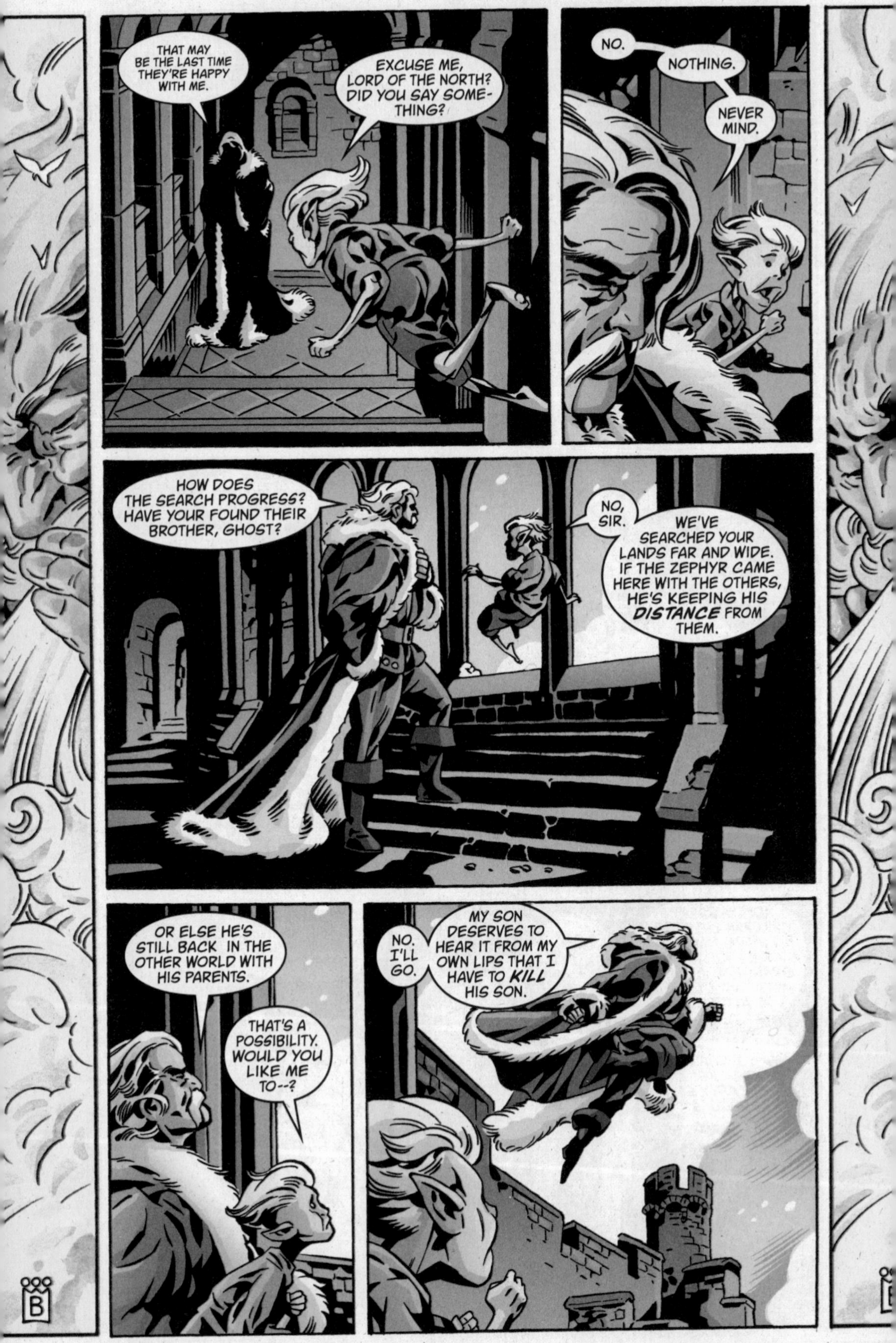
THAT MAY BE THE LAST TIME THEY'RE HAPPY WITH ME.
EXCUSE ME, LORD OF THE NORTH? DID YOU SAY SOME-THING?
NO.
NOTHING.
NEVER MIND.
HOW DOES THE SEARCH PROGRESS? HAVE YOUR FOUND THEIR BROTHER, GHOST?
NO, SIR.
WE'VE SEARCHED YOUR LANDS FAR AND WIDE. IF THE ZEPHYR CAME HERE WITH THE OTHERS, HE'S KEEPING HIS DISTANCE FROM THEM.
OR ELSE HE'S STILL BACK IN THE OTHER WORLD WITH HIS PARENTS.
THAT'S A POSSIBILITY. WOULD YOU LIKE ME TO--?
NO. I'LL GO.
MY SON DESERVES TO HEAR IT FROM MY OWN LIPS THAT I HAVE TO KILL HIS SON.

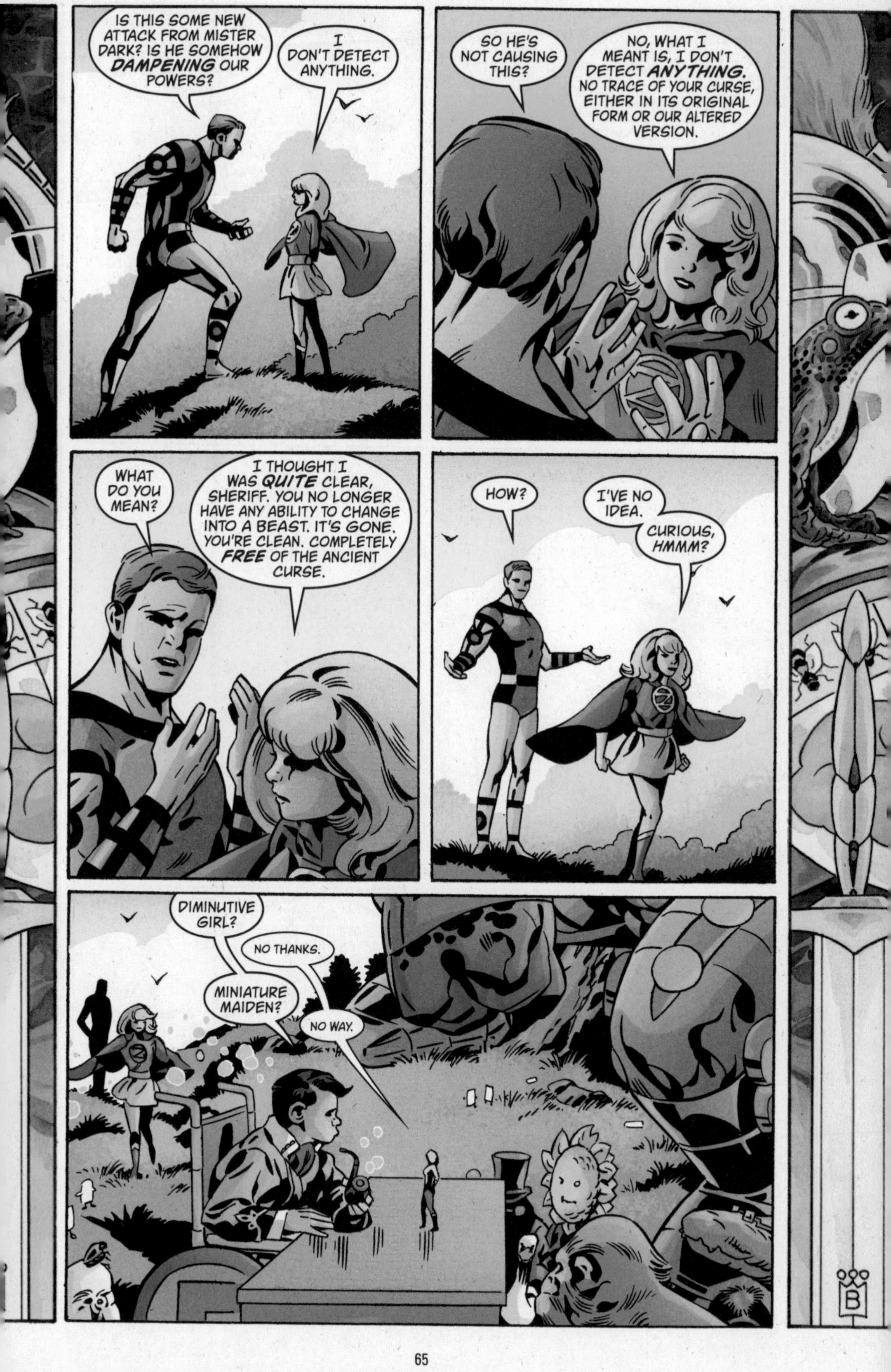
IS THIS SOME NEW ATTACK FROM MISTER DARK? IS HE SOMEHOW DAMPENING OUR POWERS?
I DON'T DETECT ANYTHING.
SO HE'S NOT CAUSING THIS?
NO, WHAT I MEANT IS, I DON'T DETECT ANYTHING. NO TRACE OF YOUR CURSE, EITHER IN ITS ORIGINAL FORM OR OUR ALTERED VERSION.
WHAT DO YOU MEAN?
I THOUGHT I WAS QUITE CLEAR, SHERIFF. YOU NO LONGER HAVE ANY ABILITY TO CHANGE INTO A BEAST. IT'S GONE. YOU'RE CLEAN. COMPLETELY FREE OF THE ANCIENT CURSE.
HOW?
I'VE NO IDEA.
CURIOUS, HMMM?
DIMINUTIVE GIRL?
NO THANKS.
MINIATURE MAIDEN?
NO WAY.

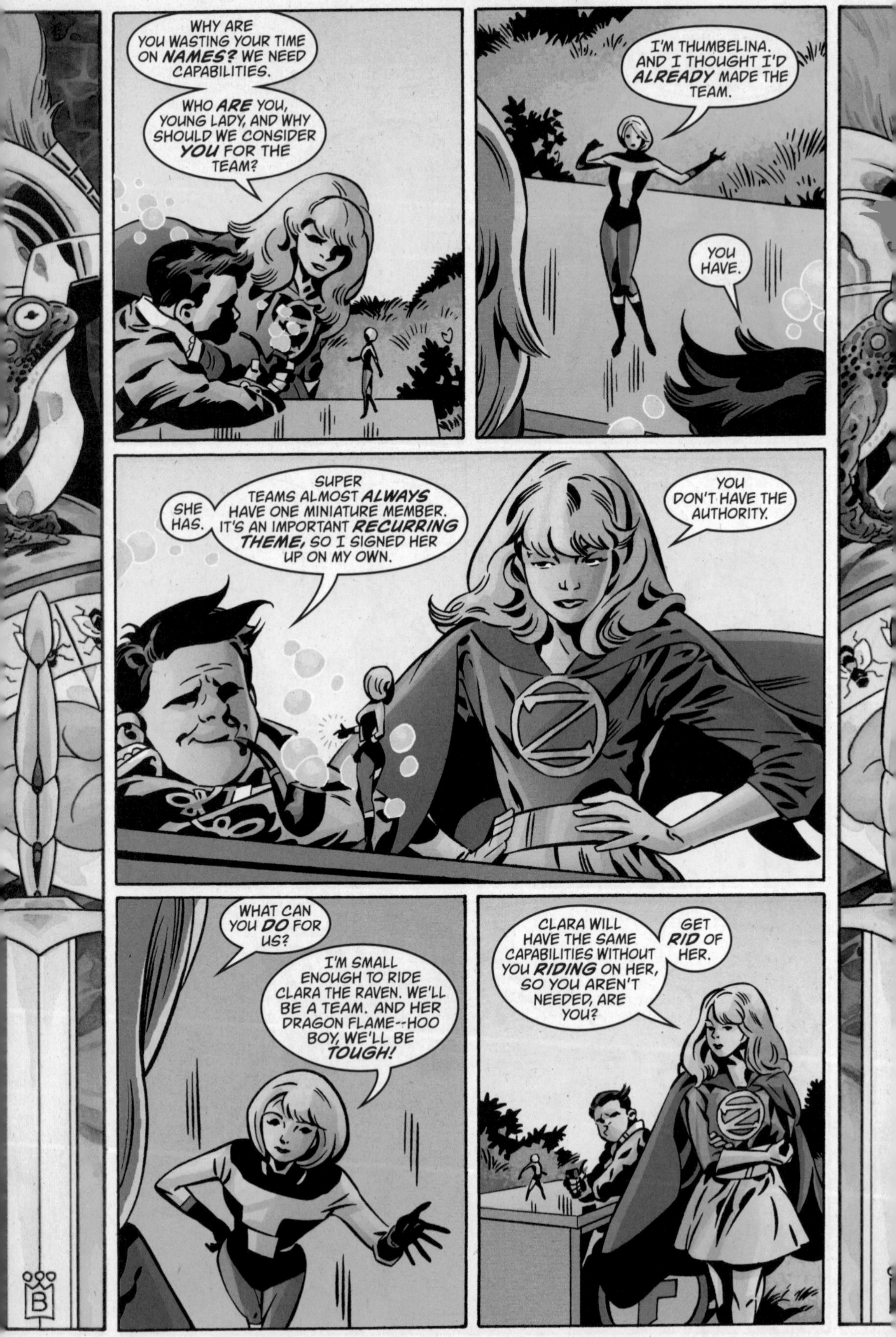
WHY ARE YOU WASTING YOUR TIME ON NAMES? WE NEED CAPABILITIES.
WHO ARE YOU, YOUNG LADY, AND WHY SHOULD WE CONSIDER YOU FOR THE TEAM?
I'M THUMBELINA. AND I THOUGHT I'D ALREADY MADE THE TEAM.
YOU HAVE.
SHE HAS.
SUPER TEAMS ALMOST ALWAYS HAVE ONE MINIATURE MEMBER. IT'S AN IMPORTANT RECURRING THEME, SO I SIGNED HER UP ON MY OWN.
YOU DON'T HAVE THE AUTHORITY.
WHAT CAN YOU DO FOR US?
I'M SMALL ENOUGH TO RIDE CLARA THE RAVEN. WE'LL BE A TEAM. AND HER DRAGON FLAME--HOO BOY, WE'LL BE TOUGH!
CLARA WILL HAVE THE SAME CAPABILITIES WITHOUT YOU RIDING ON HER, SO YOU AREN'T NEEDED, ARE YOU?
GET RID OF HER.

HOLD ON! WAIT JUST A GODDAMN *MINUTE,* OZMA!

YOU CAN'T JUST *DISMISS* HER LIKE THAT! YOU CAN'T *TREAT* PEOPLE THAT WAY!

WHY NOT? SHE'S OF NO *USE* TO US.

NONE OF THOSE STILL IN LINE ARE ANY GOOD, SO WE'RE *DONE* WITH RECRUITING.

I'VE SETTLED ON THE FINAL GROUP.

YOU CAN'T TREAT FOLKS SO CALLOUSLY, YOU LITTLE *WITCH.* THEY'RE ALL SCARED TO DEATH AND KNOW WE HAVE JUST ABOUT *ZERO* CHANCE OF BEATING THE DARK MAN, AND YET THEY *STILL* STEPPED UP TO VOLUNTEER.

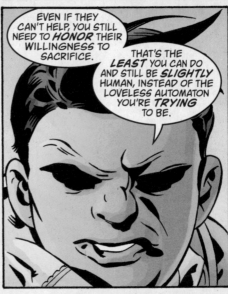

EVEN IF THEY CAN'T HELP, YOU STILL NEED TO *HONOR* THEIR WILLINGNESS TO SACRIFICE.

THAT'S THE *LEAST* YOU CAN DO AND STILL BE *SLIGHTLY* HUMAN, INSTEAD OF THE LOVELESS AUTOMATON YOU'RE *TRYING* TO BE.

I WARNED YOU BEFORE ABOUT CALLING ME NAMES.

BIG DEAL! TURN ME INTO A TOAD, OR A COCKROACH, OR ANYTHING ELSE! THAT WOULD *STILL* MAKE ME A HUNNERT-THOUSAND TIMES BETTER'N YOU!

WE'RE *DONE* TALKING. GO AWAY.

INCIDENTALLY, *YOU* DIDN'T MAKE THE TEAM EITHER.

THAT'S IT, THEN!

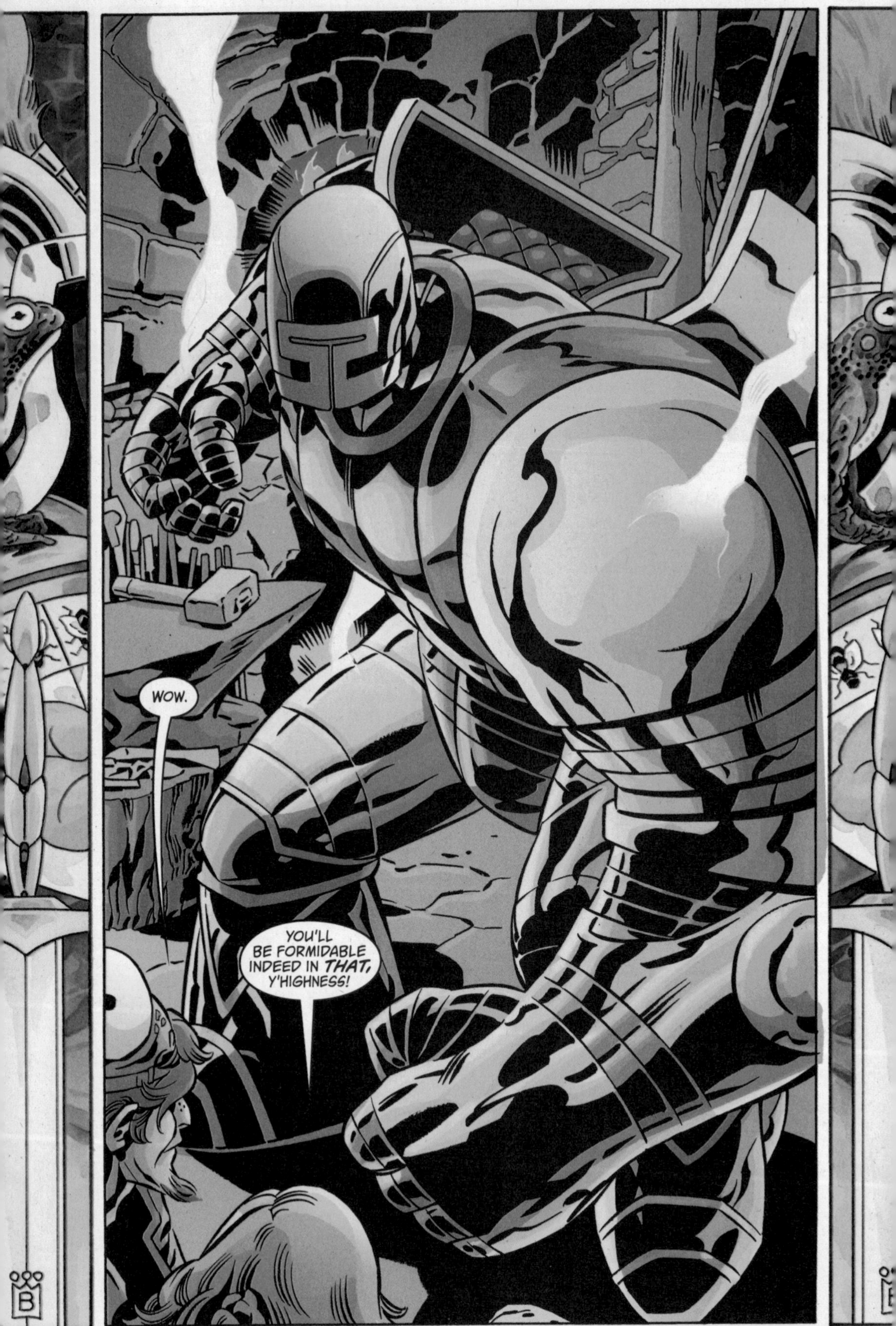
WOW.
YOU'LL BE FORMIDABLE INDEED IN *THAT*, Y'HIGHNESS!

NEXT: *THE NORTH WIND REALLY BLOWS!*

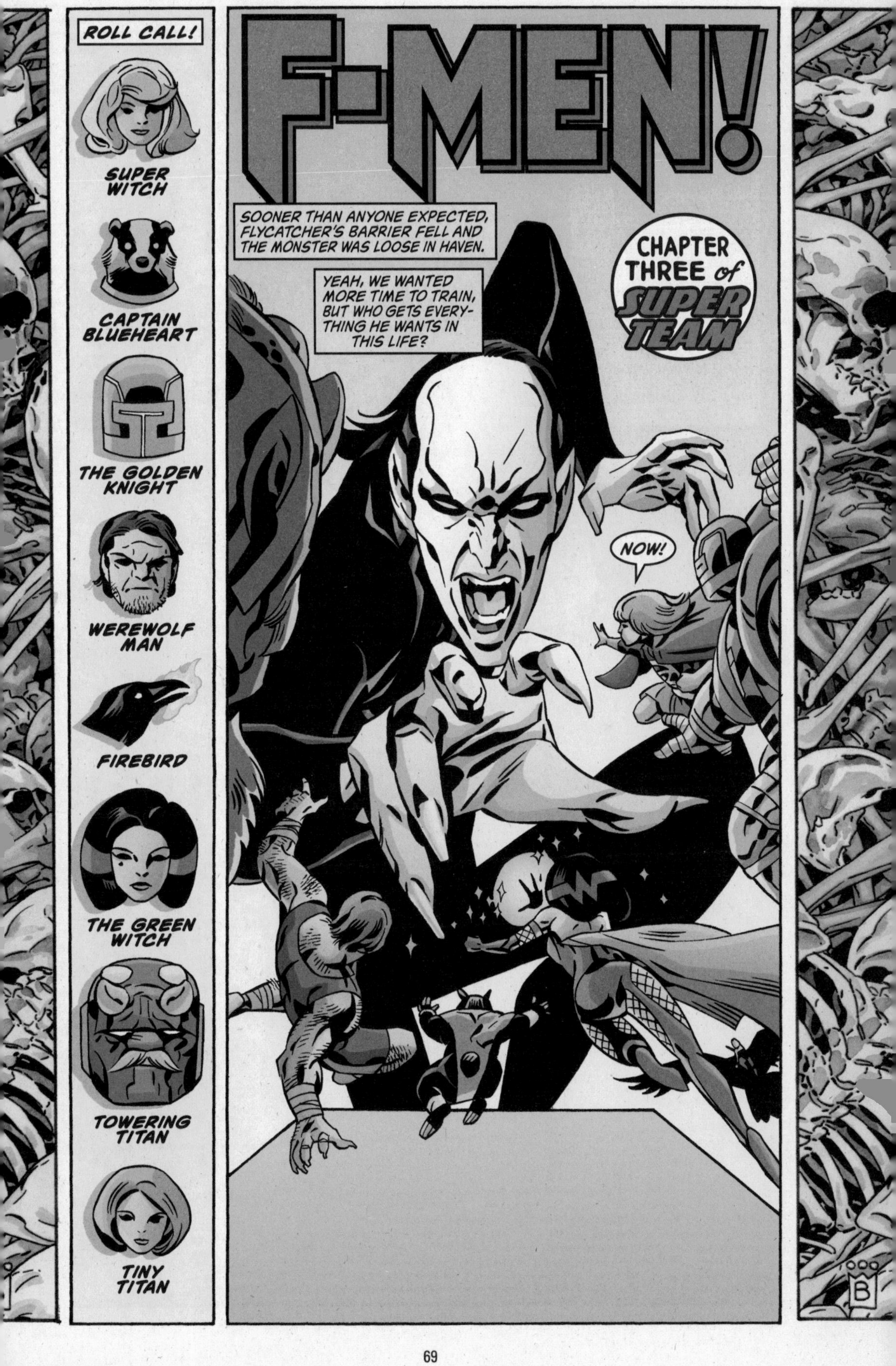
ROLL CALL!
SUPER WITCH
CAPTAIN BLUEHEART
THE GOLDEN KNIGHT
WEREWOLF MAN
FIREBIRD
THE GREEN WITCH
TOWERING TITAN
TINY TITAN
F-MEN!
SOONER THAN ANYONE EXPECTED, FLYCATCHER'S BARRIER FELL AND THE MONSTER WAS LOOSE IN HAVEN.
YEAH, WE WANTED MORE TIME TO TRAIN, BUT WHO GETS EVERYTHING HE WANTS IN THIS LIFE?
CHAPTER THREE of SUPER TEAM
NOW!

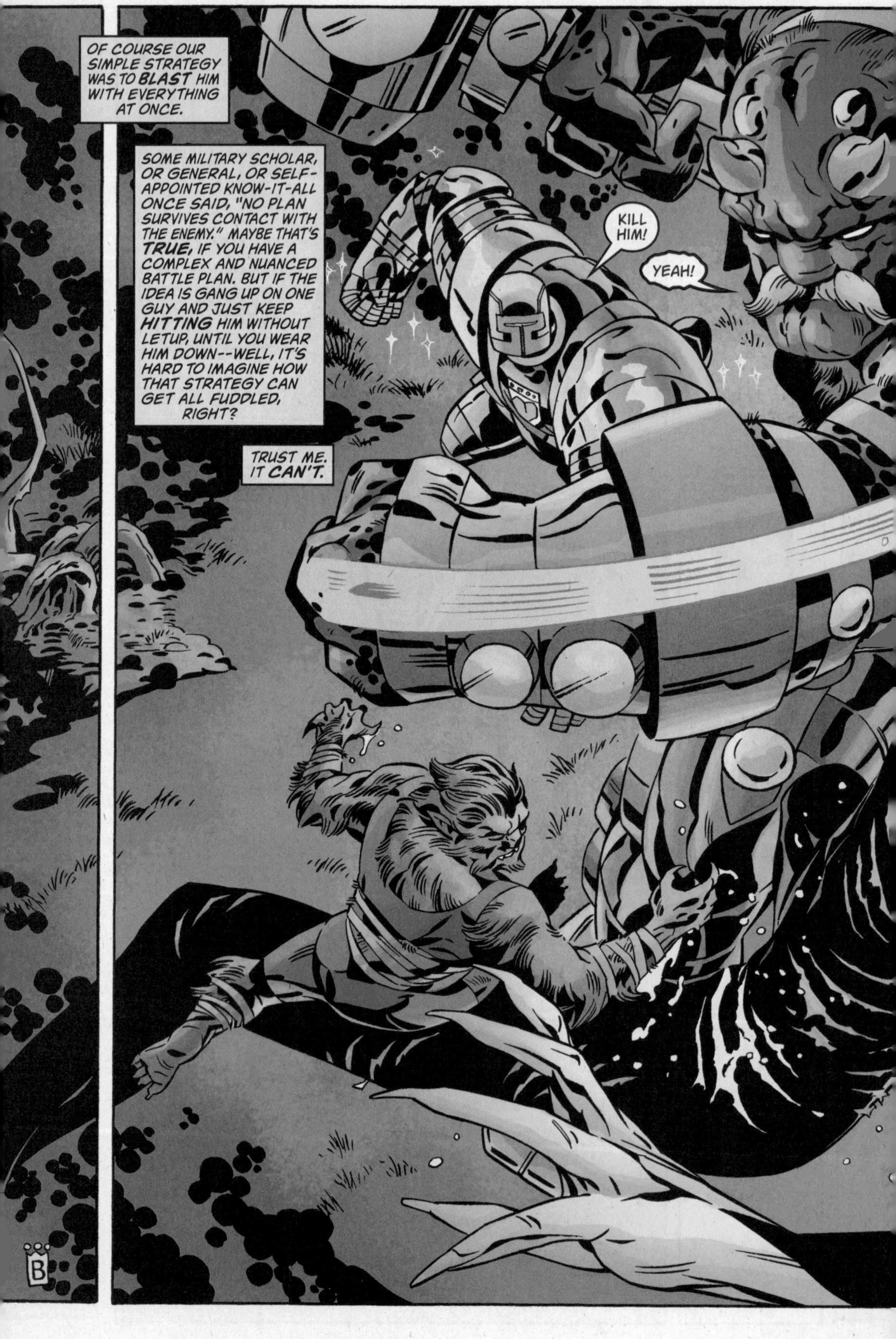

OF COURSE OUR SIMPLE STRATEGY WAS TO BLAST HIM WITH EVERYTHING AT ONCE.
SOME MILITARY SCHOLAR, OR GENERAL, OR SELF-APPOINTED KNOW-IT-ALL ONCE SAID, "NO PLAN SURVIVES CONTACT WITH THE ENEMY." MAYBE THAT'S TRUE, IF YOU HAVE A COMPLEX AND NUANCED BATTLE PLAN. BUT IF THE IDEA IS GANG UP ON ONE GUY AND JUST KEEP HITTING HIM WITHOUT LETUP, UNTIL YOU WEAR HIM DOWN--WELL, IT'S HARD TO IMAGINE HOW THAT STRATEGY CAN GET ALL FUDDLED, RIGHT?
KILL HIM!
YEAH!
TRUST ME. IT CAN'T.

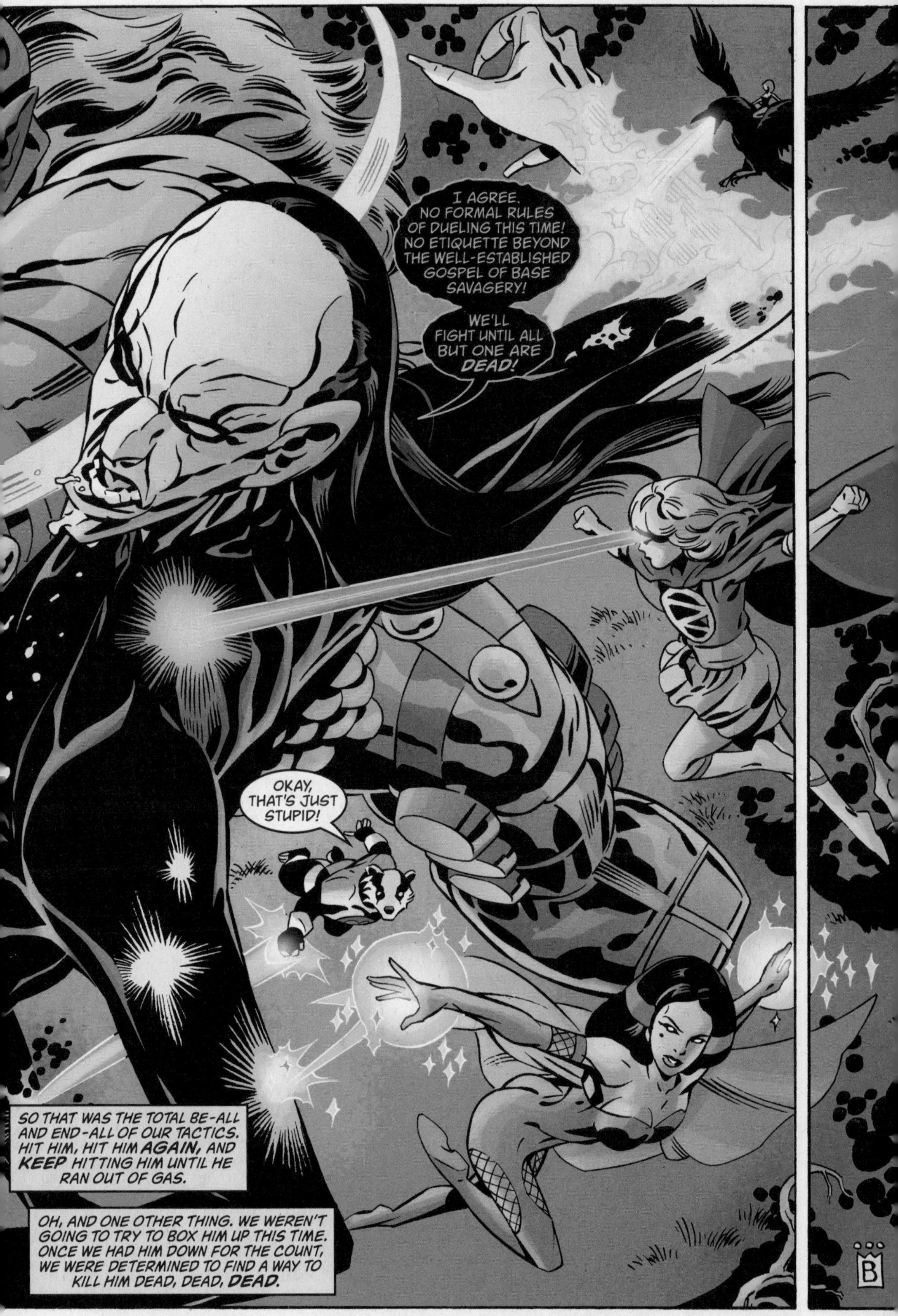
I AGREE. NO FORMAL RULES OF DUELING THIS TIME! NO ETIQUETTE BEYOND THE WELL-ESTABLISHED GOSPEL OF BASE SAVAGERY!
WE'LL FIGHT UNTIL ALL BUT ONE ARE DEAD!
OKAY, THAT'S JUST STUPID!
SO THAT WAS THE TOTAL BE-ALL AND END-ALL OF OUR TACTICS. HIT HIM, HIT HIM AGAIN, AND KEEP HITTING HIM UNTIL HE RAN OUT OF GAS.
OH, AND ONE OTHER THING. WE WEREN'T GOING TO TRY TO BOX HIM UP THIS TIME. ONCE WE HAD HIM DOWN FOR THE COUNT, WE WERE DETERMINED TO FIND A WAY TO KILL HIM DEAD, DEAD, DEAD.
B

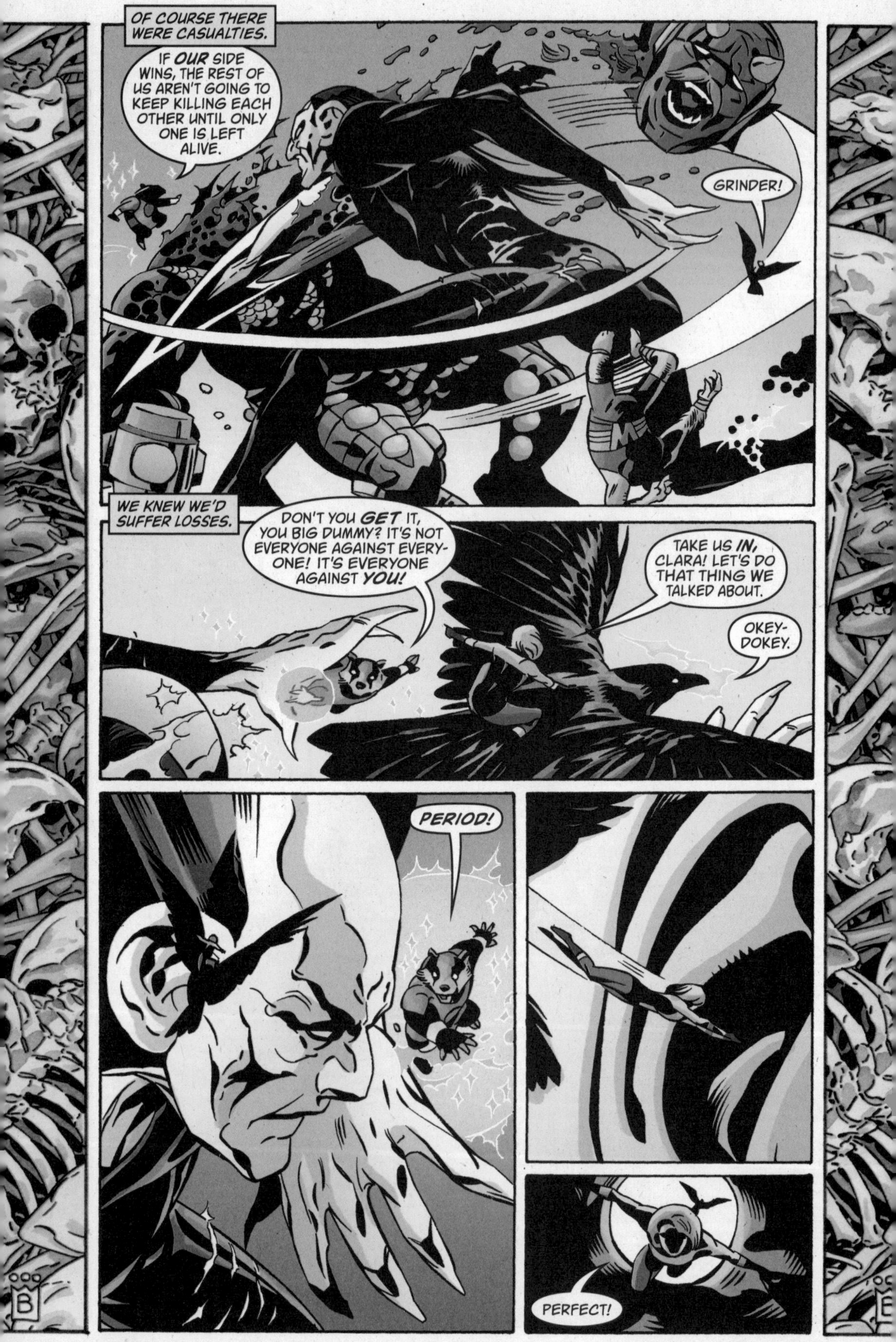
OF COURSE THERE WERE CASUALTIES.
IF OUR SIDE WINS, THE REST OF US AREN'T GOING TO KEEP KILLING EACH OTHER UNTIL ONLY ONE IS LEFT ALIVE.
GRINDER!
WE KNEW WE'D SUFFER LOSSES.
DON'T YOU GET IT, YOU BIG DUMMY? IT'S NOT EVERYONE AGAINST EVERY-ONE! IT'S EVERYONE AGAINST YOU!
TAKE US IN, CLARA! LET'S DO THAT THING WE TALKED ABOUT.
OKEY-DOKEY.
PERIOD!
PERFECT!

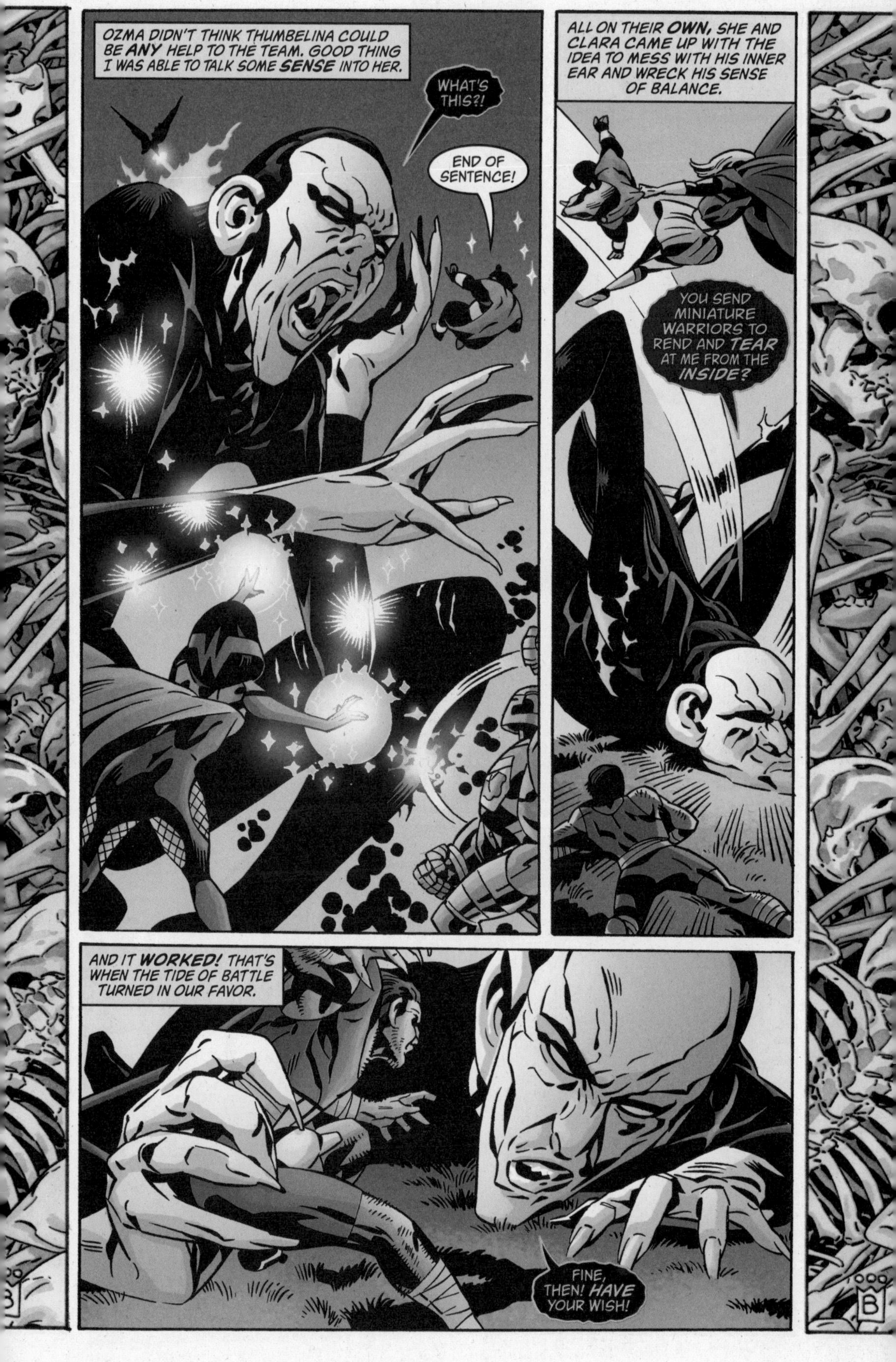

OZMA DIDN'T THINK THUMBELINA COULD BE ANY HELP TO THE TEAM. GOOD THING I WAS ABLE TO TALK SOME SENSE INTO HER.
WHAT'S THIS?!
END OF SENTENCE!
ALL ON THEIR OWN, SHE AND CLARA CAME UP WITH THE IDEA TO MESS WITH HIS INNER EAR AND WRECK HIS SENSE OF BALANCE.
YOU SEND MINIATURE WARRIORS TO REND AND TEAR AT ME FROM THE INSIDE?
AND IT WORKED! THAT'S WHEN THE TIDE OF BATTLE TURNED IN OUR FAVOR.
FINE, THEN! HAVE YOUR WISH!

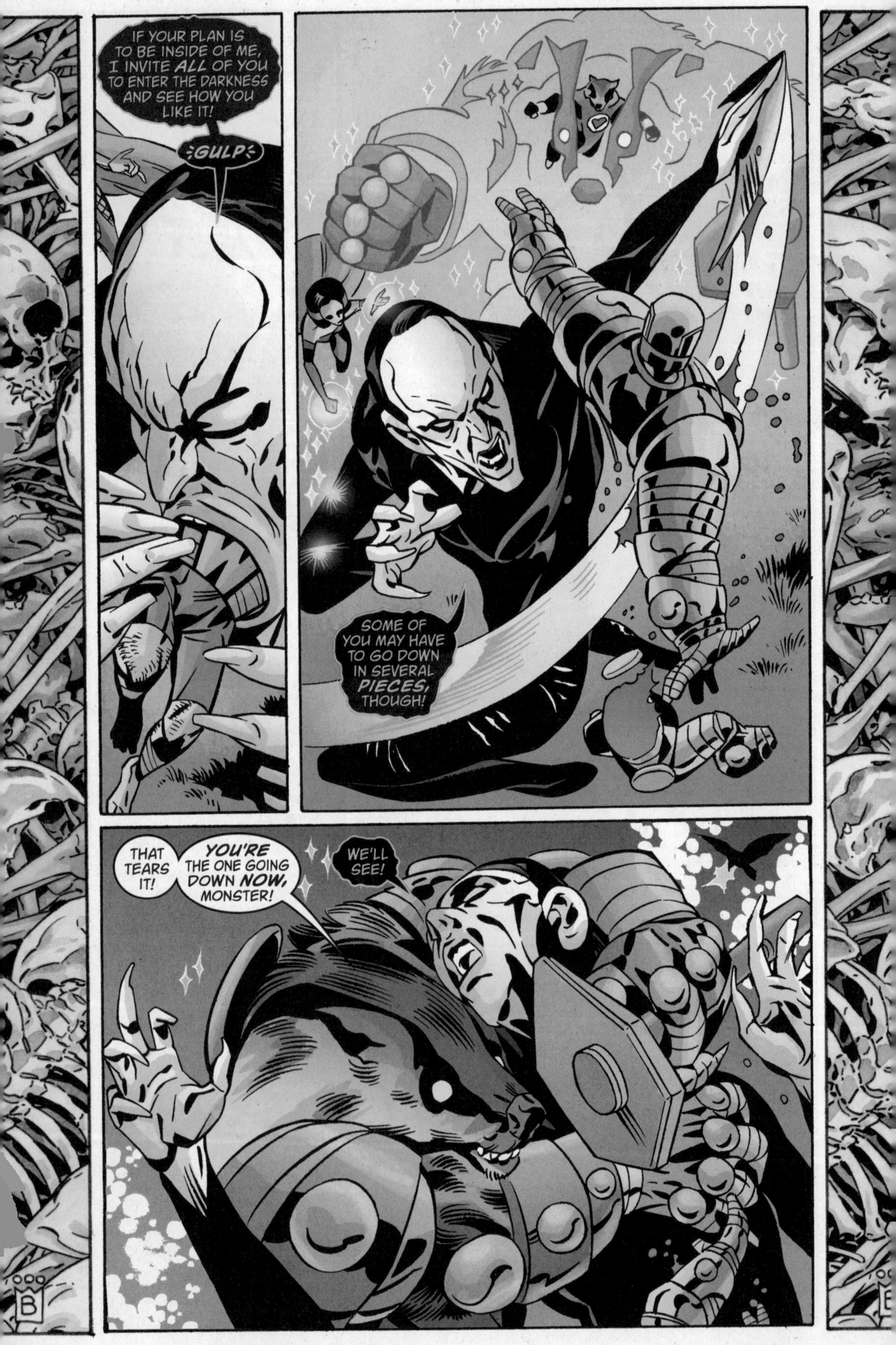
IF YOUR PLAN IS TO BE INSIDE OF ME, I INVITE ALL OF YOU TO ENTER THE DARKNESS AND SEE HOW YOU LIKE IT!
GULP
SOME OF YOU MAY HAVE TO GO DOWN IN SEVERAL PIECES, THOUGH!
THAT TEARS IT!
YOU'RE THE ONE GOING DOWN NOW, MONSTER!
WE'LL SEE!

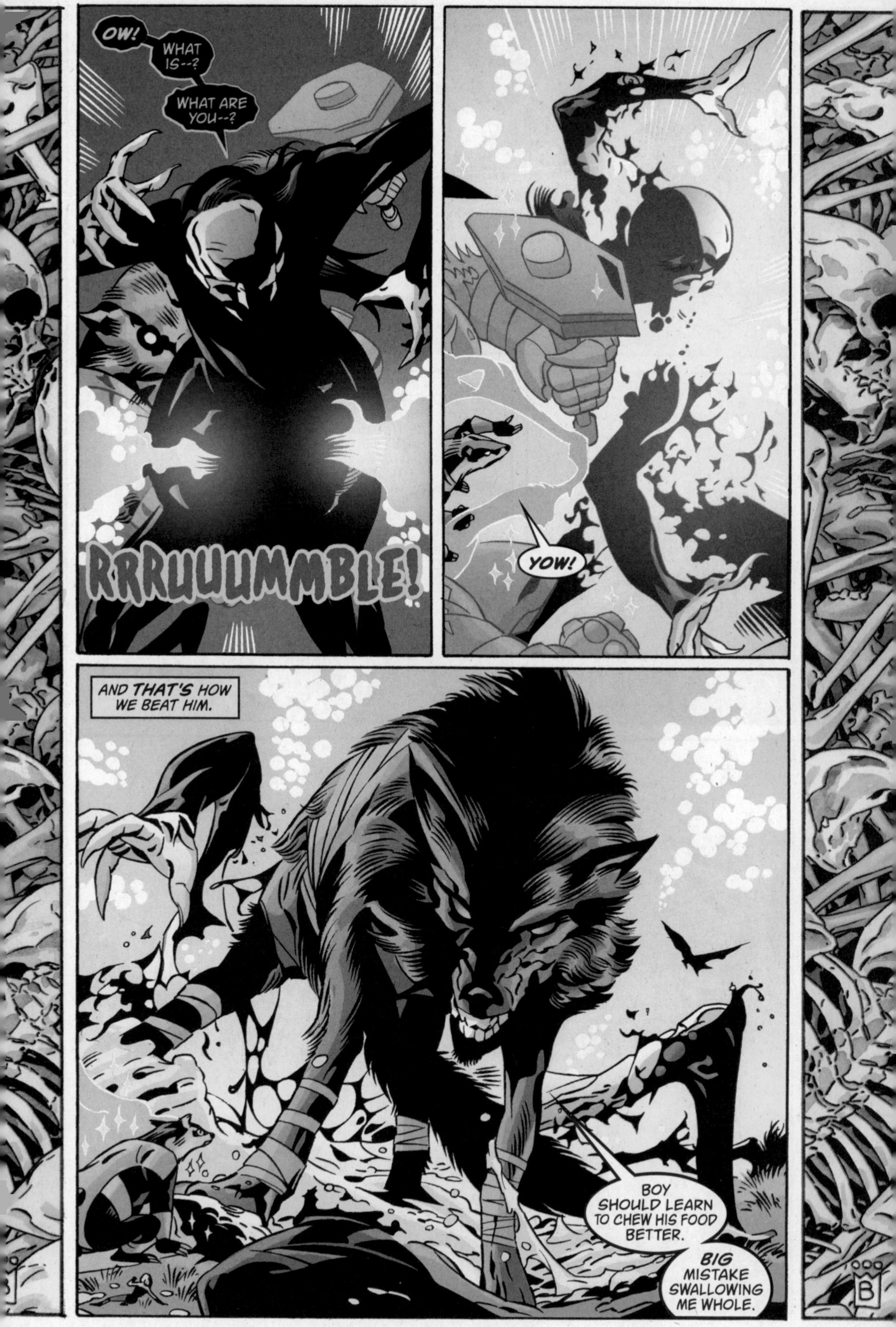
OW!
WHAT IS--?
WHAT ARE YOU--?
RRRUUUMMBLE!
YOW!
AND THAT'S HOW WE BEAT HIM.
BOY SHOULD LEARN TO CHEW HIS FOOD BETTER.
BIG MISTAKE SWALLOWING ME WHOLE.

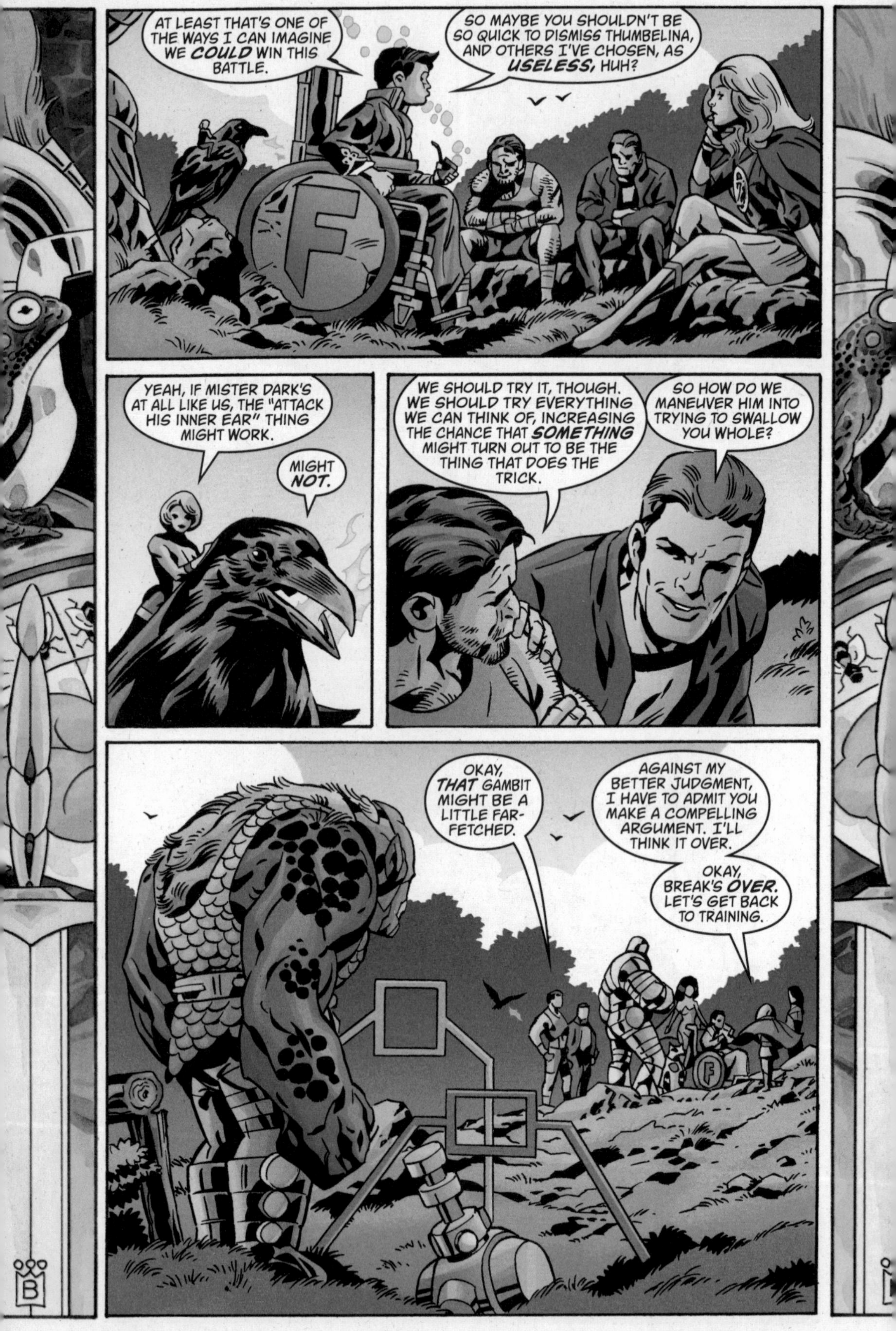
AT LEAST THAT'S ONE OF THE WAYS I CAN IMAGINE WE COULD WIN THIS BATTLE.
SO MAYBE YOU SHOULDN'T BE SO QUICK TO DISMISS THUMBELINA, AND OTHERS I'VE CHOSEN, AS USELESS, HUH?
YEAH, IF MISTER DARK'S AT ALL LIKE US, THE "ATTACK HIS INNER EAR" THING MIGHT WORK.
MIGHT NOT.
WE SHOULD TRY IT, THOUGH. WE SHOULD TRY EVERYTHING WE CAN THINK OF, INCREASING THE CHANCE THAT SOMETHING MIGHT TURN OUT TO BE THE THING THAT DOES THE TRICK.
SO HOW DO WE MANEUVER HIM INTO TRYING TO SWALLOW YOU WHOLE?
OKAY, THAT GAMBIT MIGHT BE A LITTLE FAR-FETCHED.
AGAINST MY BETTER JUDGMENT, I HAVE TO ADMIT YOU MAKE A COMPELLING ARGUMENT. I'LL THINK IT OVER.
OKAY, BREAK'S OVER. LET'S GET BACK TO TRAINING.

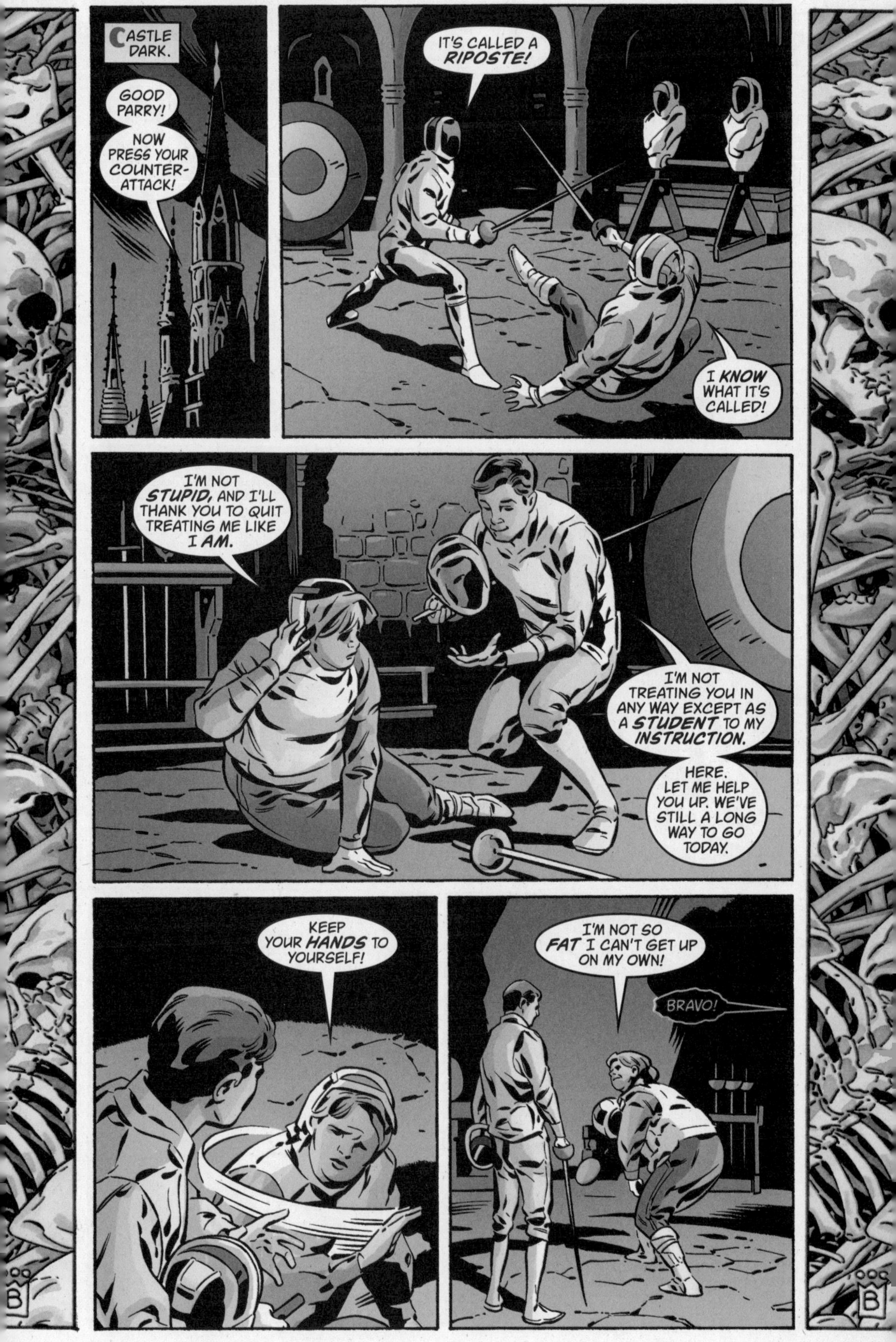
CASTLE DARK.
GOOD PARRY!
NOW PRESS YOUR COUNTER-ATTACK!
IT'S CALLED A RIPOSTE!
I KNOW WHAT IT'S CALLED!
I'M NOT STUPID, AND I'LL THANK YOU TO QUIT TREATING ME LIKE I AM.
I'M NOT TREATING YOU IN ANY WAY EXCEPT AS A STUDENT TO MY INSTRUCTION.
HERE. LET ME HELP YOU UP. WE'VE STILL A LONG WAY TO GO TODAY.
KEEP YOUR HANDS TO YOURSELF!
I'M NOT SO FAT I CAN'T GET UP ON MY OWN!
BRAVO!

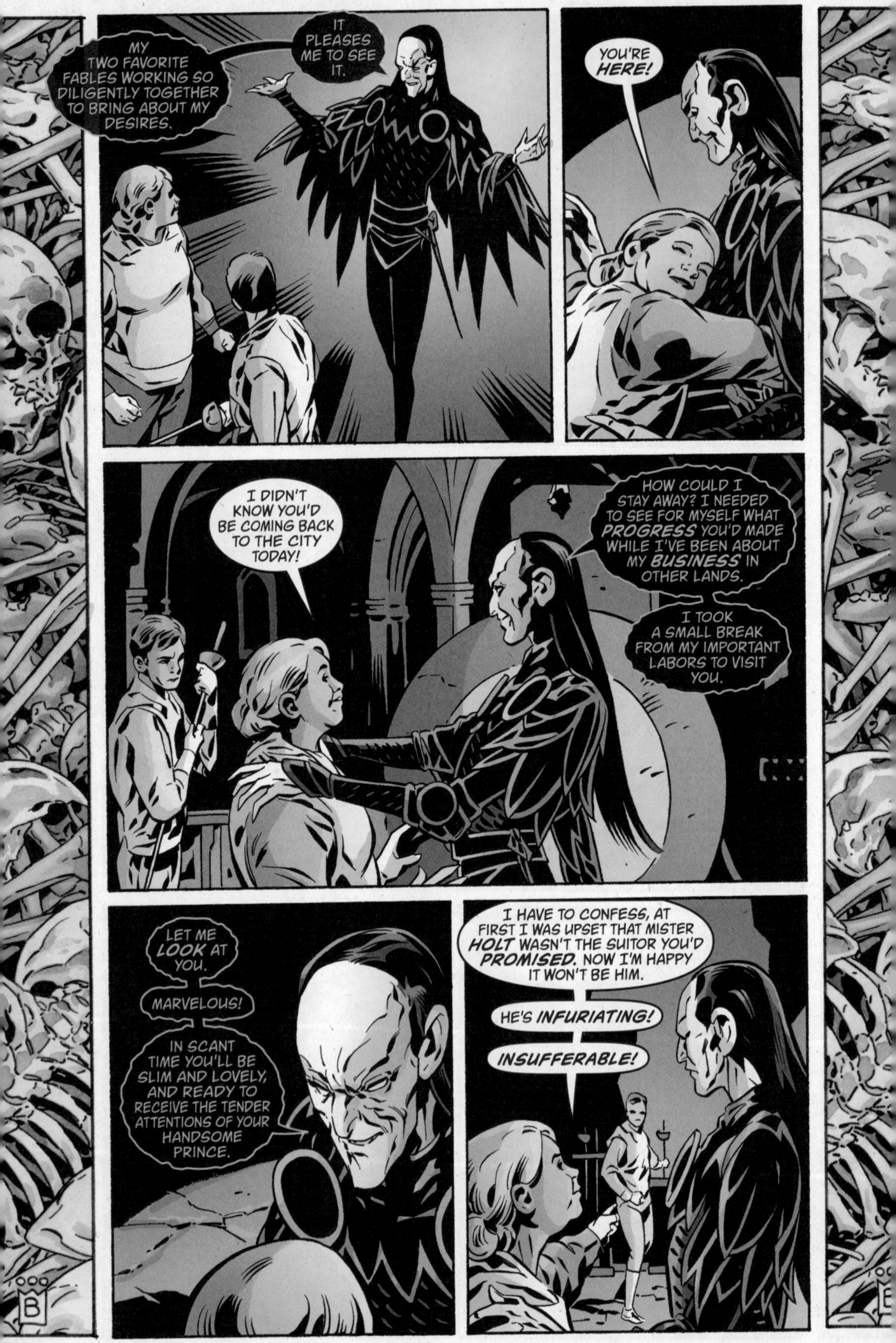
MY TWO FAVORITE FABLES WORKING SO DILIGENTLY TOGETHER TO BRING ABOUT MY DESIRES.
IT PLEASES ME TO SEE IT.
YOU'RE HERE!
I DIDN'T KNOW YOU'D BE COMING BACK TO THE CITY TODAY!
HOW COULD I STAY AWAY? I NEEDED TO SEE FOR MYSELF WHAT PROGRESS YOU'D MADE WHILE I'VE BEEN ABOUT MY BUSINESS IN OTHER LANDS.
I TOOK A SMALL BREAK FROM MY IMPORTANT LABORS TO VISIT YOU.
LET ME LOOK AT YOU.
MARVELOUS!
IN SCANT TIME YOU'LL BE SLIM AND LOVELY, AND READY TO RECEIVE THE TENDER ATTENTIONS OF YOUR HANDSOME PRINCE.
I HAVE TO CONFESS, AT FIRST I WAS UPSET THAT MISTER HOLT WASN'T THE SUITOR YOU'D PROMISED. NOW I'M HAPPY IT WON'T BE HIM.
HE'S INFURIATING!
INSUFFERABLE!

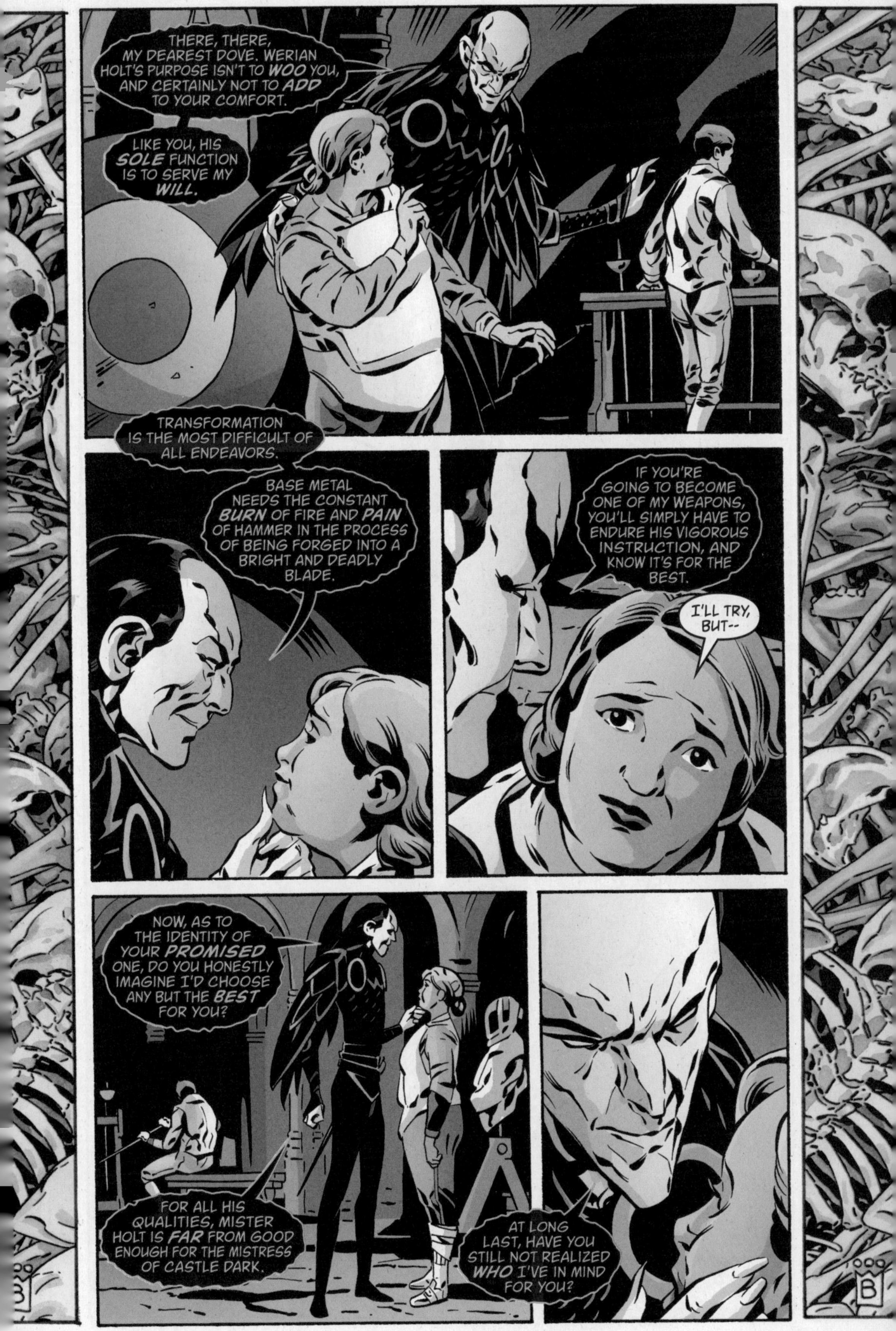
THERE, THERE, MY DEAREST DOVE. WERIAN HOLT'S PURPOSE ISN'T TO WOO YOU, AND CERTAINLY NOT TO ADD TO YOUR COMFORT.
LIKE YOU, HIS SOLE FUNCTION IS TO SERVE MY WILL.
TRANSFORMATION IS THE MOST DIFFICULT OF ALL ENDEAVORS.
BASE METAL NEEDS THE CONSTANT BURN OF FIRE AND PAIN OF HAMMER IN THE PROCESS OF BEING FORGED INTO A BRIGHT AND DEADLY BLADE.
IF YOU'RE GOING TO BECOME ONE OF MY WEAPONS, YOU'LL SIMPLY HAVE TO ENDURE HIS VIGOROUS INSTRUCTION, AND KNOW IT'S FOR THE BEST.
I'LL TRY, BUT--
NOW, AS TO THE IDENTITY OF YOUR PROMISED ONE, DO YOU HONESTLY IMAGINE I'D CHOOSE ANY BUT THE BEST FOR YOU?
FOR ALL HIS QUALITIES, MISTER HOLT IS FAR FROM GOOD ENOUGH FOR THE MISTRESS OF CASTLE DARK.
AT LONG LAST, HAVE YOU STILL NOT REALIZED WHO I'VE IN MIND FOR YOU?

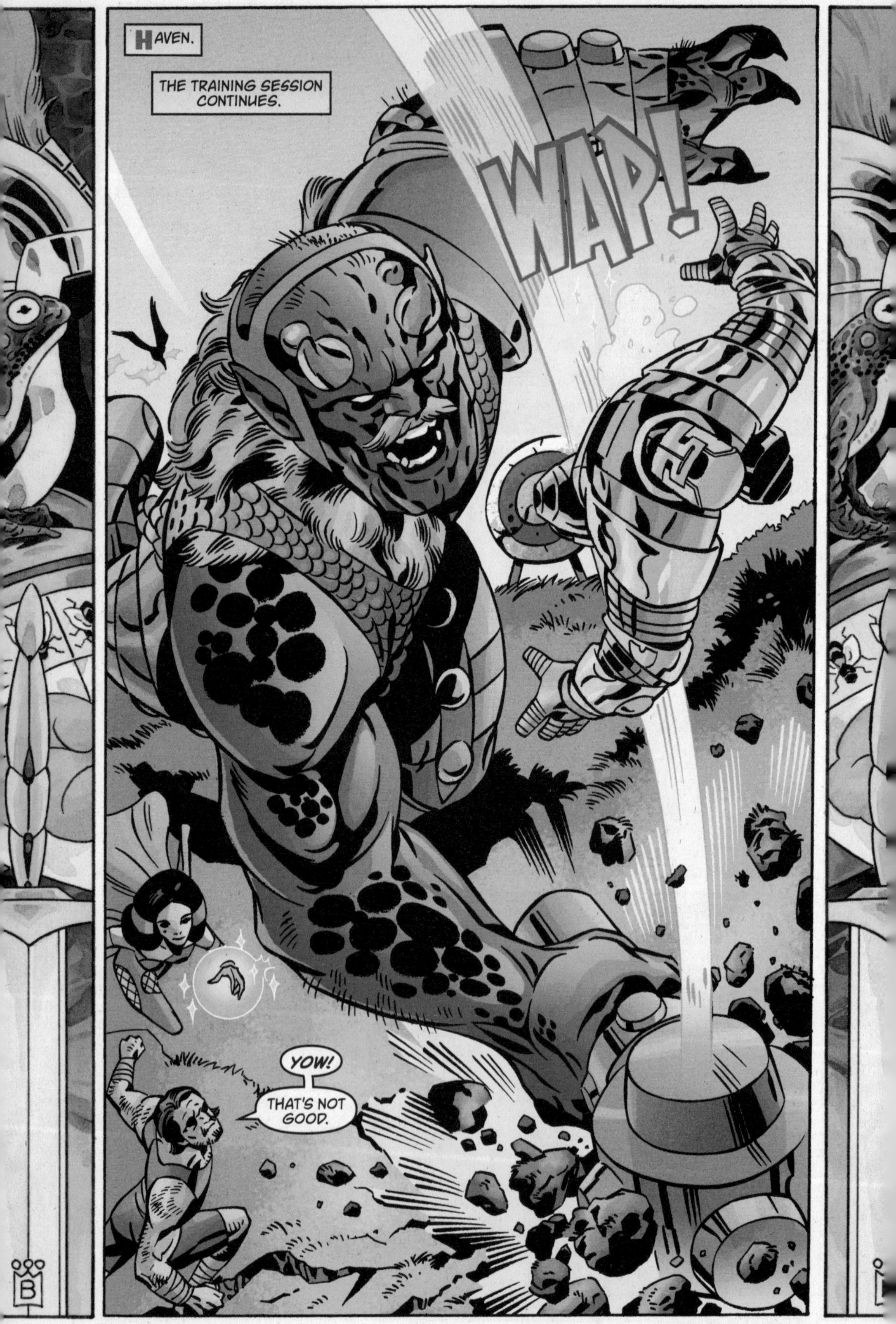
HAVEN.
THE TRAINING SESSION CONTINUES.
WAP!
YOW!
THAT'S NOT GOOD.

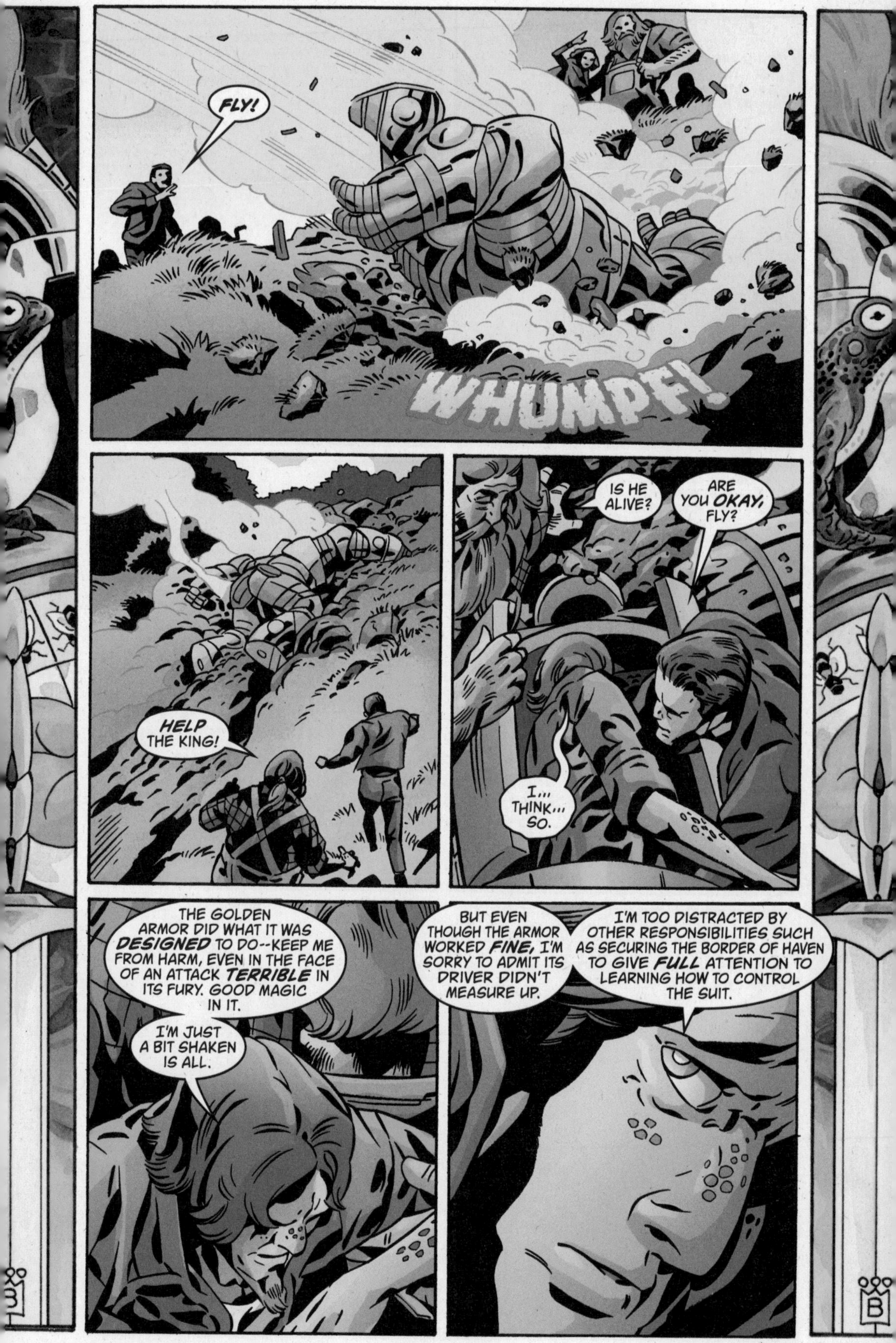
FLY!
WHUMPF!
HELP THE KING!
IS HE ALIVE?
ARE YOU OKAY, FLY?
I... THINK... SO.
THE GOLDEN ARMOR DID WHAT IT WAS DESIGNED TO DO--KEEP ME FROM HARM, EVEN IN THE FACE OF AN ATTACK TERRIBLE IN ITS FURY. GOOD MAGIC IN IT.
I'M JUST A BIT SHAKEN IS ALL.
BUT EVEN THOUGH THE ARMOR WORKED FINE, I'M SORRY TO ADMIT ITS DRIVER DIDN'T MEASURE UP.
I'M TOO DISTRACTED BY OTHER RESPONSIBILITIES SUCH AS SECURING THE BORDER OF HAVEN TO GIVE FULL ATTENTION TO LEARNING HOW TO CONTROL THE SUIT.

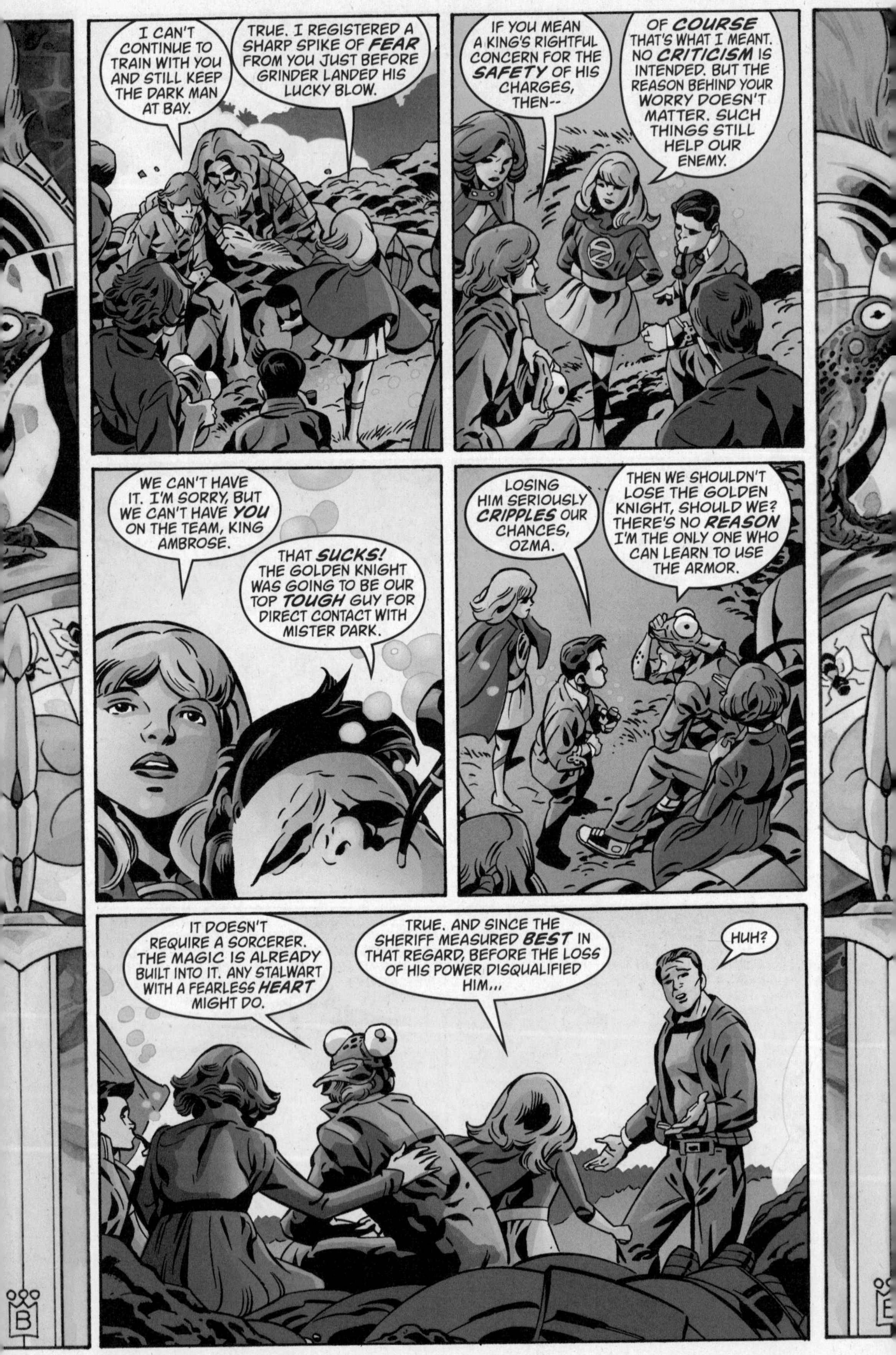

I CAN'T CONTINUE TO TRAIN WITH YOU AND STILL KEEP THE DARK MAN AT BAY.
TRUE. I REGISTERED A SHARP SPIKE OF FEAR FROM YOU JUST BEFORE GRINDER LANDED HIS LUCKY BLOW.
IF YOU MEAN A KING'S RIGHTFUL CONCERN FOR THE SAFETY OF HIS CHARGES, THEN--
OF COURSE THAT'S WHAT I MEANT. NO CRITICISM IS INTENDED. BUT THE REASON BEHIND YOUR WORRY DOESN'T MATTER. SUCH THINGS STILL HELP OUR ENEMY.
WE CAN'T HAVE IT. I'M SORRY, BUT WE CAN'T HAVE YOU ON THE TEAM, KING AMBROSE.
THAT SUCKS! THE GOLDEN KNIGHT WAS GOING TO BE OUR TOP TOUGH GUY FOR DIRECT CONTACT WITH MISTER DARK.
LOSING HIM SERIOUSLY CRIPPLES OUR CHANCES, OZMA.
THEN WE SHOULDN'T LOSE THE GOLDEN KNIGHT, SHOULD WE? THERE'S NO REASON I'M THE ONLY ONE WHO CAN LEARN TO USE THE ARMOR.
IT DOESN'T REQUIRE A SORCERER. THE MAGIC IS ALREADY BUILT INTO IT. ANY STALWART WITH A FEARLESS HEART MIGHT DO.
TRUE. AND SINCE THE SHERIFF MEASURED BEST IN THAT REGARD, BEFORE THE LOSS OF HIS POWER DISQUALIFIED HIM...
HUH?

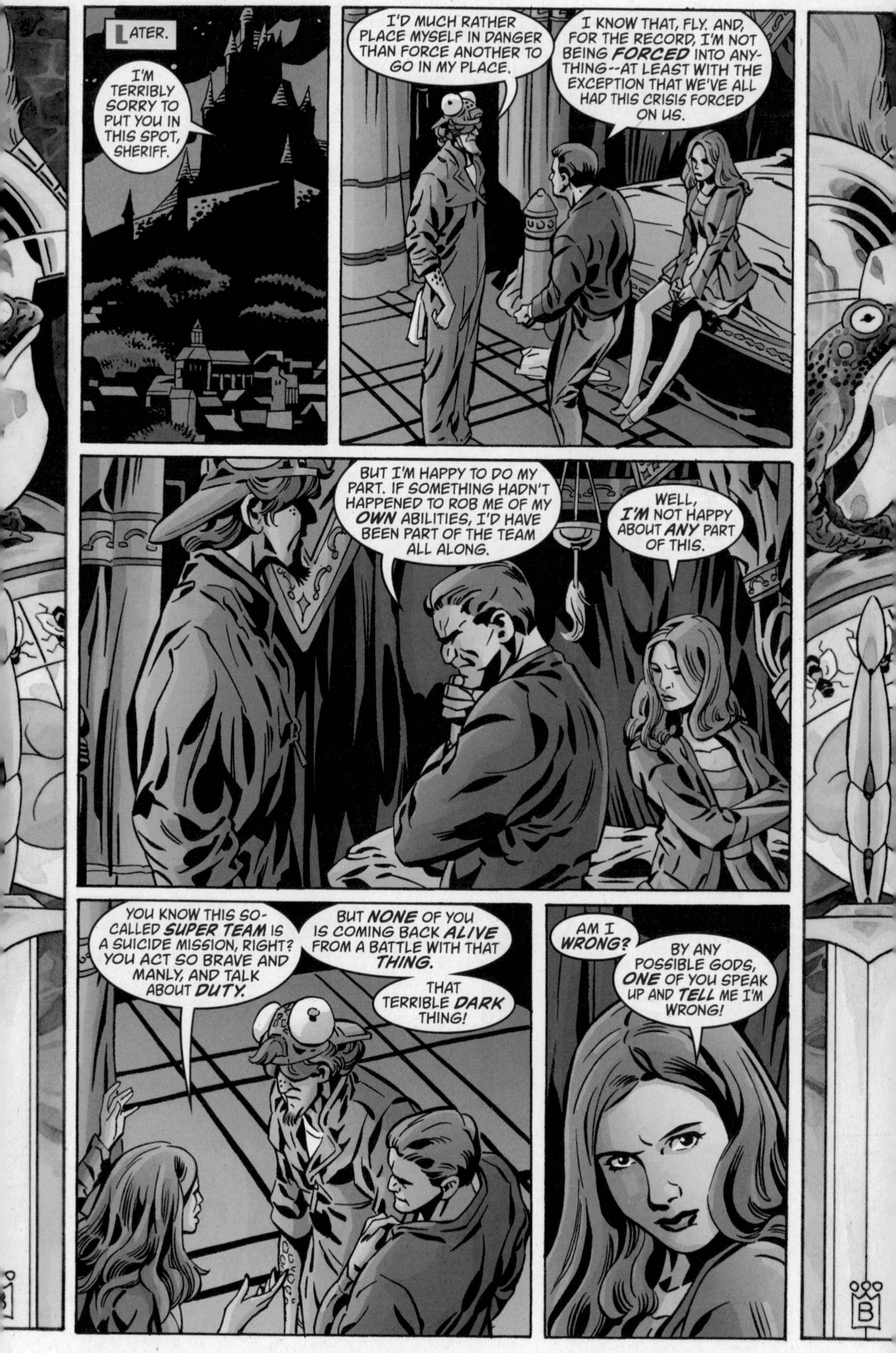
LATER.
I'M TERRIBLY SORRY TO PUT YOU IN THIS SPOT, SHERIFF.
I'D MUCH RATHER PLACE MYSELF IN DANGER THAN FORCE ANOTHER TO GO IN MY PLACE.
I KNOW THAT, FLY. AND, FOR THE RECORD, I'M NOT BEING FORCED INTO ANYTHING--AT LEAST WITH THE EXCEPTION THAT WE'VE ALL HAD THIS CRISIS FORCED ON US.
BUT I'M HAPPY TO DO MY PART. IF SOMETHING HADN'T HAPPENED TO ROB ME OF MY OWN ABILITIES, I'D HAVE BEEN PART OF THE TEAM ALL ALONG.
WELL, I'M NOT HAPPY ABOUT ANY PART OF THIS.
YOU KNOW THIS SO-CALLED SUPER TEAM IS A SUICIDE MISSION, RIGHT? YOU ACT SO BRAVE AND MANLY, AND TALK ABOUT DUTY.
BUT NONE OF YOU IS COMING BACK ALIVE FROM A BATTLE WITH THAT THING.
THAT TERRIBLE DARK THING!
AM I WRONG?
BY ANY POSSIBLE GODS, ONE OF YOU SPEAK UP AND TELL ME I'M WRONG!

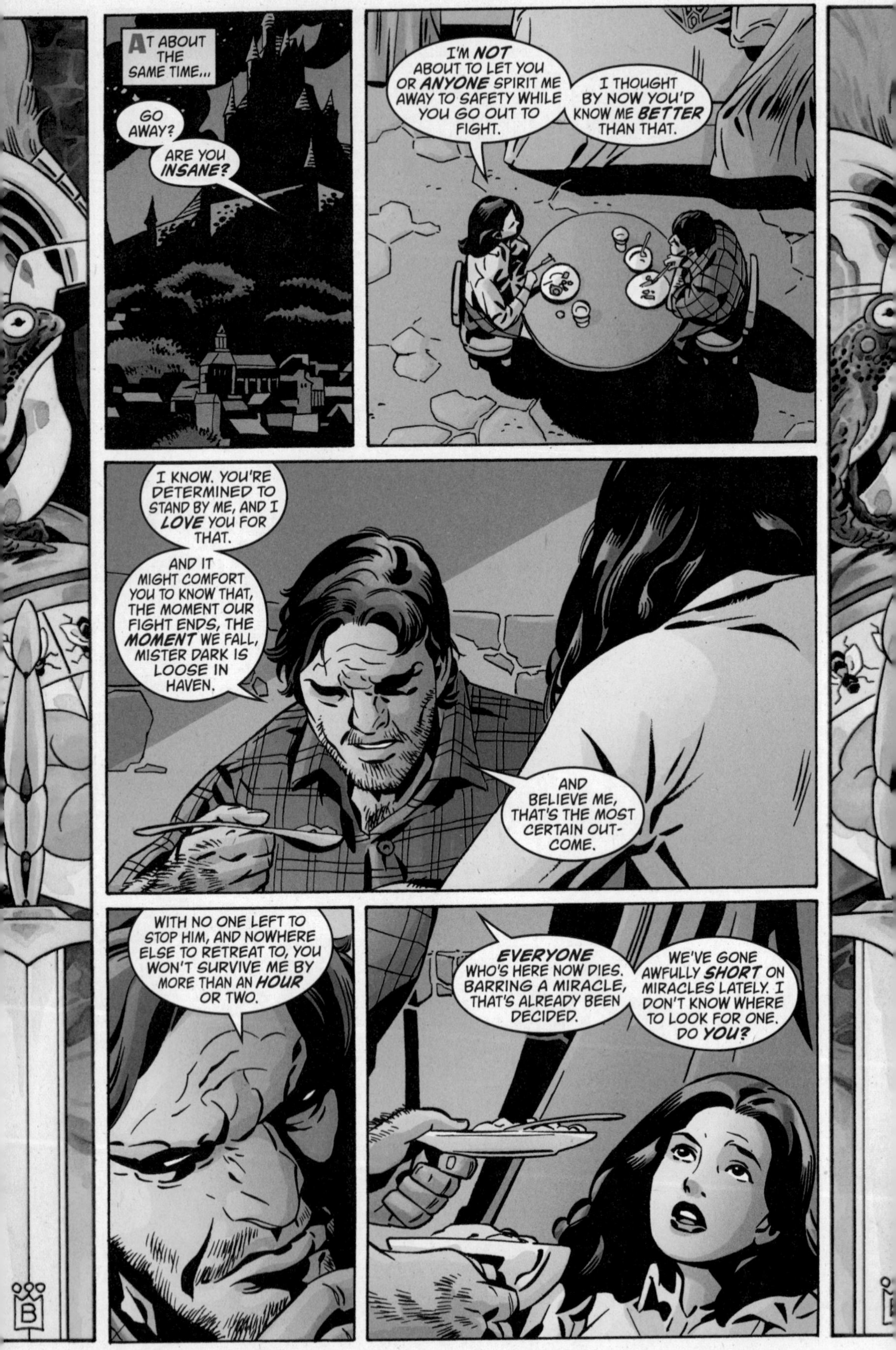

AT ABOUT THE SAME TIME...
GO AWAY?
ARE YOU INSANE?
I'M NOT ABOUT TO LET YOU OR ANYONE SPIRIT ME AWAY TO SAFETY WHILE YOU GO OUT TO FIGHT.
I THOUGHT BY NOW YOU'D KNOW ME BETTER THAN THAT.
I KNOW. YOU'RE DETERMINED TO STAND BY ME, AND I LOVE YOU FOR THAT.
AND IT MIGHT COMFORT YOU TO KNOW THAT, THE MOMENT OUR FIGHT ENDS, THE MOMENT WE FALL, MISTER DARK IS LOOSE IN HAVEN.
AND BELIEVE ME, THAT'S THE MOST CERTAIN OUT-COME.
WITH NO ONE LEFT TO STOP HIM, AND NOWHERE ELSE TO RETREAT TO, YOU WON'T SURVIVE ME BY MORE THAN AN HOUR OR TWO.
EVERYONE WHO'S HERE NOW DIES. BARRING A MIRACLE, THAT'S ALREADY BEEN DECIDED.
WE'VE GONE AWFULLY SHORT ON MIRACLES LATELY. I DON'T KNOW WHERE TO LOOK FOR ONE. DO YOU?

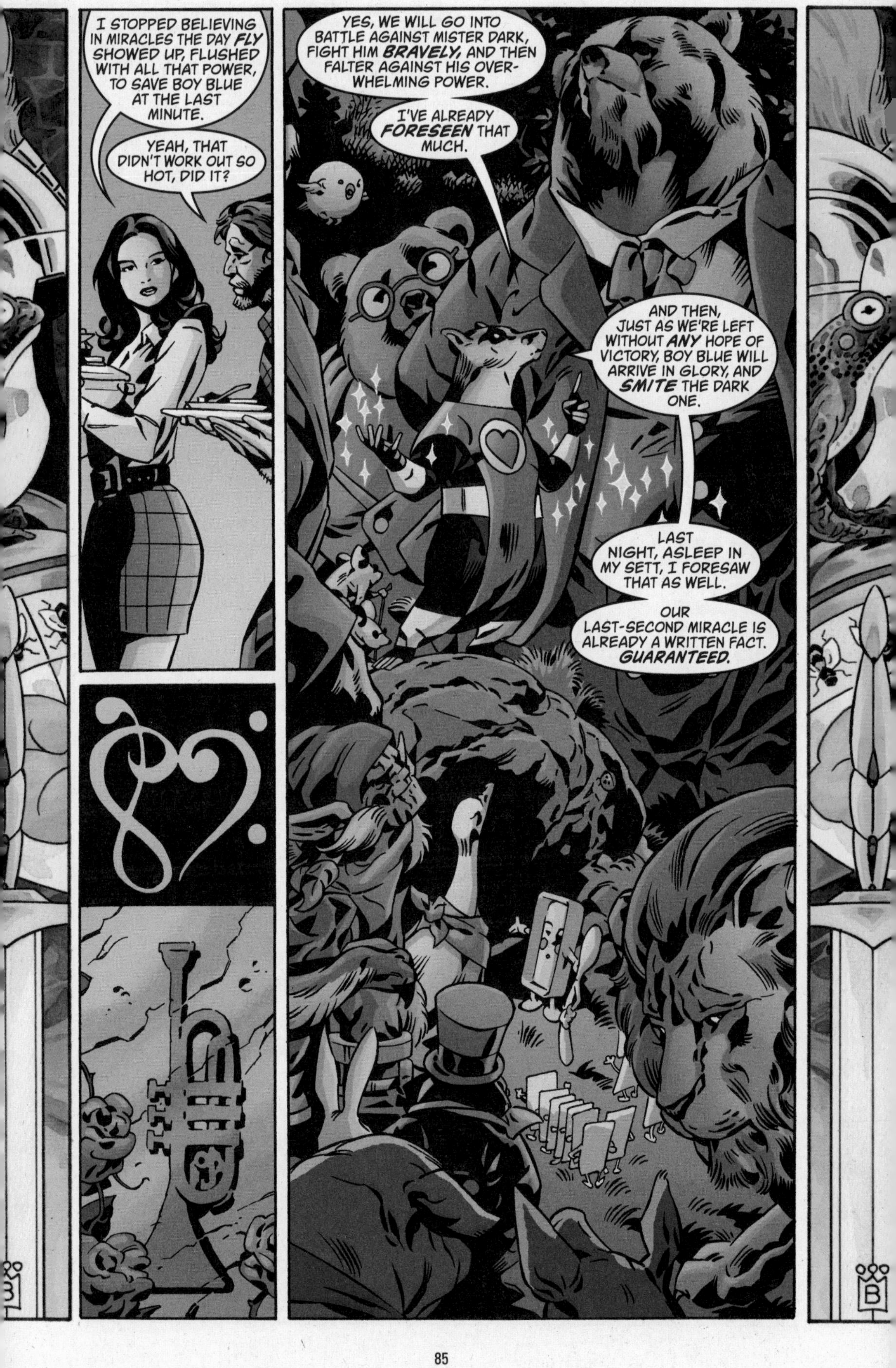
I STOPPED BELIEVING IN MIRACLES THE DAY FLY SHOWED UP, FLUSHED WITH ALL THAT POWER, TO SAVE BOY BLUE AT THE LAST MINUTE.
YEAH, THAT DIDN'T WORK OUT SO HOT, DID IT?
YES, WE WILL GO INTO BATTLE AGAINST MISTER DARK, FIGHT HIM BRAVELY, AND THEN FALTER AGAINST HIS OVER-WHELMING POWER.
I'VE ALREADY FORESEEN THAT MUCH.
AND THEN, JUST AS WE'RE LEFT WITHOUT ANY HOPE OF VICTORY, BOY BLUE WILL ARRIVE IN GLORY, AND SMITE THE DARK ONE.
LAST NIGHT, ASLEEP IN MY SETT, I FORESAW THAT AS WELL.
OUR LAST-SECOND MIRACLE IS ALREADY A WRITTEN FACT. GUARANTEED.

THANK GOODNESS OUR KIDS ARE SAFE WITH THEIR GRAND-FATHER.

TOO BAD THEY'RE NOW DOOMED TO GO THROUGH LIFE MISSING *BOTH* PARENTS, RATHER THAN ONE.

YOU CAN BE A REAL *SHITHOUSE* SOMETIMES.

FINE, SNOW. CALL ME ANY NAME YOU CAN THINK OF. GET IT ALL OUT OF YOUR SYSTEM.

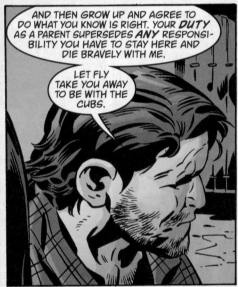

AND THEN GROW UP AND AGREE TO DO WHAT YOU KNOW IS RIGHT. YOUR *DUTY* AS A PARENT SUPERSEDES *ANY* RESPONSIBILITY YOU HAVE TO STAY HERE AND DIE BRAVELY WITH ME.

LET FLY TAKE YOU AWAY TO BE WITH THE CUBS.

I DON'T THINK--

HOLD ON!

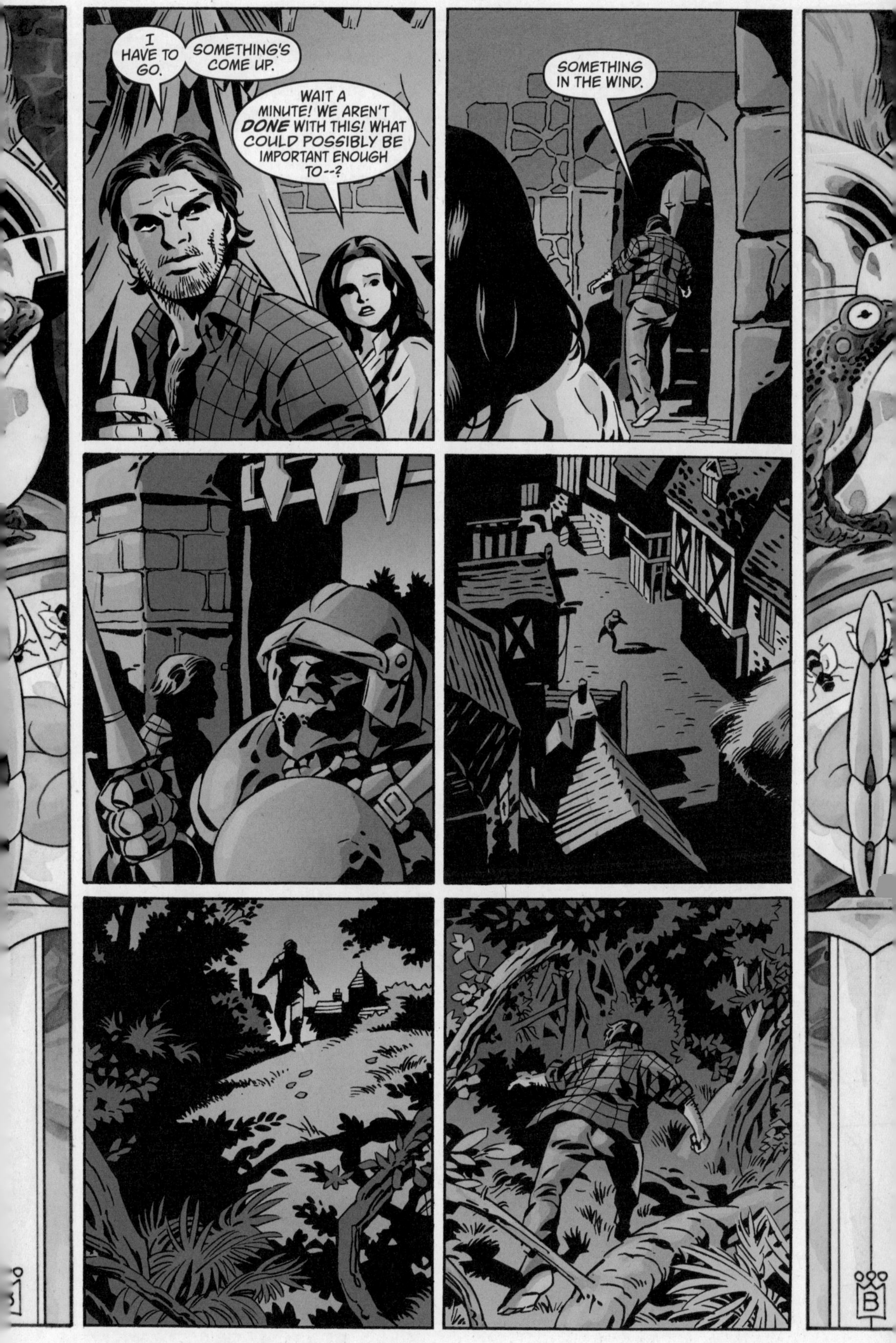
I HAVE TO GO.
SOMETHING'S COME UP.
WAIT A MINUTE! WE AREN'T **DONE** WITH THIS! WHAT COULD POSSIBLY BE IMPORTANT ENOUGH TO--?
SOMETHING IN THE WIND.

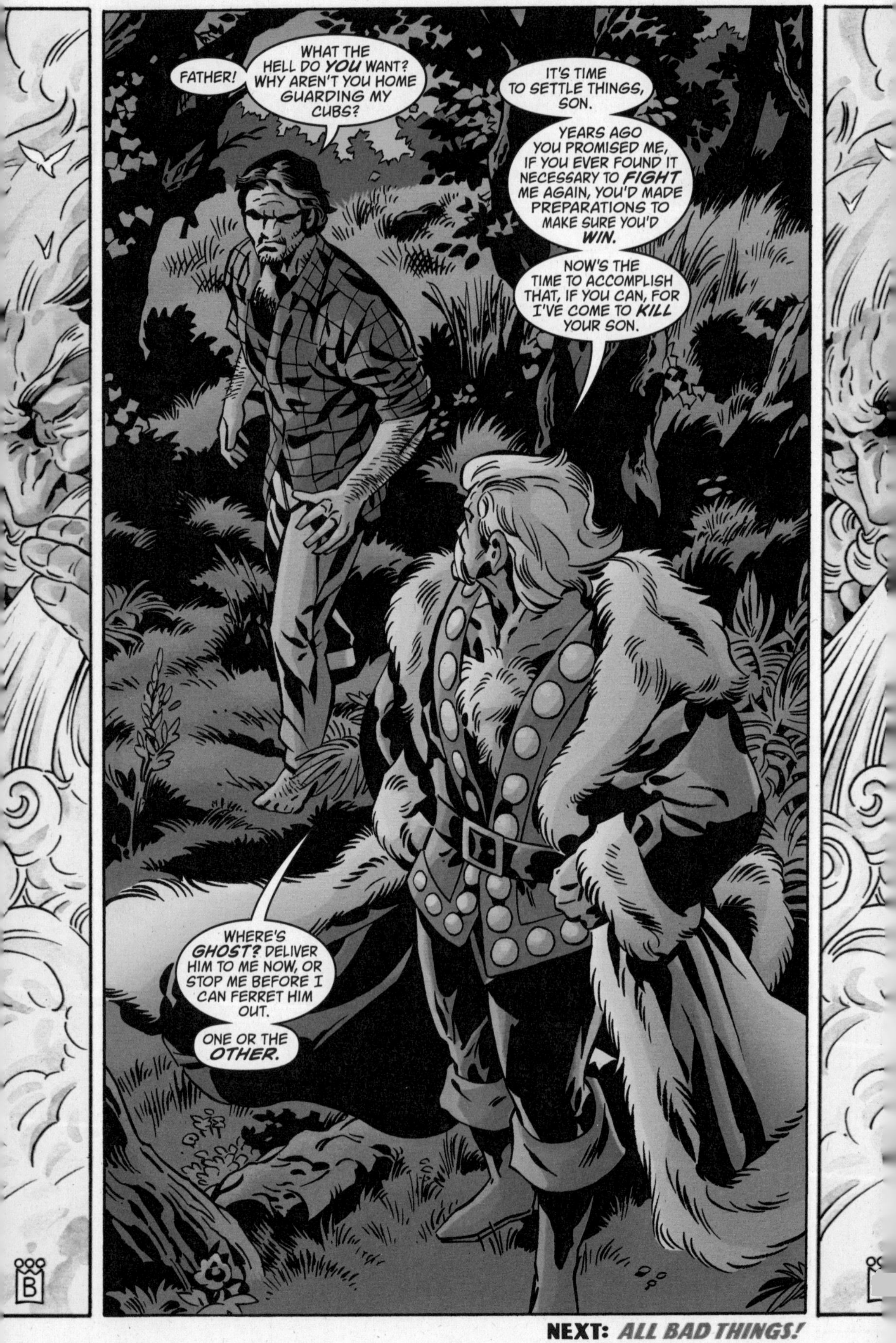
FATHER!
WHAT THE HELL DO YOU WANT? WHY AREN'T YOU HOME GUARDING MY CUBS?
IT'S TIME TO SETTLE THINGS, SON.
YEARS AGO YOU PROMISED ME, IF YOU EVER FOUND IT NECESSARY TO FIGHT ME AGAIN, YOU'D MADE PREPARATIONS TO MAKE SURE YOU'D WIN.
NOW'S THE TIME TO ACCOMPLISH THAT, IF YOU CAN, FOR I'VE COME TO KILL YOUR SON.
WHERE'S GHOST? DELIVER HIM TO ME NOW, OR STOP ME BEFORE I CAN FERRET HIM OUT.
ONE OR THE OTHER.

NEXT: ***ALL BAD THINGS!***

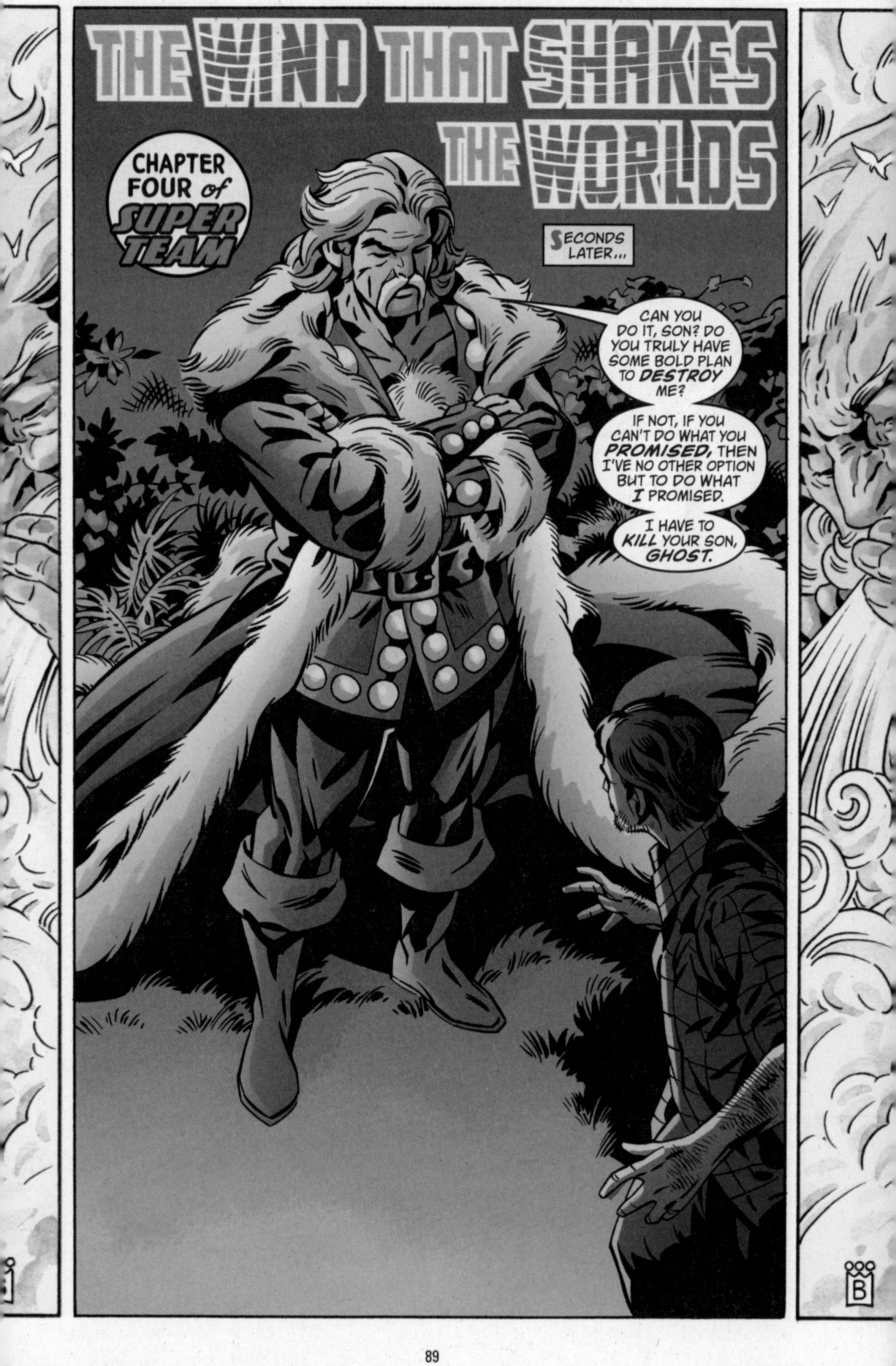
THE WIND THAT SHAKES THE WORLDS
CHAPTER FOUR of SUPER TEAM
SECONDS LATER...
CAN YOU DO IT, SON? DO YOU TRULY HAVE SOME BOLD PLAN TO DESTROY ME?
IF NOT, IF YOU CAN'T DO WHAT YOU PROMISED, THEN I'VE NO OTHER OPTION BUT TO DO WHAT I PROMISED.
I HAVE TO KILL YOUR SON, GHOST.

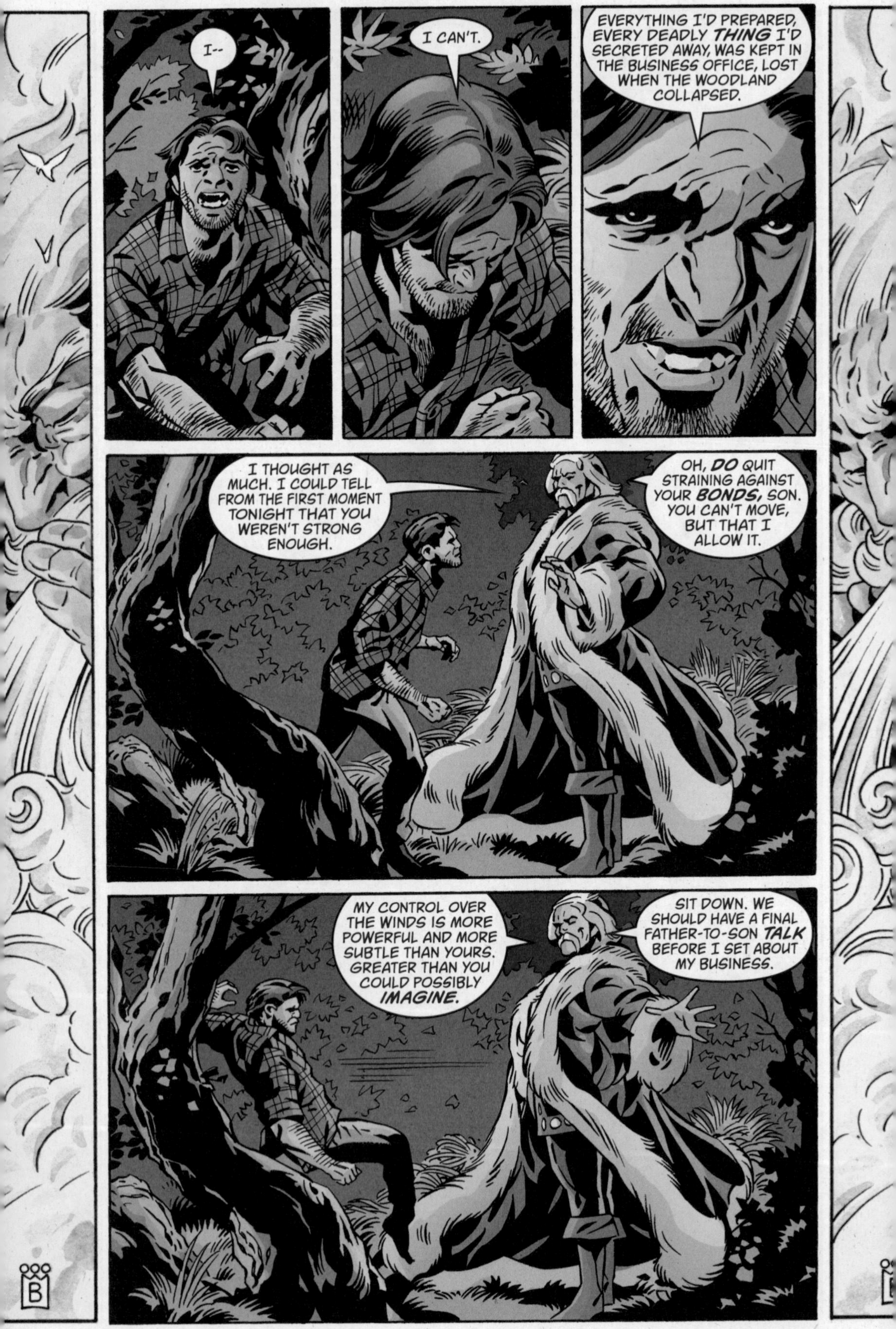
I--
I CAN'T.
EVERYTHING I'D PREPARED, EVERY DEADLY THING I'D SECRETED AWAY, WAS KEPT IN THE BUSINESS OFFICE, LOST WHEN THE WOODLAND COLLAPSED.
I THOUGHT AS MUCH. I COULD TELL FROM THE FIRST MOMENT TONIGHT THAT YOU WEREN'T STRONG ENOUGH.
OH, DO QUIT STRAINING AGAINST YOUR BONDS, SON. YOU CAN'T MOVE, BUT THAT I ALLOW IT.
MY CONTROL OVER THE WINDS IS MORE POWERFUL AND MORE SUBTLE THAN YOURS. GREATER THAN YOU COULD POSSIBLY IMAGINE.
SIT DOWN. WE SHOULD HAVE A FINAL FATHER-TO-SON TALK BEFORE I SET ABOUT MY BUSINESS.

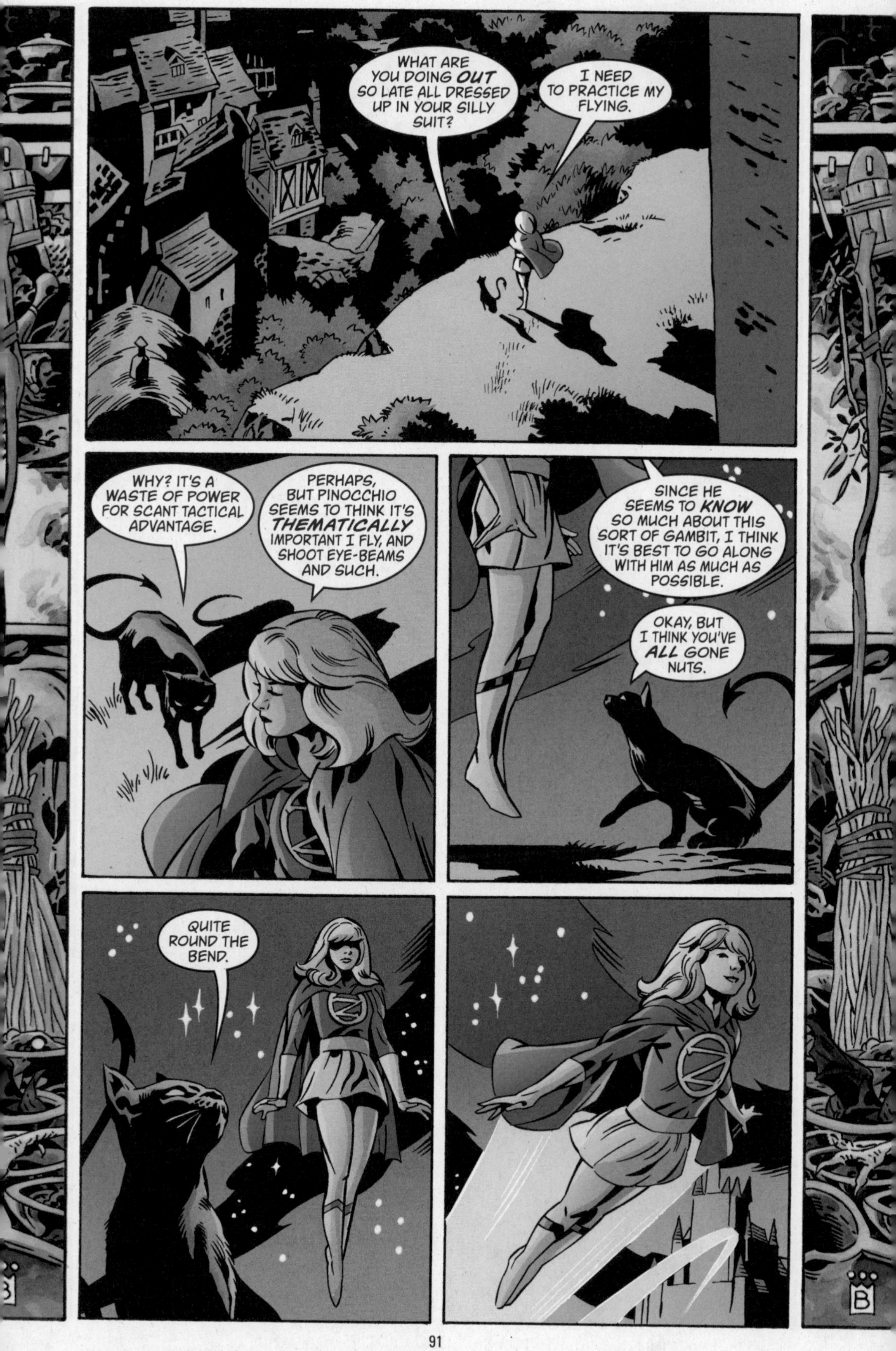

WHAT ARE YOU DOING OUT SO LATE ALL DRESSED UP IN YOUR SILLY SUIT?
I NEED TO PRACTICE MY FLYING.
WHY? IT'S A WASTE OF POWER FOR SCANT TACTICAL ADVANTAGE.
PERHAPS, BUT PINOCCHIO SEEMS TO THINK IT'S THEMATICALLY IMPORTANT I FLY, AND SHOOT EYE-BEAMS AND SUCH.
SINCE HE SEEMS TO KNOW SO MUCH ABOUT THIS SORT OF GAMBIT, I THINK IT'S BEST TO GO ALONG WITH HIM AS MUCH AS POSSIBLE.
OKAY, BUT I THINK YOU'VE ALL GONE NUTS.
QUITE ROUND THE BEND.

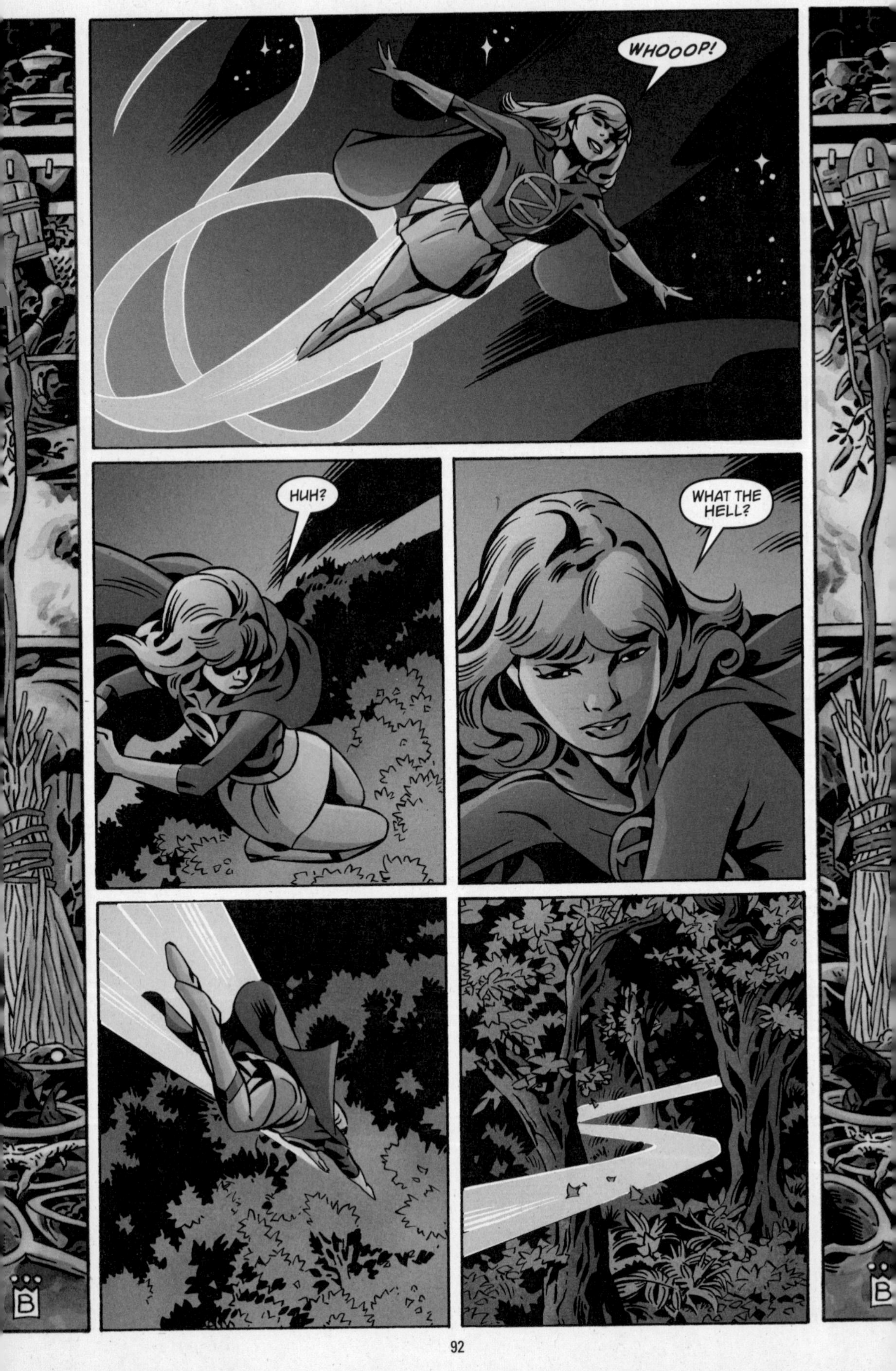
WHOOOP!
HUH?
WHAT THE HELL?

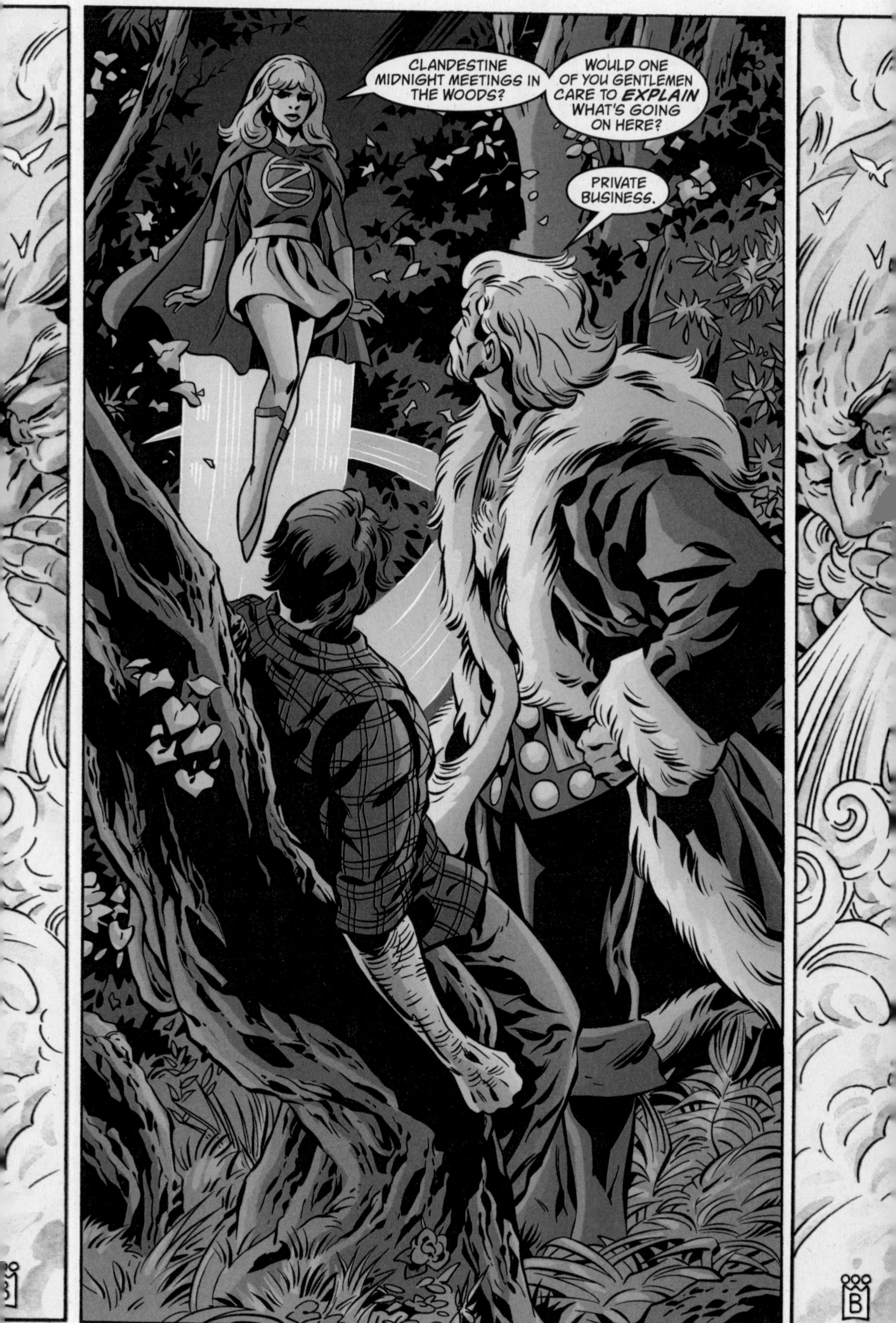
CLANDESTINE MIDNIGHT MEETINGS IN THE WOODS?
WOULD ONE OF YOU GENTLEMEN CARE TO EXPLAIN WHAT'S GOING ON HERE?
PRIVATE BUSINESS.

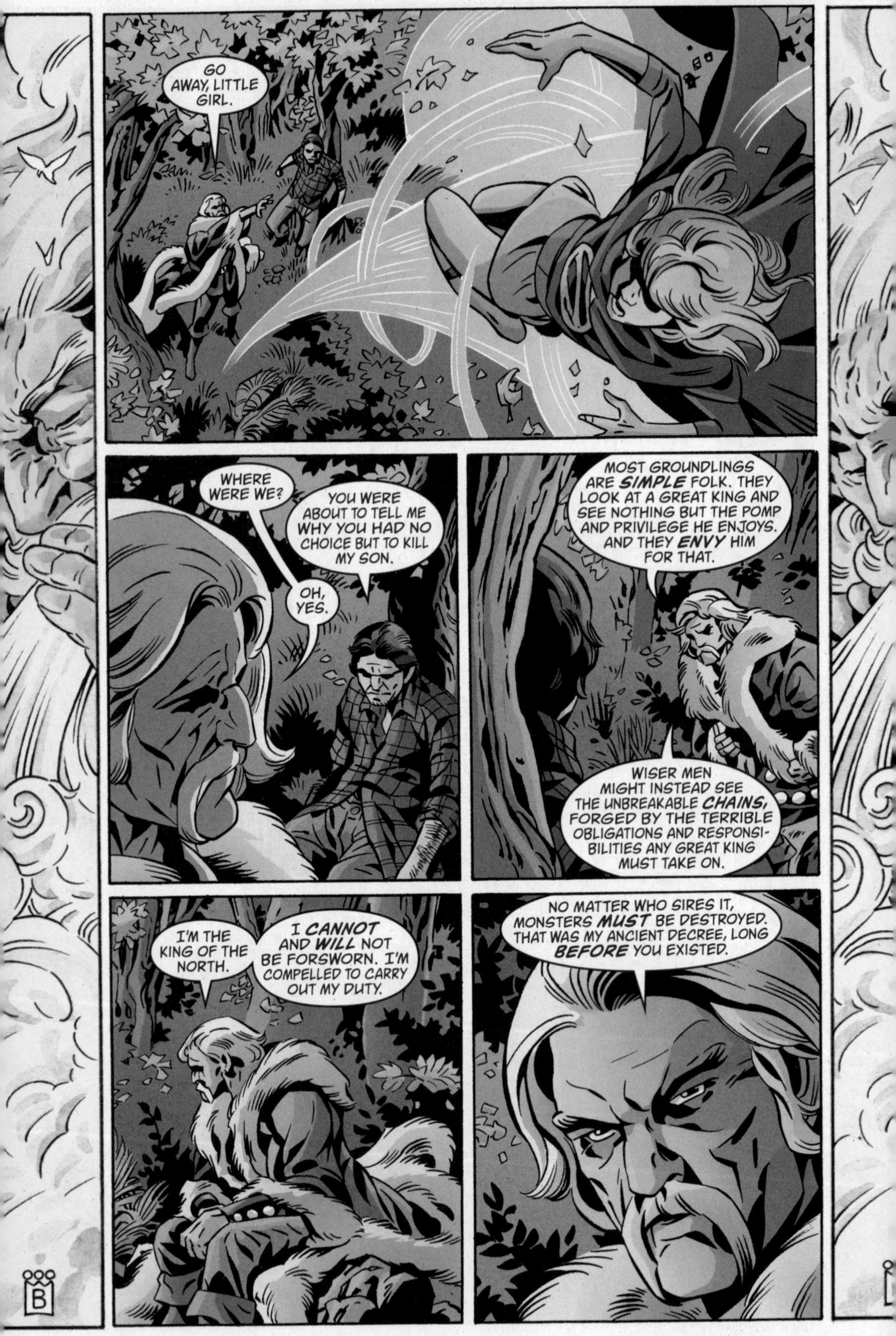
GO AWAY, LITTLE GIRL.
WHERE WERE WE?
YOU WERE ABOUT TO TELL ME WHY YOU HAD NO CHOICE BUT TO KILL MY SON.
OH, YES.
MOST GROUNDLINGS ARE SIMPLE FOLK. THEY LOOK AT A GREAT KING AND SEE NOTHING BUT THE POMP AND PRIVILEGE HE ENJOYS. AND THEY ENVY HIM FOR THAT.
WISER MEN MIGHT INSTEAD SEE THE UNBREAKABLE CHAINS, FORGED BY THE TERRIBLE OBLIGATIONS AND RESPONSI-BILITIES ANY GREAT KING MUST TAKE ON.
I'M THE KING OF THE NORTH.
I CANNOT AND WILL NOT BE FORSWORN. I'M COMPELLED TO CARRY OUT MY DUTY.
NO MATTER WHO SIRES IT, MONSTERS MUST BE DESTROYED. THAT WAS MY ANCIENT DECREE, LONG BEFORE YOU EXISTED.

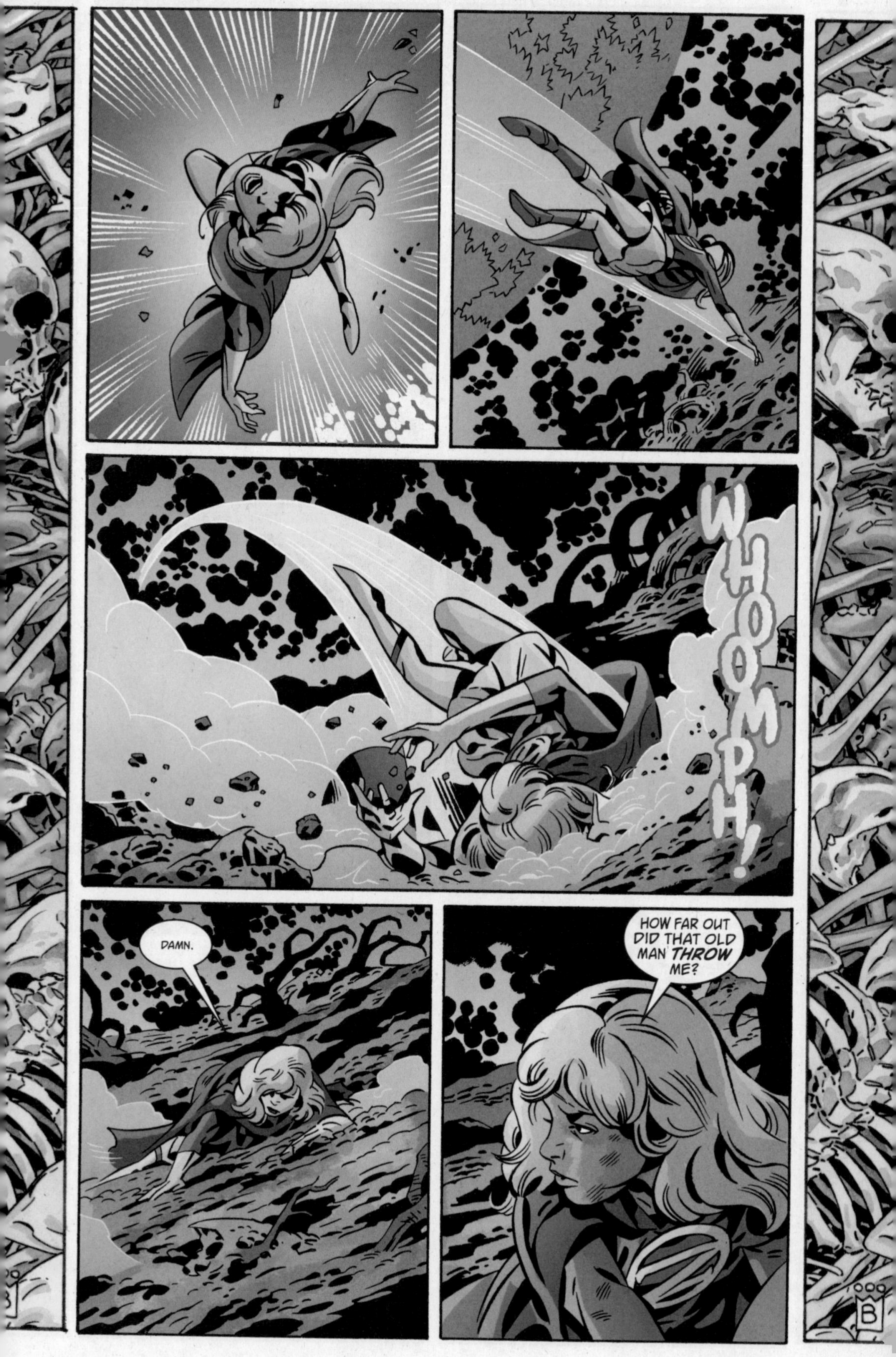
WHOOMPH!
DAMN.
HOW FAR OUT DID THAT OLD MAN THROW ME?

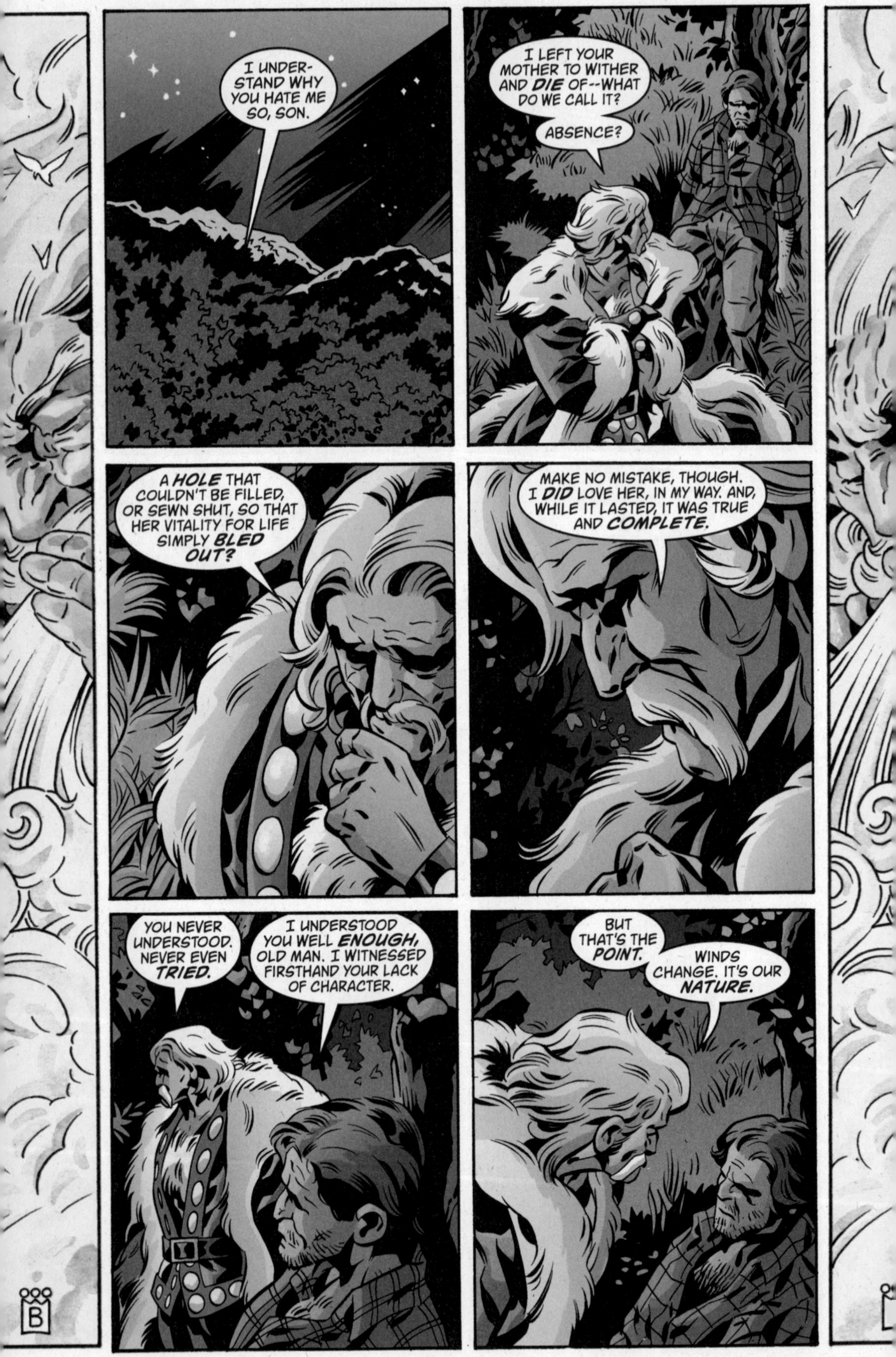

I UNDER-STAND WHY YOU HATE ME SO, SON.
I LEFT YOUR MOTHER TO WITHER AND DIE OF--WHAT DO WE CALL IT?
ABSENCE?
A HOLE THAT COULDN'T BE FILLED, OR SEWN SHUT, SO THAT HER VITALITY FOR LIFE SIMPLY BLED OUT?
MAKE NO MISTAKE, THOUGH. I DID LOVE HER, IN MY WAY. AND, WHILE IT LASTED, IT WAS TRUE AND COMPLETE.
YOU NEVER UNDERSTOOD. NEVER EVEN TRIED.
I UNDERSTOOD YOU WELL ENOUGH, OLD MAN. I WITNESSED FIRSTHAND YOUR LACK OF CHARACTER.
BUT THAT'S THE POINT.
WINDS CHANGE. IT'S OUR NATURE.

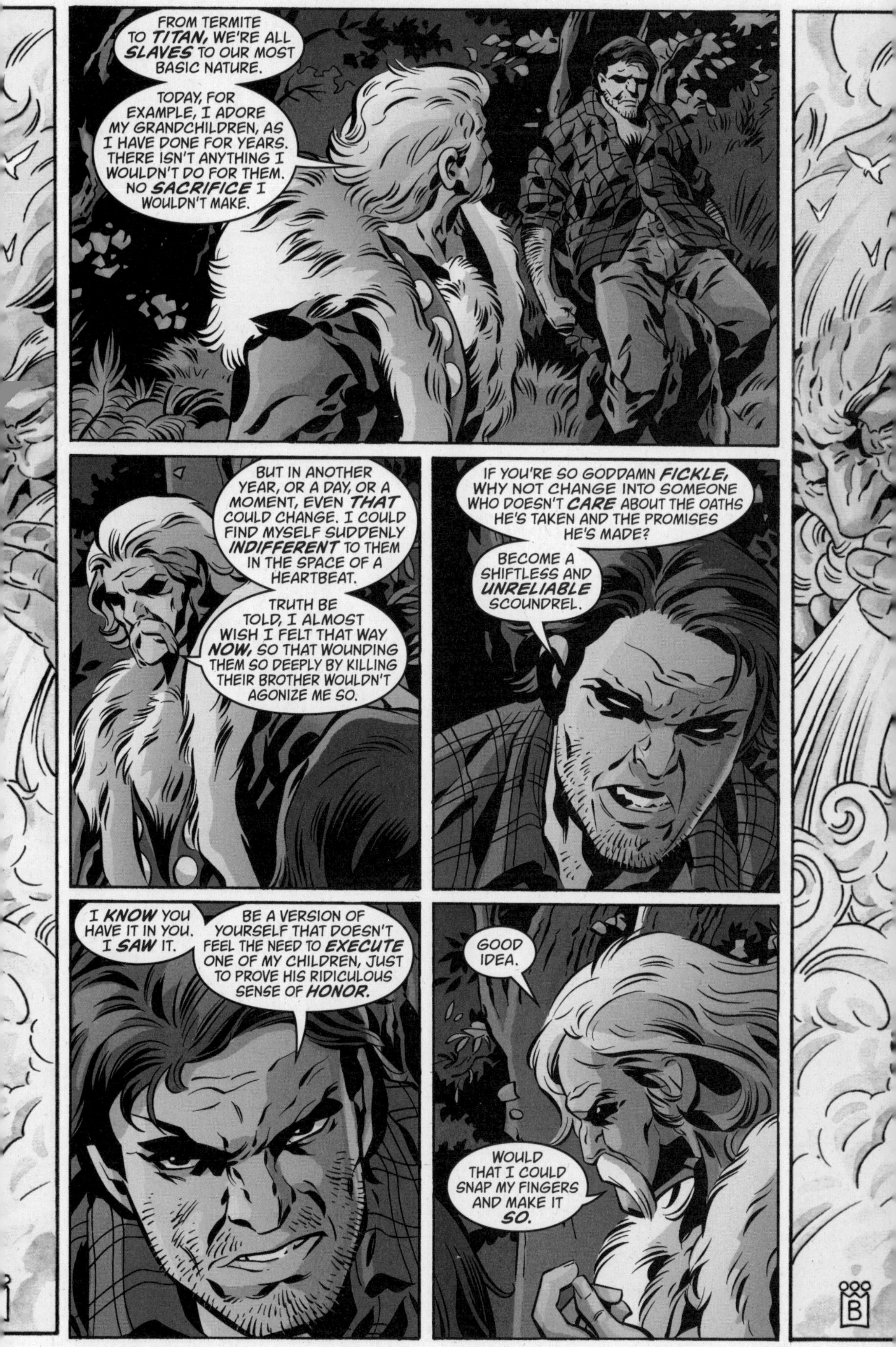
FROM TERMITE TO TITAN, WE'RE ALL SLAVES TO OUR MOST BASIC NATURE.
TODAY, FOR EXAMPLE, I ADORE MY GRANDCHILDREN, AS I HAVE DONE FOR YEARS. THERE ISN'T ANYTHING I WOULDN'T DO FOR THEM. NO SACRIFICE I WOULDN'T MAKE.
BUT IN ANOTHER YEAR, OR A DAY, OR A MOMENT, EVEN THAT COULD CHANGE. I COULD FIND MYSELF SUDDENLY INDIFFERENT TO THEM IN THE SPACE OF A HEARTBEAT.
TRUTH BE TOLD, I ALMOST WISH I FELT THAT WAY NOW, SO THAT WOUNDING THEM SO DEEPLY BY KILLING THEIR BROTHER WOULDN'T AGONIZE ME SO.
IF YOU'RE SO GODDAMN FICKLE, WHY NOT CHANGE INTO SOMEONE WHO DOESN'T CARE ABOUT THE OATHS HE'S TAKEN AND THE PROMISES HE'S MADE?
BECOME A SHIFTLESS AND UNRELIABLE SCOUNDREL.
I KNOW YOU HAVE IT IN YOU. I SAW IT.
BE A VERSION OF YOURSELF THAT DOESN'T FEEL THE NEED TO EXECUTE ONE OF MY CHILDREN, JUST TO PROVE HIS RIDICULOUS SENSE OF HONOR.
GOOD IDEA.
WOULD THAT I COULD SNAP MY FINGERS AND MAKE IT SO.

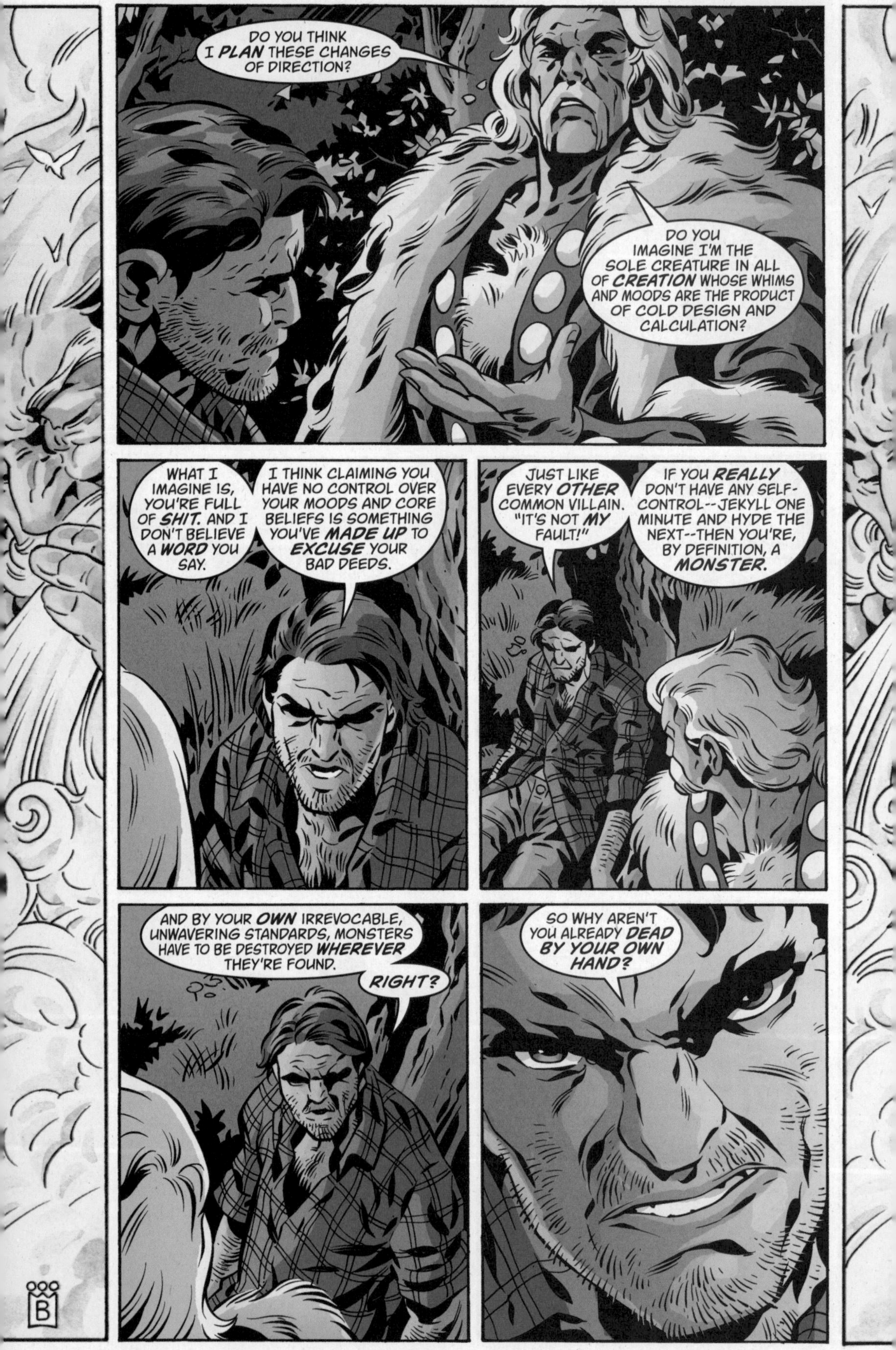
DO YOU THINK I PLAN THESE CHANGES OF DIRECTION?
DO YOU IMAGINE I'M THE SOLE CREATURE IN ALL OF CREATION WHOSE WHIMS AND MOODS ARE THE PRODUCT OF COLD DESIGN AND CALCULATION?
WHAT I IMAGINE IS, YOU'RE FULL OF SHIT. AND I DON'T BELIEVE A WORD YOU SAY.
I THINK CLAIMING YOU HAVE NO CONTROL OVER YOUR MOODS AND CORE BELIEFS IS SOMETHING YOU'VE MADE UP TO EXCUSE YOUR BAD DEEDS.
JUST LIKE EVERY OTHER COMMON VILLAIN. "IT'S NOT MY FAULT!"
IF YOU REALLY DON'T HAVE ANY SELF-CONTROL--JEKYLL ONE MINUTE AND HYDE THE NEXT--THEN YOU'RE, BY DEFINITION, A MONSTER.
AND BY YOUR OWN IRREVOCABLE, UNWAVERING STANDARDS, MONSTERS HAVE TO BE DESTROYED WHEREVER THEY'RE FOUND.
RIGHT?
SO WHY AREN'T YOU ALREADY DEAD BY YOUR OWN HAND?

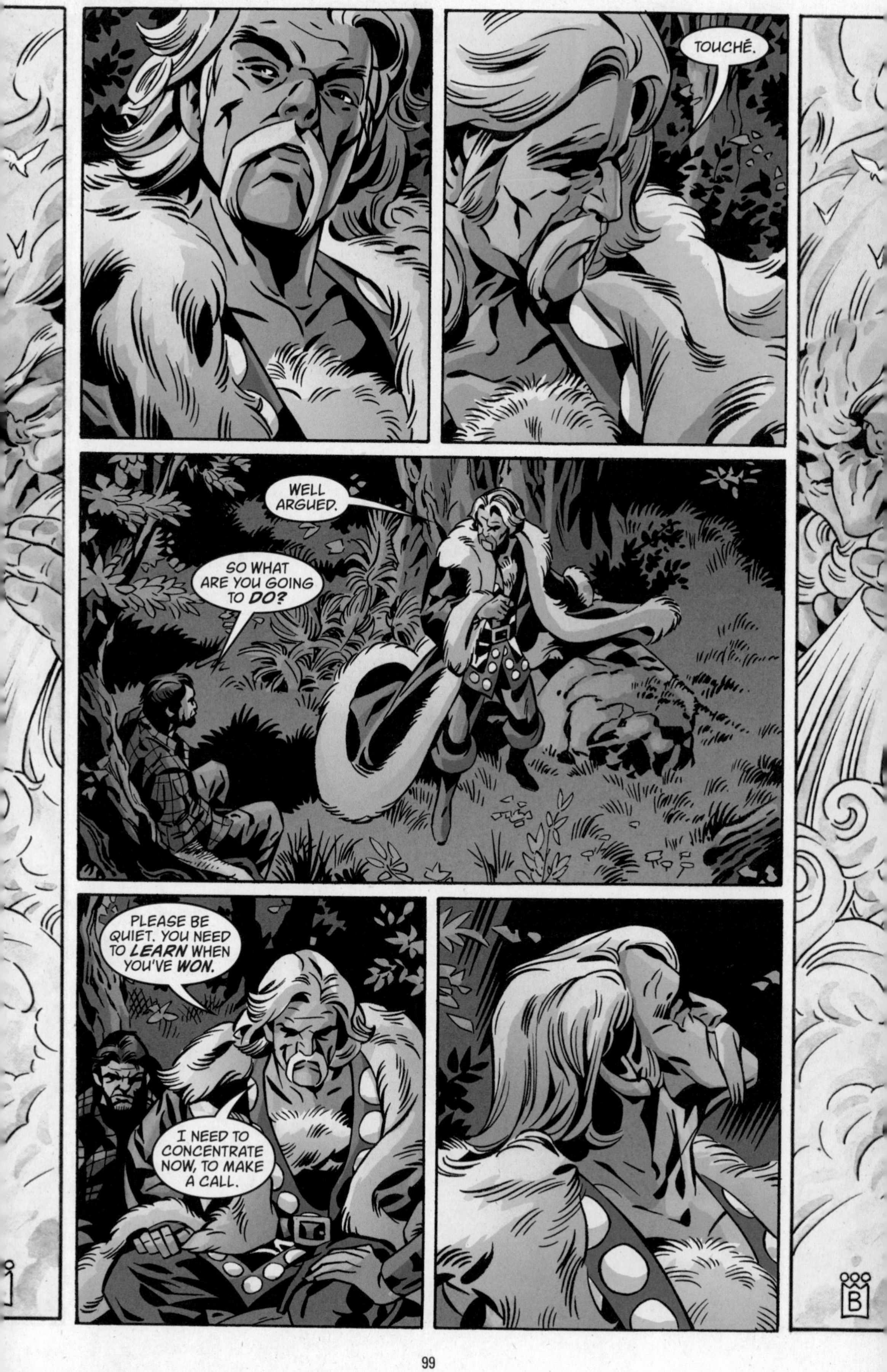

TOUCHÉ.
WELL ARGUED.
SO WHAT ARE YOU GOING TO *DO?*
PLEASE BE QUIET. YOU NEED TO *LEARN* WHEN YOU'VE *WON.*
I NEED TO CONCENTRATE NOW, TO MAKE A CALL.

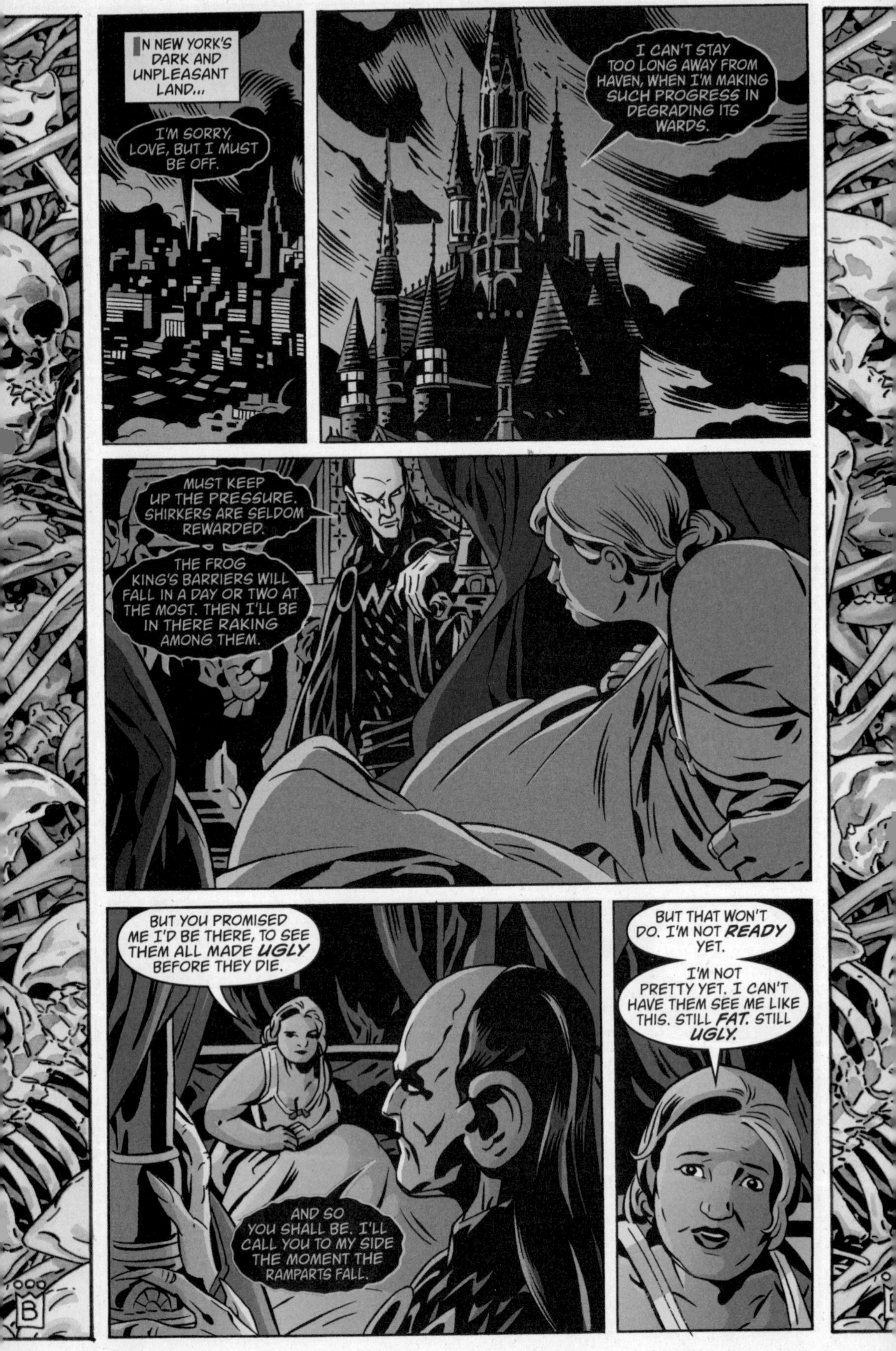
IN NEW YORK'S DARK AND UNPLEASANT LAND...
I'M SORRY, LOVE, BUT I MUST BE OFF.
I CAN'T STAY TOO LONG AWAY FROM HAVEN, WHEN I'M MAKING SUCH PROGRESS IN DEGRADING ITS WARDS.
MUST KEEP UP THE PRESSURE. SHIRKERS ARE SELDOM REWARDED.
THE FROG KING'S BARRIERS WILL FALL IN A DAY OR TWO AT THE MOST. THEN I'LL BE IN THERE RAKING AMONG THEM.
BUT YOU PROMISED ME I'D BE THERE, TO SEE THEM ALL MADE UGLY BEFORE THEY DIE.
AND SO YOU SHALL BE. I'LL CALL YOU TO MY SIDE THE MOMENT THE RAMPARTS FALL.
BUT THAT WON'T DO. I'M NOT READY YET.
I'M NOT PRETTY YET. I CAN'T HAVE THEM SEE ME LIKE THIS. STILL FAT. STILL UGLY.

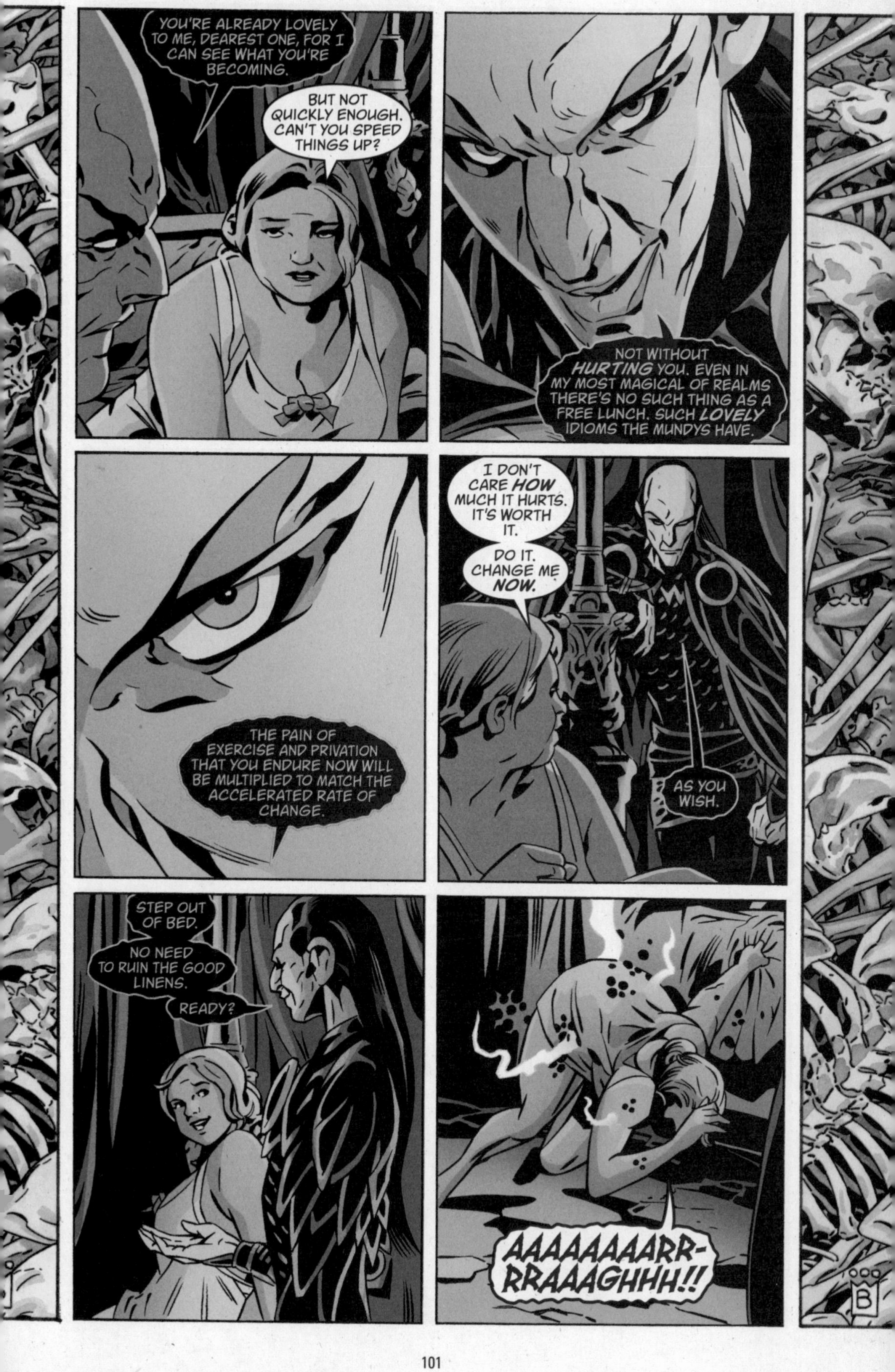
YOU'RE ALREADY LOVELY TO ME, DEAREST ONE, FOR I CAN SEE WHAT YOU'RE BECOMING.
BUT NOT QUICKLY ENOUGH. CAN'T YOU SPEED THINGS UP?
NOT WITHOUT HURTING YOU. EVEN IN MY MOST MAGICAL OF REALMS THERE'S NO SUCH THING AS A FREE LUNCH. SUCH LOVELY IDIOMS THE MUNDYS HAVE.
THE PAIN OF EXERCISE AND PRIVATION THAT YOU ENDURE NOW WILL BE MULTIPLIED TO MATCH THE ACCELERATED RATE OF CHANGE.
I DON'T CARE HOW MUCH IT HURTS. IT'S WORTH IT.
DO IT. CHANGE ME NOW.
AS YOU WISH.
STEP OUT OF BED.
NO NEED TO RUIN THE GOOD LINENS.
READY?
AAAAAAAARR-RRAAAGHHH!!

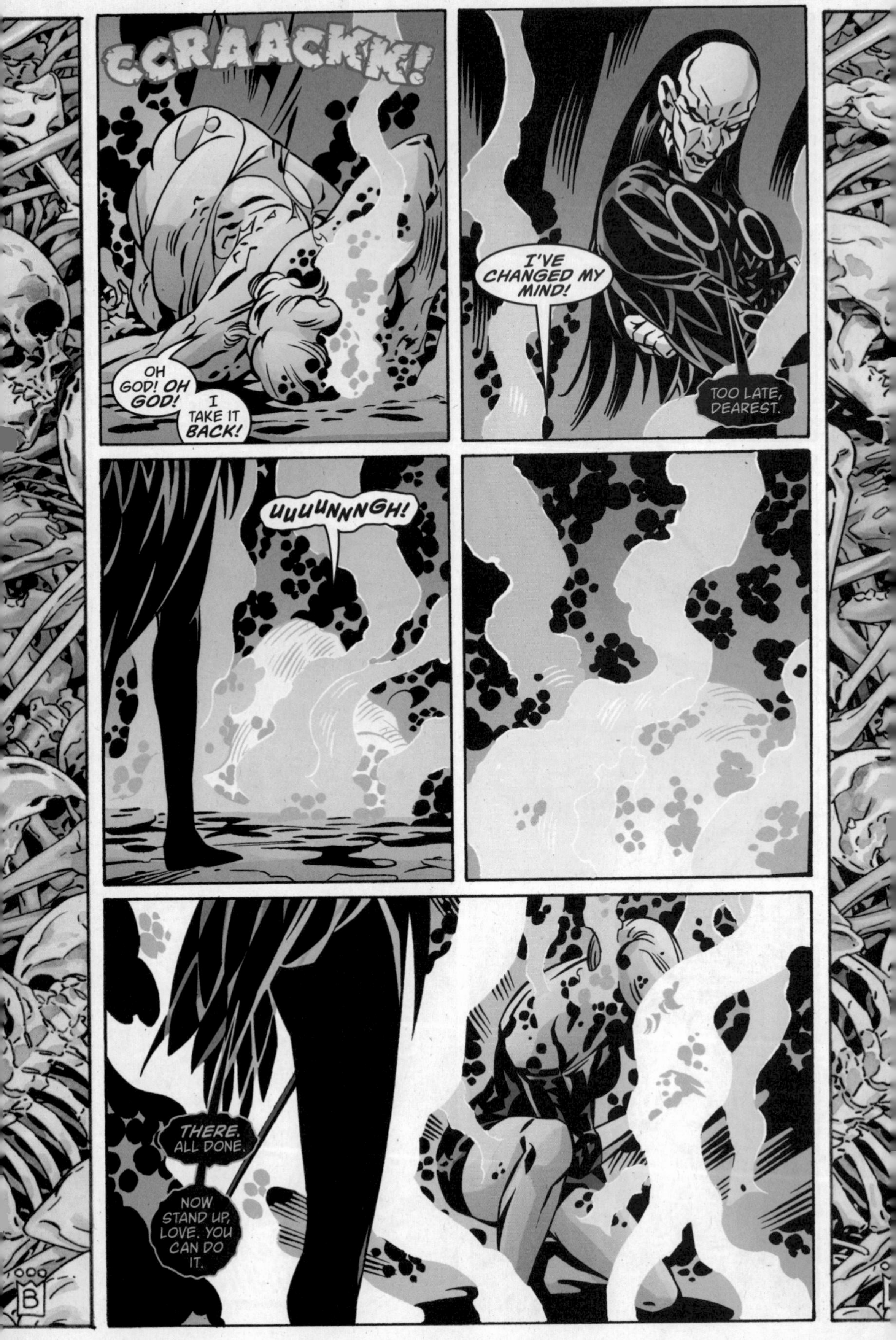
CCRAACKK!
OH GOD! OH GOD!
I TAKE IT BACK!
I'VE CHANGED MY MIND!
TOO LATE, DEAREST.
UUUUNNNGH!
THERE. ALL DONE.
NOW STAND UP, LOVE. YOU CAN DO IT.

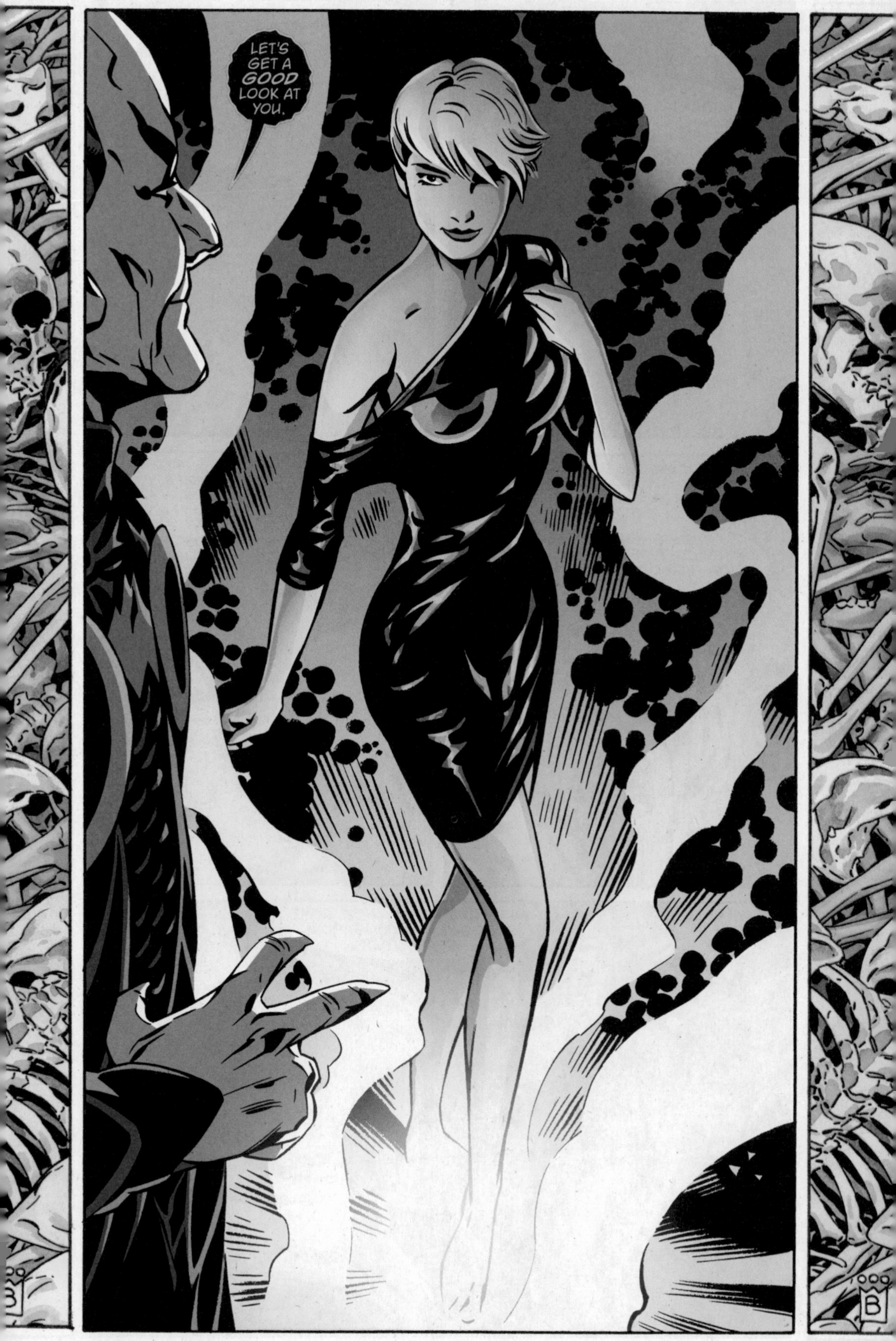
LET'S GET A GOOD LOOK AT YOU.

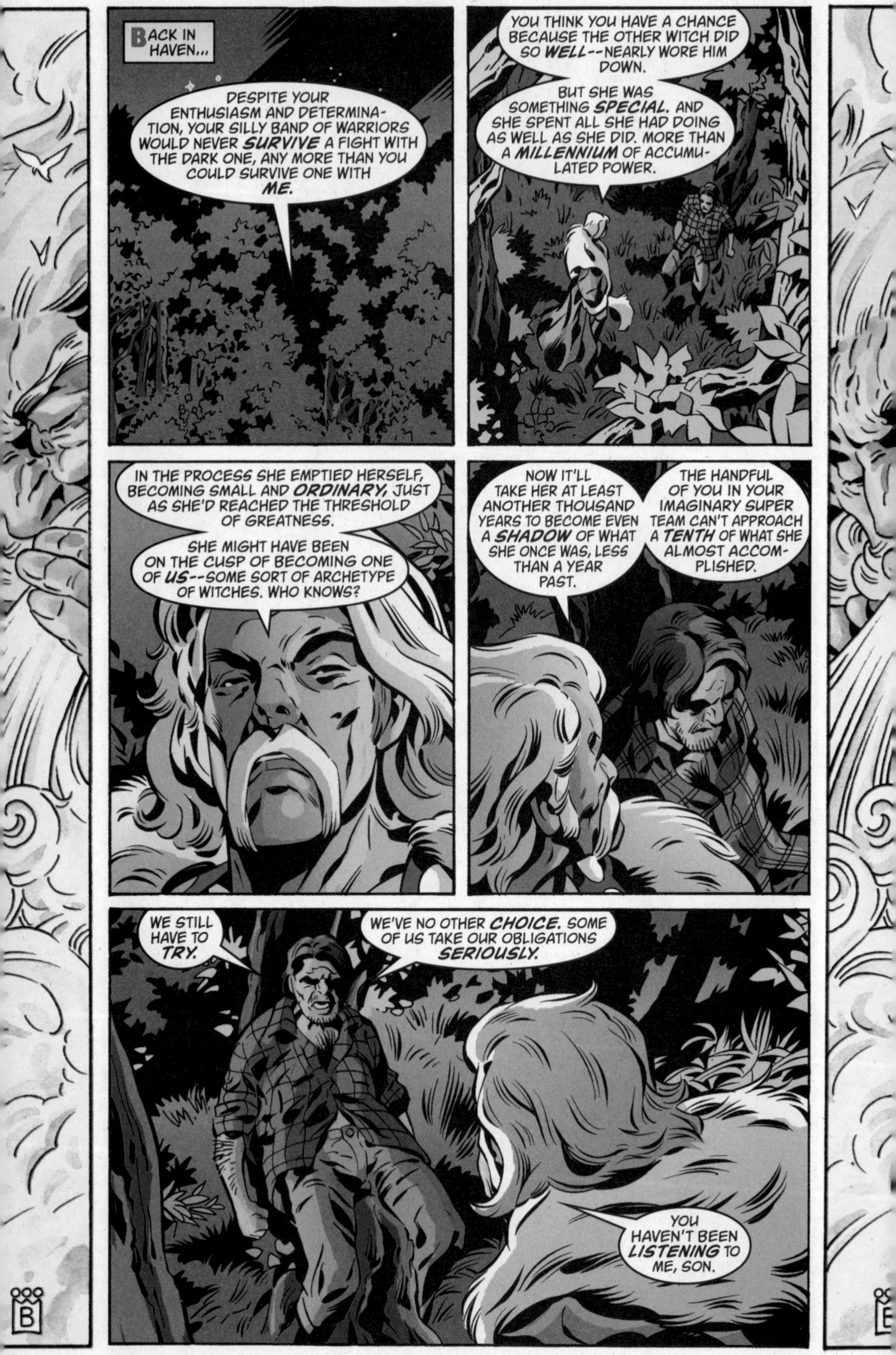
BACK IN HAVEN...
DESPITE YOUR ENTHUSIASM AND DETERMINATION, YOUR SILLY BAND OF WARRIORS WOULD NEVER SURVIVE A FIGHT WITH THE DARK ONE, ANY MORE THAN YOU COULD SURVIVE ONE WITH ME.
YOU THINK YOU HAVE A CHANCE BECAUSE THE OTHER WITCH DID SO WELL--NEARLY WORE HIM DOWN.
BUT SHE WAS SOMETHING SPECIAL. AND SHE SPENT ALL SHE HAD DOING AS WELL AS SHE DID. MORE THAN A MILLENNIUM OF ACCUMULATED POWER.
IN THE PROCESS SHE EMPTIED HERSELF, BECOMING SMALL AND ORDINARY, JUST AS SHE'D REACHED THE THRESHOLD OF GREATNESS.
SHE MIGHT HAVE BEEN ON THE CUSP OF BECOMING ONE OF US--SOME SORT OF ARCHETYPE OF WITCHES. WHO KNOWS?
NOW IT'LL TAKE HER AT LEAST ANOTHER THOUSAND YEARS TO BECOME EVEN A SHADOW OF WHAT SHE ONCE WAS, LESS THAN A YEAR PAST.
THE HANDFUL OF YOU IN YOUR IMAGINARY SUPER TEAM CAN'T APPROACH A TENTH OF WHAT SHE ALMOST ACCOMPLISHED.
WE STILL HAVE TO TRY.
WE'VE NO OTHER CHOICE. SOME OF US TAKE OUR OBLIGATIONS SERIOUSLY.
YOU HAVEN'T BEEN LISTENING TO ME, SON.

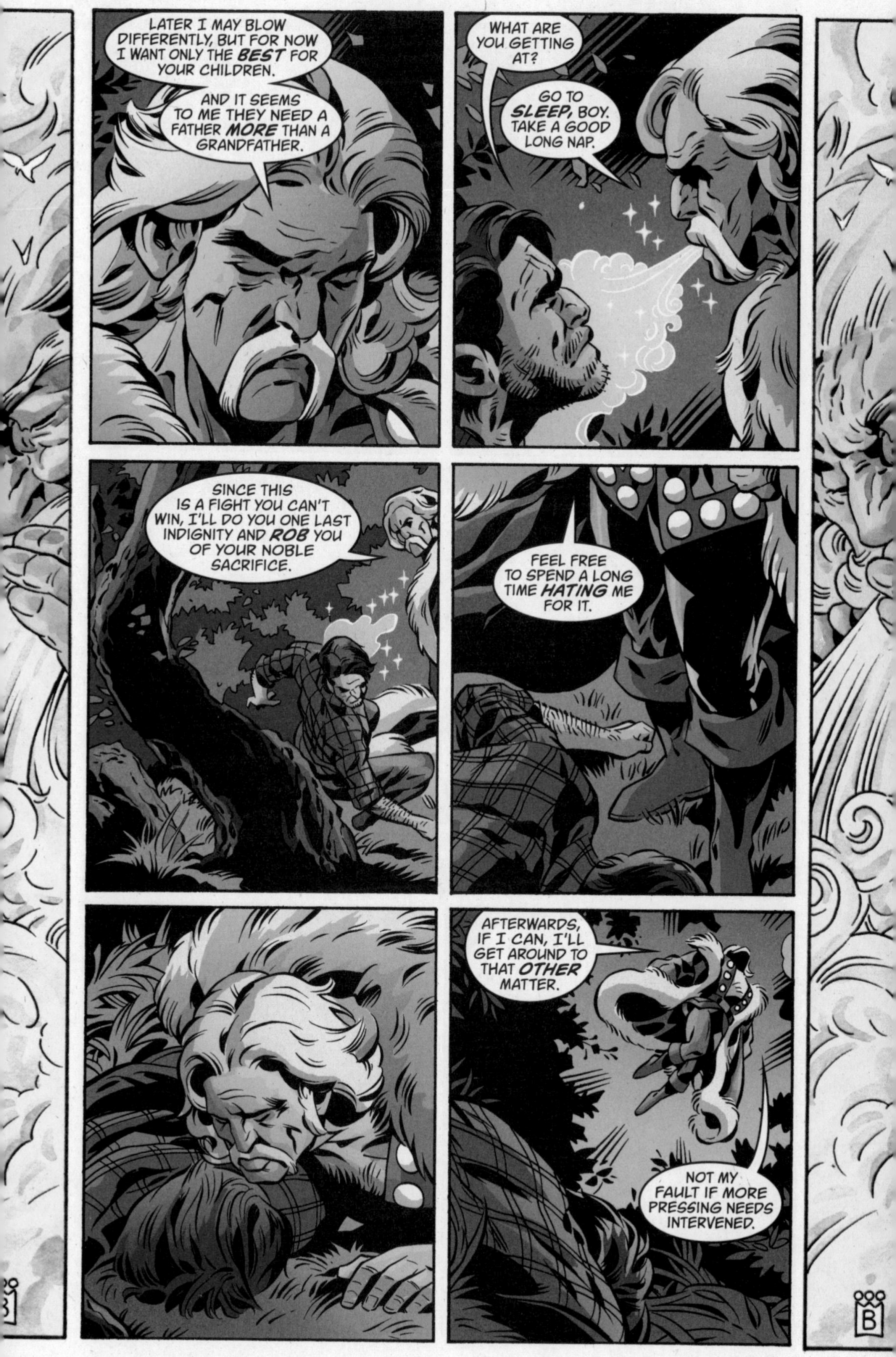
LATER I MAY BLOW DIFFERENTLY, BUT FOR NOW I WANT ONLY THE BEST FOR YOUR CHILDREN.
AND IT SEEMS TO ME THEY NEED A FATHER MORE THAN A GRANDFATHER.
WHAT ARE YOU GETTING AT?
GO TO SLEEP, BOY. TAKE A GOOD LONG NAP.
SINCE THIS IS A FIGHT YOU CAN'T WIN, I'LL DO YOU ONE LAST INDIGNITY AND ROB YOU OF YOUR NOBLE SACRIFICE.
FEEL FREE TO SPEND A LONG TIME HATING ME FOR IT.
AFTERWARDS, IF I CAN, I'LL GET AROUND TO THAT OTHER MATTER.
NOT MY FAULT IF MORE PRESSING NEEDS INTERVENED.

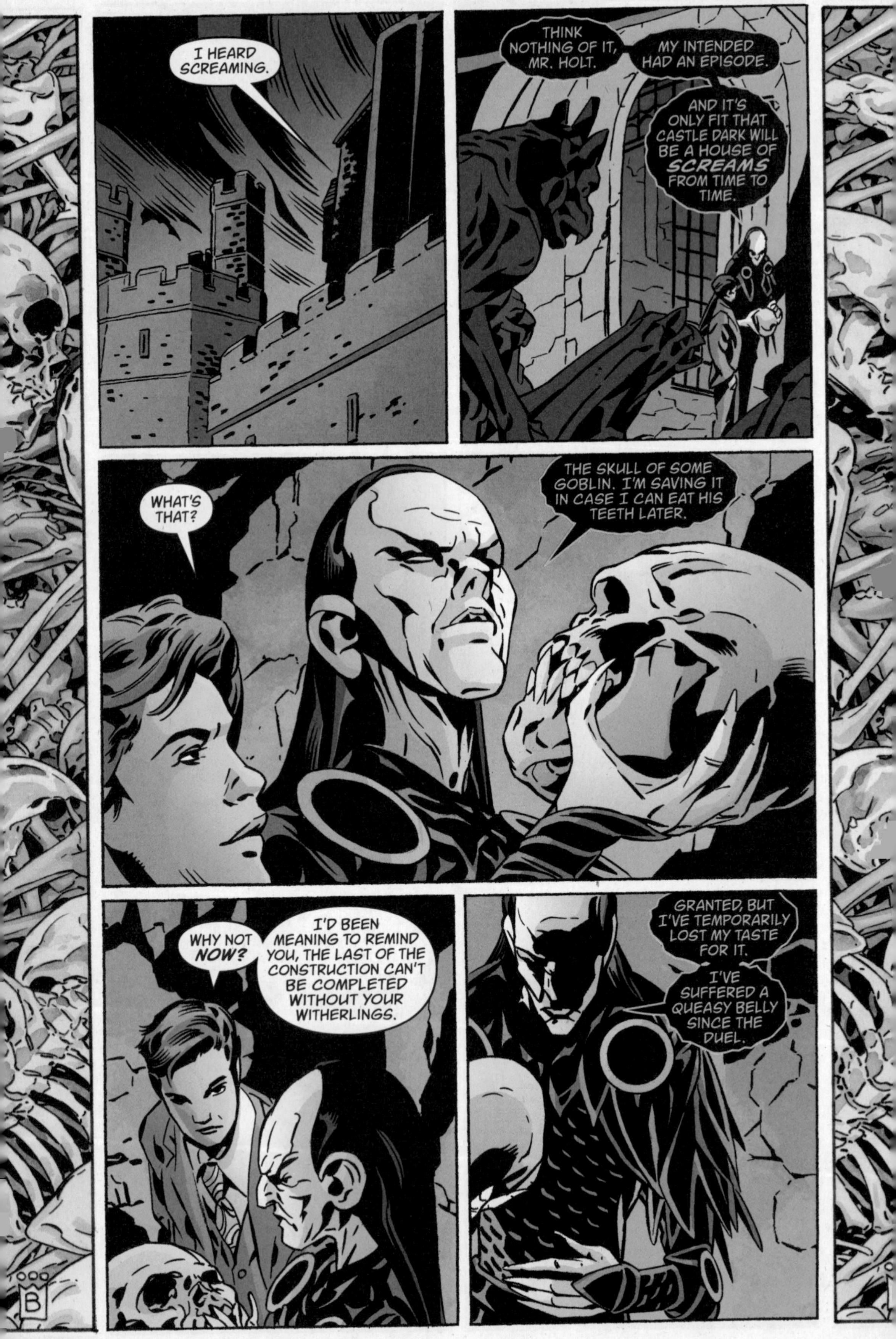
I HEARD SCREAMING.
THINK NOTHING OF IT, MR. HOLT.
MY INTENDED HAD AN EPISODE.
AND IT'S ONLY FIT THAT CASTLE DARK WILL BE A HOUSE OF SCREAMS FROM TIME TO TIME.
WHAT'S THAT?
THE SKULL OF SOME GOBLIN. I'M SAVING IT IN CASE I CAN EAT HIS TEETH LATER.
WHY NOT NOW?
I'D BEEN MEANING TO REMIND YOU, THE LAST OF THE CONSTRUCTION CAN'T BE COMPLETED WITHOUT YOUR WITHERLINGS.
GRANTED, BUT I'VE TEMPORARILY LOST MY TASTE FOR IT.
I'VE SUFFERED A QUEASY BELLY SINCE THE DUEL.

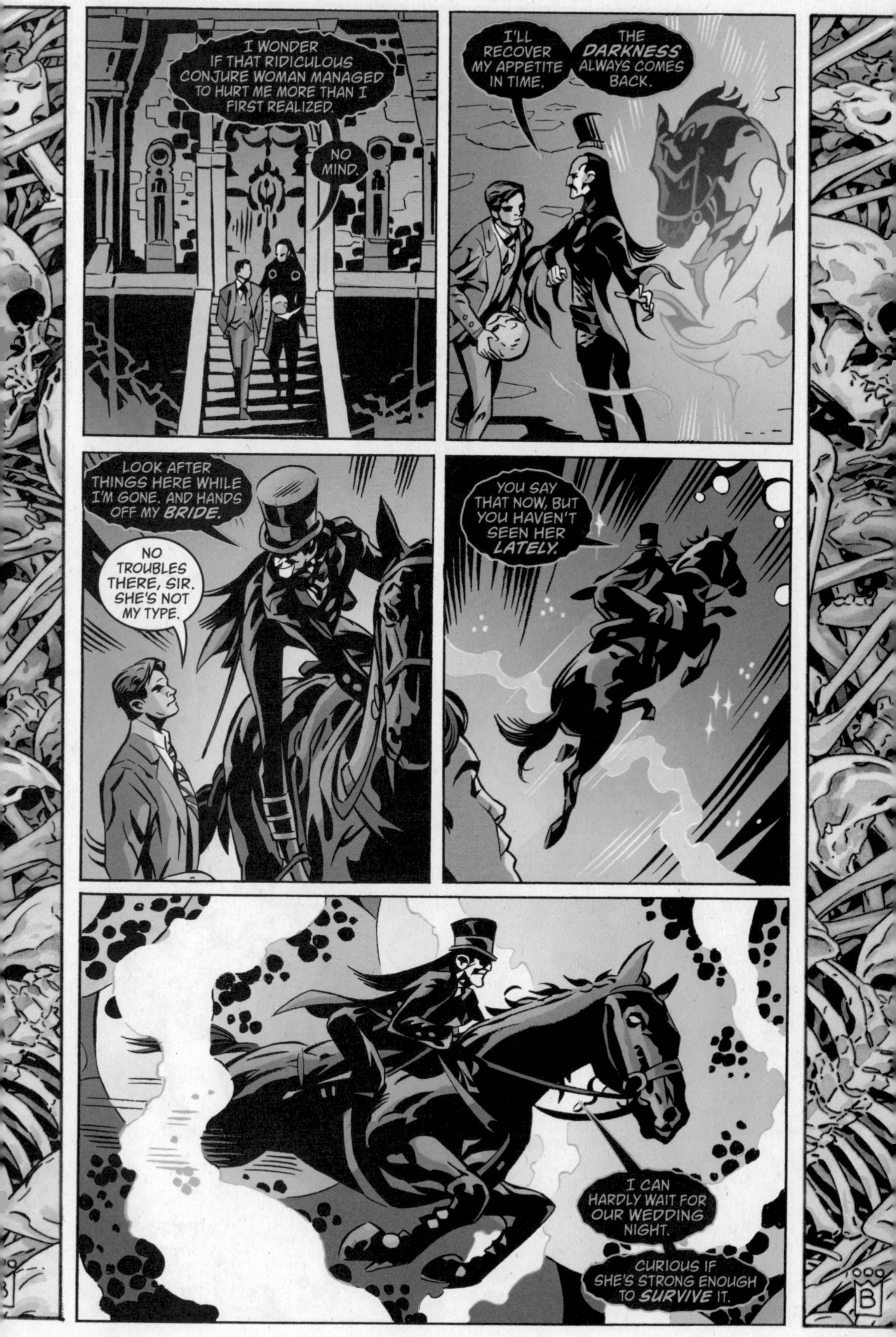
I WONDER IF THAT RIDICULOUS CONJURE WOMAN MANAGED TO HURT ME MORE THAN I FIRST REALIZED.
NO MIND.
I'LL RECOVER MY APPETITE IN TIME.
THE DARKNESS ALWAYS COMES BACK.
LOOK AFTER THINGS HERE WHILE I'M GONE. AND HANDS OFF MY BRIDE.
NO TROUBLES THERE, SIR. SHE'S NOT MY TYPE.
YOU SAY THAT NOW, BUT YOU HAVEN'T SEEN HER LATELY.
I CAN HARDLY WAIT FOR OUR WEDDING NIGHT.
CURIOUS IF SHE'S STRONG ENOUGH TO SURVIVE IT.

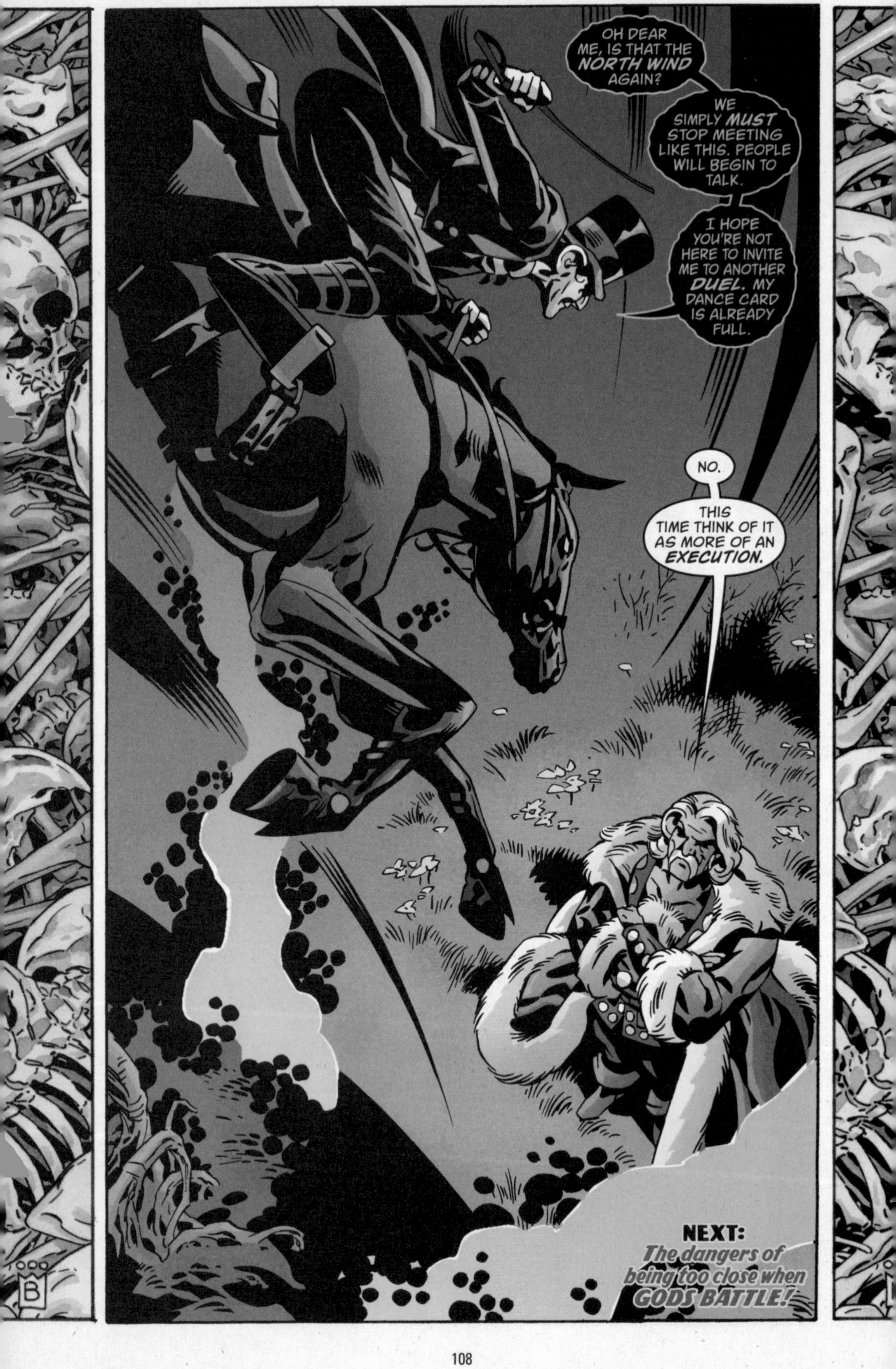
OH DEAR ME, IS THAT THE NORTH WIND AGAIN?
WE SIMPLY MUST STOP MEETING LIKE THIS. PEOPLE WILL BEGIN TO TALK.
I HOPE YOU'RE NOT HERE TO INVITE ME TO ANOTHER DUEL. MY DANCE CARD IS ALREADY FULL.
NO.
THIS TIME THINK OF IT AS MORE OF AN EXECUTION.
NEXT: The dangers of being too close when GODS BATTLE!

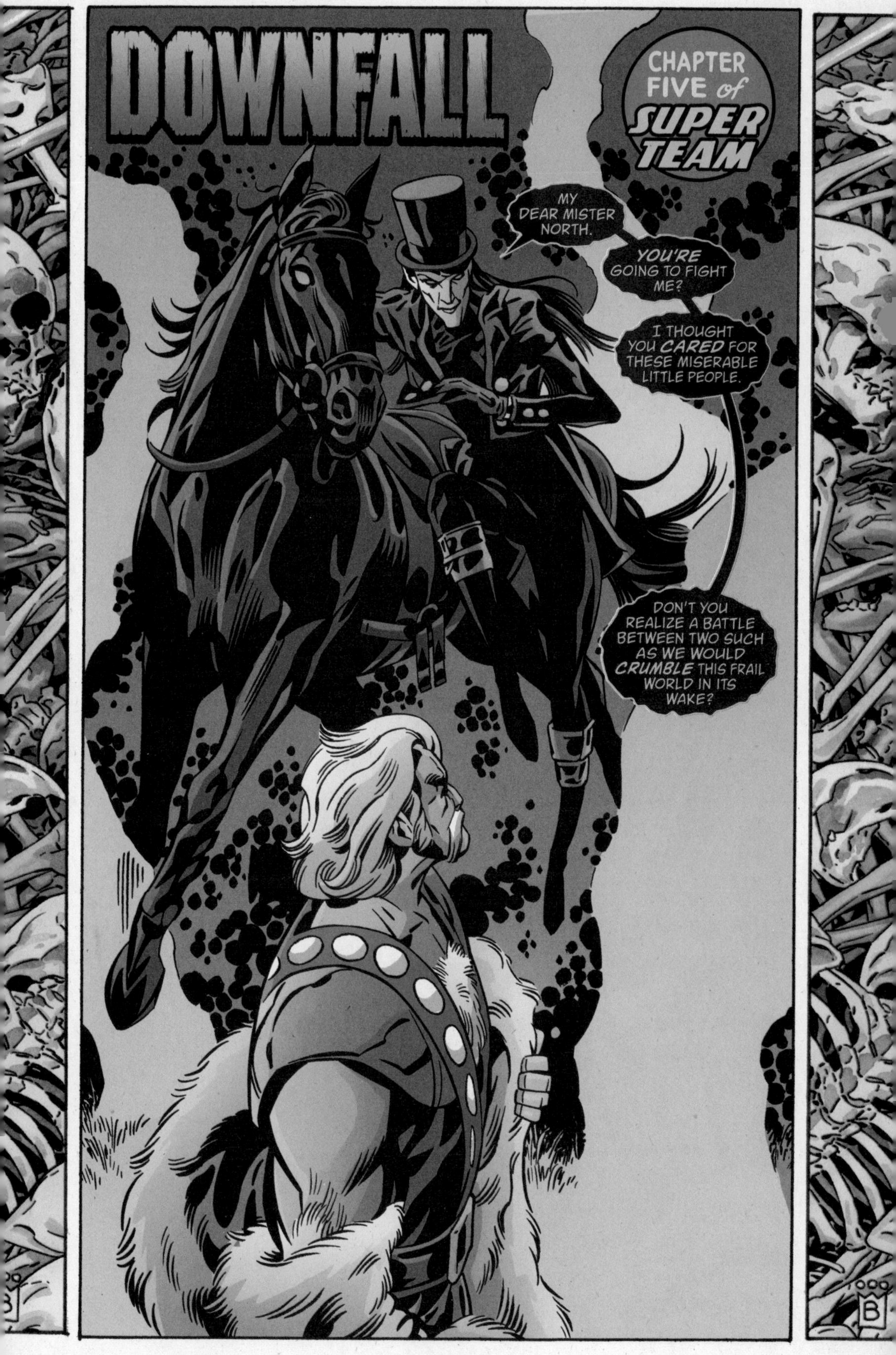
DOWNFALL
CHAPTER FIVE of SUPER TEAM
MY DEAR MISTER NORTH.
YOU'RE GOING TO FIGHT ME?
I THOUGHT YOU CARED FOR THESE MISERABLE LITTLE PEOPLE.
DON'T YOU REALIZE A BATTLE BETWEEN TWO SUCH AS WE WOULD CRUMBLE THIS FRAIL WORLD IN ITS WAKE?

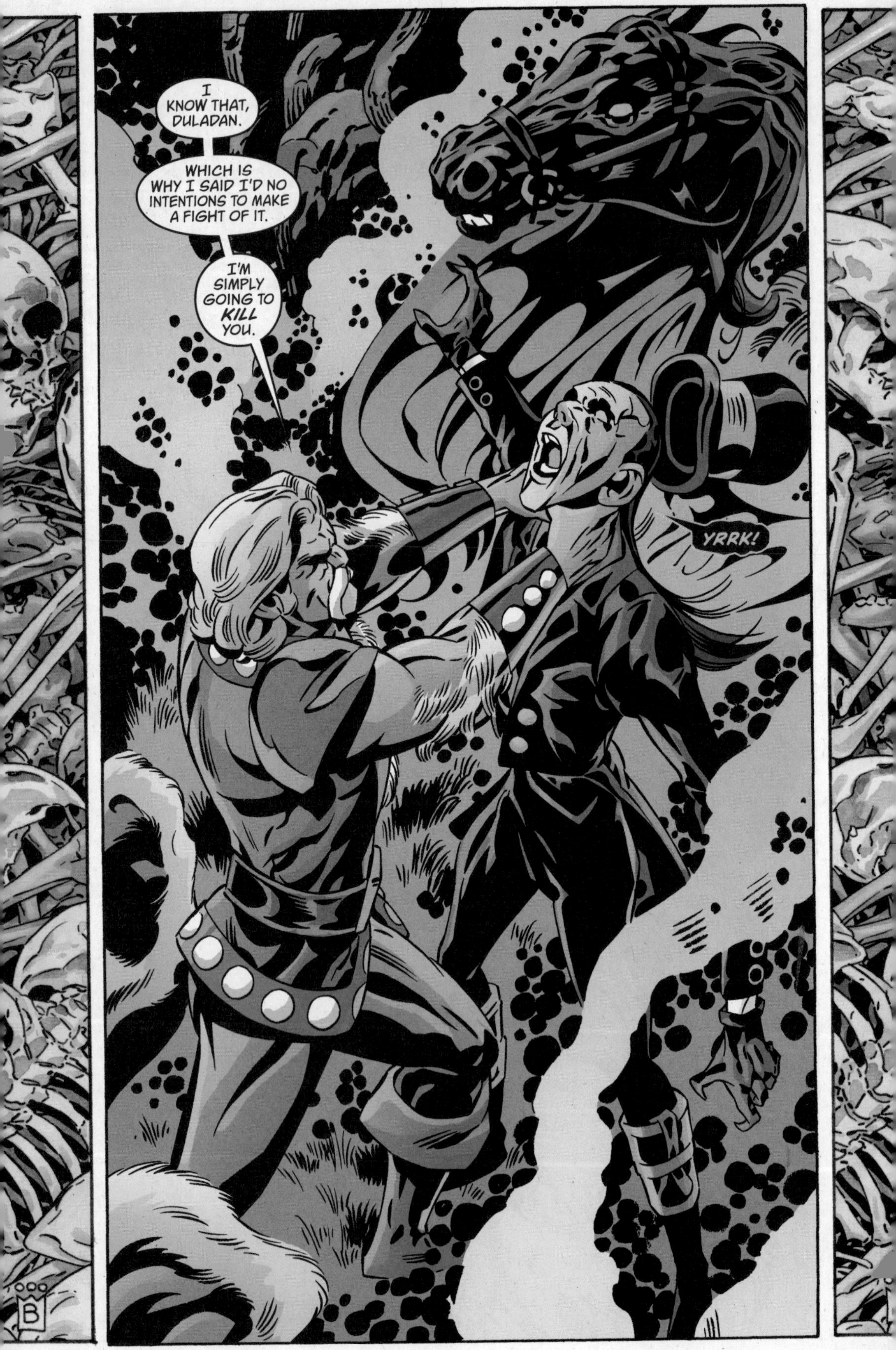
I KNOW THAT, DULADAN.
WHICH IS WHY I SAID I'D NO INTENTIONS TO MAKE A FIGHT OF IT.
I'M SIMPLY GOING TO KILL YOU.
YRRK!

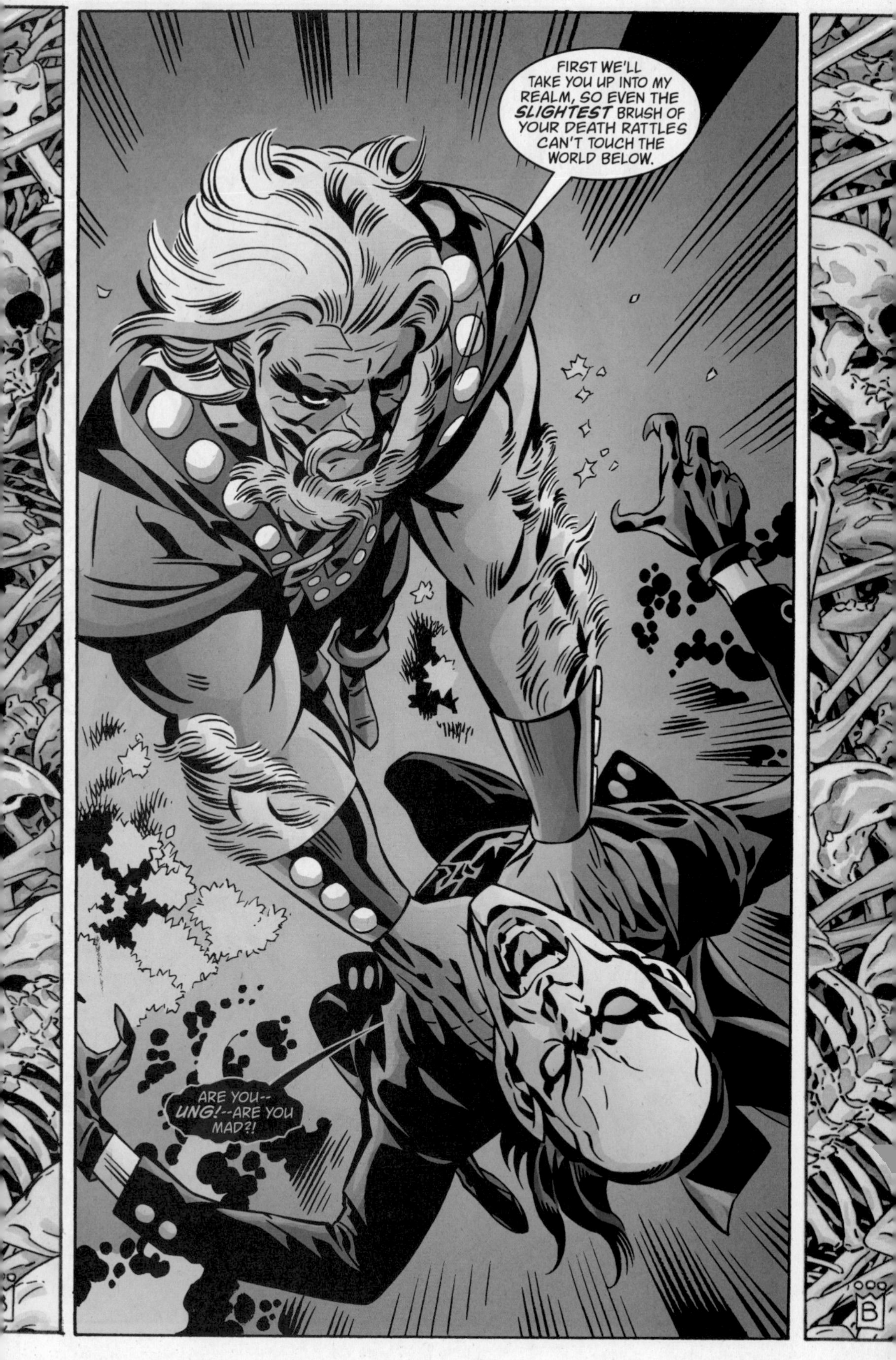
FIRST WE'LL TAKE YOU UP INTO MY REALM, SO EVEN THE SLIGHTEST BRUSH OF YOUR DEATH RATTLES CAN'T TOUCH THE WORLD BELOW.
ARE YOU-- UNG!--ARE YOU MAD?!

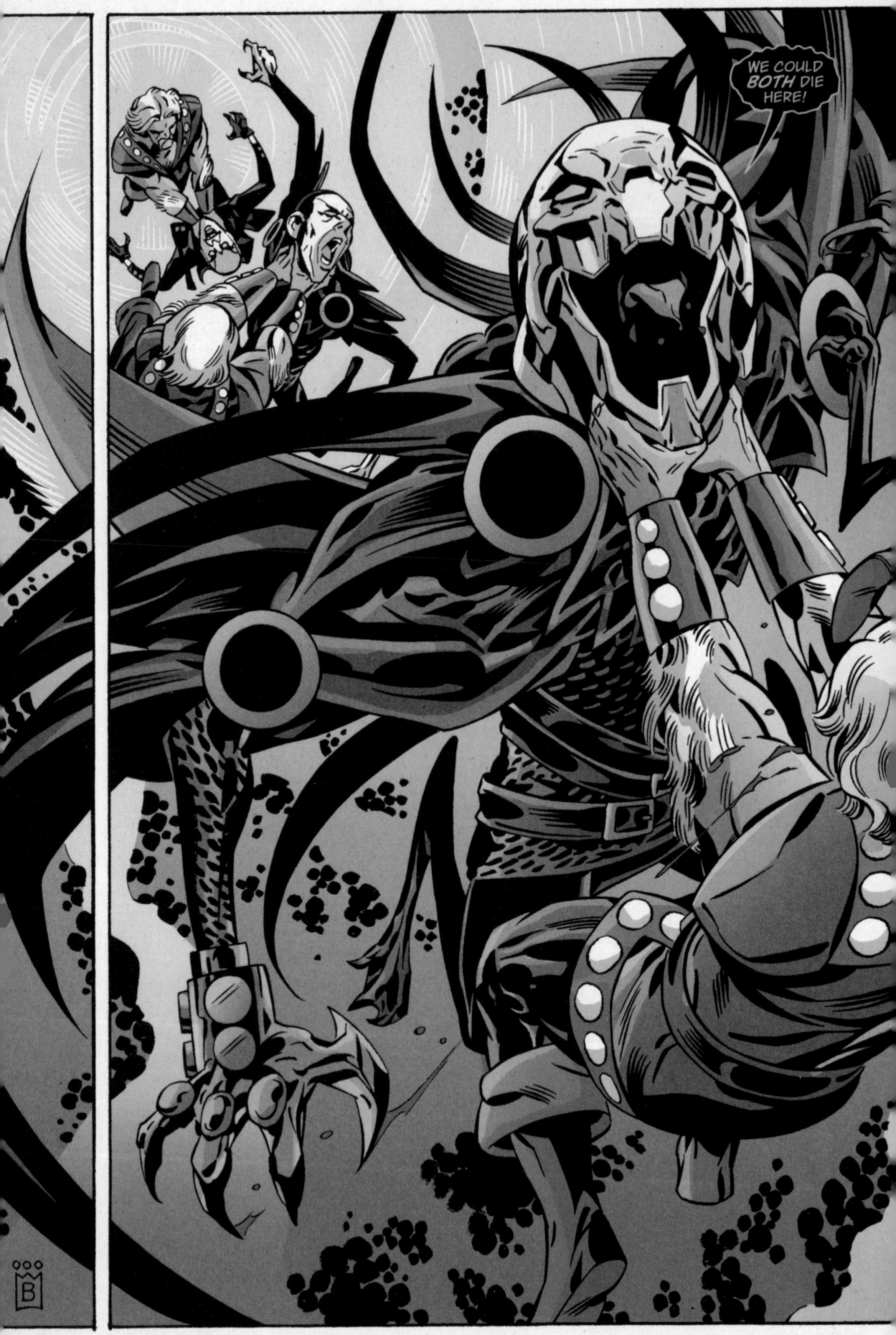
WE COULD BOTH DIE HERE!

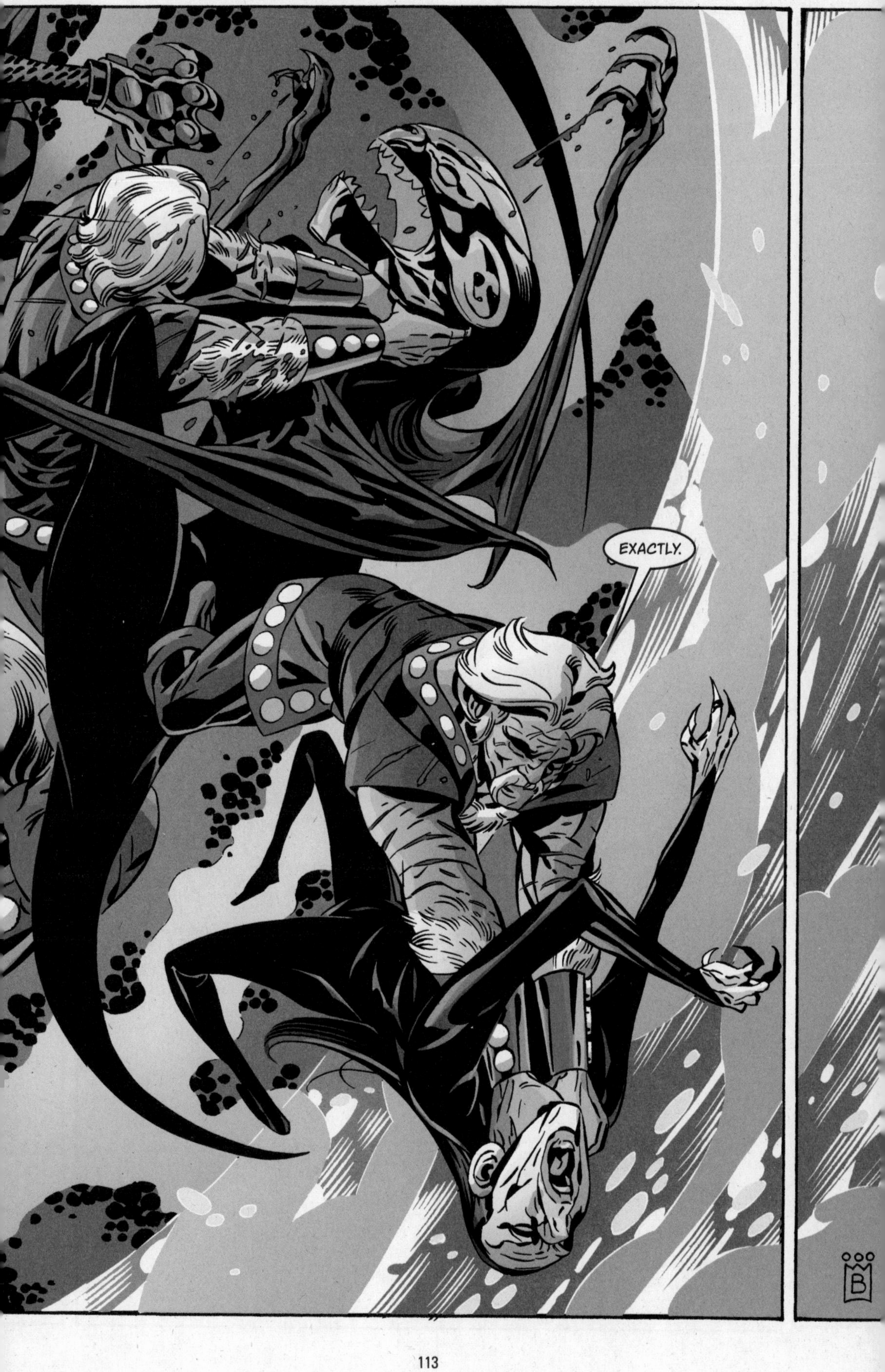
EXACTLY.

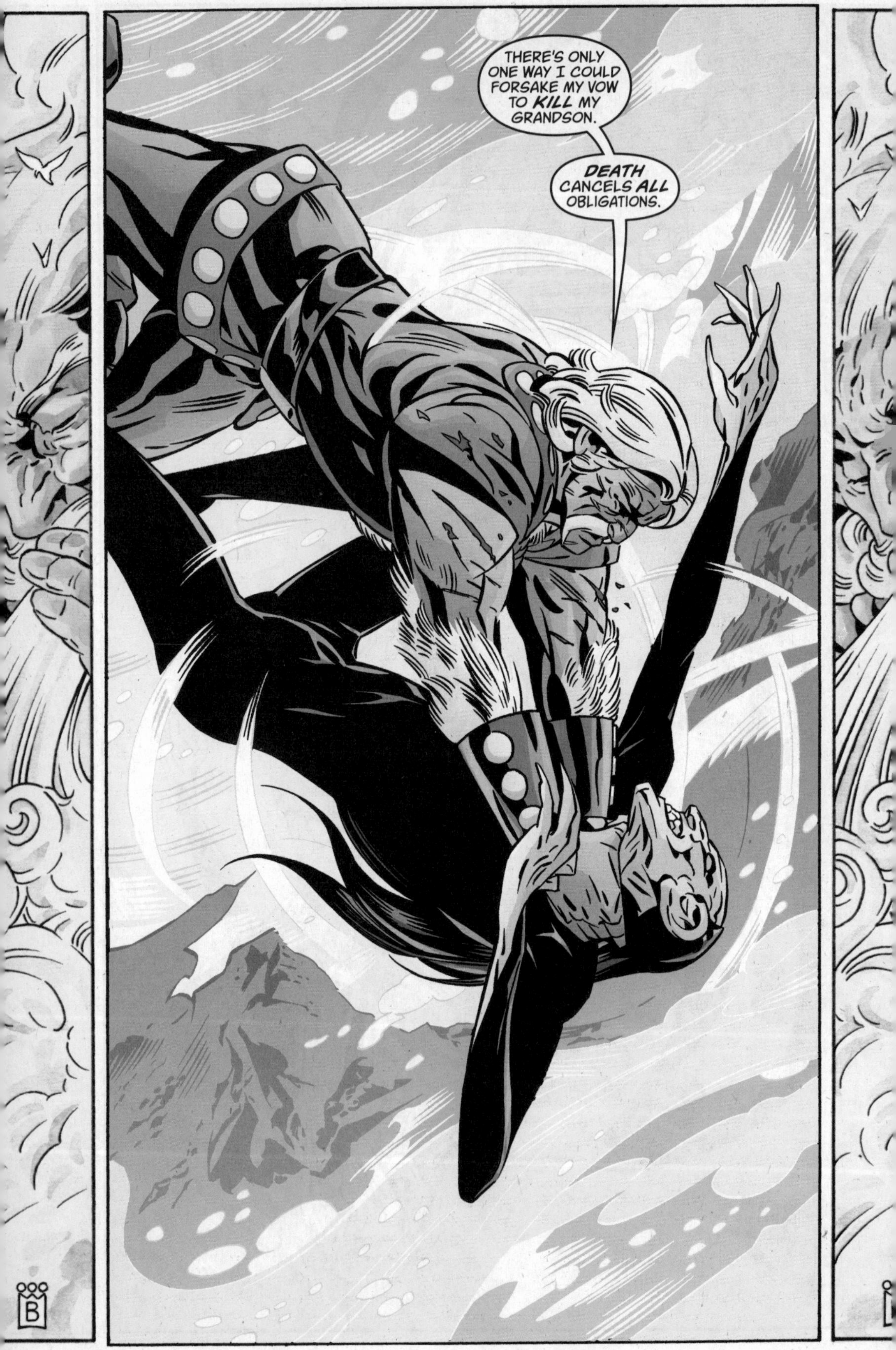
THERE'S ONLY ONE WAY I COULD FORSAKE MY VOW TO **KILL** MY GRANDSON.
DEATH CANCELS **ALL** OBLIGATIONS.

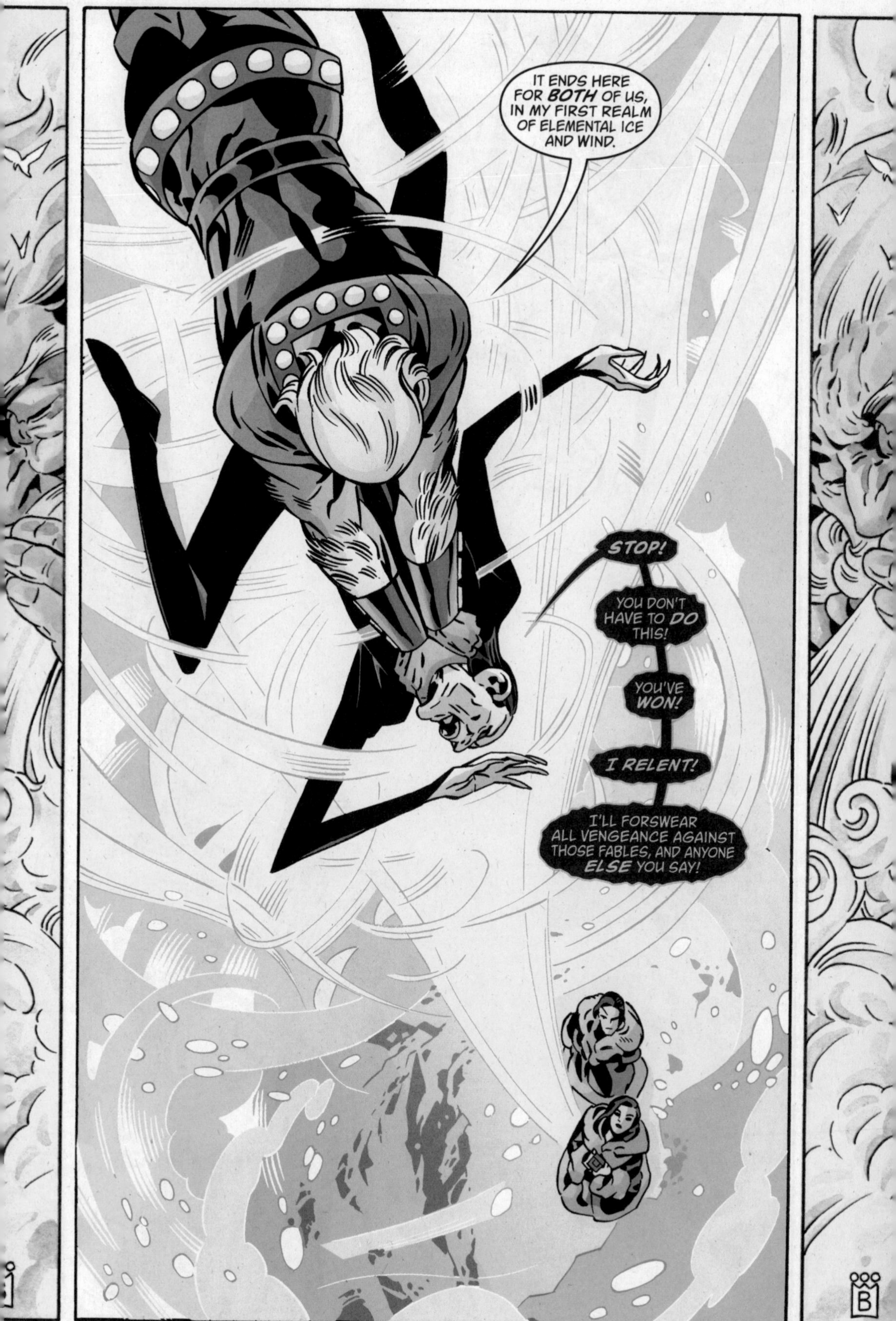
IT ENDS HERE FOR BOTH OF US, IN MY FIRST REALM OF ELEMENTAL ICE AND WIND.
STOP!
YOU DON'T HAVE TO DO THIS!
YOU'VE WON!
I RELENT!
I'LL FORSWEAR ALL VENGEANCE AGAINST THOSE FABLES, AND ANYONE ELSE YOU SAY!

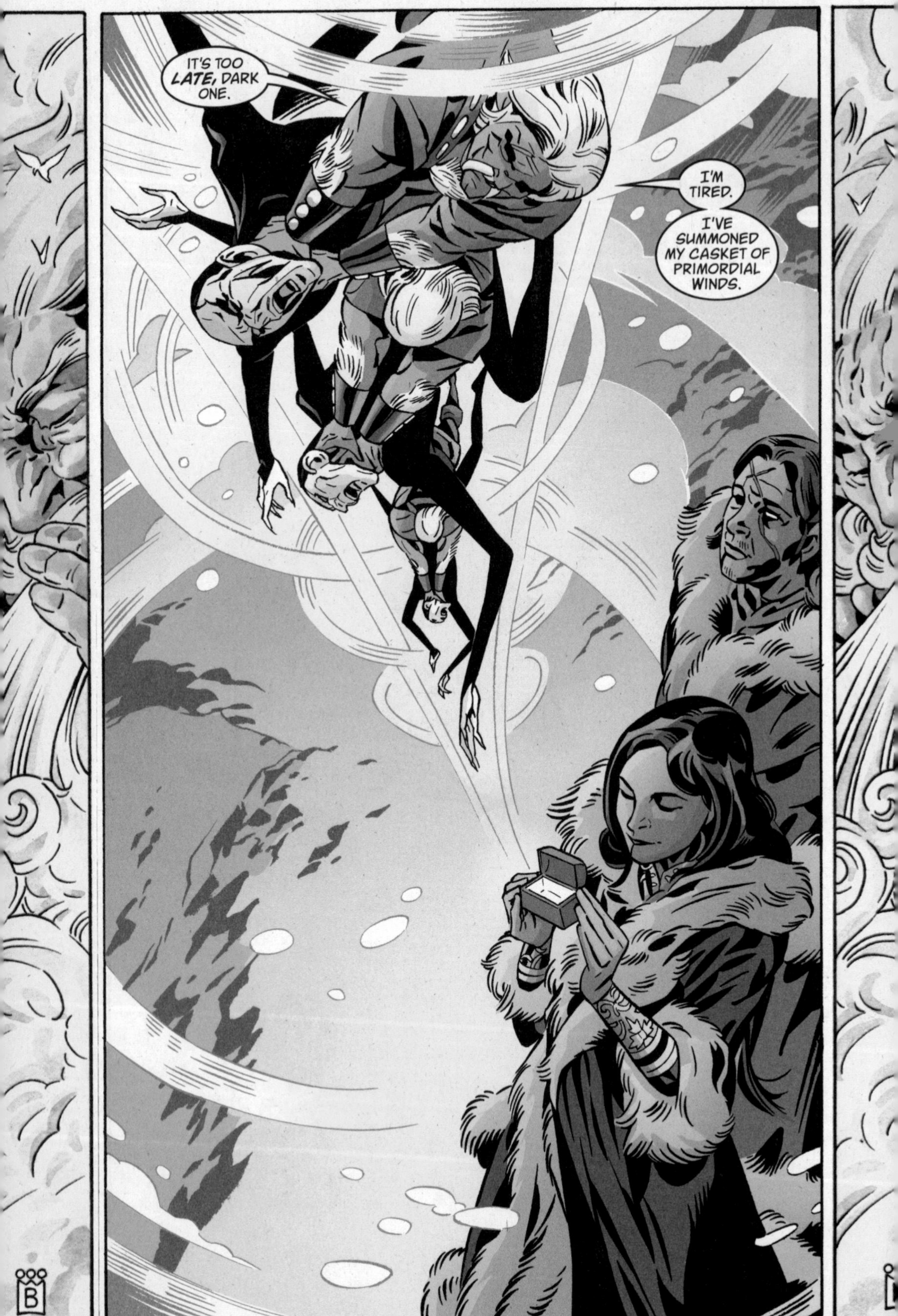

IT'S TOO LATE, DARK ONE.
I'M TIRED.
I'VE SUMMONED MY CASKET OF PRIMORDIAL WINDS.

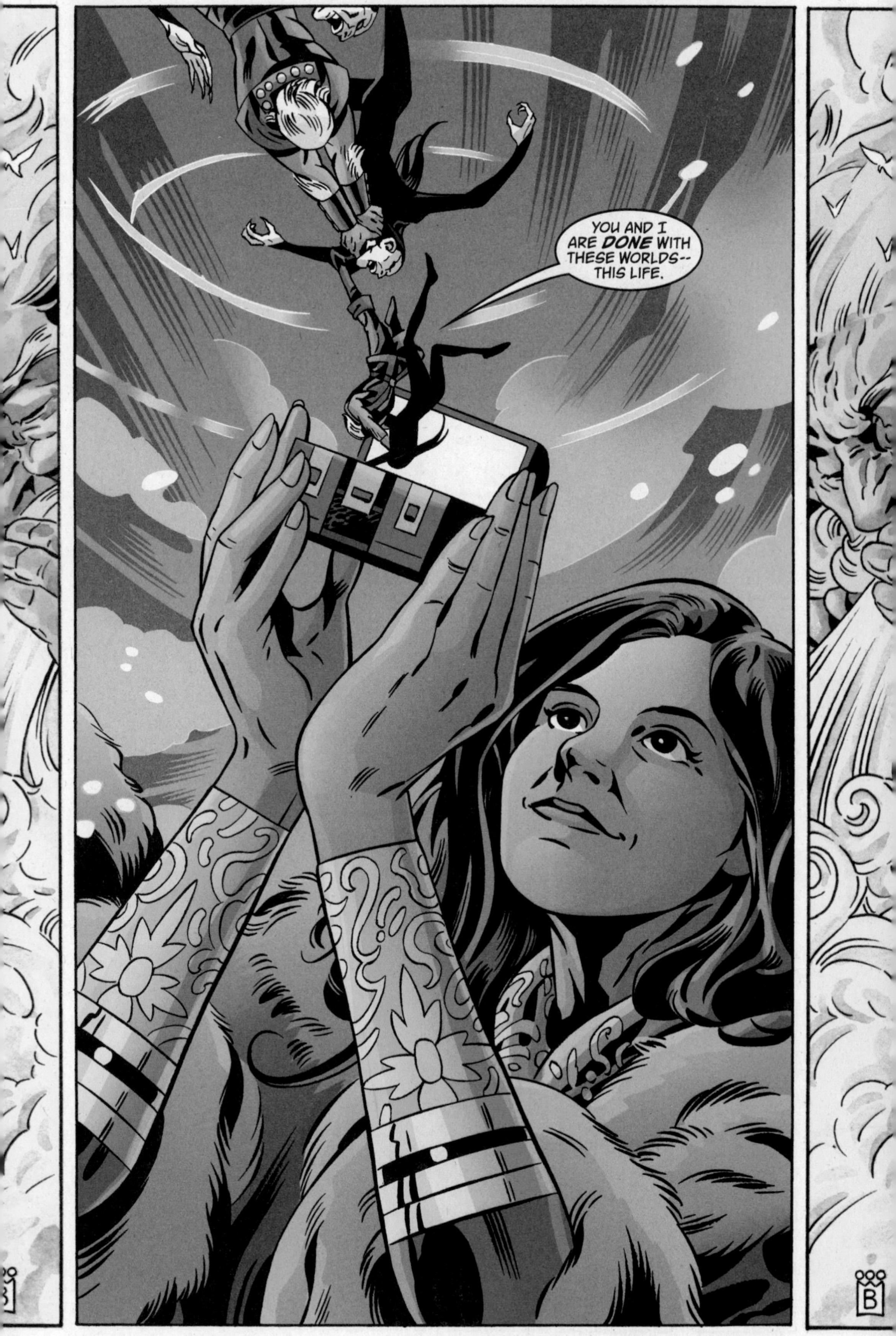
YOU AND I ARE DONE WITH THESE WORLDS-- THIS LIFE.

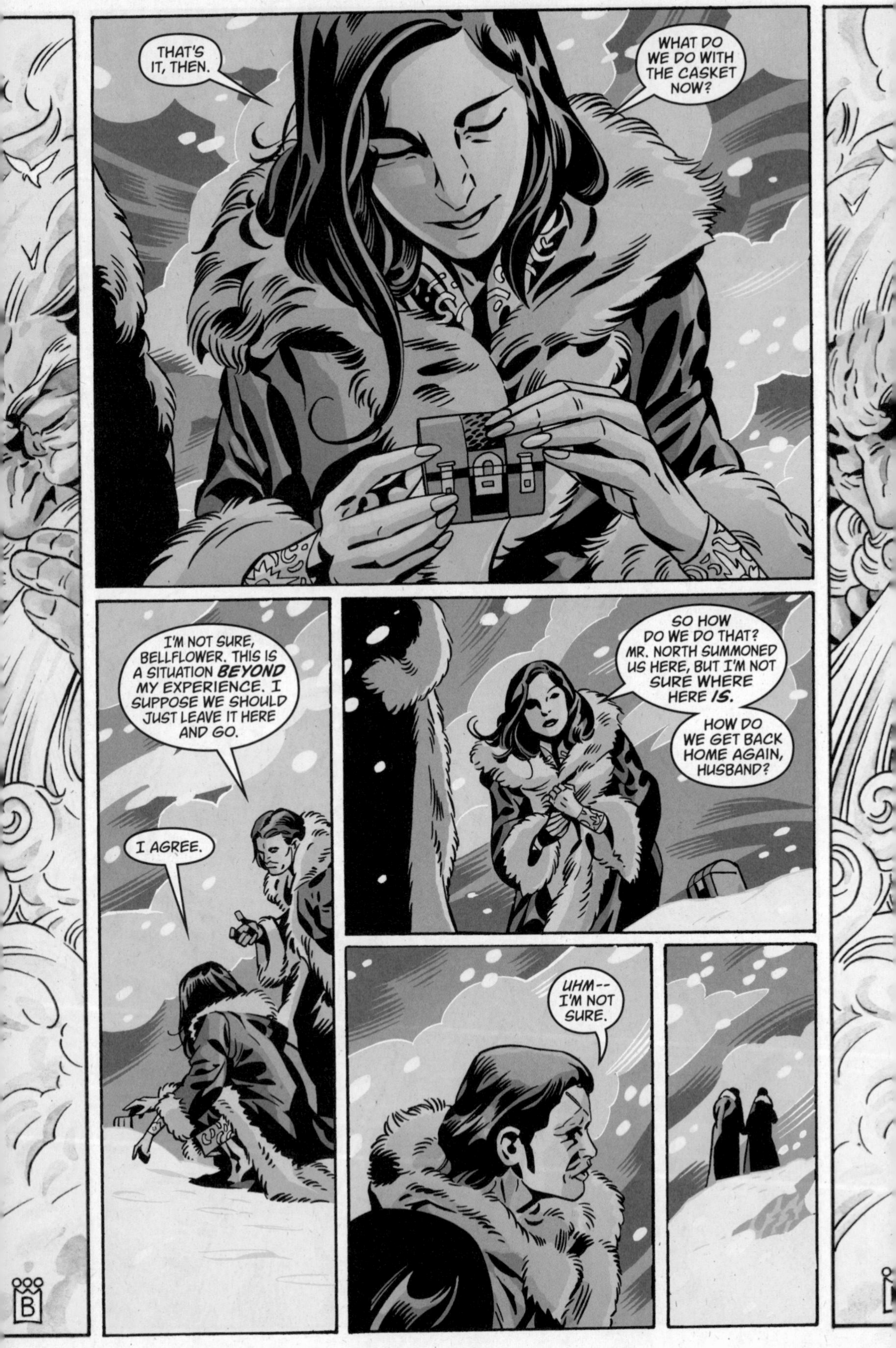
THAT'S IT, THEN.
WHAT DO WE DO WITH THE CASKET NOW?
I'M NOT SURE, BELLFLOWER. THIS IS A SITUATION BEYOND MY EXPERIENCE. I SUPPOSE WE SHOULD JUST LEAVE IT HERE AND GO.
I AGREE.
SO HOW DO WE DO THAT? MR. NORTH SUMMONED US HERE, BUT I'M NOT SURE WHERE HERE IS.
HOW DO WE GET BACK HOME AGAIN, HUSBAND?
UHM-- I'M NOT SURE.

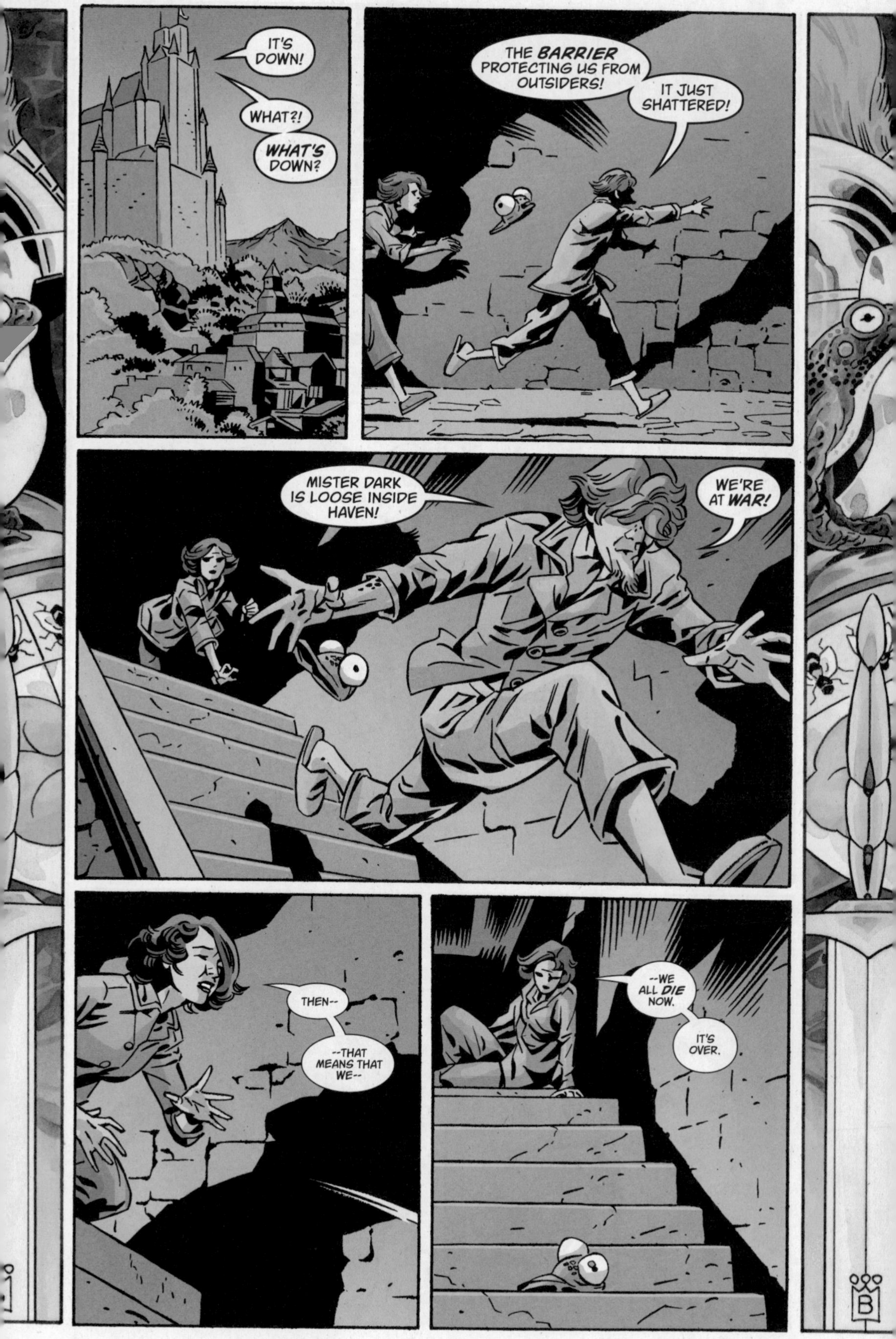

IT'S DOWN!
WHAT?! WHAT'S DOWN?
THE BARRIER PROTECTING US FROM OUTSIDERS!
IT JUST SHATTERED!
MISTER DARK IS LOOSE INSIDE HAVEN!
WE'RE AT WAR!
THEN--
--THAT MEANS THAT WE--
--WE ALL DIE NOW.
IT'S OVER.

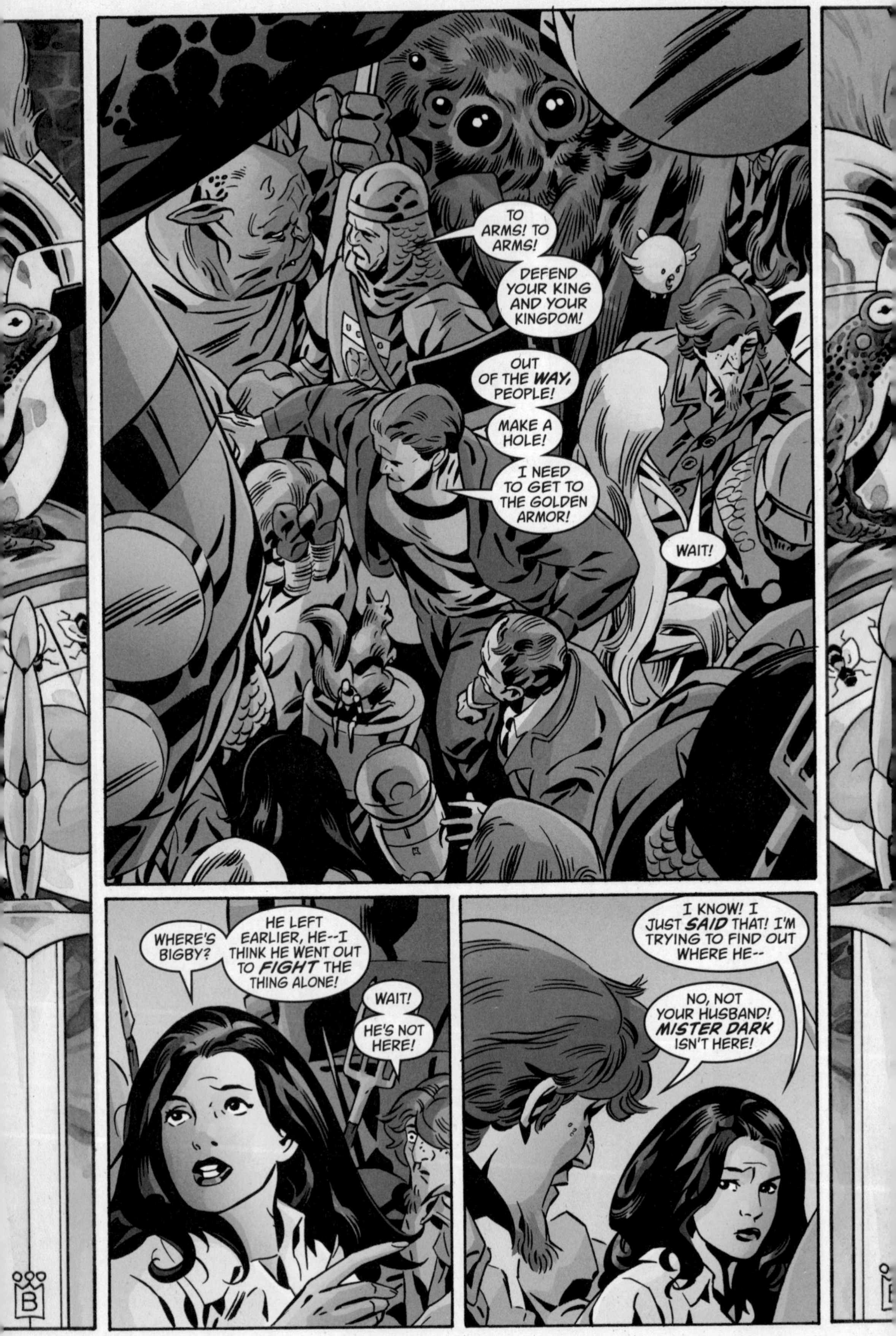
TO ARMS! TO ARMS!
DEFEND YOUR KING AND YOUR KINGDOM!
OUT OF THE WAY, PEOPLE!
MAKE A HOLE!
I NEED TO GET TO THE GOLDEN ARMOR!
WAIT!
WHERE'S BIGBY?
HE LEFT EARLIER, HE--I THINK HE WENT OUT TO FIGHT THE THING ALONE!
WAIT!
HE'S NOT HERE!
I KNOW! I JUST SAID THAT! I'M TRYING TO FIND OUT WHERE HE--
NO, NOT YOUR HUSBAND! MISTER DARK ISN'T HERE!

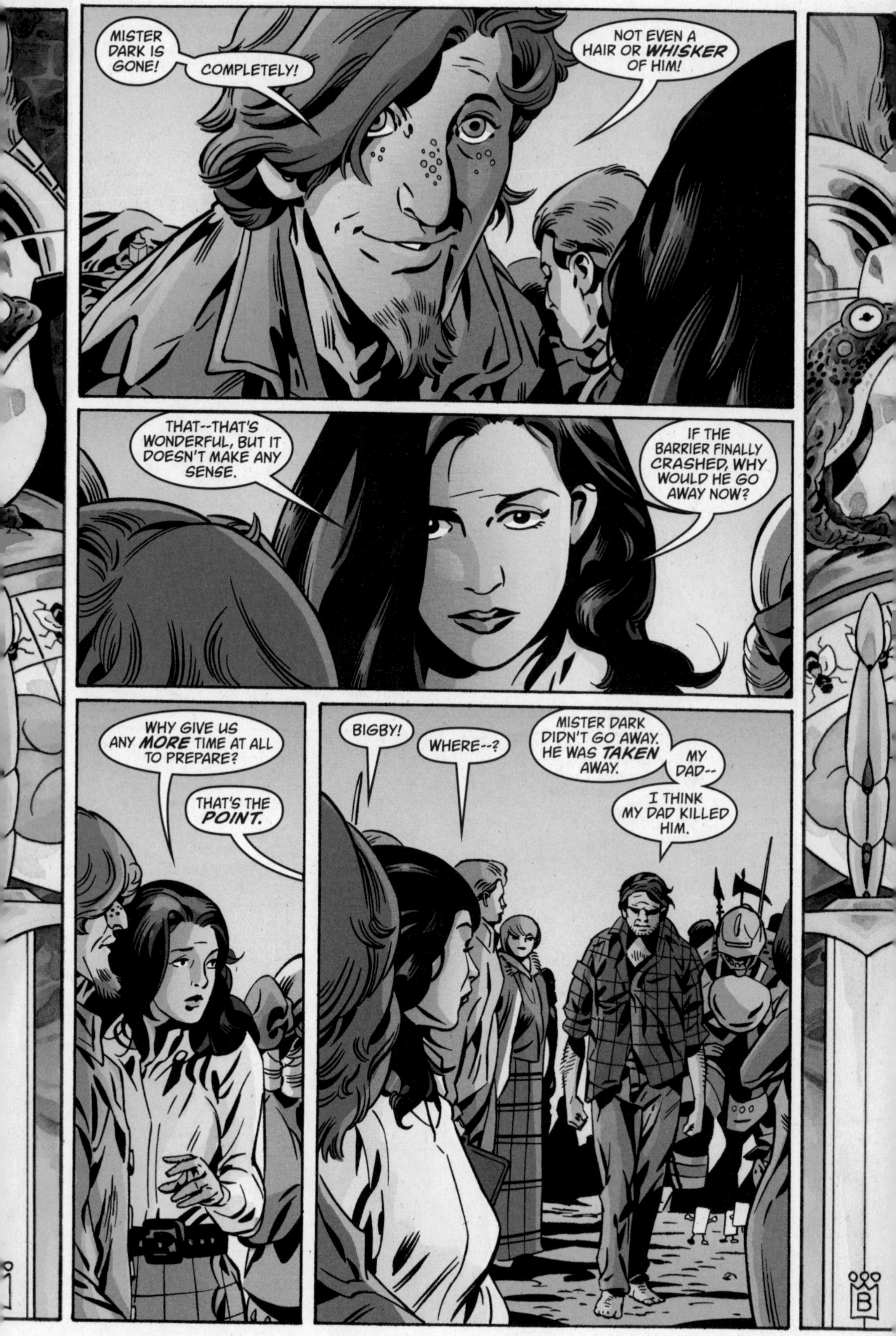
MISTER DARK IS GONE!
COMPLETELY!
NOT EVEN A HAIR OR WHISKER OF HIM!
THAT--THAT'S WONDERFUL, BUT IT DOESN'T MAKE ANY SENSE.
IF THE BARRIER FINALLY CRASHED, WHY WOULD HE GO AWAY NOW?
WHY GIVE US ANY MORE TIME AT ALL TO PREPARE?
THAT'S THE POINT.
BIGBY!
WHERE--?
MISTER DARK DIDN'T GO AWAY. HE WAS TAKEN AWAY.
MY DAD--
I THINK MY DAD KILLED HIM.

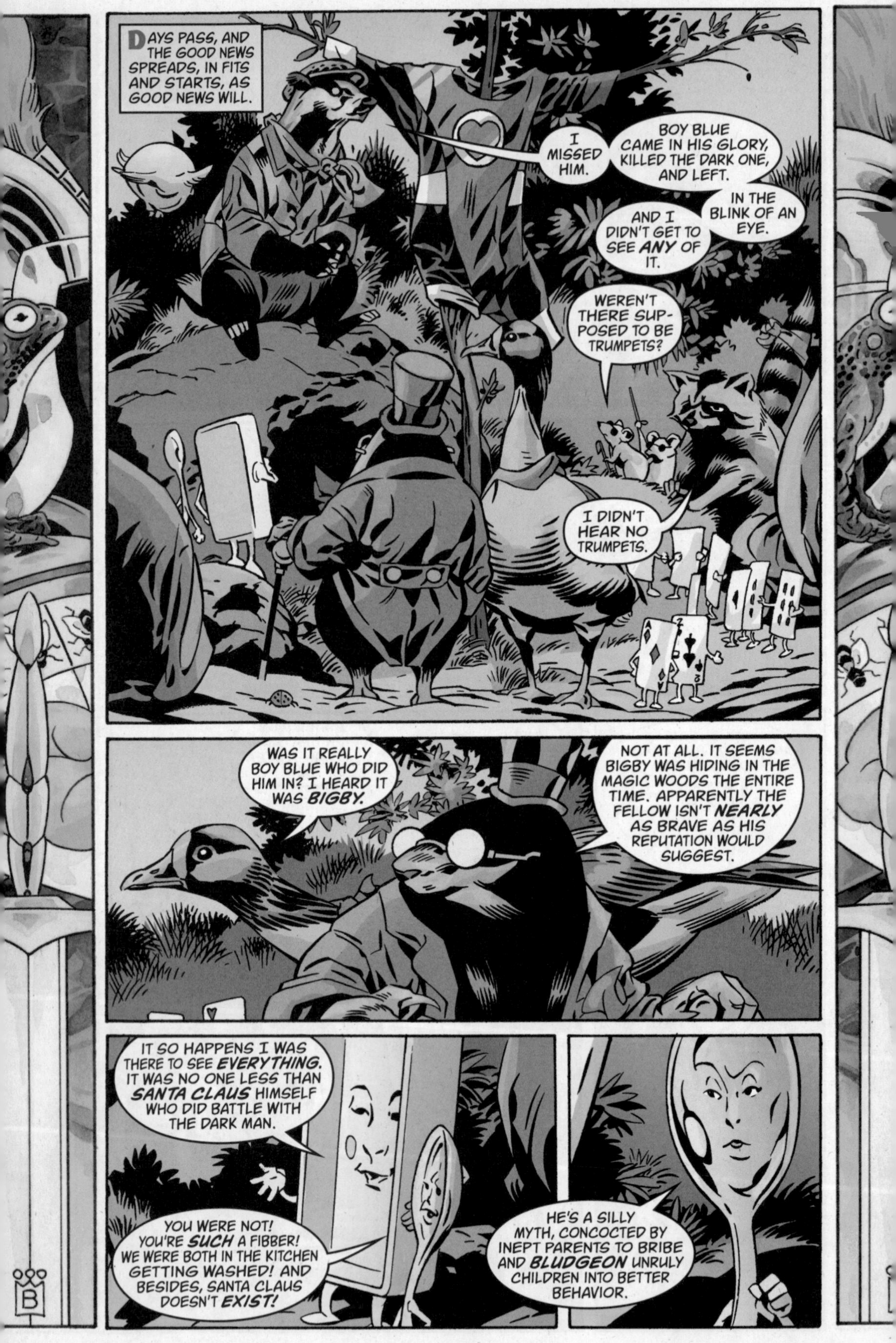
DAYS PASS, AND THE GOOD NEWS SPREADS, IN FITS AND STARTS, AS GOOD NEWS WILL.
I MISSED HIM.
BOY BLUE CAME IN HIS GLORY, KILLED THE DARK ONE, AND LEFT.
IN THE BLINK OF AN EYE.
AND I DIDN'T GET TO SEE ANY OF IT.
WEREN'T THERE SUP-POSED TO BE TRUMPETS?
I DIDN'T HEAR NO TRUMPETS.
WAS IT REALLY BOY BLUE WHO DID HIM IN? I HEARD IT WAS BIGBY.
NOT AT ALL. IT SEEMS BIGBY WAS HIDING IN THE MAGIC WOODS THE ENTIRE TIME. APPARENTLY THE FELLOW ISN'T NEARLY AS BRAVE AS HIS REPUTATION WOULD SUGGEST.
IT SO HAPPENS I WAS THERE TO SEE EVERYTHING. IT WAS NO ONE LESS THAN SANTA CLAUS HIMSELF WHO DID BATTLE WITH THE DARK MAN.
YOU WERE NOT! YOU'RE SUCH A FIBBER! WE WERE BOTH IN THE KITCHEN GETTING WASHED! AND BESIDES, SANTA CLAUS DOESN'T EXIST!
HE'S A SILLY MYTH, CONCOCTED BY INEPT PARENTS TO BRIBE AND BLUDGEON UNRULY CHILDREN INTO BETTER BEHAVIOR.

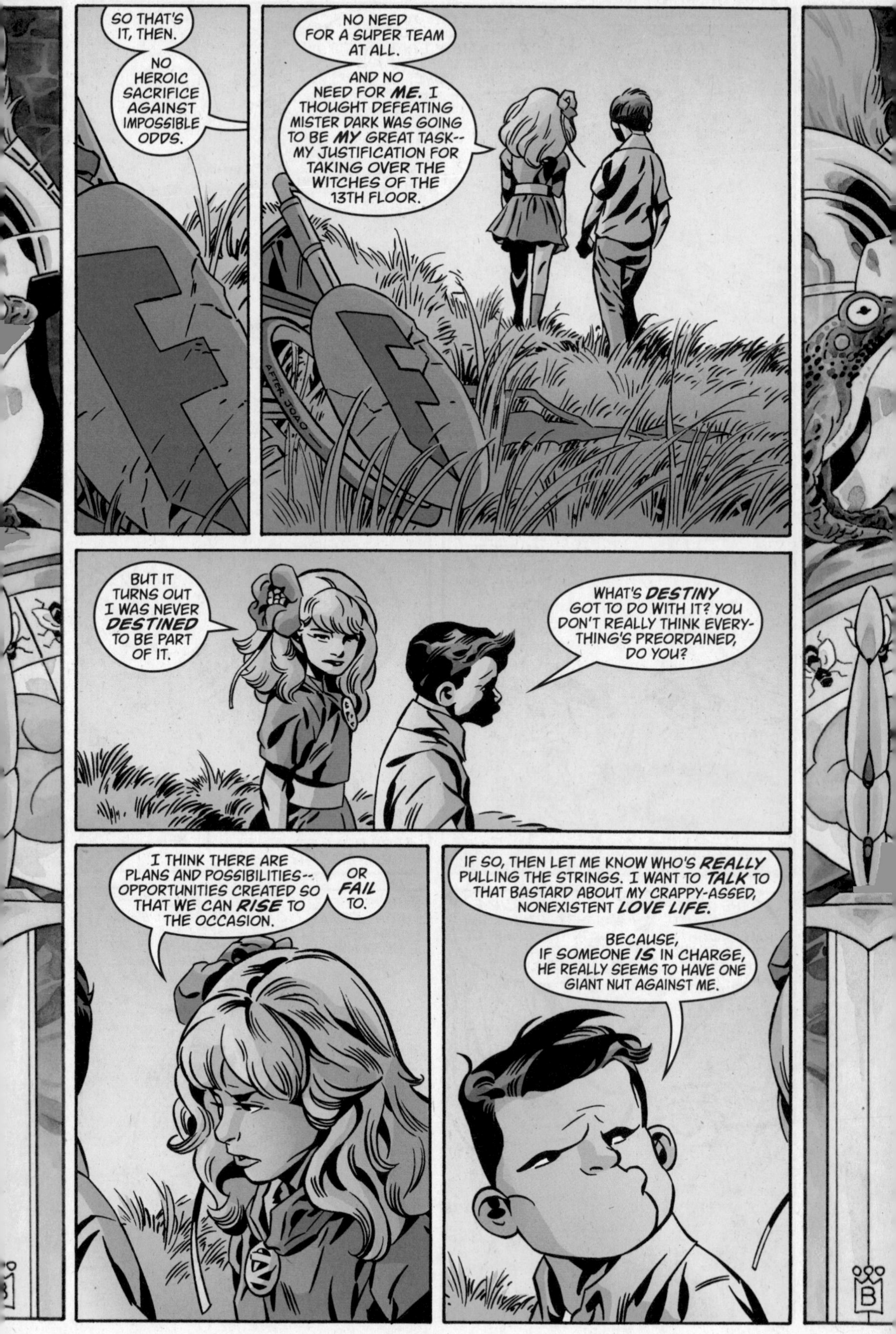
SO THAT'S IT, THEN.
NO HEROIC SACRIFICE AGAINST IMPOSSIBLE ODDS.
NO NEED FOR A SUPER TEAM AT ALL.
AND NO NEED FOR ME. I THOUGHT DEFEATING MISTER DARK WAS GOING TO BE MY GREAT TASK-- MY JUSTIFICATION FOR TAKING OVER THE WITCHES OF THE 13TH FLOOR.
AFTER JOAO
BUT IT TURNS OUT I WAS NEVER DESTINED TO BE PART OF IT.
WHAT'S DESTINY GOT TO DO WITH IT? YOU DON'T REALLY THINK EVERYTHING'S PREORDAINED, DO YOU?
I THINK THERE ARE PLANS AND POSSIBILITIES-- OPPORTUNITIES CREATED SO THAT WE CAN RISE TO THE OCCASION.
OR FAIL TO.
IF SO, THEN LET ME KNOW WHO'S REALLY PULLING THE STRINGS. I WANT TO TALK TO THAT BASTARD ABOUT MY CRAPPY-ASSED, NONEXISTENT LOVE LIFE.
BECAUSE, IF SOMEONE IS IN CHARGE, HE REALLY SEEMS TO HAVE ONE GIANT NUT AGAINST ME.

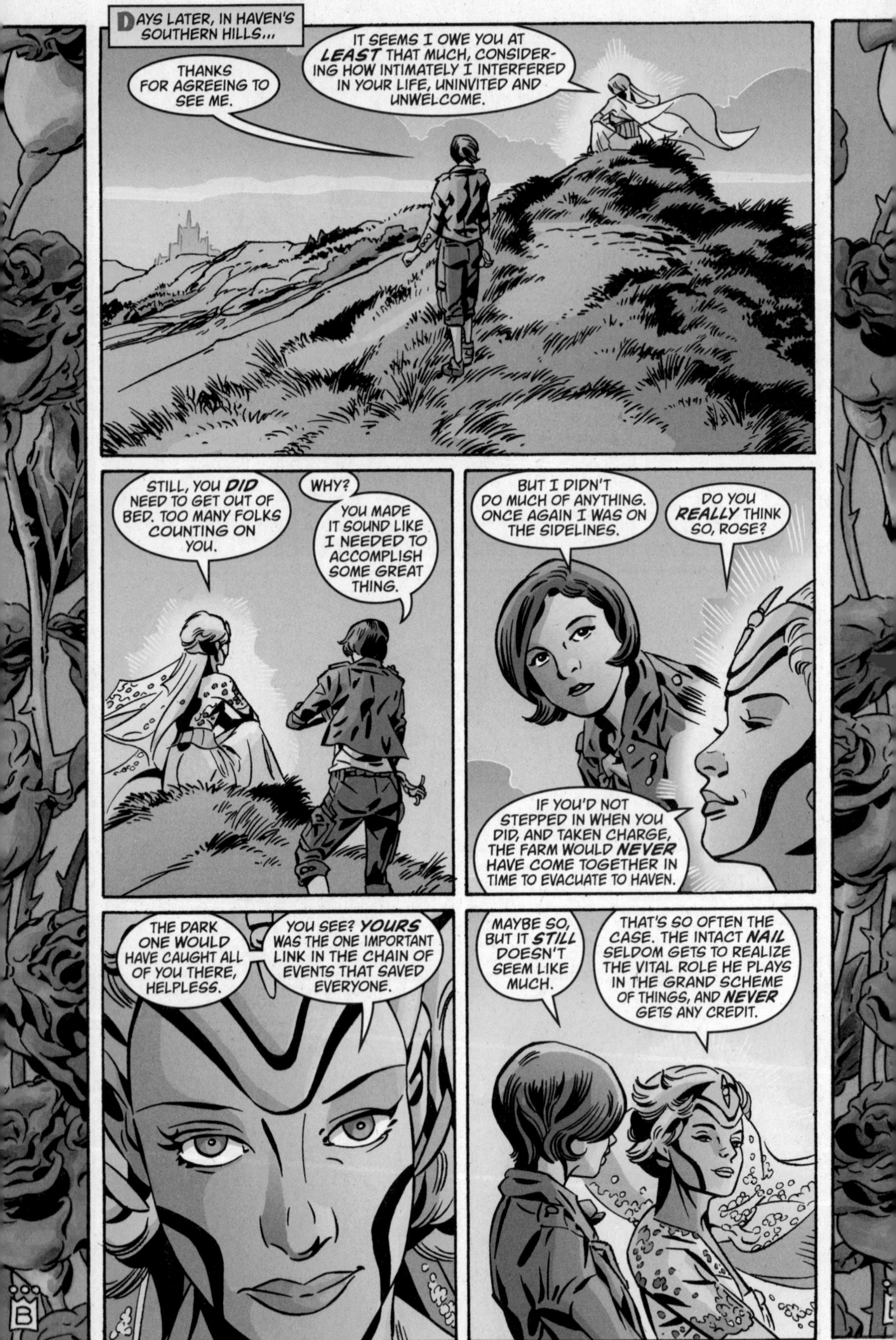
DAYS LATER, IN HAVEN'S SOUTHERN HILLS...
THANKS FOR AGREEING TO SEE ME.
IT SEEMS I OWE YOU AT LEAST THAT MUCH, CONSIDER-ING HOW INTIMATELY I INTERFERED IN YOUR LIFE, UNINVITED AND UNWELCOME.
STILL, YOU DID NEED TO GET OUT OF BED. TOO MANY FOLKS COUNTING ON YOU.
WHY?
YOU MADE IT SOUND LIKE I NEEDED TO ACCOMPLISH SOME GREAT THING.
BUT I DIDN'T DO MUCH OF ANYTHING. ONCE AGAIN I WAS ON THE SIDELINES.
DO YOU REALLY THINK SO, ROSE?
IF YOU'D NOT STEPPED IN WHEN YOU DID, AND TAKEN CHARGE, THE FARM WOULD NEVER HAVE COME TOGETHER IN TIME TO EVACUATE TO HAVEN.
THE DARK ONE WOULD HAVE CAUGHT ALL OF YOU THERE, HELPLESS.
YOU SEE? YOURS WAS THE ONE IMPORTANT LINK IN THE CHAIN OF EVENTS THAT SAVED EVERYONE.
MAYBE SO, BUT IT STILL DOESN'T SEEM LIKE MUCH.
THAT'S SO OFTEN THE CASE. THE INTACT NAIL SELDOM GETS TO REALIZE THE VITAL ROLE HE PLAYS IN THE GRAND SCHEME OF THINGS, AND NEVER GETS ANY CREDIT.

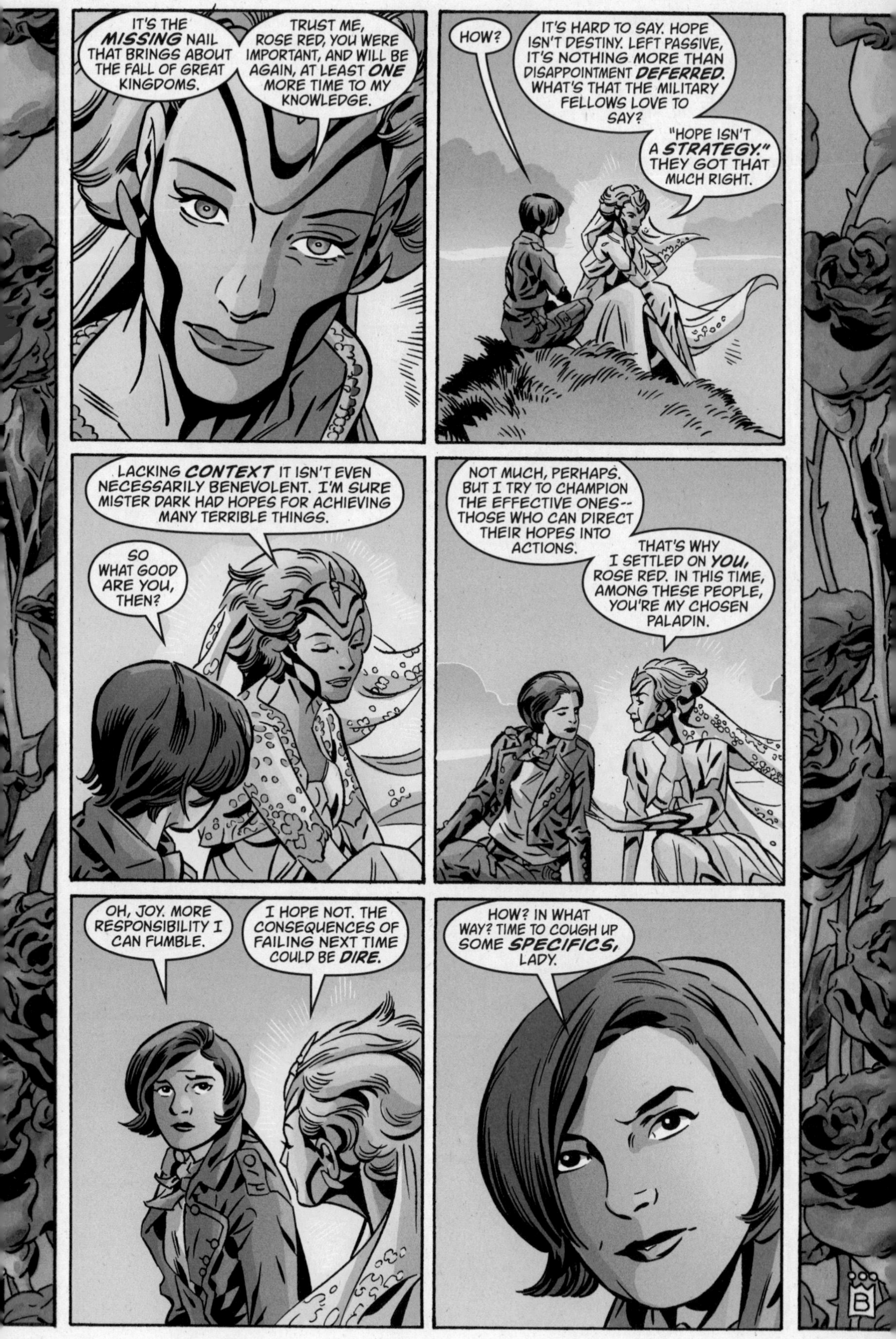
IT'S THE MISSING NAIL THAT BRINGS ABOUT THE FALL OF GREAT KINGDOMS.
TRUST ME, ROSE RED, YOU WERE IMPORTANT, AND WILL BE AGAIN, AT LEAST ONE MORE TIME TO MY KNOWLEDGE.
HOW?
IT'S HARD TO SAY. HOPE ISN'T DESTINY. LEFT PASSIVE, IT'S NOTHING MORE THAN DISAPPOINTMENT DEFERRED. WHAT'S THAT THE MILITARY FELLOWS LOVE TO SAY?
"HOPE ISN'T A STRATEGY." THEY GOT THAT MUCH RIGHT.
LACKING CONTEXT IT ISN'T EVEN NECESSARILY BENEVOLENT. I'M SURE MISTER DARK HAD HOPES FOR ACHIEVING MANY TERRIBLE THINGS.
SO WHAT GOOD ARE YOU, THEN?
NOT MUCH, PERHAPS. BUT I TRY TO CHAMPION THE EFFECTIVE ONES-- THOSE WHO CAN DIRECT THEIR HOPES INTO ACTIONS.
THAT'S WHY I SETTLED ON YOU, ROSE RED. IN THIS TIME, AMONG THESE PEOPLE, YOU'RE MY CHOSEN PALADIN.
OH, JOY. MORE RESPONSIBILITY I CAN FUMBLE.
I HOPE NOT. THE CONSEQUENCES OF FAILING NEXT TIME COULD BE DIRE.
HOW? IN WHAT WAY? TIME TO COUGH UP SOME SPECIFICS, LADY.

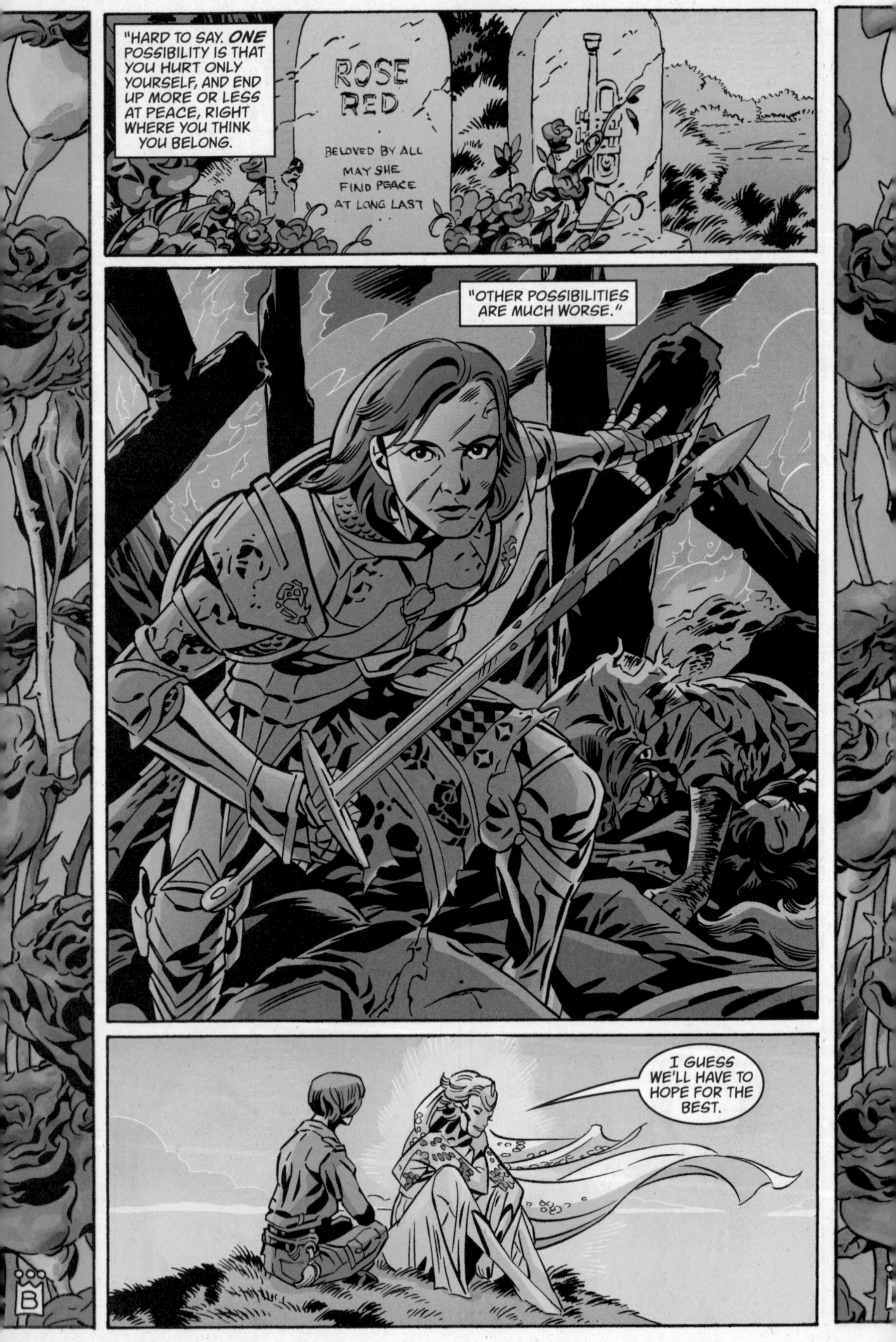
"HARD TO SAY. ONE POSSIBILITY IS THAT YOU HURT ONLY YOURSELF, AND END UP MORE OR LESS AT PEACE, RIGHT WHERE YOU THINK YOU BELONG.
ROSE RED
BELOVED BY ALL MAY SHE FIND PEACE AT LONG LAST
"OTHER POSSIBILITIES ARE MUCH WORSE."
I GUESS WE'LL HAVE TO HOPE FOR THE BEST.

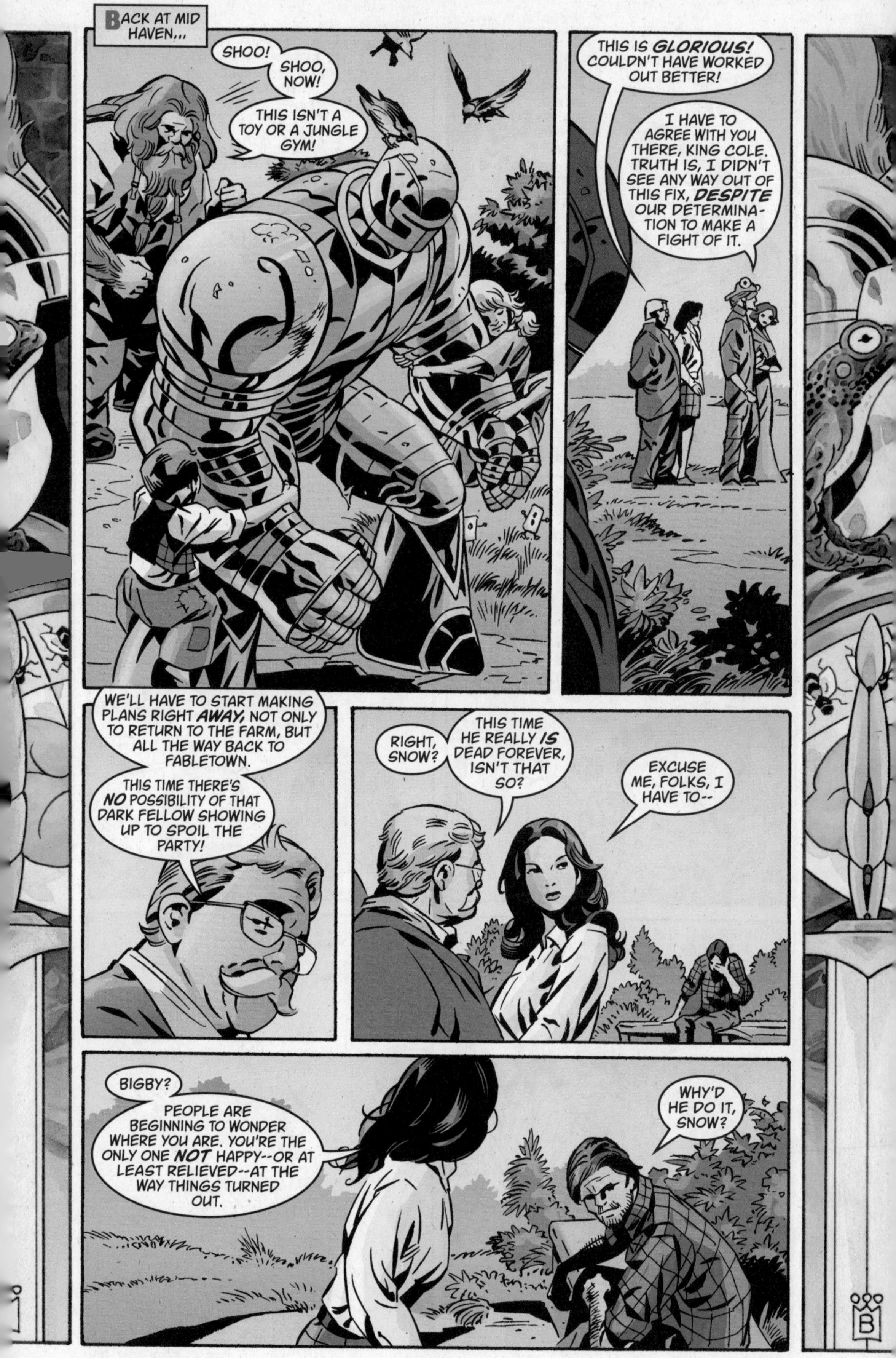
BACK AT MID HAVEN...
SHOO!
SHOO, NOW!
THIS ISN'T A TOY OR A JUNGLE GYM!
THIS IS GLORIOUS! COULDN'T HAVE WORKED OUT BETTER!
I HAVE TO AGREE WITH YOU THERE, KING COLE. TRUTH IS, I DIDN'T SEE ANY WAY OUT OF THIS FIX, DESPITE OUR DETERMINATION TO MAKE A FIGHT OF IT.
WE'LL HAVE TO START MAKING PLANS RIGHT AWAY, NOT ONLY TO RETURN TO THE FARM, BUT ALL THE WAY BACK TO FABLETOWN.
THIS TIME THERE'S NO POSSIBILITY OF THAT DARK FELLOW SHOWING UP TO SPOIL THE PARTY!
THIS TIME HE REALLY IS DEAD FOREVER, ISN'T THAT SO?
RIGHT, SNOW?
EXCUSE ME, FOLKS, I HAVE TO--
BIGBY?
PEOPLE ARE BEGINNING TO WONDER WHERE YOU ARE. YOU'RE THE ONLY ONE NOT HAPPY--OR AT LEAST RELIEVED--AT THE WAY THINGS TURNED OUT.
WHY'D HE DO IT, SNOW?

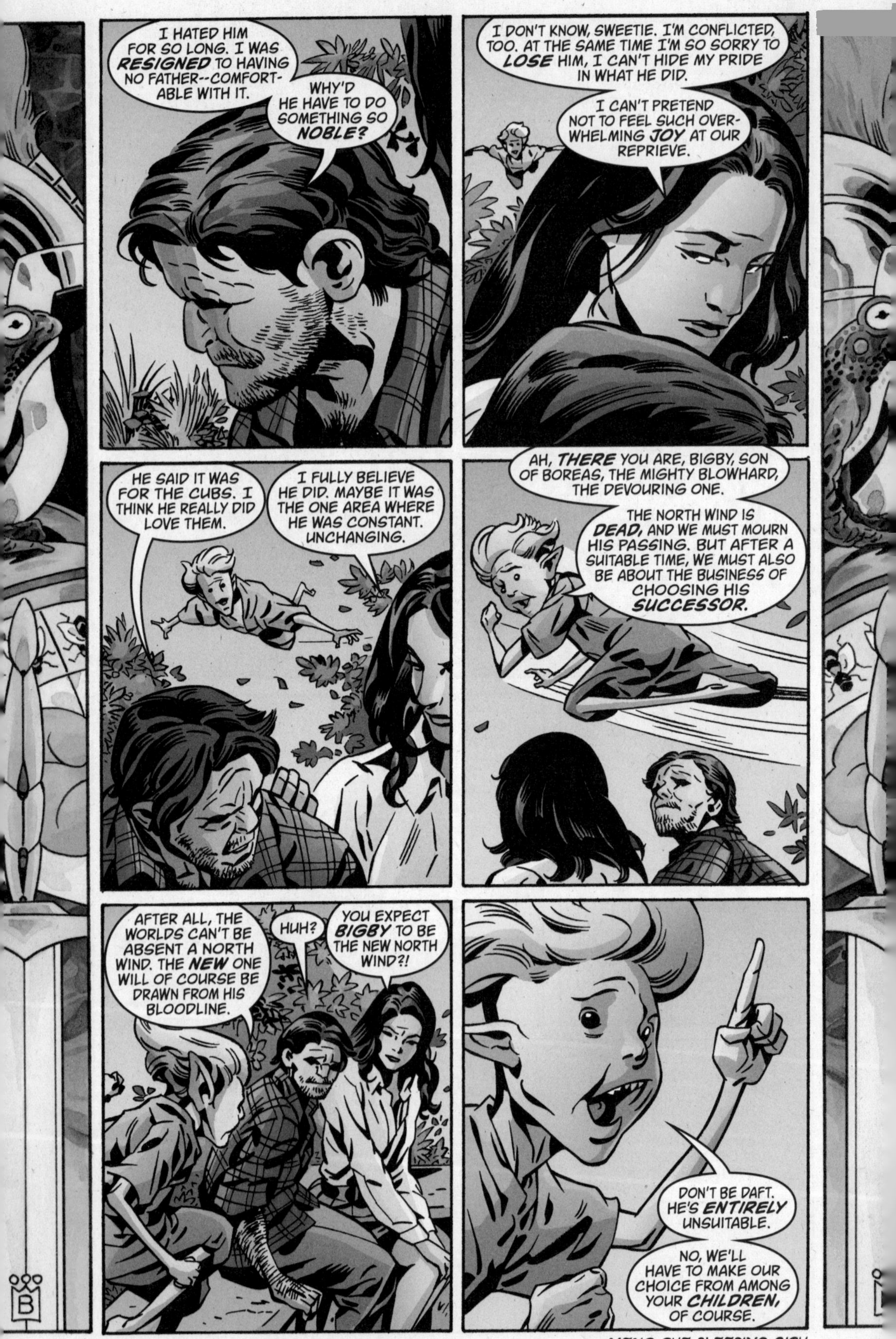
I HATED HIM FOR SO LONG. I WAS RESIGNED TO HAVING NO FATHER--COMFORTABLE WITH IT.
WHY'D HE HAVE TO DO SOMETHING SO NOBLE?
I DON'T KNOW, SWEETIE. I'M CONFLICTED, TOO. AT THE SAME TIME I'M SO SORRY TO LOSE HIM, I CAN'T HIDE MY PRIDE IN WHAT HE DID.
I CAN'T PRETEND NOT TO FEEL SUCH OVERWHELMING JOY AT OUR REPRIEVE.
HE SAID IT WAS FOR THE CUBS. I THINK HE REALLY DID LOVE THEM.
I FULLY BELIEVE HE DID. MAYBE IT WAS THE ONE AREA WHERE HE WAS CONSTANT. UNCHANGING.
AH, THERE YOU ARE, BIGBY, SON OF BOREAS, THE MIGHTY BLOWHARD, THE DEVOURING ONE.
THE NORTH WIND IS DEAD, AND WE MUST MOURN HIS PASSING. BUT AFTER A SUITABLE TIME, WE MUST ALSO BE ABOUT THE BUSINESS OF CHOOSING HIS SUCCESSOR.
AFTER ALL, THE WORLDS CAN'T BE ABSENT A NORTH WIND. THE NEW ONE WILL OF COURSE BE DRAWN FROM HIS BLOODLINE.
HUH?
YOU EXPECT BIGBY TO BE THE NEW NORTH WIND?!
DON'T BE DAFT. HE'S ENTIRELY UNSUITABLE.
NO, WE'LL HAVE TO MAKE OUR CHOICE FROM AMONG YOUR CHILDREN, OF COURSE.

NEXT: THE SLEEPING CITY

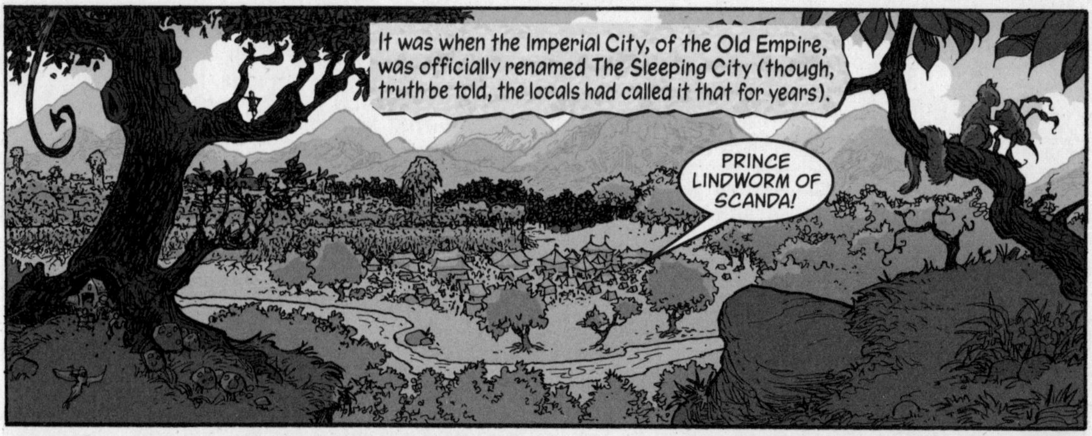
It was when the Imperial City, of the Old Empire, was officially renamed The Sleeping City (though, truth be told, the locals had called it that for years).
PRINCE LINDWORM OF SCANDA!

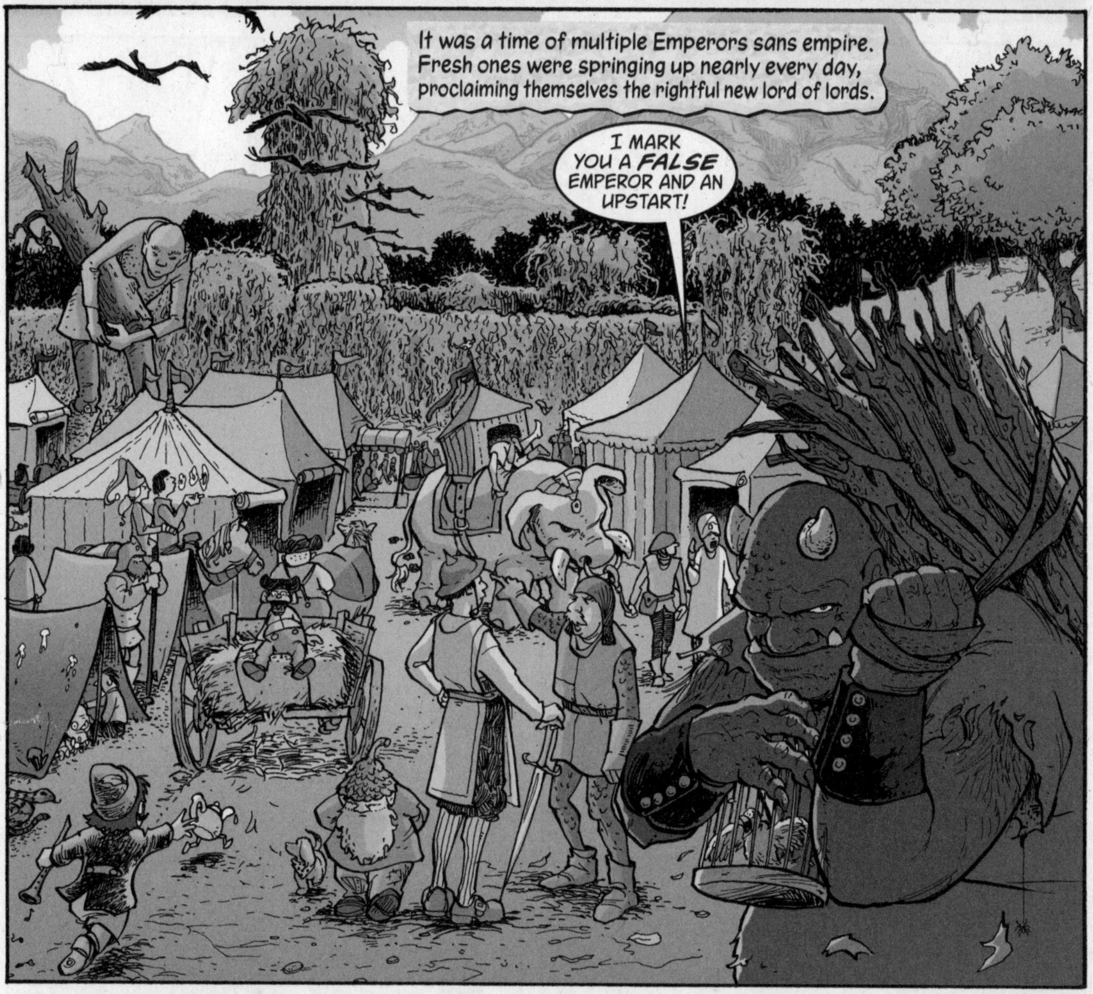
It was a time of multiple Emperors sans empire. Fresh ones were springing up nearly every day, proclaiming themselves the rightful new lord of lords.
I MARK YOU A *FALSE* EMPEROR AND AN UPSTART!

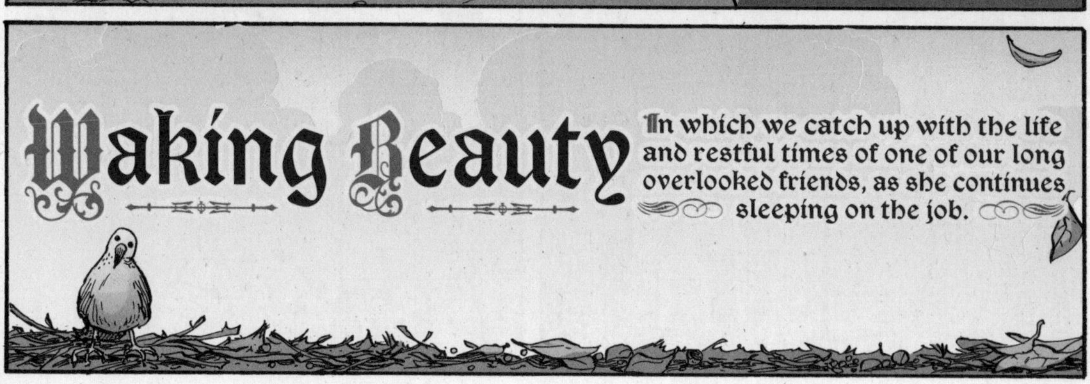
Waking Beauty
In which we catch up with the life and restful times of one of our long overlooked friends, as she continues sleeping on the job.

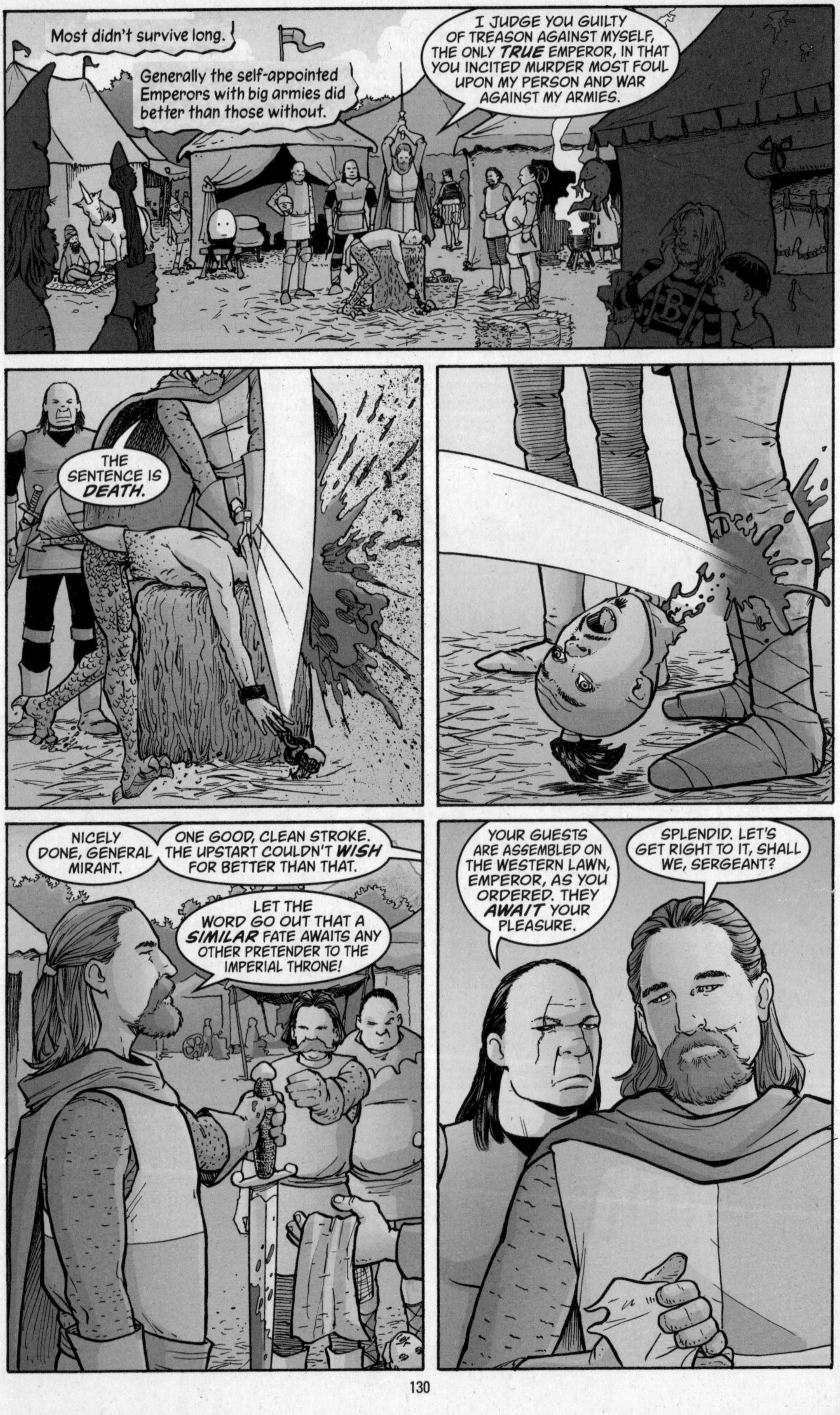
Most didn't survive long.
Generally the self-appointed Emperors with big armies did better than those without.
I JUDGE YOU GUILTY OF TREASON AGAINST MYSELF, THE ONLY TRUE EMPEROR, IN THAT YOU INCITED MURDER MOST FOUL UPON MY PERSON AND WAR AGAINST MY ARMIES.
THE SENTENCE IS DEATH.
NICELY DONE, GENERAL MIRANT.
ONE GOOD, CLEAN STROKE. THE UPSTART COULDN'T WISH FOR BETTER THAN THAT.
LET THE WORD GO OUT THAT A SIMILAR FATE AWAITS ANY OTHER PRETENDER TO THE IMPERIAL THRONE!
YOUR GUESTS ARE ASSEMBLED ON THE WESTERN LAWN, EMPEROR, AS YOU ORDERED. THEY AWAIT YOUR PLEASURE.
SPLENDID. LET'S GET RIGHT TO IT, SHALL WE, SERGEANT?

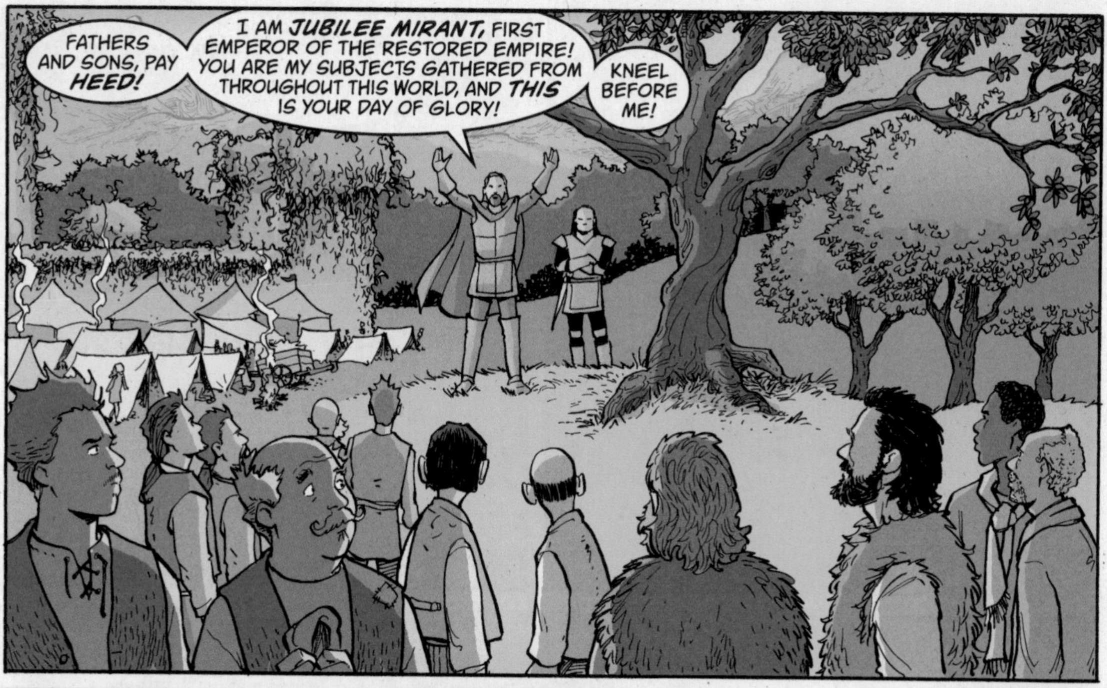
FATHERS AND SONS, PAY HEED!
I AM JUBILEE MIRANT, FIRST EMPEROR OF THE RESTORED EMPIRE! YOU ARE MY SUBJECTS GATHERED FROM THROUGHOUT THIS WORLD, AND THIS IS YOUR DAY OF GLORY!
KNEEL BEFORE ME!

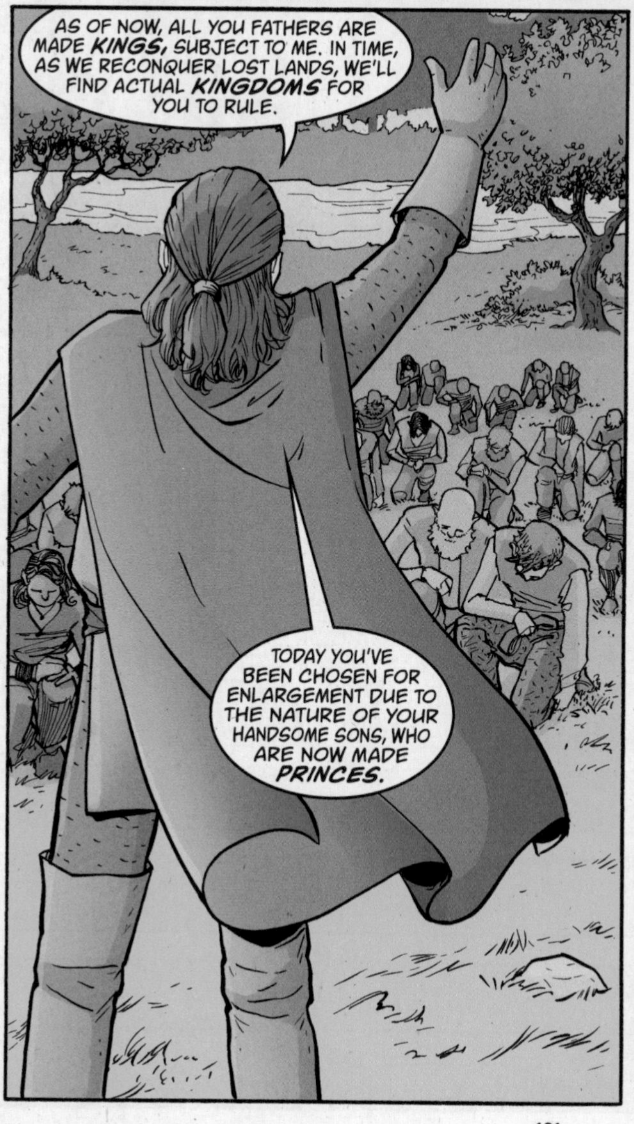
AS OF NOW, ALL YOU FATHERS ARE MADE KINGS, SUBJECT TO ME. IN TIME, AS WE RECONQUER LOST LANDS, WE'LL FIND ACTUAL KINGDOMS FOR YOU TO RULE.
TODAY YOU'VE BEEN CHOSEN FOR ENLARGEMENT DUE TO THE NATURE OF YOUR HANDSOME SONS, WHO ARE NOW MADE PRINCES.

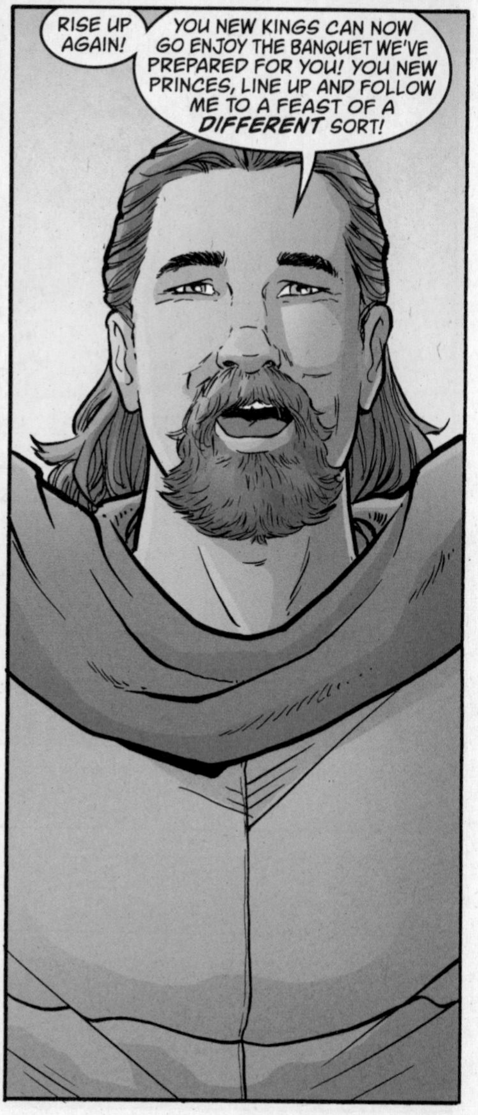
RISE UP AGAIN!
YOU NEW KINGS CAN NOW GO ENJOY THE BANQUET WE'VE PREPARED FOR YOU! YOU NEW PRINCES, LINE UP AND FOLLOW ME TO A FEAST OF A DIFFERENT SORT!

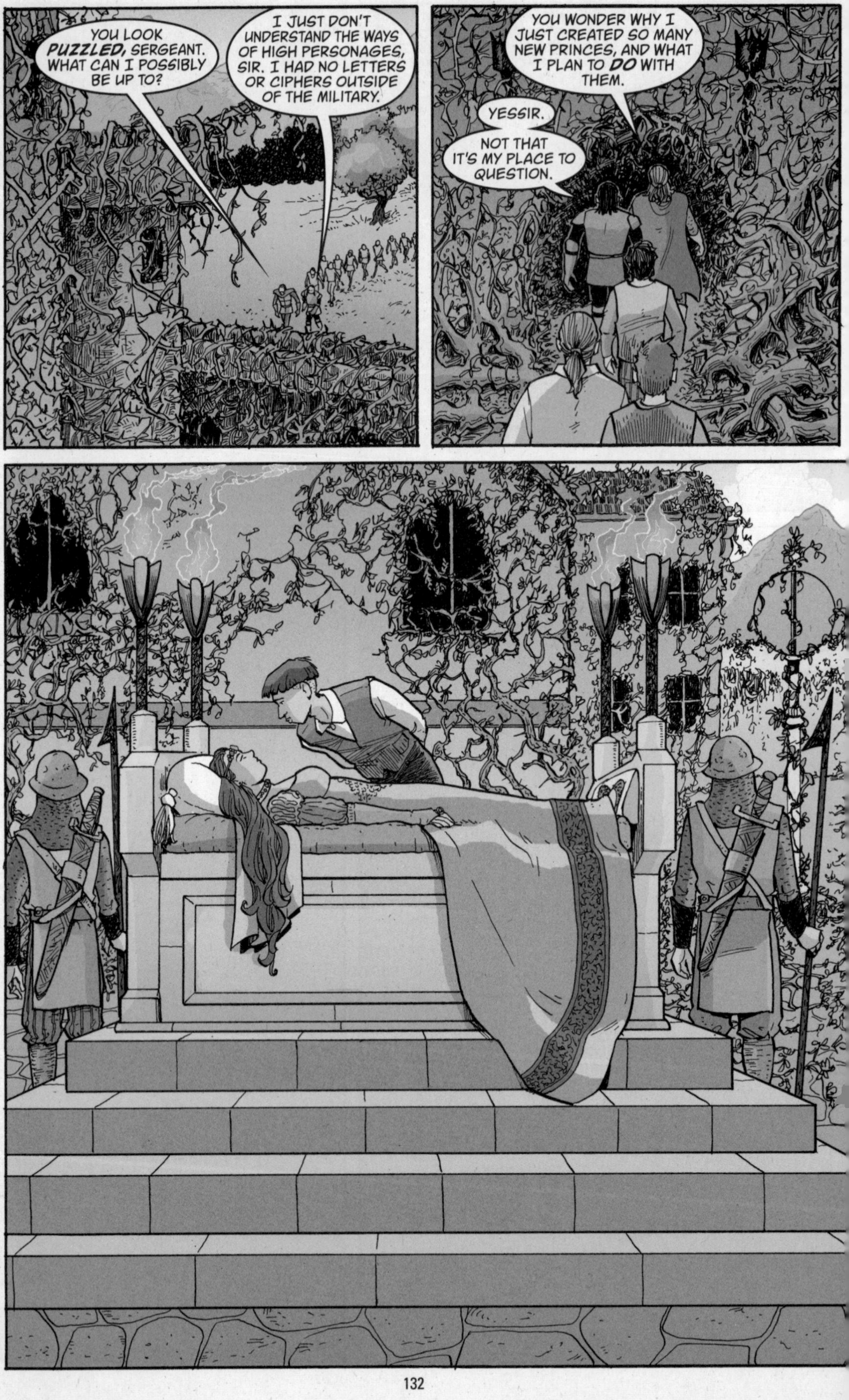
YOU LOOK PUZZLED, SERGEANT. WHAT CAN I POSSIBLY BE UP TO?
I JUST DON'T UNDERSTAND THE WAYS OF HIGH PERSONAGES, SIR. I HAD NO LETTERS OR CIPHERS OUTSIDE OF THE MILITARY.
YOU WONDER WHY I JUST CREATED SO MANY NEW PRINCES, AND WHAT I PLAN TO DO WITH THEM.
YESSIR.
NOT THAT IT'S MY PLACE TO QUESTION.

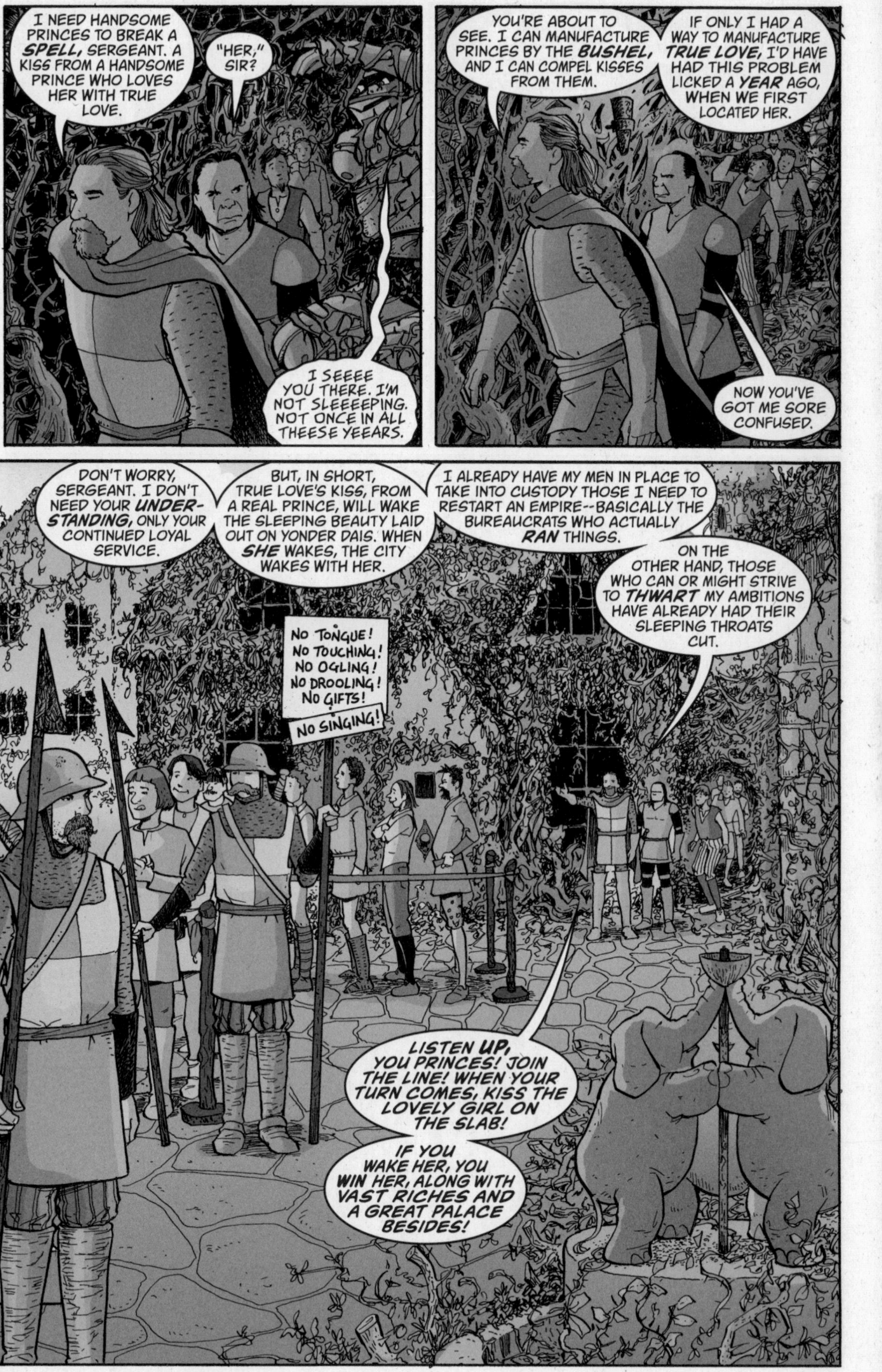

I NEED HANDSOME PRINCES TO BREAK A **SPELL,** SERGEANT. A KISS FROM A HANDSOME PRINCE WHO LOVES HER WITH TRUE LOVE.
"HER," SIR?
I SEEEE YOU THERE. I'M NOT SLEEEEPING. NOT ONCE IN ALL THEESE YEEARS.
YOU'RE ABOUT TO SEE. I CAN MANUFACTURE PRINCES BY THE **BUSHEL,** AND I CAN COMPEL KISSES FROM THEM.
IF ONLY I HAD A WAY TO MANUFACTURE **TRUE LOVE,** I'D HAVE HAD THIS PROBLEM LICKED A **YEAR** AGO, WHEN WE FIRST LOCATED HER.
NOW YOU'VE GOT ME SORE CONFUSED.
DON'T WORRY, SERGEANT. I DON'T NEED YOUR **UNDERSTANDING,** ONLY YOUR CONTINUED LOYAL SERVICE.
BUT, IN SHORT, TRUE LOVE'S KISS, FROM A REAL PRINCE, WILL WAKE THE SLEEPING BEAUTY LAID OUT ON YONDER DAIS. WHEN **SHE** WAKES, THE CITY WAKES WITH HER.
I ALREADY HAVE MY MEN IN PLACE TO TAKE INTO CUSTODY THOSE I NEED TO RESTART AN EMPIRE--BASICALLY THE BUREAUCRATS WHO ACTUALLY **RAN** THINGS.
ON THE OTHER HAND, THOSE WHO CAN OR MIGHT STRIVE TO **THWART** MY AMBITIONS HAVE ALREADY HAD THEIR SLEEPING THROATS CUT.
NO TONGUE! NO TOUCHING! NO OGLING! NO DROOLING! NO GIFTS!
NO SINGING!
LISTEN **UP,** YOU PRINCES! JOIN THE LINE! WHEN YOUR TURN COMES, KISS THE LOVELY GIRL ON THE SLAB!
IF YOU WAKE HER, YOU **WIN** HER, ALONG WITH **VAST RICHES** AND A GREAT PALACE BESIDES!

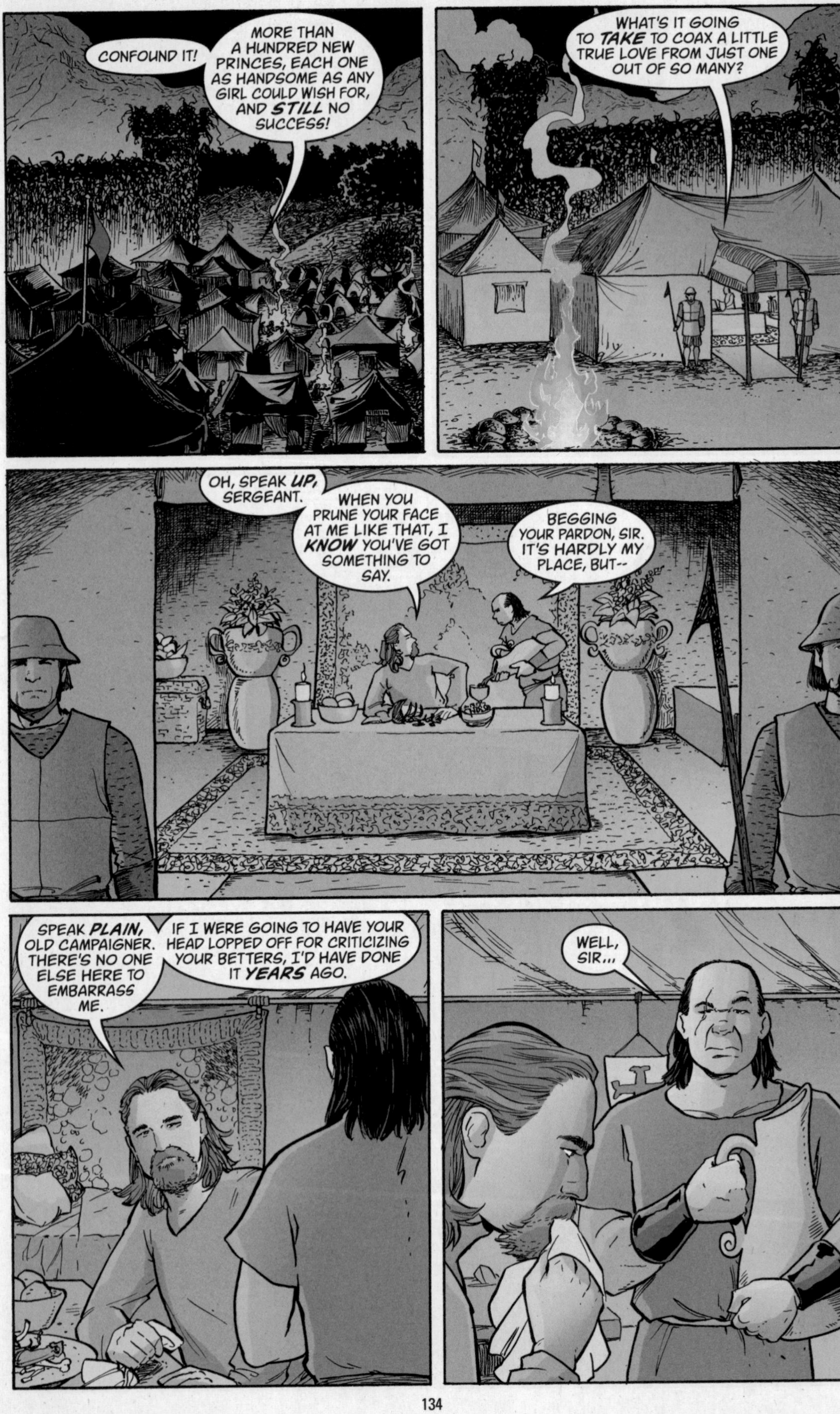
CONFOUND IT!
MORE THAN A HUNDRED NEW PRINCES, EACH ONE AS HANDSOME AS ANY GIRL COULD WISH FOR, AND STILL NO SUCCESS!
WHAT'S IT GOING TO TAKE TO COAX A LITTLE TRUE LOVE FROM JUST ONE OUT OF SO MANY?
OH, SPEAK UP, SERGEANT.
WHEN YOU PRUNE YOUR FACE AT ME LIKE THAT, I KNOW YOU'VE GOT SOMETHING TO SAY.
BEGGING YOUR PARDON, SIR. IT'S HARDLY MY PLACE, BUT--
SPEAK PLAIN, OLD CAMPAIGNER. THERE'S NO ONE ELSE HERE TO EMBARRASS ME.
IF I WERE GOING TO HAVE YOUR HEAD LOPPED OFF FOR CRITICIZING YOUR BETTERS, I'D HAVE DONE IT YEARS AGO.
WELL, SIR...

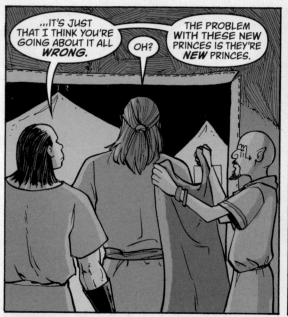

...IT'S JUST THAT I THINK YOU'RE GOING ABOUT IT ALL **WRONG.**

OH?

THE PROBLEM WITH THESE NEW PRINCES IS THEY'RE *NEW* PRINCES.

THEY WON'T BE THINKING ABOUT LOVE AND MARRIAGE AND SUCH-- NOT ON THE SAME DAY THEY'VE BEEN SO ENLARGED.

I'D SUSPECT INSTEAD THAT THEIR MINDS ARE ALL AWHIRL WITH THE POMP AND *ADVENTURE* OF THEIR SUDDENLY TRANSFORMED LIVES.

I DON'T KNOW ABOUT THE HIGH AFFAIRS OF KINGS AND EMPIRES, BUT I KNOW THE WAYS OF ORDINARY MEN. I'VE SPENT A LIFETIME TURNING BOYS INTO SOLDIERS.

Y'SEE, SIR, I THINK YOU WERE WRONG TODAY. I THINK YOU *CAN* MANUFACTURE TRUE LOVE--OR AT LEAST DRUM IT INTO THESE FELLERS.

LET ME TAKE OVER THEIR TRAINING. I'LL ROUST THEM EVERY MORNING BEFORE FIRST SUN, WORK THEM ALL DAY, AND RETURN THEM *EXHAUSTED* TO THEIR COTS EACH NIGHT.

AND I'LL ISOLATE THEM FROM THE FAIRER SEX.

NEVER SO MUCH AS A LOCAL MILKMAID WILL THEY SEE.

THEN, IN A FEW WEEKS, WE'LL START BEDDING THEM DOWN IN THE CITY COURTYARD, IN *SIGHT* OF THE SLEEPING BEAUTY.

BUT, FROM NOW ON, IT'S STRICTLY *LOOK* BUT DON'T TOUCH.

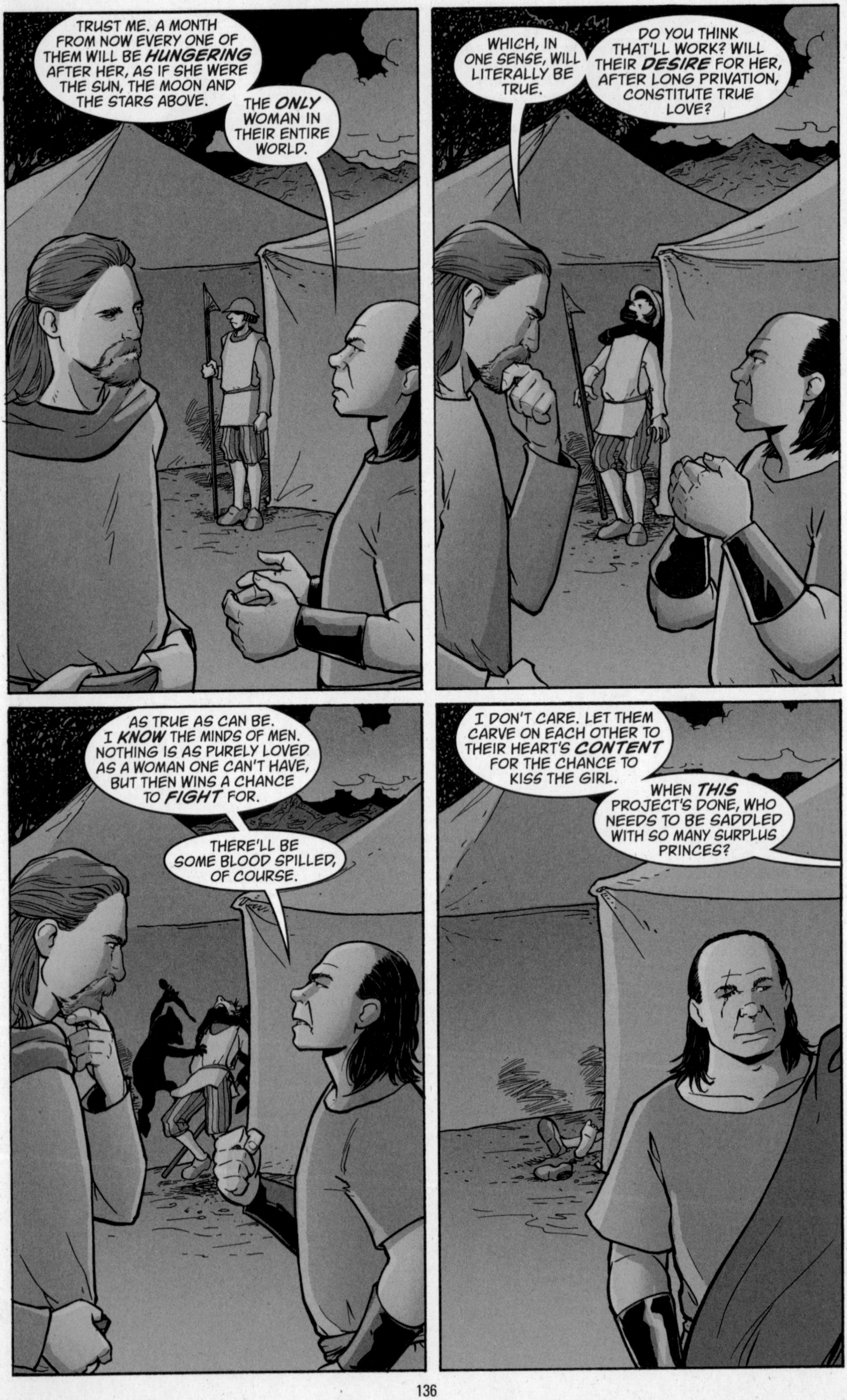

TRUST ME. A MONTH FROM NOW EVERY ONE OF THEM WILL BE *HUNGERING* AFTER HER, AS IF SHE WERE THE SUN, THE MOON AND THE STARS ABOVE.
THE *ONLY* WOMAN IN THEIR ENTIRE WORLD.
WHICH, IN ONE SENSE, WILL LITERALLY BE TRUE.
DO YOU THINK THAT'LL WORK? WILL THEIR *DESIRE* FOR HER, AFTER LONG PRIVATION, CONSTITUTE TRUE LOVE?
AS TRUE AS CAN BE. I *KNOW* THE MINDS OF MEN. NOTHING IS AS PURELY LOVED AS A WOMAN ONE CAN'T HAVE, BUT THEN WINS A CHANCE TO *FIGHT* FOR.
THERE'LL BE SOME BLOOD SPILLED, OF COURSE.
I DON'T CARE. LET THEM CARVE ON EACH OTHER TO THEIR HEART'S *CONTENT* FOR THE CHANCE TO KISS THE GIRL.
WHEN *THIS* PROJECT'S DONE, WHO NEEDS TO BE SADDLED WITH SO MANY SURPLUS PRINCES?

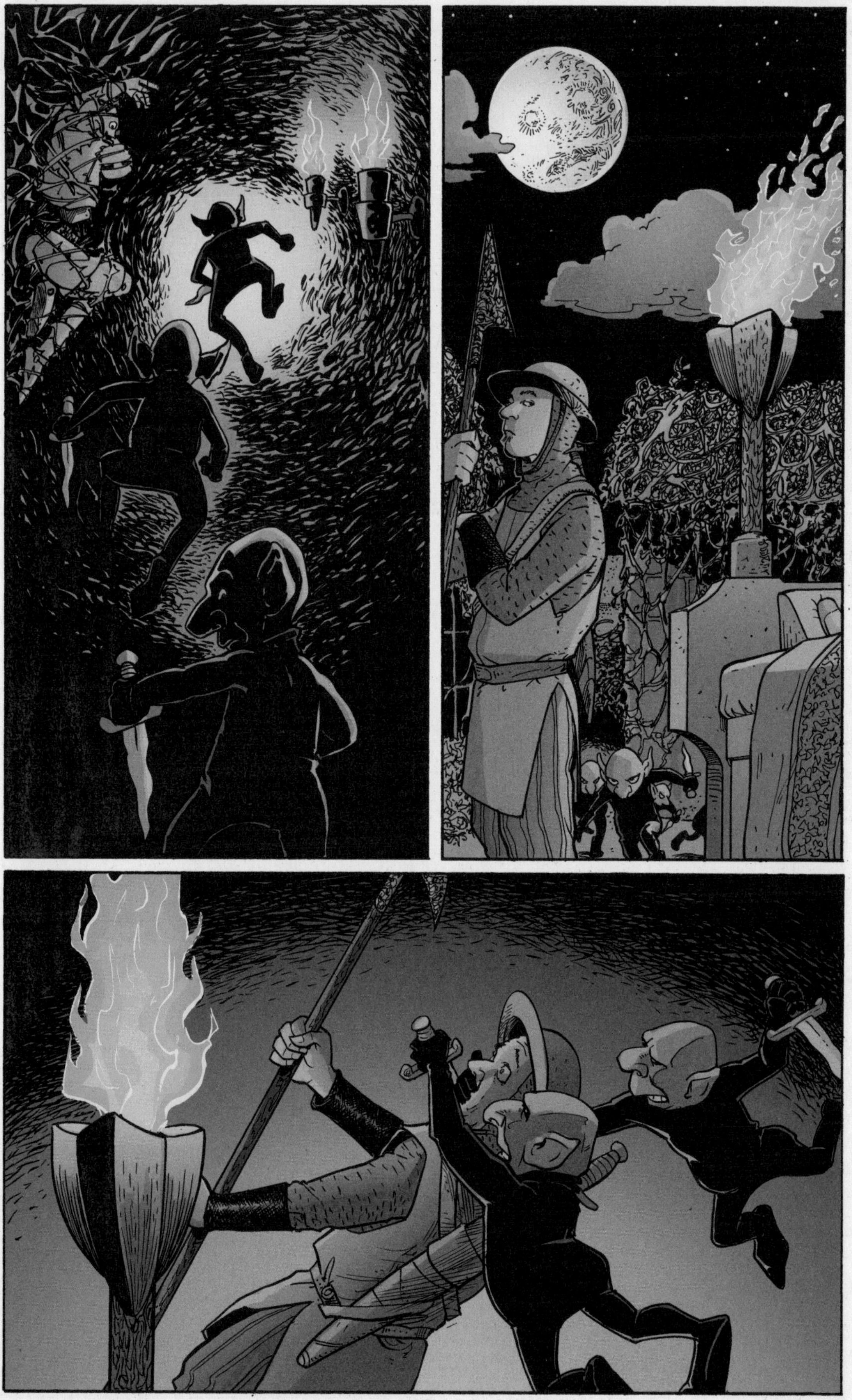

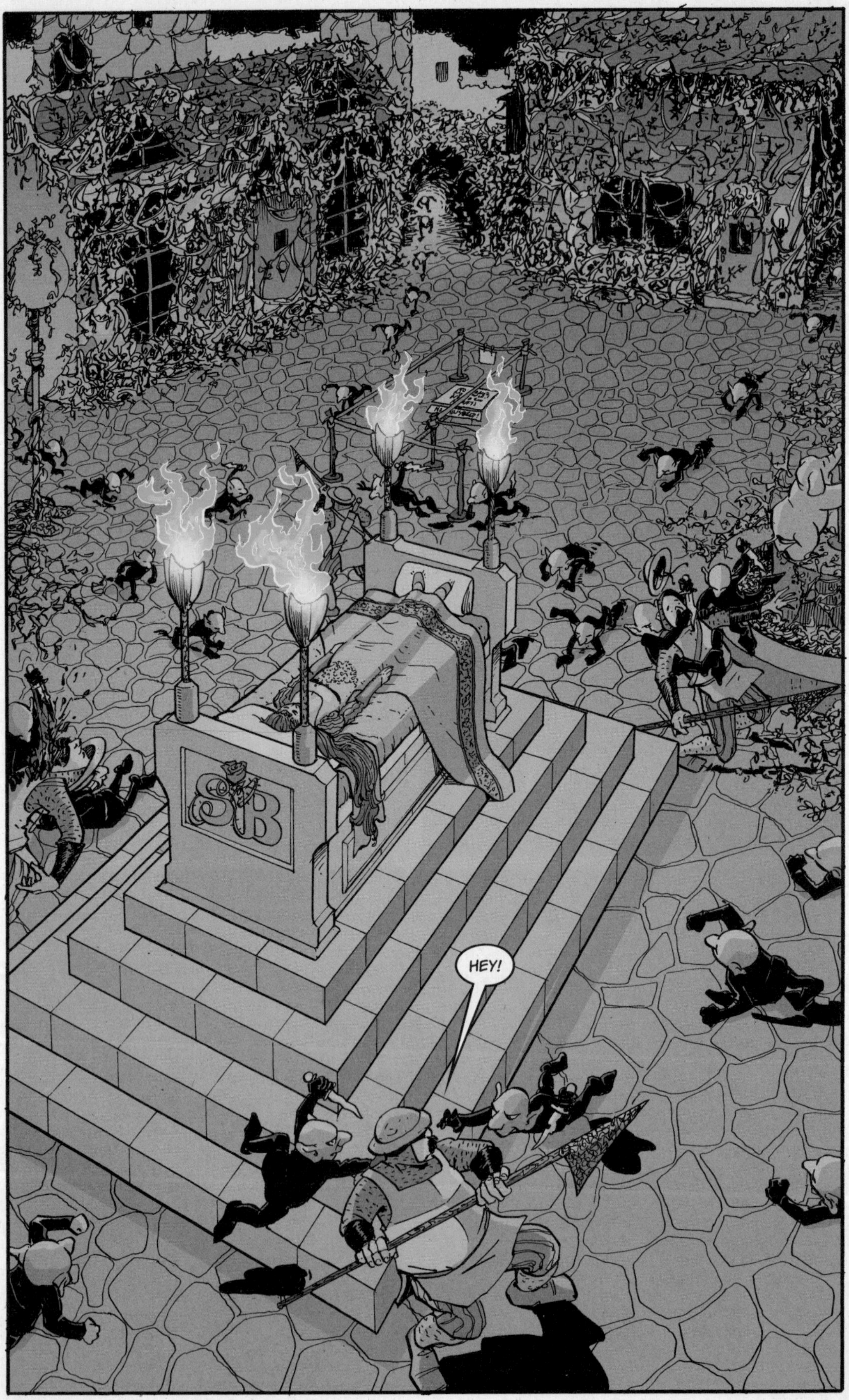
HEY!

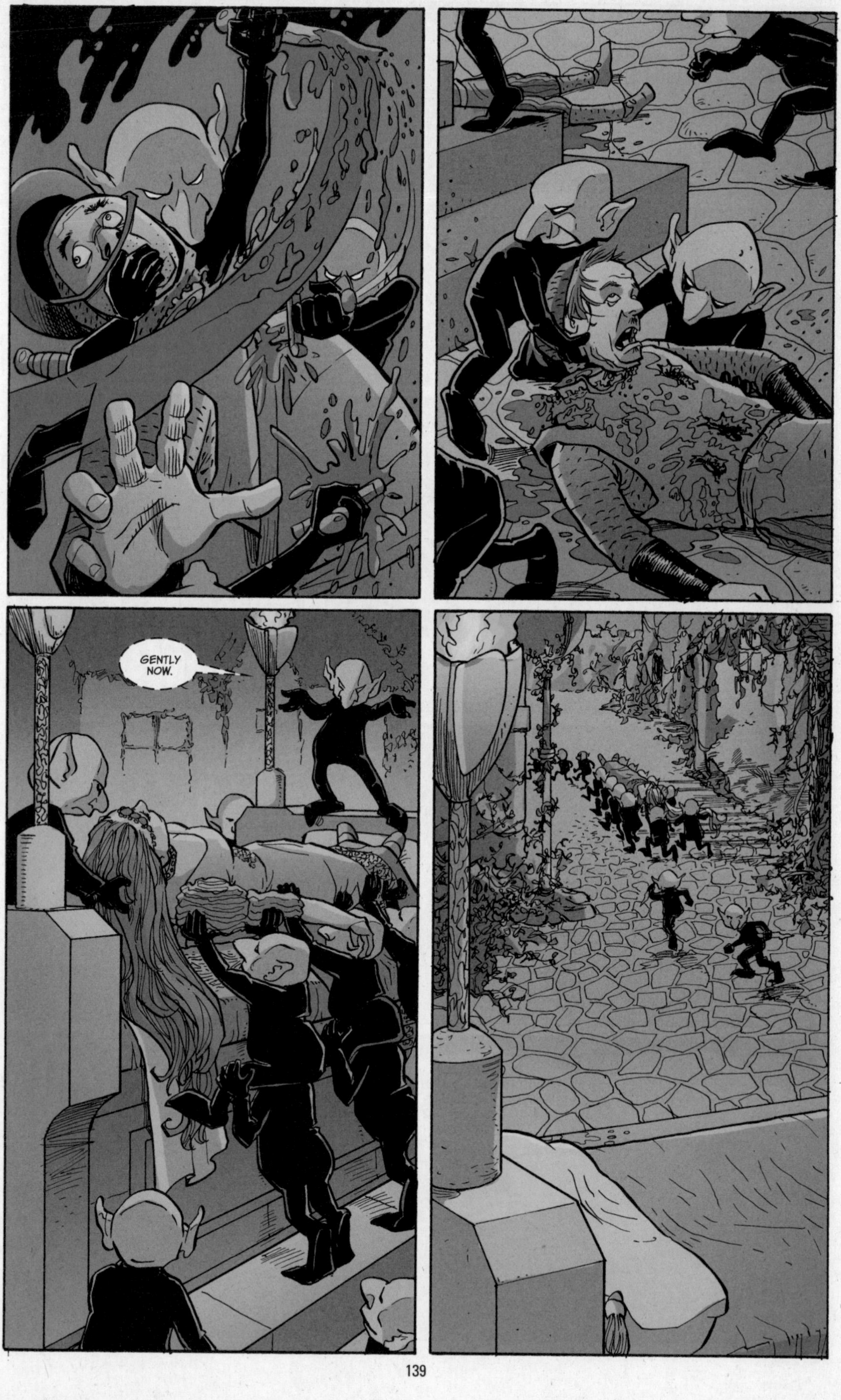
GENTLY NOW.

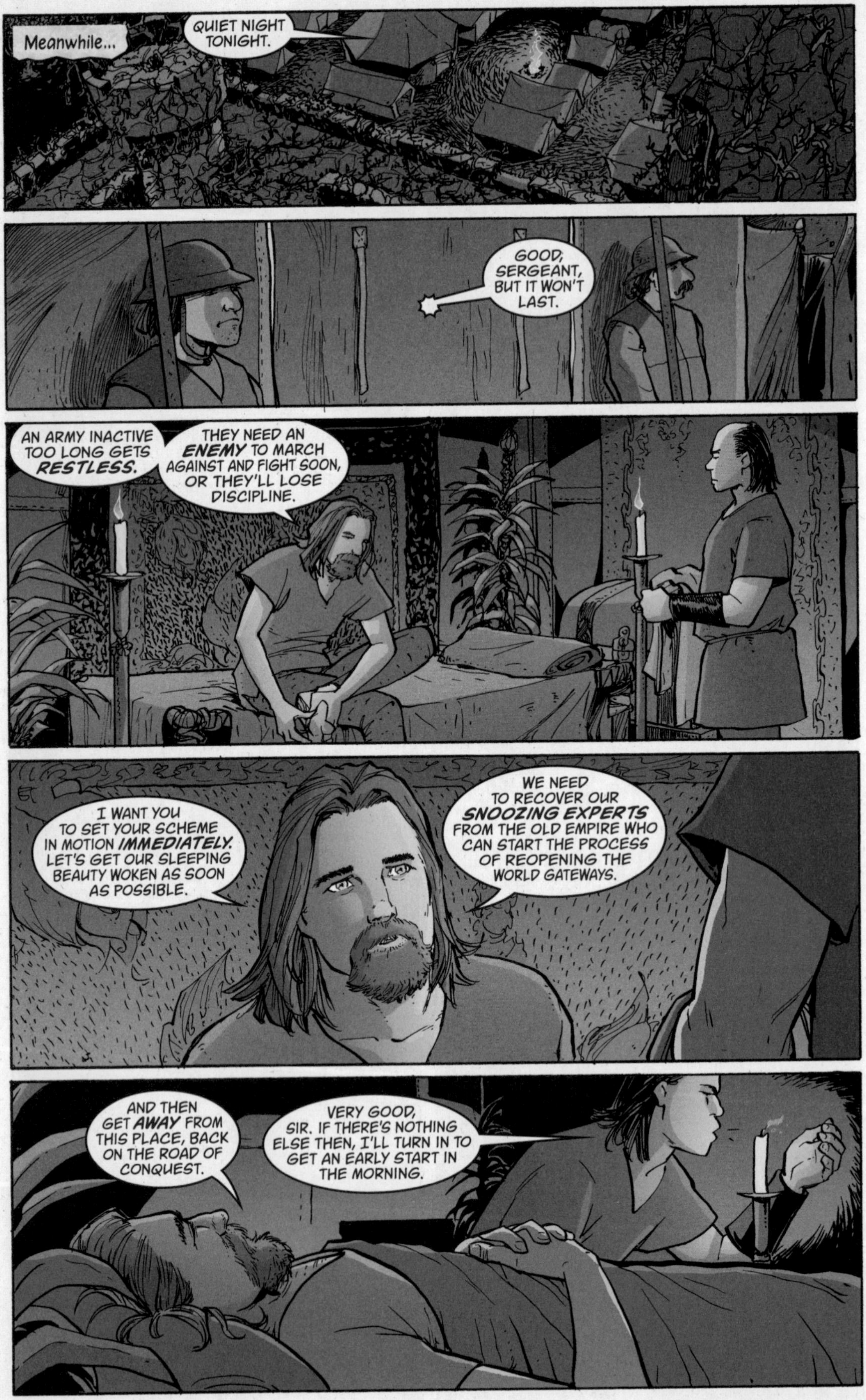
Meanwhile...
QUIET NIGHT TONIGHT.
GOOD, SERGEANT, BUT IT WON'T LAST.
AN ARMY INACTIVE TOO LONG GETS RESTLESS.
THEY NEED AN ENEMY TO MARCH AGAINST AND FIGHT SOON, OR THEY'LL LOSE DISCIPLINE.
I WANT YOU TO SET YOUR SCHEME IN MOTION IMMEDIATELY. LET'S GET OUR SLEEPING BEAUTY WOKEN AS SOON AS POSSIBLE.
WE NEED TO RECOVER OUR SNOOZING EXPERTS FROM THE OLD EMPIRE WHO CAN START THE PROCESS OF REOPENING THE WORLD GATEWAYS.
AND THEN GET AWAY FROM THIS PLACE, BACK ON THE ROAD OF CONQUEST.
VERY GOOD, SIR. IF THERE'S NOTHING ELSE THEN, I'LL TURN IN TO GET AN EARLY START IN THE MORNING.

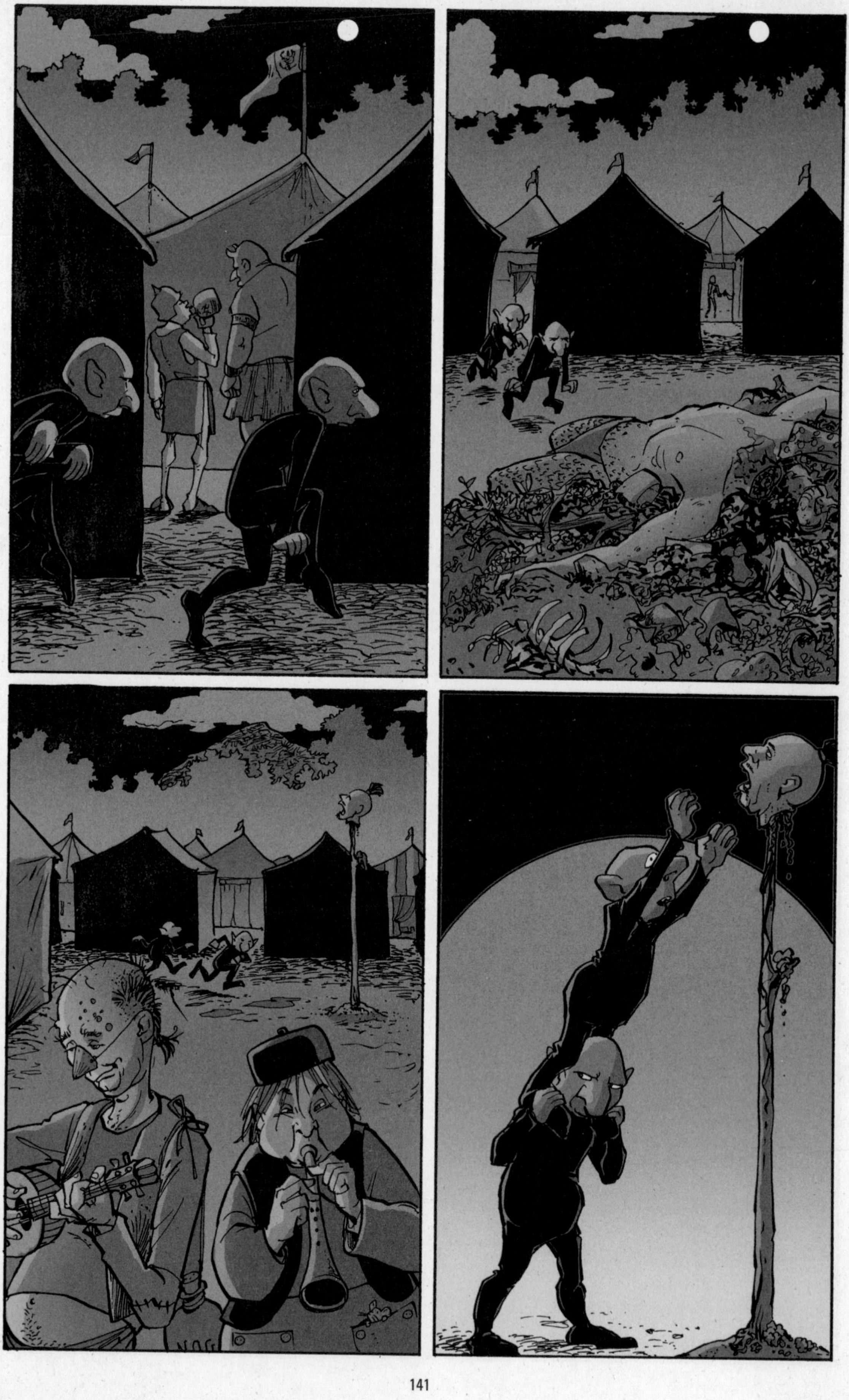

Elsewhere, at another, more humble encampment...

START STRIKING THE CAMP. PACK UP.

THEY'LL BE BACK SOON.

HERE THEY COME NOW!

EXCELLENT WORK!

WERE YOU SPOTTED? FOLLOWED?

OF COURSE NOT, COMMANDER.

GOOD. PROP UP THE BODY.

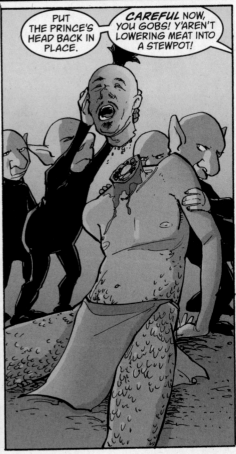

PUT THE PRINCE'S HEAD BACK IN PLACE.

CAREFUL NOW, YOU GOBS! Y'AREN'T LOWERING MEAT INTO A STEWPOT!

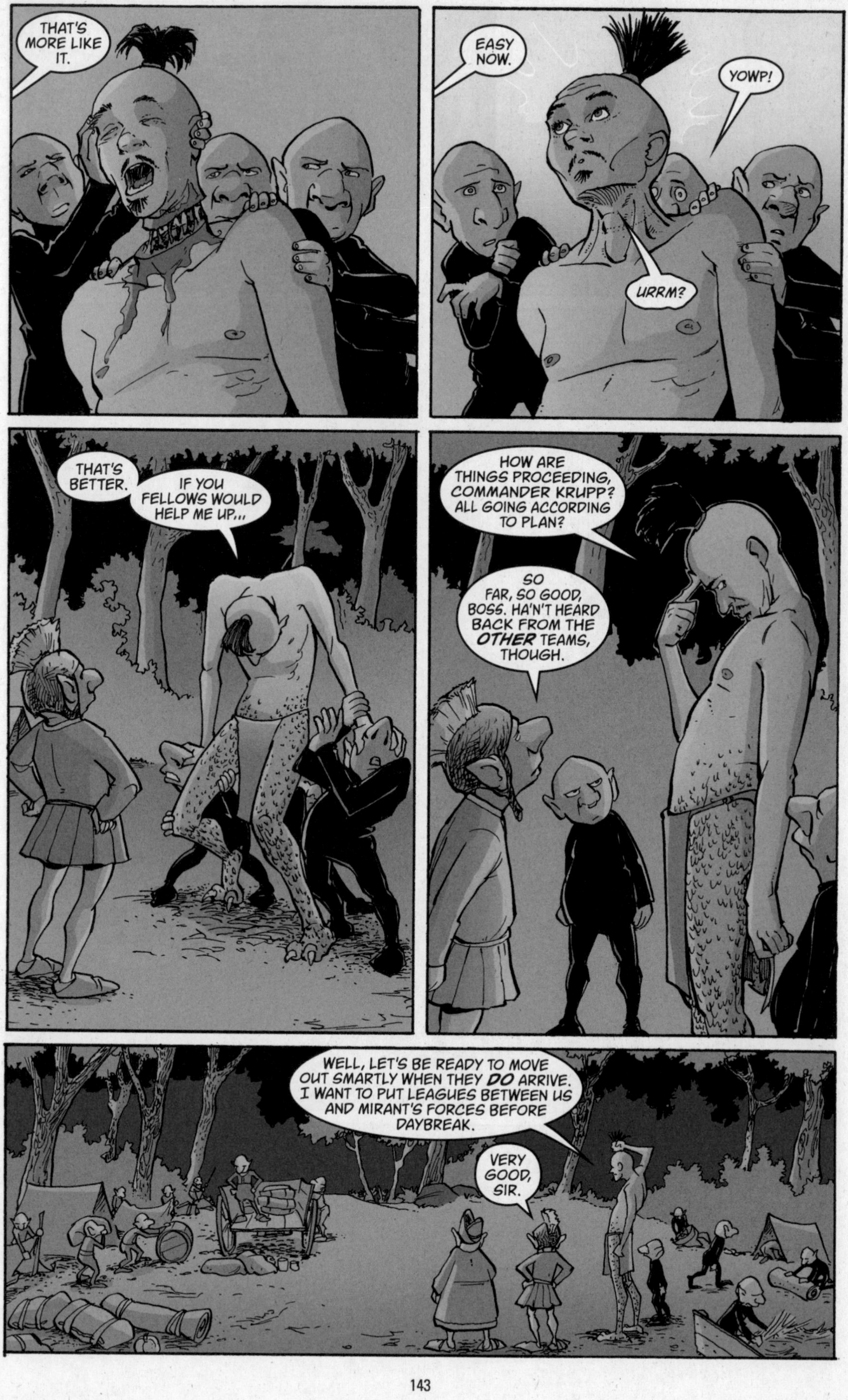
THAT'S MORE LIKE IT.
EASY NOW.
YOWP!
URRM?
THAT'S BETTER.
IF YOU FELLOWS WOULD HELP ME UP...
HOW ARE THINGS PROCEEDING, COMMANDER KRUPP? ALL GOING ACCORDING TO PLAN?
SO FAR, SO GOOD, BOSS. HA'N'T HEARD BACK FROM THE OTHER TEAMS, THOUGH.
WELL, LET'S BE READY TO MOVE OUT SMARTLY WHEN THEY DO ARRIVE. I WANT TO PUT LEAGUES BETWEEN US AND MIRANT'S FORCES BEFORE DAYBREAK.
VERY GOOD, SIR.

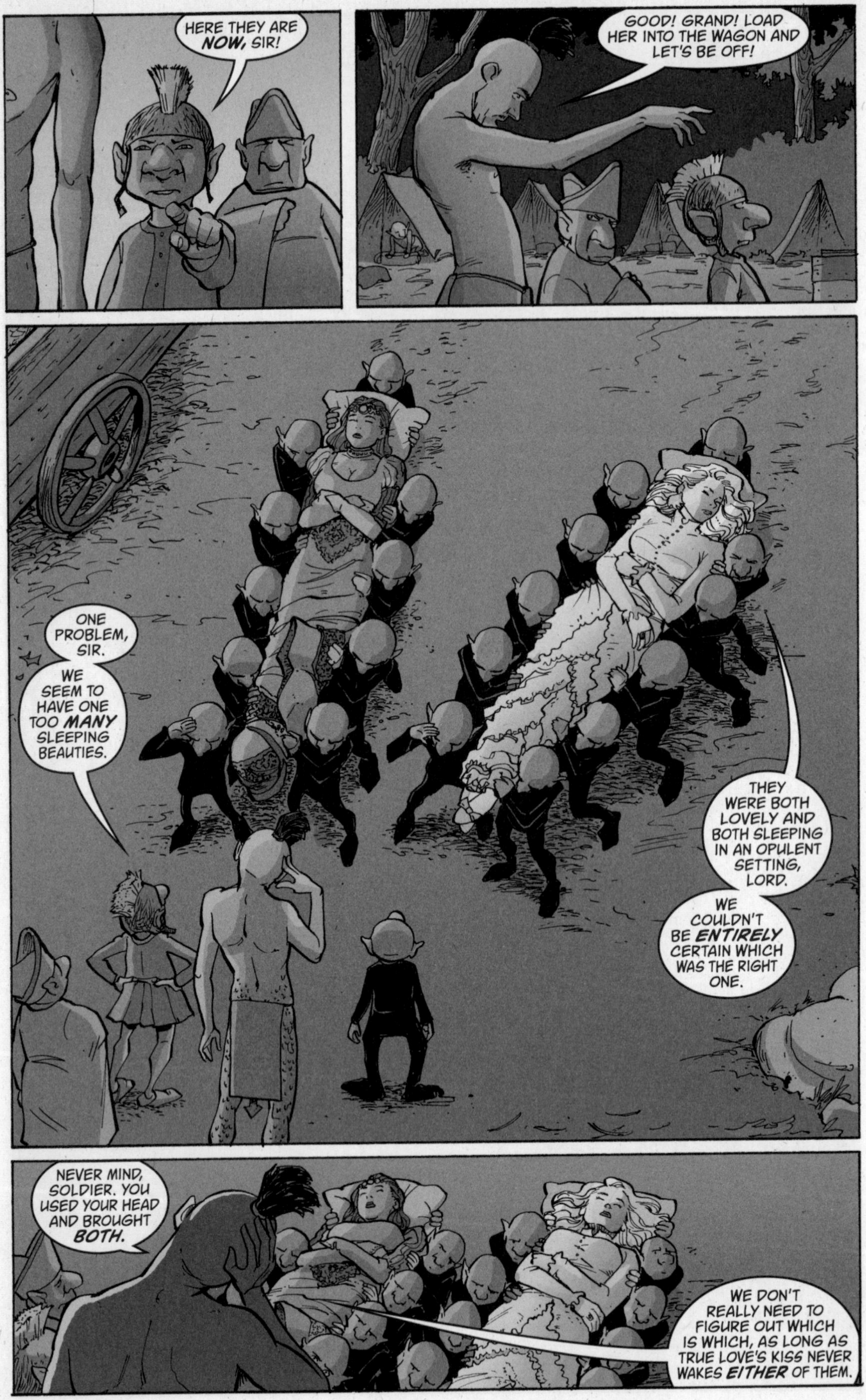
HERE THEY ARE NOW, SIR!
GOOD! GRAND! LOAD HER INTO THE WAGON AND LET'S BE OFF!
ONE PROBLEM, SIR.
WE SEEM TO HAVE ONE TOO MANY SLEEPING BEAUTIES.
THEY WERE BOTH LOVELY AND BOTH SLEEPING IN AN OPULENT SETTING, LORD.
WE COULDN'T BE ENTIRELY CERTAIN WHICH WAS THE RIGHT ONE.
NEVER MIND, SOLDIER. YOU USED YOUR HEAD AND BROUGHT BOTH.
WE DON'T REALLY NEED TO FIGURE OUT WHICH IS WHICH, AS LONG AS TRUE LOVE'S KISS NEVER WAKES EITHER OF THEM.

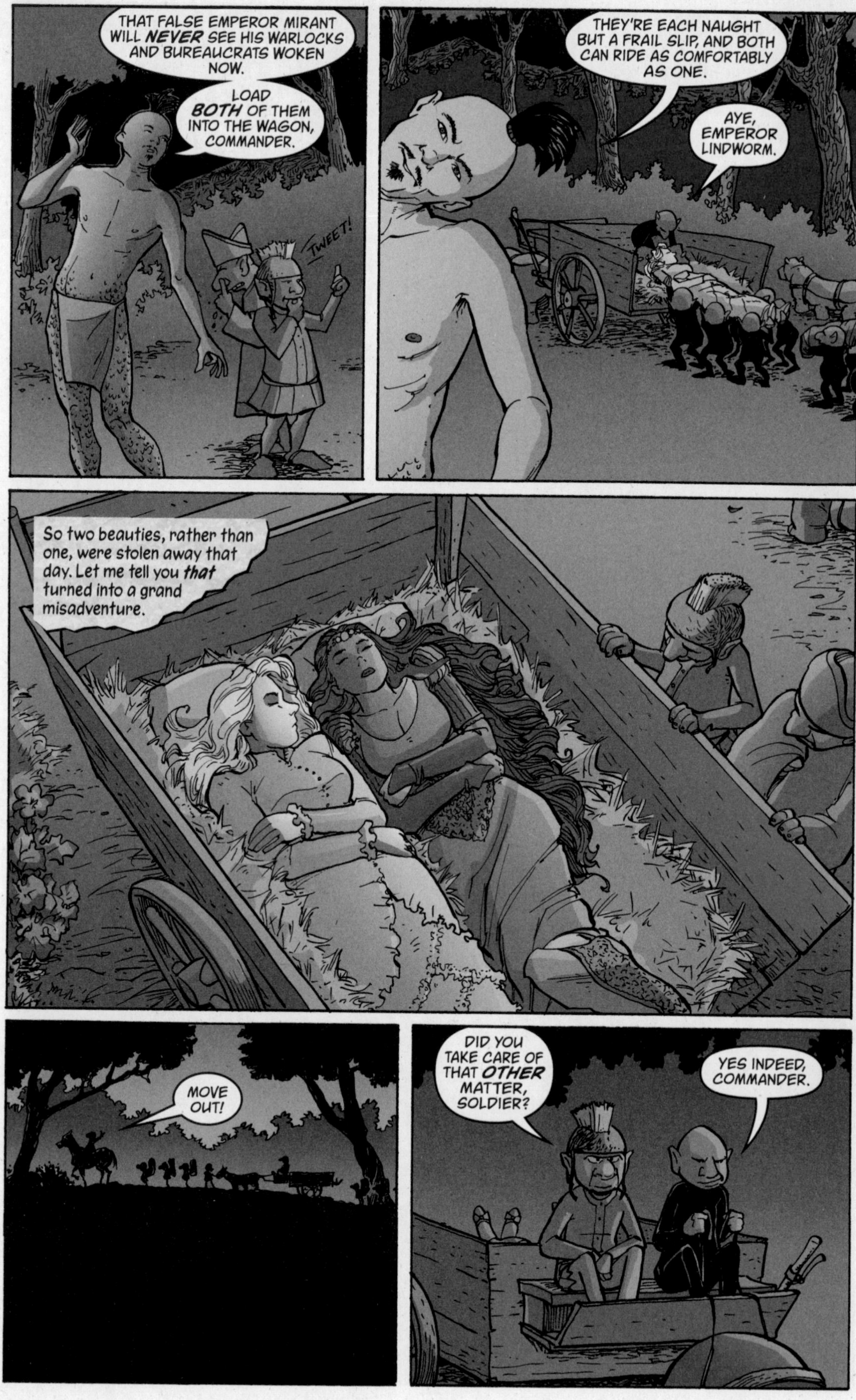
THAT FALSE EMPEROR MIRANT WILL NEVER SEE HIS WARLOCKS AND BUREAUCRATS WOKEN NOW.
LOAD BOTH OF THEM INTO THE WAGON, COMMANDER.
TWEET!
THEY'RE EACH NAUGHT BUT A FRAIL SLIP, AND BOTH CAN RIDE AS COMFORTABLY AS ONE.
AYE, EMPEROR LINDWORM.
So two beauties, rather than one, were stolen away that day. Let me tell you that turned into a grand misadventure.
MOVE OUT!
DID YOU TAKE CARE OF THAT OTHER MATTER, SOLDIER?
YES INDEED, COMMANDER.

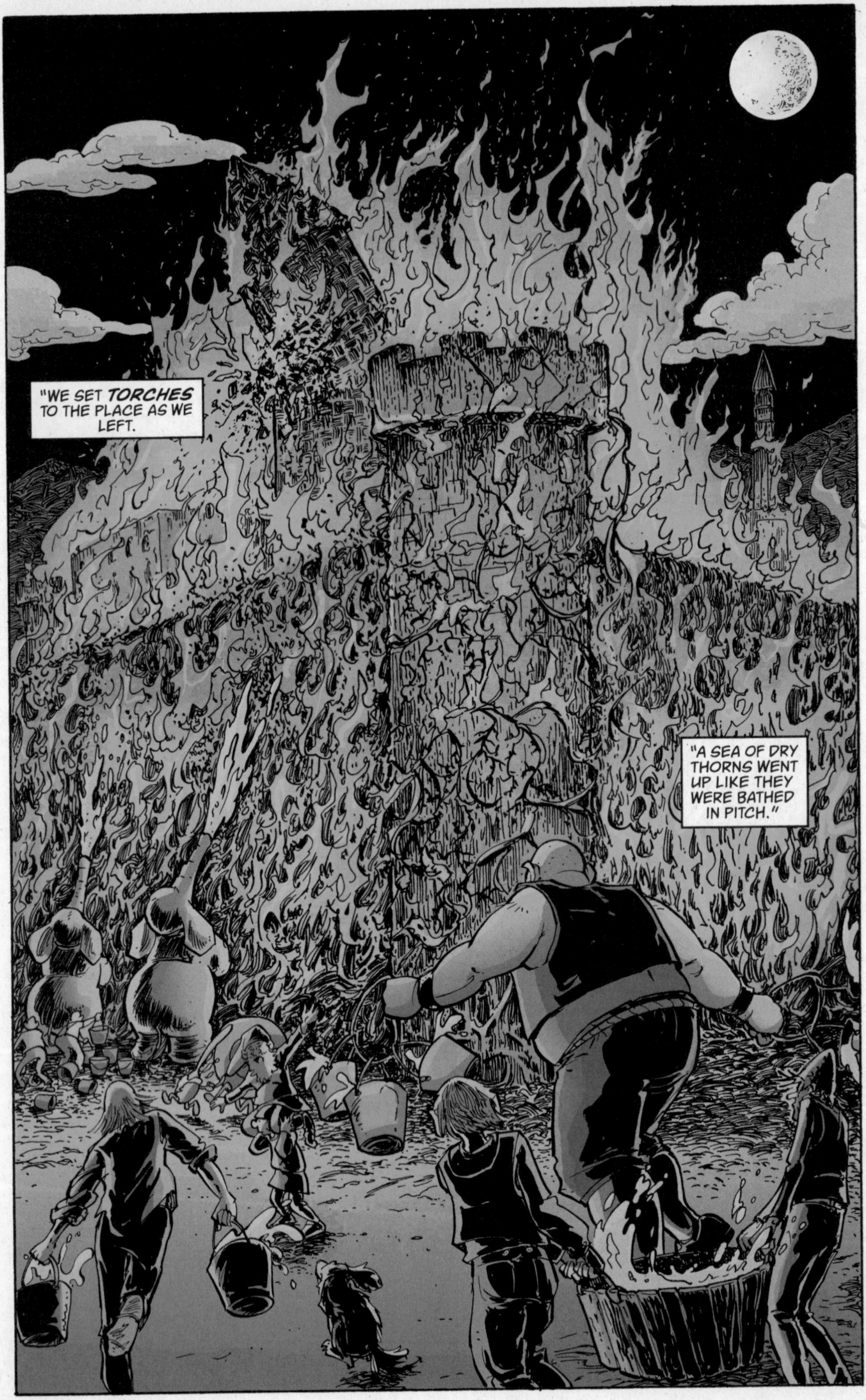
"WE SET *TORCHES* TO THE PLACE AS WE LEFT.
"A SEA OF DRY THORNS WENT UP LIKE THEY WERE BATHED IN PITCH."

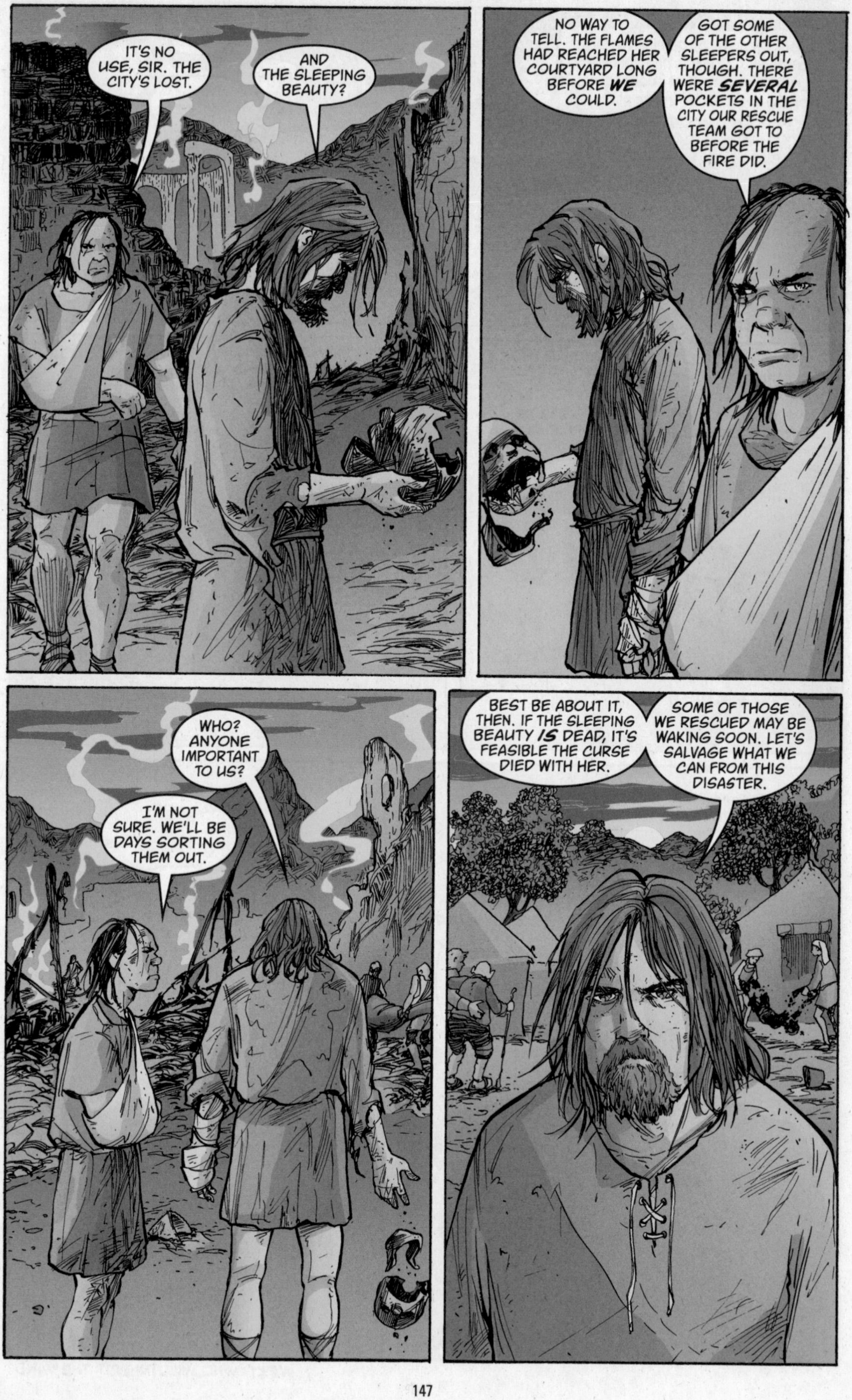

IT'S NO USE, SIR. THE CITY'S LOST.
AND THE SLEEPING BEAUTY?
NO WAY TO TELL. THE FLAMES HAD REACHED HER COURTYARD LONG BEFORE *WE* COULD.
GOT SOME OF THE OTHER SLEEPERS OUT, THOUGH. THERE WERE *SEVERAL* POCKETS IN THE CITY OUR RESCUE TEAM GOT TO BEFORE THE FIRE DID.
WHO? ANYONE IMPORTANT TO US?
I'M NOT SURE. WE'LL BE DAYS SORTING THEM OUT.
BEST BE ABOUT IT, THEN. IF THE SLEEPING BEAUTY *IS* DEAD, IT'S FEASIBLE THE CURSE DIED WITH HER.
SOME OF THOSE WE RESCUED MAY BE WAKING SOON. LET'S SALVAGE WHAT WE CAN FROM THIS DISASTER.

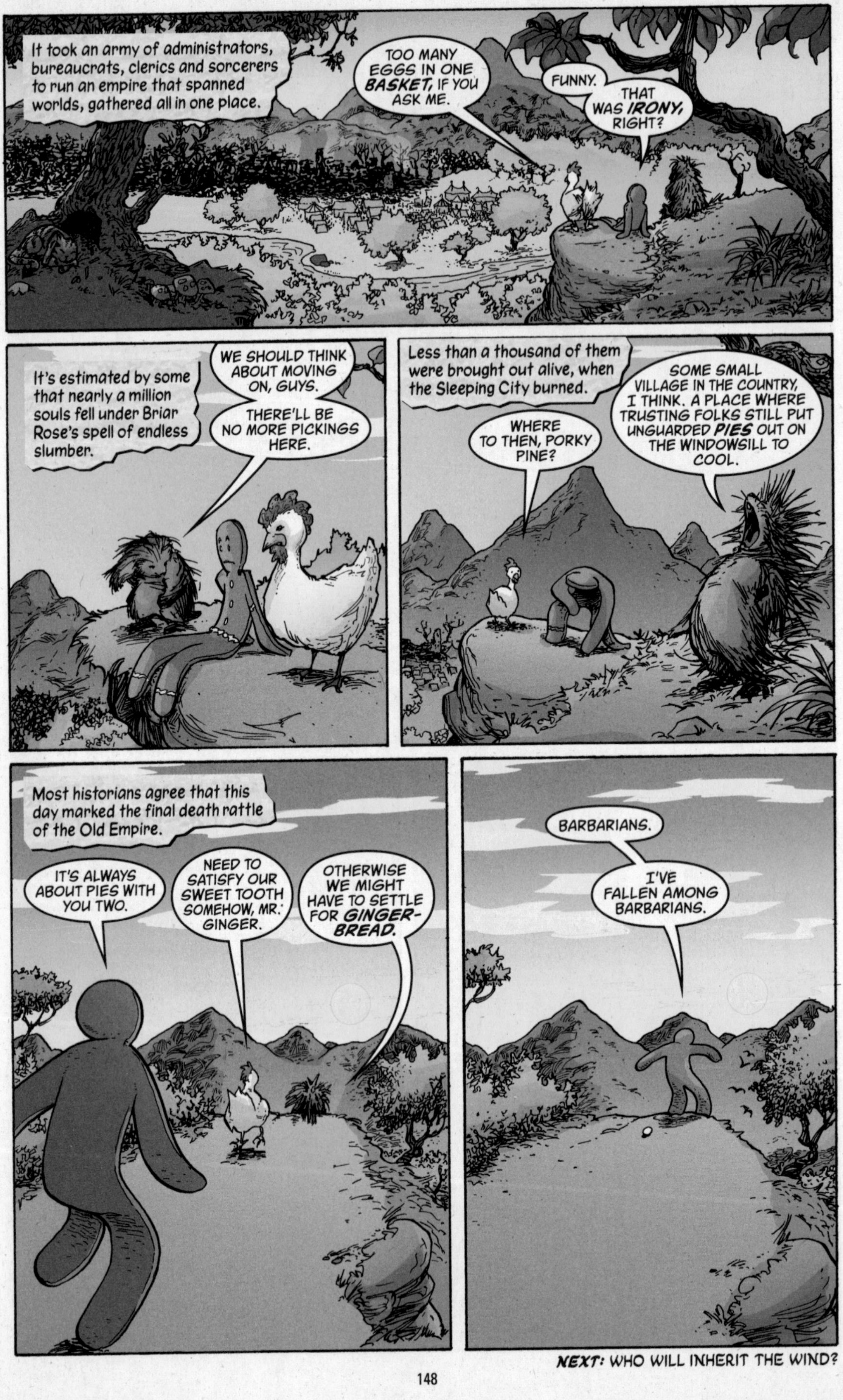
It took an army of administrators, bureaucrats, clerics and sorcerers to run an empire that spanned worlds, gathered all in one place.
TOO MANY EGGS IN ONE BASKET, IF YOU ASK ME.
FUNNY.
THAT WAS IRONY, RIGHT?
It's estimated by some that nearly a million souls fell under Briar Rose's spell of endless slumber.
WE SHOULD THINK ABOUT MOVING ON, GUYS.
THERE'LL BE NO MORE PICKINGS HERE.
Less than a thousand of them were brought out alive, when the Sleeping City burned.
WHERE TO THEN, PORKY PINE?
SOME SMALL VILLAGE IN THE COUNTRY, I THINK. A PLACE WHERE TRUSTING FOLKS STILL PUT UNGUARDED PIES OUT ON THE WINDOWSILL TO COOL.
Most historians agree that this day marked the final death rattle of the Old Empire.
IT'S ALWAYS ABOUT PIES WITH YOU TWO.
NEED TO SATISFY OUR SWEET TOOTH SOMEHOW, MR. GINGER.
OTHERWISE WE MIGHT HAVE TO SETTLE FOR GINGER-BREAD.
BARBARIANS.
I'VE FALLEN AMONG BARBARIANS.

NEXT: WHO WILL INHERIT THE WIND?

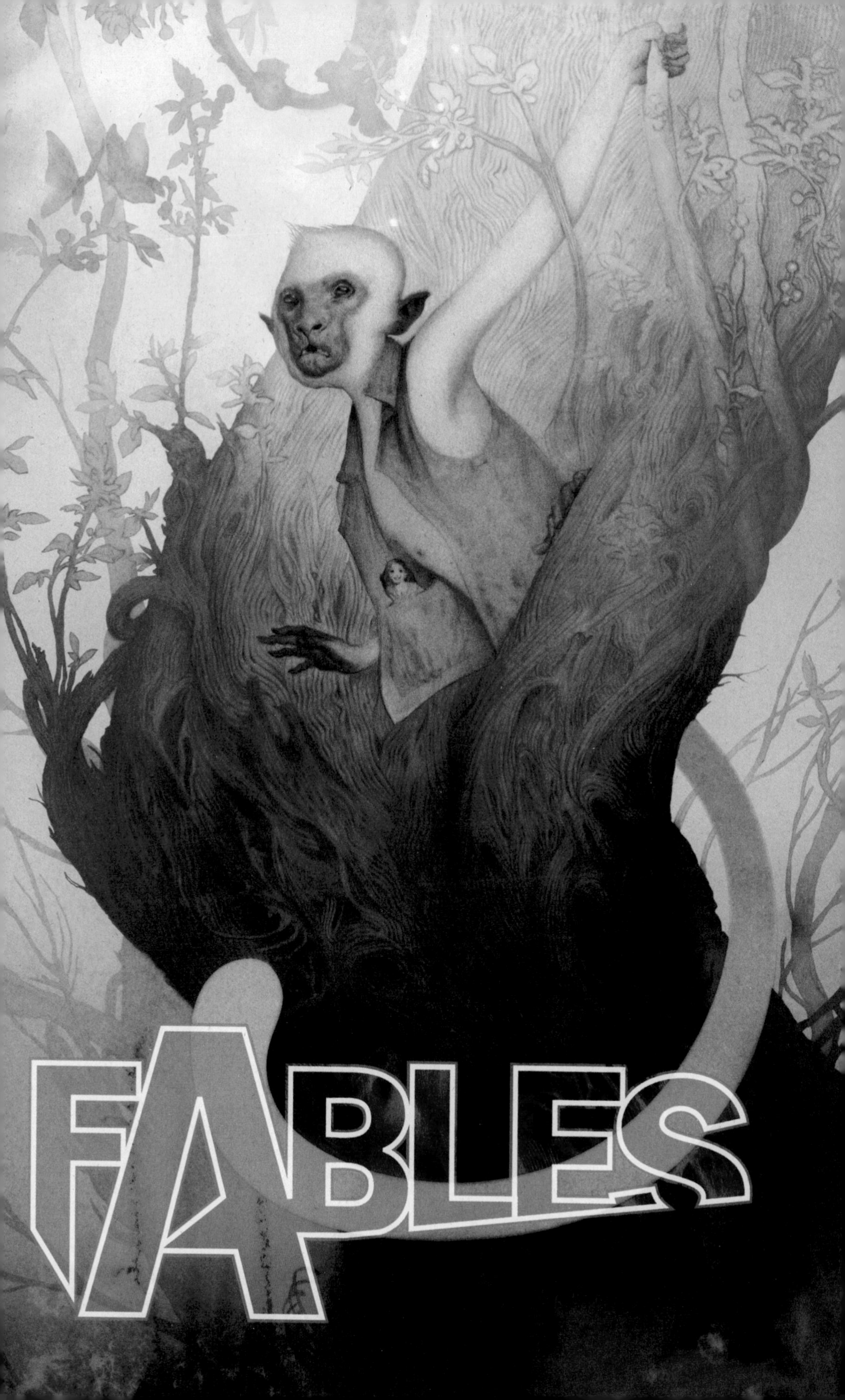
FABLES

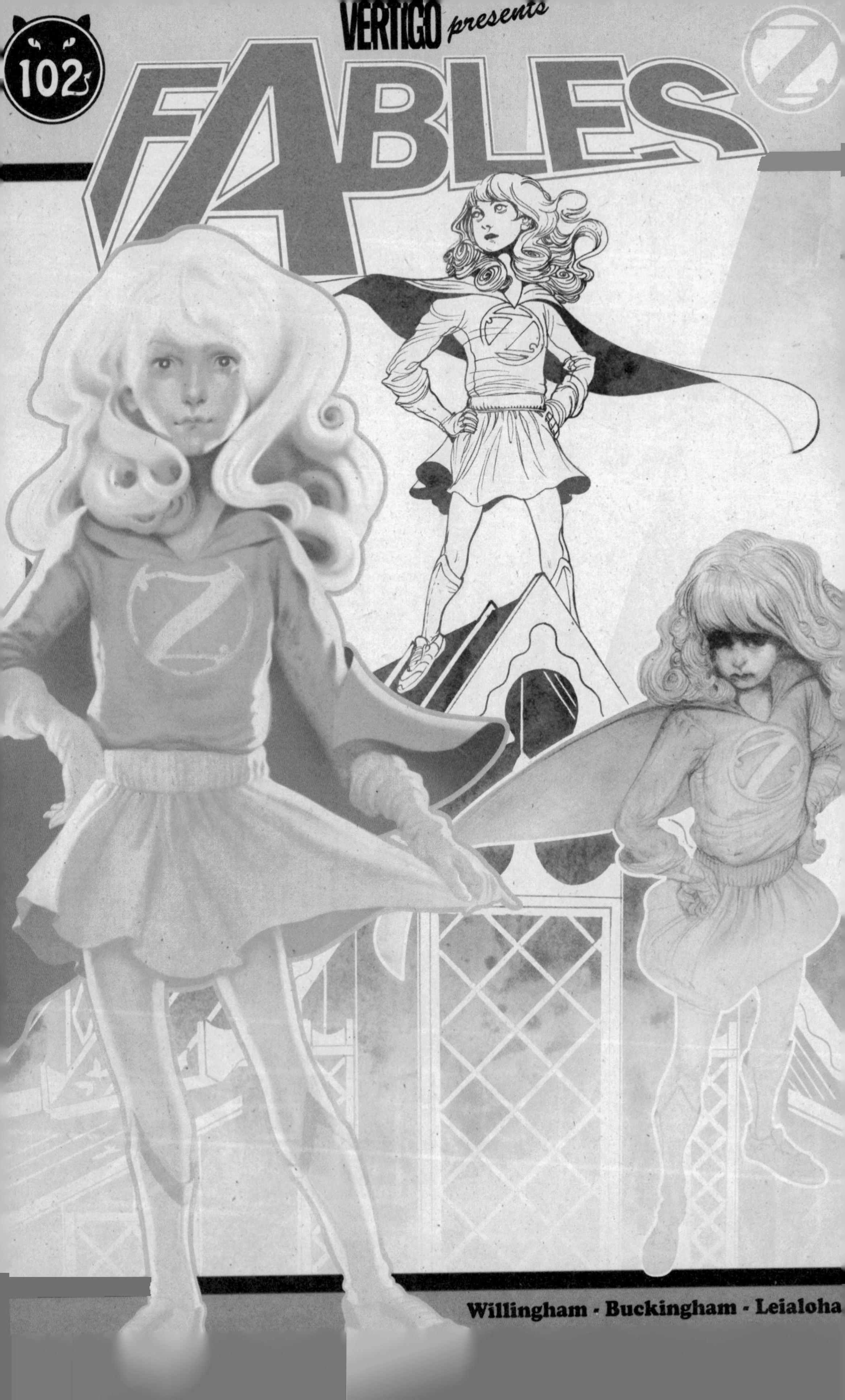
VERTIGO presents
102
FABLES
Willingham - Buckingham - Leialoha

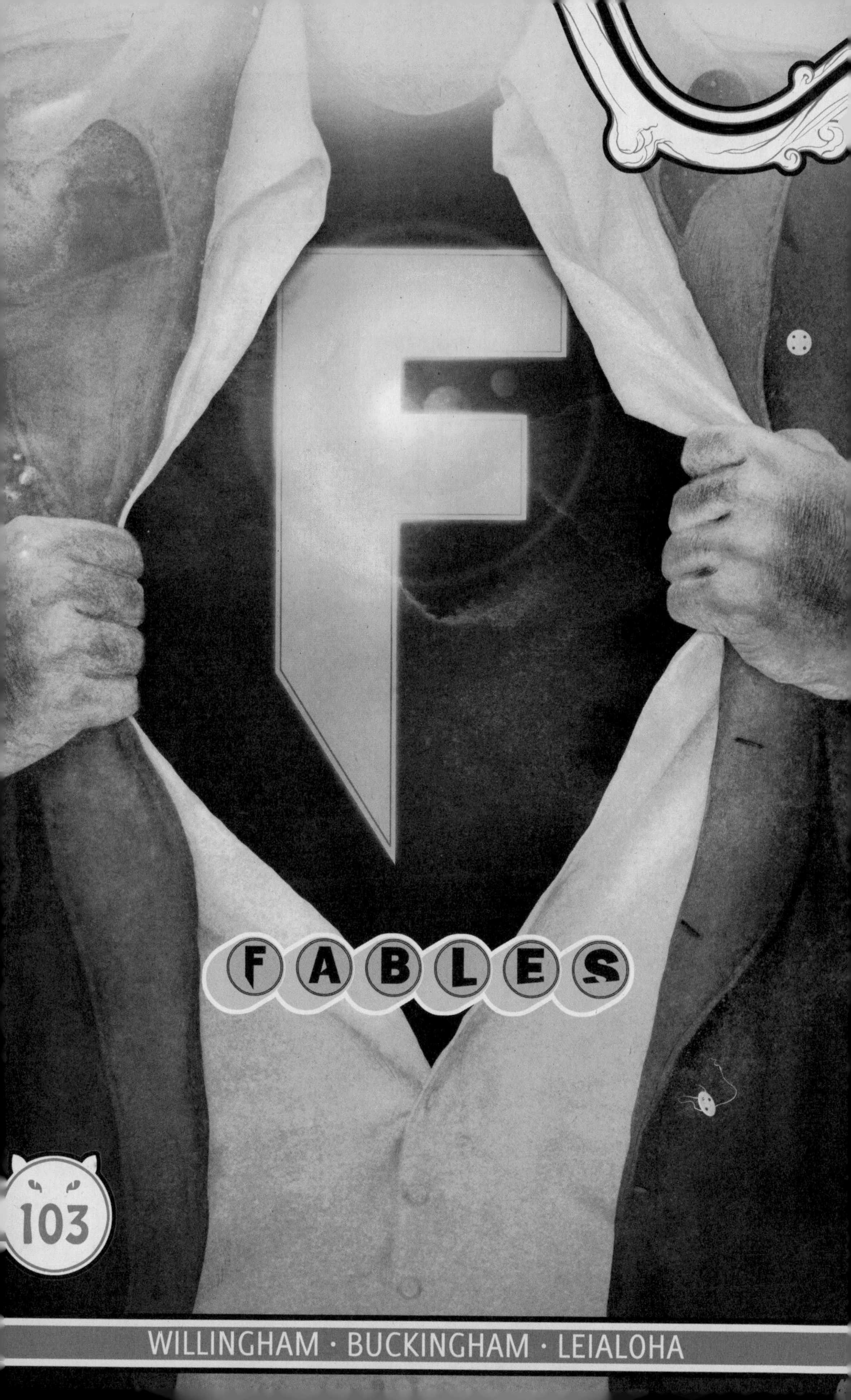
FABLES
103
WILLINGHAM · BUCKINGHAM · LEIALOHA

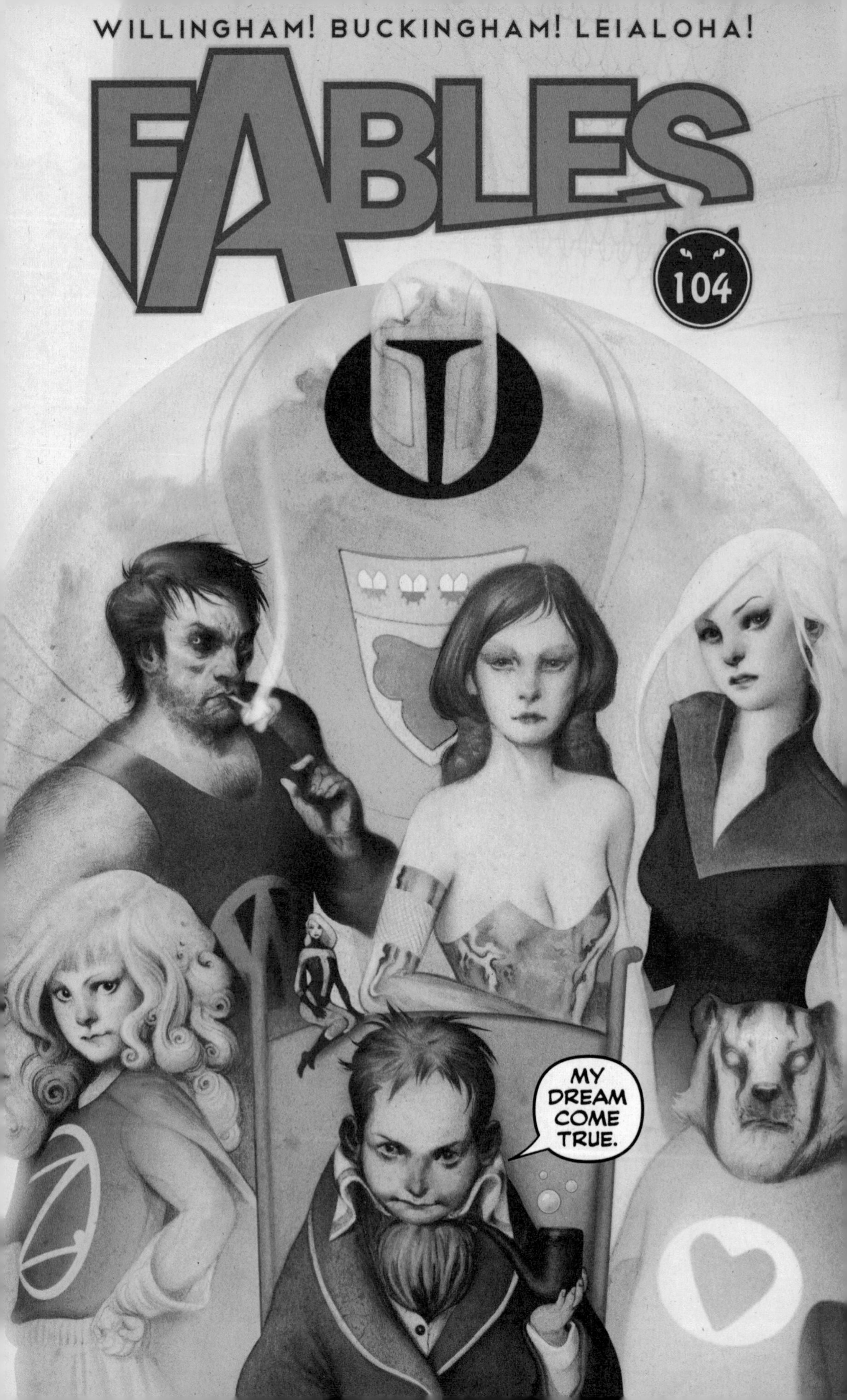
WILLINGHAM! BUCKINGHAM! LEIALOHA!
FABLES
104
MY DREAM COME TRUE.

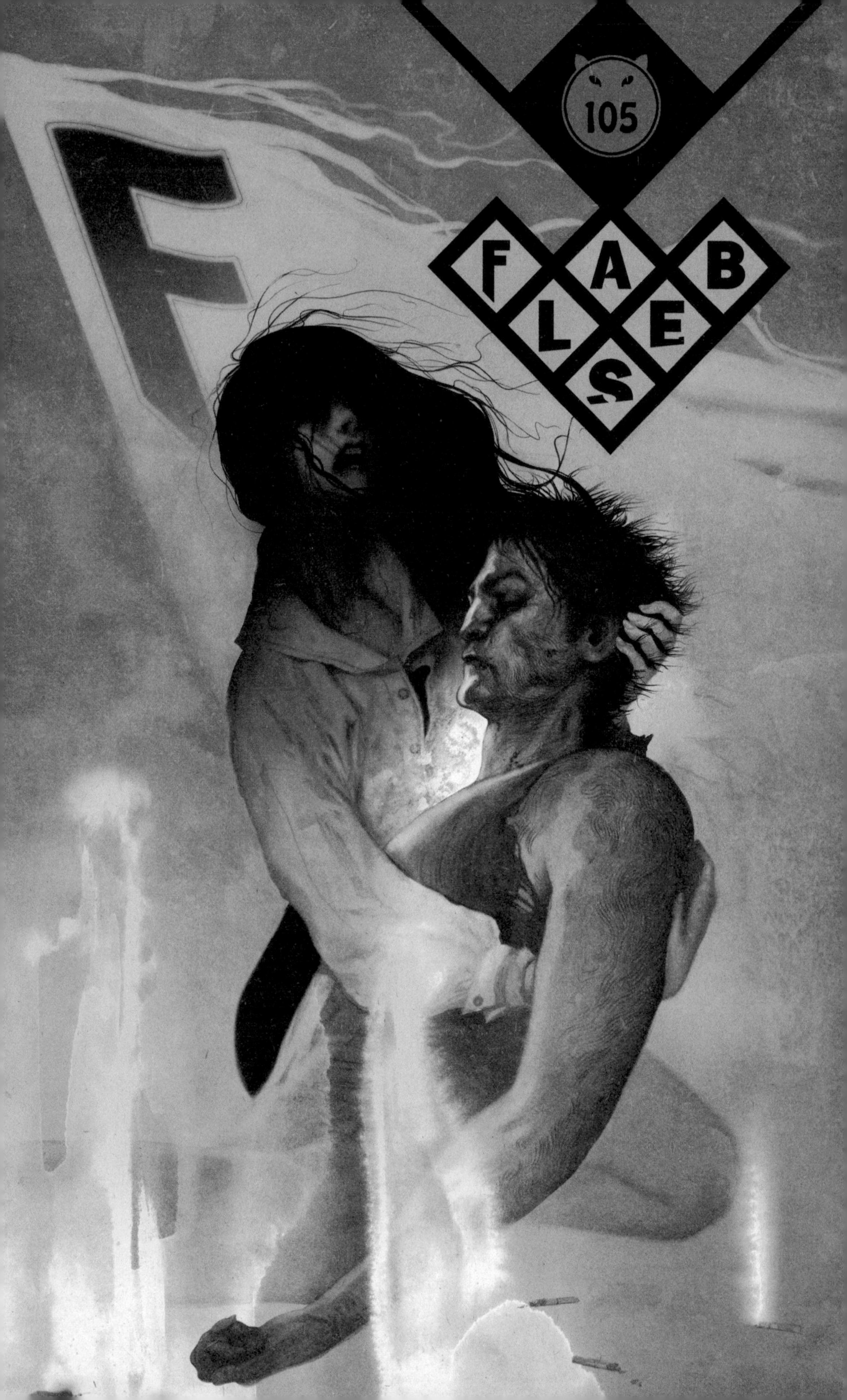
105
FABLES

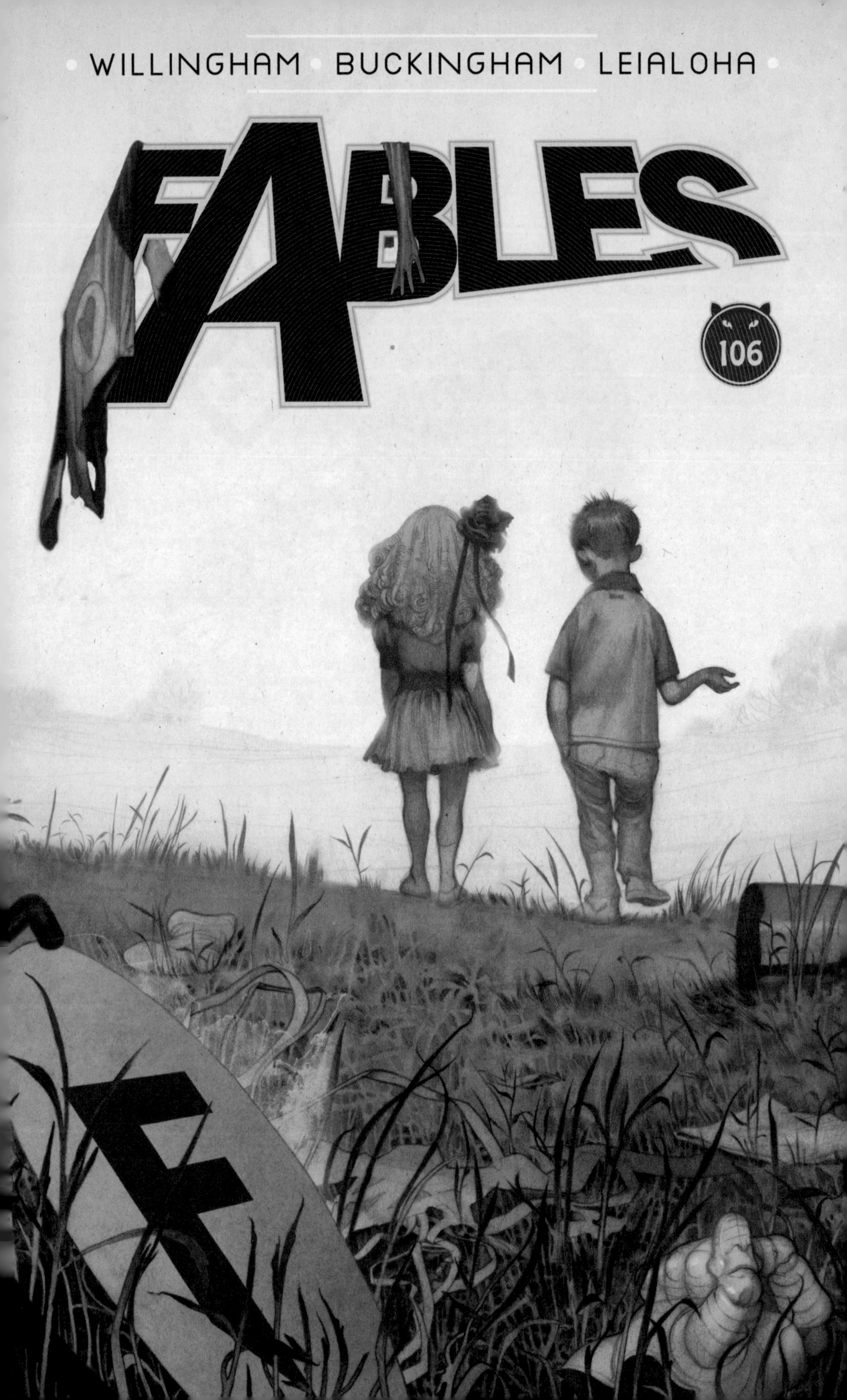
WILLINGHAM • BUCKINGHAM • LEIALOHA
FABLES
106

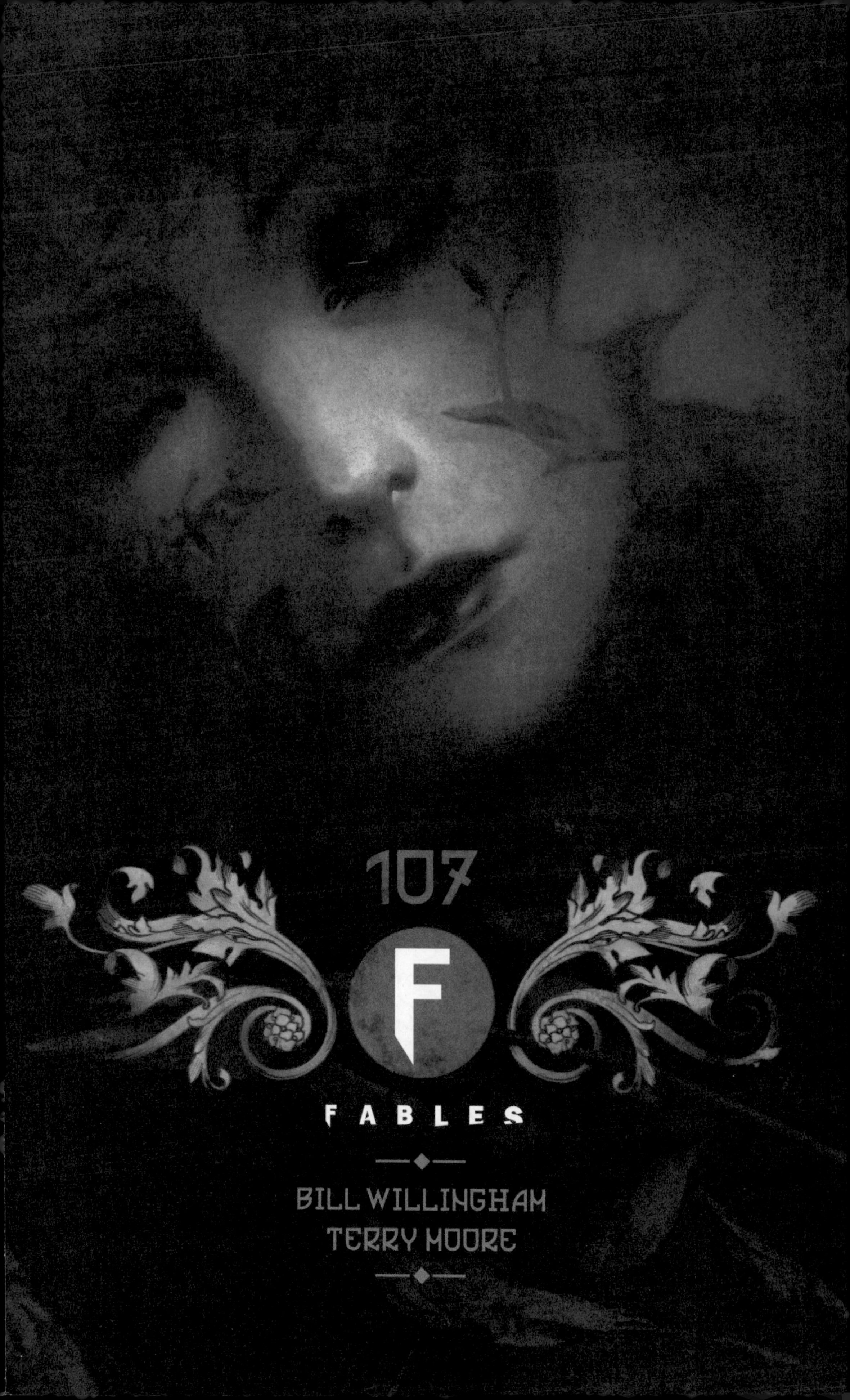
107
F
FABLES
BILL WILLINGHAM
TERRY MOORE

FABLES ASSEMBLE!

DESIGNS AND SKETCHES BY MARK BUCKINGHAM

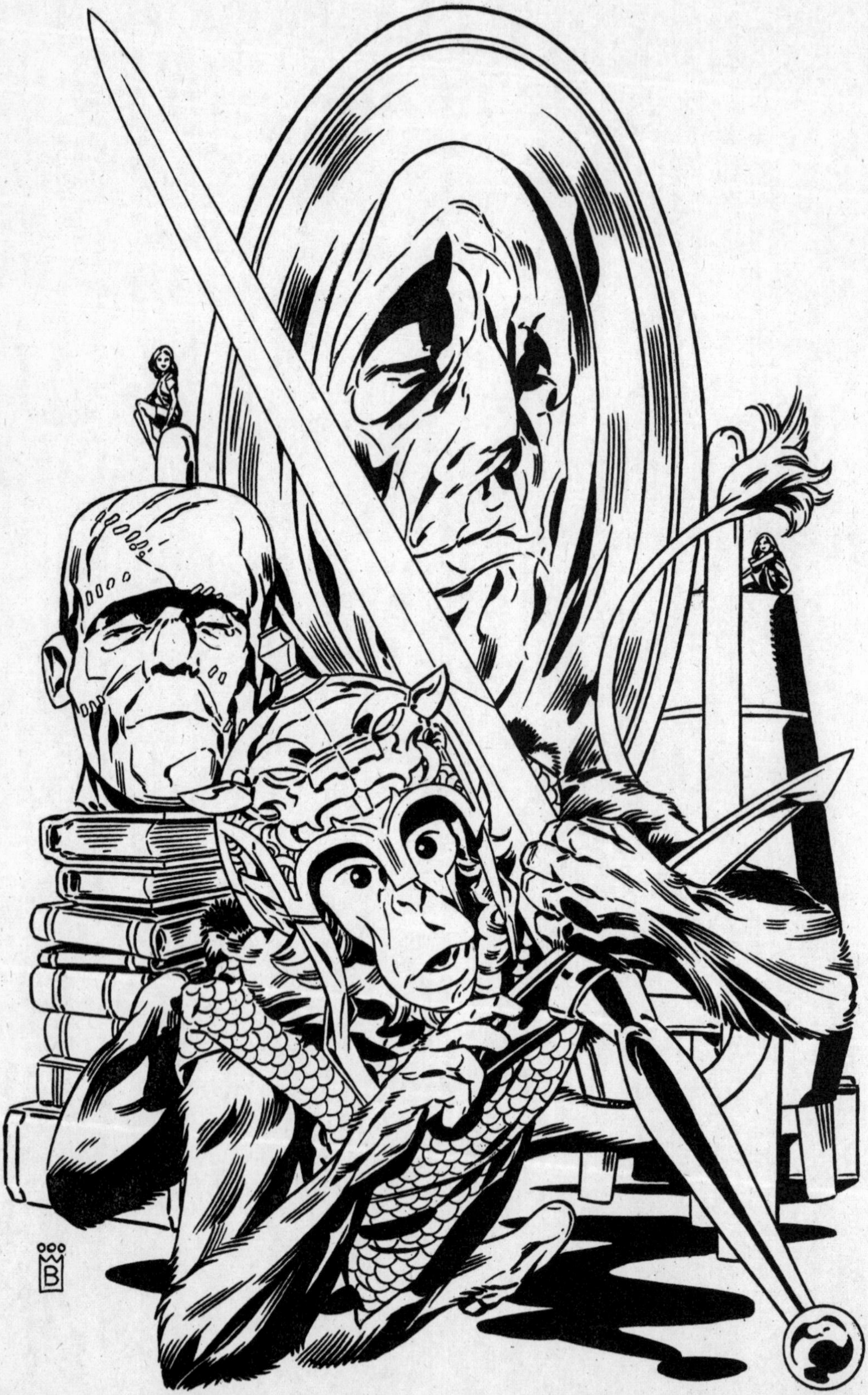

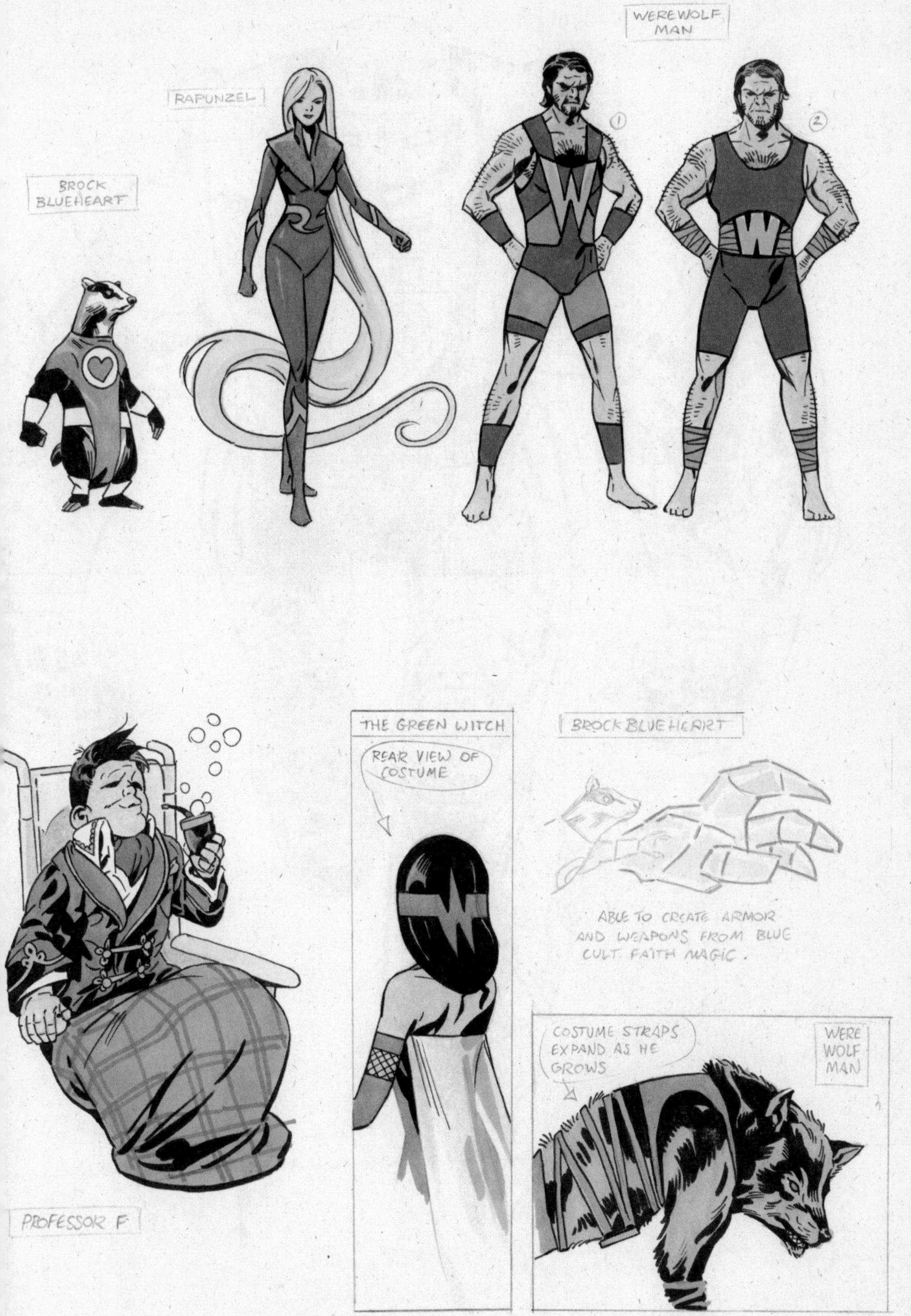
BROCK BLUEHEART
RAPUNZEL
WEREWOLF MAN
1
2
PROFESSOR F
THE GREEN WITCH
REAR VIEW OF COSTUME
BROCK BLUEHEART
ABLE TO CREATE ARMOR AND WEAPONS FROM BLUE CULT FAITH MAGIC.
COSTUME STRAPS EXPAND AS HE GROWS
WERE WOLF MAN

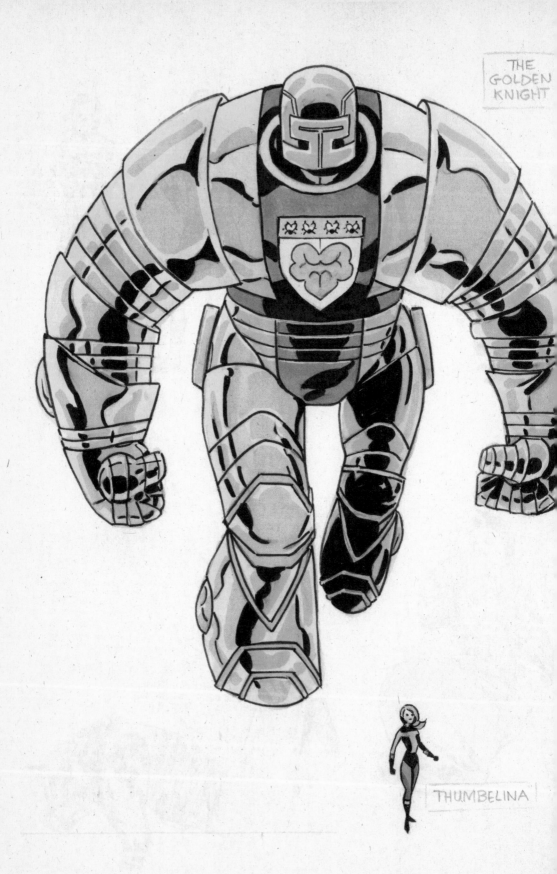

THE
GOLDEN
KNIGHT

THUMBELINA

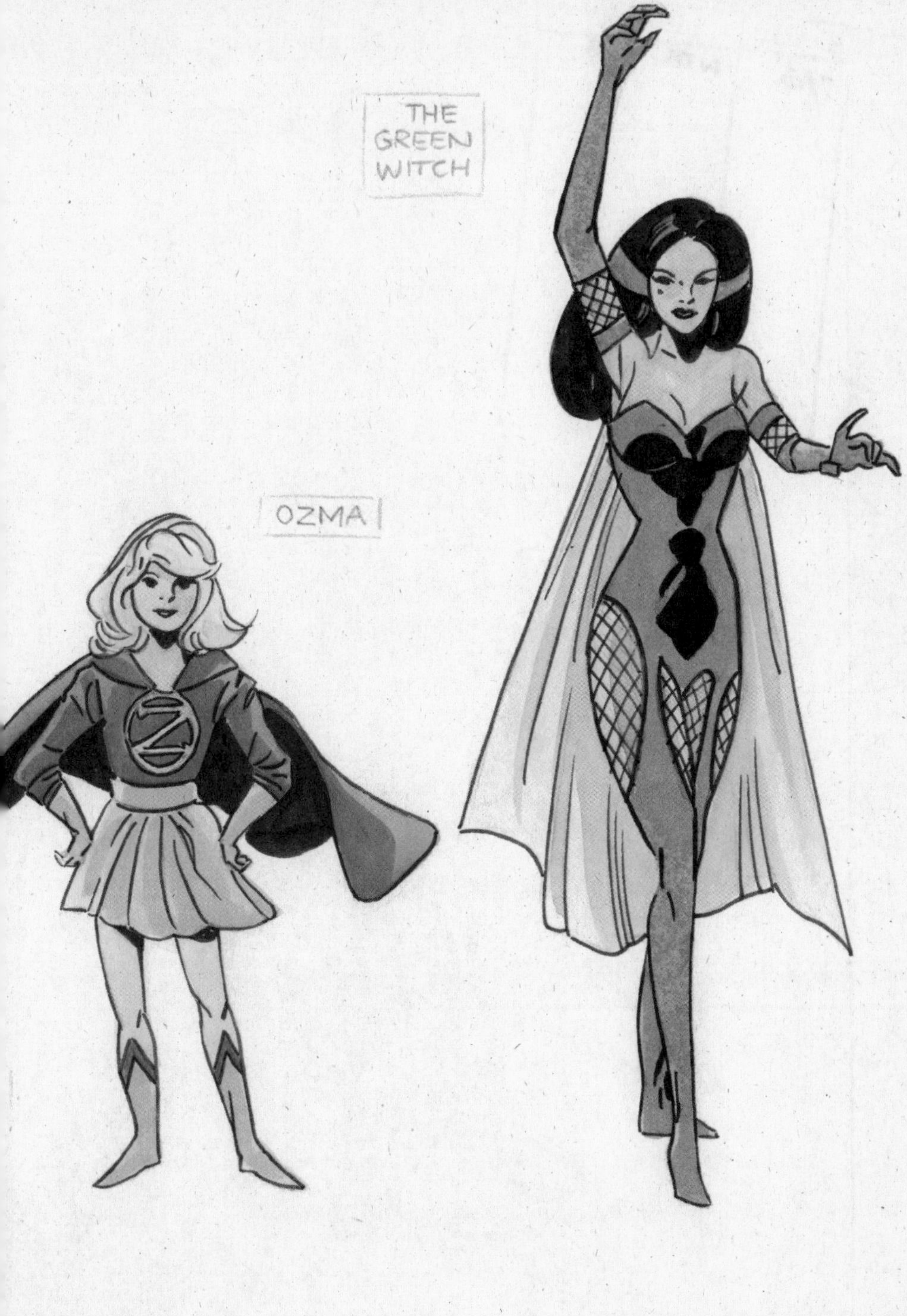
THE GREEN WITCH
OZMA

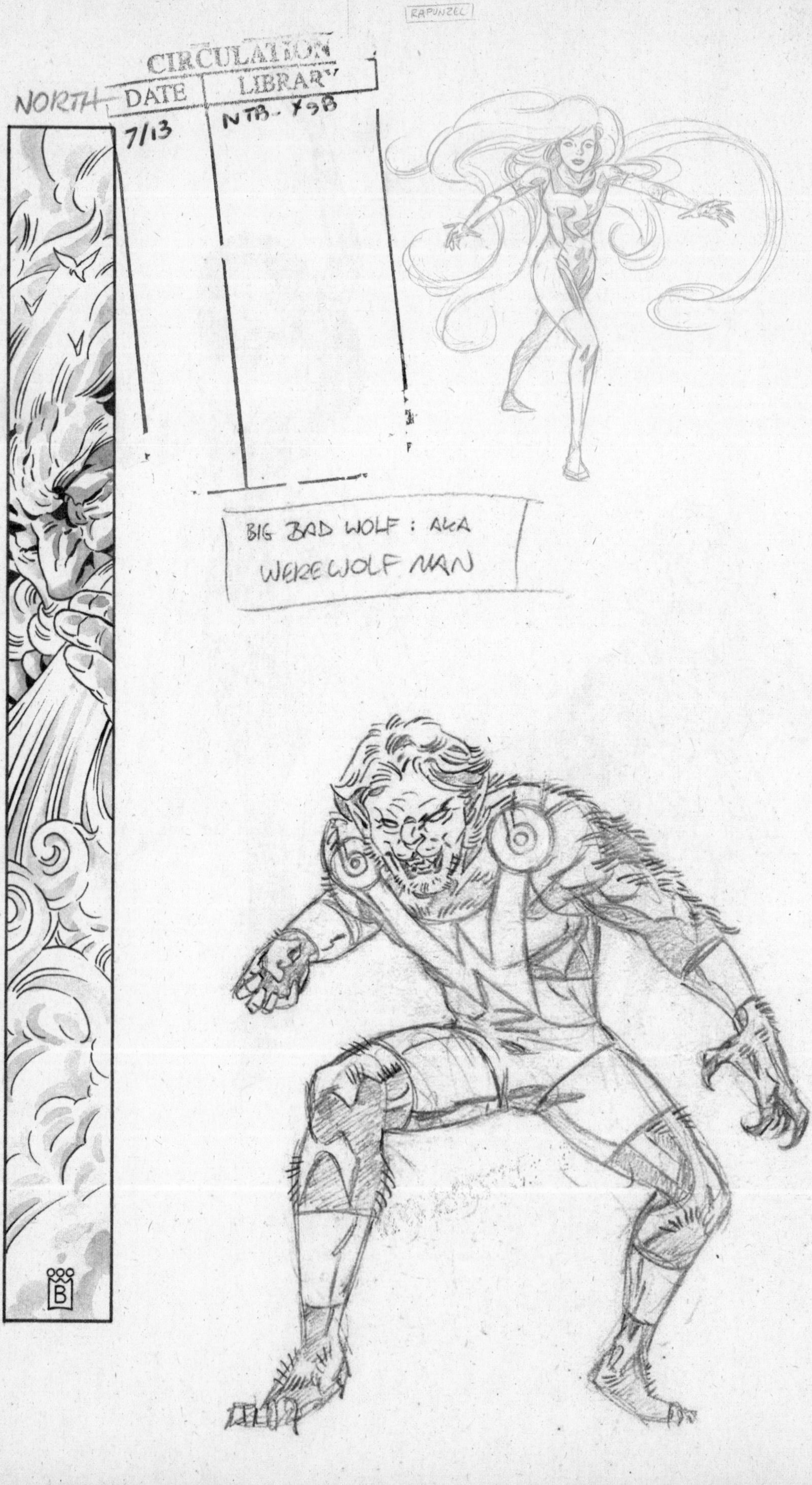
RAPUNZEL
CIRCULATION
NORTH
DATE
LIBRARY
7/13
BIG BAD WOLF : AKA
WEREWOLF MAN